The Woman Question

in Classical Sociological Theory

The Woman Question

in Classical Sociological Theory

Terry R. Kandal

Florida International University Press / Miami

Library of Congress Cataloging in Publication Data

Kandal, Terry R.
  The woman question in classical sociological
theory.
     p. cm.
  Bibliography: p.
  Includes index.
  ISBN 0-8130-0796-8
  1. Feminism.   2. Sociology.   3. Women.
I. Title.
HQ1206.K36   1987
305.4′2—dc19   87-18616
                                                      CIP

This book is for sale in the United States, its possessions, Canada, and the British Commonwealth only.

Permissions from authors and publishers to quote excerpts from copyrighted material may be found on the continuation of the copyright page following the index.

UNIVERSITY PRESSES OF FLORIDA is the central agency for scholarly publishing of the State of Florida's university system, producing books selected for publication by the faculty editorial committees of Florida's nine public universities: Florida A&M University (Tallahassee), Florida Atlantic University (Boca Raton), Florida International University (Miami), Florida State University (Tallahassee), University of Central Florida (Orlando), University of Florida (Gainesville), University of North Florida (Jacksonville), University of South Florida (Tampa), University of West Florida (Pensacola).

ORDERS for books published by all member presses should be addressed to University Presses of Florida, 15 NW 15th Street, Gainesville, FL 32603.

Printed in the U.S.A. on acid-free paper. ∞

To my mother, Gertrude

Contents

Abbreviations, ix
Preface, xiii
Acknowledgments, xvii

1. Introduction, 1
   Contemporary Feminism and Classical Sociological
      Theory, 1
   Historical Context of the "Woman Question," 4

2. England, 10
   Feminism and Liberal Social Theory, 10
   The English Theorists, 22
      John Stuart Mill, 22
      Herbert Spencer, 32

3. France, 49
   Revolutionary Feminism and Sociological Moralism, 49
   The French Theorists, 67
      Alexis de Tocqueville, 68
      Auguste Comte, 74
      Émile Durkheim, 79

4. Germany, 89
   Die Frauenfrage and Historical Sociology, 89
      Socialist Feminism, 90
      Liberal Feminism, 99
      The Erotic Movement, 108
      Socialism, Feminism, and the Fate of the Weimar
         Republic, 118
   The German Theorists, 126
      Max Weber, 126
      Georg Simmel, 156
      Ferdinand Tönnies, 177
      Karl Mannheim, 182

5. Italy, 186
   Women, Sexuality, and the Tradition of Machiavelli, 186
   The Italian Theorists, 192
      Vilfredo Pareto, 193
      Robert Michels, 201

6. The United States, 212
   Contrasting Versions of the Sociological Tradition on Sex
      Roles, 212
   The U.S. Theorists, 228
      Talcott Parsons, 228
      C. Wright Mills, 235

7. Conclusion, 245
   Evaluation, 250
   Theoretical Issues, 262
   Historical Alternatives, 271

Notes, 281

Bibliography, 317

Index, 333

Abbreviations

Work of Auguste Comte

SPP   *System of Positive Polity.* 1851. First published in English in London in 1875. Translated by John Henry Bridges. Vol. 1. New York: Burt Franklin, n.d.

Works of Émile Durkheim

DLS   *The Division of Labor in Society.* 1893. Translated by George Simpson. New York: Free Press, 1964.

S   *Suicide: A Study in Sociology.* 1897. Translated by John A. Spaulding and George Simpson. Glencoe, Ill.: Free Press, 1951.

Work of Karl Mannheim

ESC   *Essays on the Sociology of Culture.* Edited by Ernest Manheim, in cooperation with Paul Kecskemeti. London: Routledge and Kegan Paul, 1956.

Works of Robert Michels

PP   *Political Parties: A Sociological Study of the Oligarchical Tendencies of Modern Democracy.* 1911. Translated by Eden Paul and Cedar Paul. Introduction by Seymour Martin Lipset. New York: Collier Books, 1962.

SE   *Sexual Ethics: A Study of Borderland Questions.* 1911.
              New York: Charles Scribner's Sons, 1915.

                           Work of John Stuart Mill
SW   *The Subjection of Women. 1869.* In *Essays on Sex
              Equality,* by John Stuart Mill and Harriet Taylor Mill,
              edited by Alice S. Rossi. Chicago: University of Chicago
              Press, 1970.

                           Works of C. Wright Mills
"PTFS"   "Plain Talk on Fancy Sex." 1952. In *Power, Politics, and
              People: The Collected Essays of C. Wright Mills,* edited
              by Irving Louis Horowitz. New York: Ballantine Books,
              1963.
WC   *White Collar: The American Middle Classes.* New York:
              Oxford University Press, 1956.
"WDLS"   "Women: The Darling Little Slaves." 1953. A review of
              Simone de Beauvoir's *The Second Sex.* In *Power, Poli-
              tics, and People: The Collected Essays of C. Wright
              Mills,* edited by Irving Louis Horowitz. New York: Bal-
              lantine Books, 1963.

                           Work of Vilfredo Pareto
MS   *The Mind and Society.* 1916. Edited by Arthur Living-
              ston. Translated by Andrew Bongiorno and Arthur
              Livingston, with the advice and active cooperation of
              James Harvey Rogers. 4 vols. New York: Harcourt
              Brace and Company, 1935.

                           Works of Talcott Parsons
"AS"   "Age and Sex in the Social Structure of the United
              States." *American Sociological Review* 7 (October 1942):
              604–16.
FSIP   *Family, Socialization, and Interaction Process.* By Tal-
              cott Parsons and Robert Bales, in collaboration with
              James Olds, Morris Zelditch, Jr., and Philip E. Slater.
              Glencoe, Ill.: Free Press, 1955.

                           Works of Georg Simmel
CW   *Conflict and the Web of Group Affiliations.* Translated
              by Kurt H. Wolff and Reinhard Bendix. New York: Free
              Press, 1964.
SISF   *Georg Simmel on Individuality and Social Forms.*

Edited by Donald N. Levine. Chicago: University of
Chicago Press, 1971.

"SNC" Passages from Simmel's works as quoted in "Simmel's
Neglected Contributions to the Sociology of Women."
By Lewis A. Coser. *Signs: A Journal of Women in Cul-
ture and Society* 2, no. 4 (Summer 1977): 869–76.

SGS *The Sociology of Georg Simmel.* Edited and translated
by Kurt H. Wolff. New York: Free Press, 1964.

Works of Herbert Spencer

PS *The Principles of Sociology.* 1876. 3d ed. Vol. 1. New
York: D. Appleton and Company, 1899.

SS *Social Statics; or, The Conditions Essential to Human
Happiness Specified and the First of Them Developed.*
1851. New York: Augustus M. Kelley Publishers, 1969.

SSoc *The Study of Sociology.* 1873. Introduction by Talcott
Parsons. Ann Arbor: University of Michigan Press,
1961.

Work of Alexis de Tocqueville

DA *Democracy in America.* 1835. Translated by George
Lawrence. Edited by J. P. Mayer and Max Lerner. New
York: Harper and Row, 1966.

Works of Ferdinand Tönnies

CA *Community and Association.* 1887. Translated by
Charles P. Loomis. London: Routledge and Kegan
Paul, 1955.

OS *Ferdinand Tönnies on Sociology: Pure, Applied, and
Empirical, Selected Writings.* Edited by Werner J.
Cahnman and Rudolf Heberle. Chicago: University of
Chicago Press, 1971.

Works of Max Weber

GEH *General Economic History.* 1924. Translated by Frank
H. Knight. Glencoe, Ill.: Free Press, 1950.

"HC" "The Household Community." Translated by Ferdi-
nand Kolegar from *Wirtschaft und Gesellschaft.* 1922.
In *Theories of Society: Foundations of Modern So-
ciological Theory,* edited by Talcott Parsons, Edward
Shils, Kasper D. Naegele, Jesse R. Pitts. New York:
Free Press, 1965.

"RR"   "Religious Rejections of the World and Their Direc-
            tions." 1915. In *From Max Weber: Essays in Sociology,*
            edited and translated by H. H. Gerth and C. Wright
            Mills. New York: Oxford University Press, 1958.
SR   *Sociology of Religion.* 1922. Translated by Ephraim
            Fischoff. Boston: Beacon Press, 1963.

Preface

This book grew out of an intellectual puzzle. In the context of a quarter-century of women's struggles for equal rights and individual dignity and of a swelling wave of feminist scholarship, I could think of no major history of sociological theory that suggested that the classical theorists had written anything of substance about women. I knew that some of them had. I was versed in some of the classics of the Marxist tradition on the "woman question," especially Engels's. My consciousness about gender issues was shaped in discussion groups in San Francisco and Berkeley during the early 1960s, in which criticism and self-criticism around the problem of what was then termed male chauvinism were voiced. As a consequence of my political background, it was years later before I familiarized myself with the debate among feminist theorists about Freud's work.

My search through and rereading of the works of the classical (non-Marxist) sociological theorists was guided at first by what I would call a radical-feminist hunch—namely, that I would discover that they were, to a man, ideologically antifeminist. The matter turned out to be more complex; the theorists displayed some diversity of attitudes toward the position of women in society. More intriguing were changes of interest in and analysis of the "woman question" and changes in attitudes toward feminist movements within the careers of certain theorists. These shifts indicated clearly the thus far neglected impact of feminism on classical theory. As I came to better understand the historical and feminist contexts of, and the biographical facts relevant to, the theorists' writings on women and the relations of the sexes, my thinking about the material became more personal in character, and the material took on more and more meaning for me.

This book is deeply influenced by the lives of my parents. My father's background as a son of Norwegian immigrants, his work as a tool-and-die maker, trade-union organizer, and participant in the left wing of the working-class movement from the 1930s to the present have strongly influenced my work. My mother's origins in a German Lutheran family of small businessmen in part accounts for the length of the chapter on Germany. She was to become a woman of the working class and presently is a member of the Ada James Chapter of the National Organization for Women (Richland Center, Wisconsin). The organization of the historical materials along class lines stems from my reading of the evidence and my reading of it in light of my own history. And thus the dedication of this book to my mother, Gertrude.

Feminist critical discourse has raised the epistemological question of whether one must be a woman in order to contribute to an authentic sociology of or for women. Obviously, having written this book, my answer is: not necessarily. Although a man cannot experience what it means to be a woman, this does not preclude making a contribution to the sociology of women. William James's distinction between "knowing" and "knowing about" is apropos. Oppression seems to me to have transgender aspects, which those who have experienced it can communicate.

Several caveats are in order. It was not my intention to write complete histories of women's movements in modern European capitalist societies. Rather, my purpose was to provide sketches of the historical contexts surrounding the classical theorists' writings on women, selecting the works of the historians that best served this purpose. Therefore, I attempted to avoid joining issues in feminist historiography—with full awareness that the facts I selected do not speak exactly for themselves.

For consistency and conformity to contemporary usage, I have used the terms *feminist* and *feminism* to describe the movements for extensions of rights to women and proposals to alter fundamentally the relationships of the sexes, once again knowing full well that such characterizations were not used throughout the period covered here, nor uniformly.

Finally, I do not offer a theory of the relations of women and men. Therefore I do not address contemporary research on and argument about the biological and physiological differences between women and men, differences stressed by some feminists as well as antifeminists. What I have stressed of necessity are the ways in which conventional and "scientific" biological ideas about women's nature were used by nineteenth- and early twentieth-century classical sociologists to determine the "proper" social sphere of women and as a result to see them with a theoretically blurred vision. In the final chapter I offer my evaluations of the theorists, an argument for a theoretically informed comparison of histories as the only route to a sociology of the sexes, and my judgments of what the historical cases covered here tell us about variations in the oppression and liberation of women.

In this book I present what thirteen male classical sociologists wrote about the social position of women, the relationships of the sexes, and the feminist movements of their times—in short, the theoretical treatment of women by the founding fathers of classical sociological theory. To convey the original flavor of their texts, I have chosen to use extensive quotations from their writings rather than summary paraphrase and interpretation.

Quotations from the works of the theorists are cited in the text after citation in a note at first mention. A list of abbreviations of the titles and information about the editions used follows the table of contents. Other sources, particularly in the historical sketches, are cited in notes at the end of the book. Within paragraphs, when it was possible to do so and still be clear, citations were combined in one note referenced at the end of the paragraph; page numbers of quotations are listed in order of their appearance in the paragraph, followed by page numbers of references to general discussions.

Acknowledgments

There are several people without whom this work might neither have been published nor acquired whatever virtues it possesses. Chuck Elkins provided the sounding board some years ago and the initial encouragement to go ahead with the idea of the book. He gave freely of his skills with the English language and his wide range of intellectual resources to get the early draft into presentable shape. Unbeknownst to me, he submitted it to the editorial board of Florida International University Press (Miami). Elliott Currie gave me added confidence to carry out the project and offered valuable suggestions at the beginning and in the last phases of my work, pushing me to sharpen formulations. Randall Collins unselfishly displayed his professional commitment by giving me a thorough critique of the initial conception of the work; he also shared with me his extensive knowledge of Weber and suggested I develop more detailed pictures of the historical contexts of the classical theorists' writings on women. I was honored to have Rose Laub Coser review the manuscript and take my work seriously.

I also wish to thank especially Bob Dunn for his critical comments on an early draft of the book and a later draft of the conclusion. He generously allowed me to use the wonderful library of feminist scholarship of the late Harriet Older. It was Harriet (whose tragic death entwined with the historical subjects in these pages) who introduced me to the work of Sheila Rowbotham. Jon Snodgrass offered valuable suggestions for revising the tone of the initial draft of the manuscript. He shared his psychoanalytic training in the section on Weber and so many of his books. Mary Jane Elkins directed me to Spencer's biography to find clues to his shift from support of equal rights for women in his first book to the (in)famous antifeminist stance of his later work.

A number of my colleagues in the Department of Sociology at California State University, Los Angeles, gave continuous support. I thank Ralph Thomlinson, Paul Rowan, Eui-Young Yu, Larry Hong, Janice Marie Allard, Steve Gordon, Marion Dearman, and Fred Lynch (for suggestions on Mills). From outside my department, I want to thank Norma Pratt for pointing me in the right direction on the historiography of German socialist feminism, and Don Dewey, dean of the School of Natural and Social Sciences, for special encouragement on two occasions. Although it is impossible for me to thank individually all of my friends and colleagues throughout the university for their enthusiastic response to and concern for my work, I hope they will accept my gratitude. The Faculty Awards and Leaves Subcommittee recommended me for two grants that the CSULA Foundation awarded me to defray the costs of manuscript preparation. I am grateful for these awards, which allayed worries that otherwise would have interfered with my work. Harriet McNeeking typed a good part of the revised version of the manuscript. I was heartened that the material touched her. I cannot forget my students for their interest, encouraging responses, and patient anticipation. The personnel of University Presses of Florida have been unusually supportive.

I also wish to thank my friend Harry Orr for his persistent interest and prodding, my sister Kathryn Ann Kandal for her confidence in my way of thinking about the issues, and Tom Peters for helping me to build my own confidence.

I also thank my seventeen-year-old son Josh for his interest, pride in my work, and mostly for his patience. For five years, he lived with me and my work on the book. My wish and hope is that the world in which he lives will be one of peace, equality, and dignity for all persons and that he will experience the end to the oppression of women and the war between the sexes.

From Anita Aurora Acosta I came to understand more fully the personal and interpersonal costs to women and men of the victimization of women and how deeply sexism is embedded in the language of everyday life. She educated me in what it all means in practice.

1

Introduction

Contemporary Feminism and Classical Sociological Theory

Most recent social theories about the oppression of women take as their starting points the works of Karl Marx and/or Sigmund Freud.[1] These theories usually omit the treatment of women's roles by the founding fathers of nineteenth- and twentieth-century classical sociological theory. This lacuna is puzzling in light of current professional concern about the status of women in sociology and because of the general issue of the role of ideology in the development of sociological theory.[2] It is also puzzling because within the social sciences and the humanities in general, and in social theory in particular, a universe of discourse has emerged concerning the position of women in society, a universe of discourse composed of the separate but related vocabularies of various disciplines—for example, anthropology, historiography, and literary criticism—each with its distinctive subject matter and traditions.[3]

Much feminist writing has consisted of critiques of traditional

1

and contemporary scholarship and theory about women, or the absence thereof, highlighting how good or bad in an ideological sense such work is on what used to be referred to as the "woman question." Such concerns remain tacit but never too far below the surface in the following chapters. Feminist scholars are committed to rewriting "herstory," to include women, in the same way that Karl Marx forced the retelling of history from the point of view of the exploited classes; and feminist theorists of patriarchy, drawing on Freud's work, have constructed explanations of male domination over women. In Gayle Rubin's characterization, "The literature on women—both feminist and anti-feminist—is a long rumination on the question of the nature and genesis of women's oppression and social subordination."[4] Although not widely recognized, the texts of classical sociological theory of the nineteenth and twentieth centuries are part of this literature.

Sociologist Eloise C. Snyder wrote in 1979: "What is important to note here is not only the inferior position accorded to women in society by social theorists but the fact that for years no significant recognition was given to the prescriptive quality that such descriptions have. Even more important is the fact that during the many, many years that such pronouncements about women were being made, in spite of the changes that were occurring in women's roles, few writers found it important enough to address the manner in which women were portrayed in 'classical' theory. Recently, however, such reassessments are being made through feminist scholarship and are contributing a great deal more to our understanding of women in society than the entire collection of writings about women has done in the past."[5] Although such reassessment may be going on in a piecemeal way, to this day there exists no major history of classical sociological theory in which the impact of nineteenth- and twentieth-century debate and controversy over the "woman question" and of feminist movements on the sociological tradition is recognized, acknowledged, and evaluated.[6] The purpose of this work is to contribute to such a reassessment of classical sociological theory, which, after all, provides the foundation of the discipline.

The contemporary debate over feminism, as in the nineteenth century, has brought to the fore the issue of "woman's nature." Sociobiology, for example, assumes the universality of male aggression and dominance over women in its genetic-evolutionary theory of human behavior. The family—its nature and its relationship to

the social structure, the economy, work, and other institutions—
has been a second major issue in the contemporary controversies
surrounding feminism. Conservative thinkers going back to Comte
and Spencer argue for, or fear for, the autonomy of the family, and
Freudians view it as a determinative—if not *the* determinative—
social institution. On both sides of the feminist divide are to be
found assertions of the universality, if not the inevitability, of the
patriarchal family. However, some historical sociologists and eth-
nologists show that forms of the family and degrees of oppression or
equality of women vary with historical conditions and types of social organization of work, authority, and force. And in individual
lives, women and men strive to create or re-create alternative forms
of family life. A related theoretical dispute centers on the relative
importance of sex/gender and social class in producing and repro-
ducing the oppression of women. Closely linked to these issues are
analyses of the historical circumstances in which women's movements for equality occur—their relationships to reform and revolutionary movements of other oppressed groups, and the forces favoring or hindering their success.[7] Some of the first contemporary
discussions of these issues are to be found in the classical tradition
of sociological theory. Turning back to read and to critically evaluate
these discussions seems particularly appropriate in our time, when
women "are suffering under a resurgence of femininity."[8]

In feminist criticism, sociology is faulted for its exclusion of
women in most of its subject matter and for its preference for "hard"
methods of inquiry that are alleged to disguise its masculine bias.
Feminist criticism (explored in the concluding chapter of this book)
argues, in effect, that sociology is constructed on male-dominated
categories of understanding and perspective. What is missing in
feminist scholarship is an assessment of the treatment of women in
the history of classical sociological theory. For the most part, we are
offered merely cursory, generalized, and unhistorical references to
the sexism of classical theorists. Sociology, feminist and nonfeminist,
apparently knows only its contemporary self. In this study, I attempt
to explore in greater depth the puzzle of the missing link between
contemporary feminism and the treatment of women in classical
theory, by noting the debates in classical sociological theory about
the inequality and subjection of women and by examining the historical context in which this theory was formed.

Historical Context of the "Woman Question"

The omission in major secondary historical and theoretical analysis
of the classical theorists' treatment of women is striking for another
reason: the formation and development of classical sociological theory occurred, after all, as a response to social, political, and intellectual changes arising with or from the Industrial Revolution, the
French Revolution, and the Enlightenment. Thus, classical sociological theory originated in the same historical epoch as the long
swell of modern feminism, flowing in pulses and lulls roughly from
the eighteenth century to the present. Sheila Ryan Johansson has
referred to the first wave when she speaks of "the great nineteenth-
century flowering of feminist thought."[9]

Chiding standard historiography for its virtual neglect of feminist movements in the nineteenth and early twentieth centuries,
Theodore Roszak wrote: "A fair survey of feminism would see the
pressure for woman's emancipation building from the 1830s and
1840s and reaching out well beyond the issue of the ballot. . . . By
the late nineteenth century—in the wake of at least two generations of feminist organization and crusading—this supposedly mar-
ginal curiosity called the 'woman problem' had become one of the
most earth-shaking debates in the Western world, fully as explosive
an issue as the class or national conflicts of the day. . . . One would
be hard pressed to find many major figures of the period in any cultural field who did not address themselves passionately to the rights
of women."[10] By the late 1920s and early 1930s, "the last great feminist wave of the late nineteenth century finally faded,"[11] not to be
revived worldwide until the 1960s and 1970s. For the most inclusive
contexts of the beginnings of feminism, however, we must go back
beyond the 1830s, to the two revolutions of the last years of the
eighteenth century—the French Revolution and the Industrial
Revolution.

"Feminism came, like socialism, out of the tangled, confused
response of men and women to capitalism," Sheila Rowbotham has
argued.[12] The Industrial Revolution, which occurred first and with
purest effect in England, involved the separation of the workplace
from the home, thereby producing roles for women as workers distinct from their roles in the family. As a result, women were subjected to a double oppression—at home and in the workplace—or
they were faced with "an unprecedented choice between home and
children on the one hand, and the continued possibility of earning a

cash wage, however meager, on the other." The conflict caused by the demands of these two roles "survives in the twentieth century as perhaps the most enduring legacy of the Victorian period."[13] Although the earlier development of capitalism had weakened the position of working women, associated "women's work" with low pay, and restricted middle-class women to the household, the Industrial Revolution created the potential material basis for women's emancipation by drawing them back into social production separate from family life, thereby altering the prevailing relationships of the sexes. Opportunities were created for weakening patriarchal authority in working-class households, for financial independence for women, and for women to fight collectively for new rights as workers and citizens.

The Enlightenment and the French Revolution provided the ideas for feminist protest and the forms of political activity in which to express them. The moral and political aspirations of the Enlightenment were captured in ideas such as *progress, contract, nature, reason,* and in the Enlightenment's central theme, the "release of the individual from ancient social ties and of the mind from fettering traditions."[14] For the thinkers of the Enlightenment, nature and reason demanded recognition of the inalienable rights of the individual, including the right of equality. The Marquis de Condorcet, an aristocratic supporter of the French Revolution who became one of its victims, joined the feminists in stating the case for the equality of the sexes:

> Among the various sorts of mental progress most important for the general good, we must count the total destruction of those prejudices which have established between the two sexes an inequality of rights fatal to even that one which it favors. We shall search in vain for motives to justify it in differences of physical organization, or in differences we should like to find in power of intellect or moral sensibility. That inequality has had no other origin than the abuse of strength, and it is in vain that we have tried since to excuse it through sophisms.
>
> We shall show to what degrees the abolition of the practices authorized by this prejudice and of the laws which it has dictated can contribute to the increased happiness of families, to rendering common the domestic virtues, the first foundation of all the others; to favoring the progress of instruction, and especially to making it truly general, either because it

should be extended to both sexes with greater equality, or because it cannot become general, even for the men, without the
concurrence of the mothers of families. Would not this tardy
homage paid finally to equity and good sense dry up a too
fruitful source of injustice, cruelty, and crime, by doing away
with so dangerous an opposition between man's most active
natural propensity, and the most difficult to suppress, and his
duties, or the interests of society? Would it not produce, finally, what has hitherto been only a dream, national manners
of a gentle and blameless character, built, not on proud priva-
tions, on hypocritical appearances, on reservations imposed
by fear of shame or religious terrors, but on habits freely con-
tracted, inspired by nature, and avowed by reason?[15]

Condorcet was, of course, a rare exception among male revolutionary leaders, most of whom believed that women should serve the
revolution as wives and mothers. Nevertheless, the revolutionary
tradition was an inspiration to feminists in France, England, Germany, Italy, and the United States. As Rowbotham has pointed out,
"By the 1840s connection between social revolution and the liberation of women had been made."[16] Classical sociological theory took
shape against the background of revolutionary upheaval and capitalist industrialization, along with the concomitant "explosive expansion of state bureaucracies" and the surveillance and regulation
of public and private life by the state, subjecting women and men
"to a host of new strictures."[17]

Articulating a view shared by many feminists, Erna Olafson
Hellerstein, Leslie Parker Hume, and Karen M. Offen have argued
that "modern 'objective' social science, born during the Victorian
period, both incorporated and legitimized Victorian prejudices
about gender, the family, work, and the division between public
and private spheres." Further, they have contended that an "extreme polarization of sex roles" emerged during this period: "In
both practice and prescription the male and female spheres became
increasingly separated, and the roles of men and women became
even more frozen. Social scientists by and large sanctified the separation of spheres and consigned women to the domestic, private
sphere."[18] Similarly, Snyder has argued that sociological theories
"tended either to ignore women or to place them in extremely inferior roles. Such predominantly male orientations are evident in
the writings of almost all the classical theorists, such as Comte,

Durkheim, Pareto, Tönnies, and Weber."[19] These assessments omit both the complexities and contradictions of the effects of the two revolutions on the lives of women and on relationships of men and women of different classes, of the new class and sexual divisions of labor under capitalism, and—of chief concern here—of the responses of classical sociologists to the "woman question."

In the following five chapters, the central representatives of five national traditions or variants of classical sociological theory— English, French, German, Italian, and North American—are examined for their analyses of the social position of women and their responses to movements for women's emancipation. Each chapter begins with a historical sketch followed by sections on that nation's theorists selected for study. I will discuss the English themes of "woman's nature," the struggle for women's suffrage, and access for middle-class women to equal education and to the professions expressed in John Stuart Mill's liberal social theory; and I will explore Herbert Spencer's shift, in response to currents of evolutionary naturalism and pressures for women's rights, from a profeminist to an antifeminist position.

Next I will turn to France to observe the moralistic and political responses of Alexis de Tocqueville and Auguste Comte to the revolutionary feminism of the period 1830–48 and Émile Durkheim's move from a functionalist to a conflict perspective on the relations of men and women in post–Paris Commune France, in which the struggle for women's rights to divorce, education, and suffrage took nonrevolutionary forms.

In Germany, feminist and class struggles occurred in telescoped historical processes, and the tradition of sociological theory there is rich in feminist concerns. For these reasons, the German case is the centerpiece of the story, containing as it does the confrontation of bourgeois theory and Marxism, the theory and practice of socialist feminism, the conflict of socialist feminism with liberal feminism, and the patriarchal reaction against both of them. I will explore the effect of the erotic and feminist movements on Max Weber's sociological interests, life, and personal values, Georg Simmel's preoccupation over nearly three decades with the social psychology of women and the relations of the sexes in their social and cultural dimensions, the modification of Ferdinand Tönnies' conception of womanly *Gemeinschaft* and "woman's nature" in the light of capitalist development, and Karl Mannheim's historical-structural analyses of male sexuality and variations in marital relationships.

Vilfredo Pareto's sociological theory, written around the time of the First World War, mirroring the relative backwardness of Italian capitalism, commented on feminism outside of Italy more than within it and also discussed sexuality and prostitution. His work exhibits a hostile and fearful response to the battle for women's suffrage. Robert Michels's shift from Marxist socialism to Italian nationalism is prefigured in his writings on prostitution, sexuality, and flirtation. His *Sexual Ethics* documents the debates about sexuality and the relations of the sexes in turn-of-the-century Europe.

In the chapter on sociological theory in the United States, the contrasting versions of classical theory in the writings of Talcott Parsons and C. Wright Mills about women are summarized against the background of the history of feminism in the United States and the rise of corporate capitalism.

The concluding chapter contains an evaluation of the classical theorists' writings about women, a comparison of alternative theoretical accounts of the subjection of women derived from Marx and Freud, and some suggestions for a comparative-historical sociology of women. By assessing classical theory in light of contemporary feminist concerns, I hope to bring to light a neglected but crucial aspect of the sociological tradition.

The approach adopted draws on the perspectives of the sociology of knowledge and of ideology, modes of inquiry that seek to trace the interplay of social structure and theoretical consciousness. Each chapter therefore begins with a historical sketch of the national (and sometimes international) context of the works of the classical sociologists. In this way, differences can be specified in intellectual traditions, in conceptions of feminine nature, and in the timing, size, degree of militancy, class, and political characteristics of particular movements for women's emancipation. These, along with a modest attempt to link biography and history, may offer clues to help explain what the theorists said, and did not say, about the condition and "nature" of women and their responses to women's struggles for freedom and equality.

The larger theoretical issues of the sources of the oppression of women are not new issues but have their modern roots in the nineteenth and early twentieth centuries, including the sociological theory of that period. The topics, then as now, include the relationships of class and sex (and at times, race); the nature of the family and its relationship to changes in social structures; sexuality; as well as the related but more specific and practical issues of the exclusion of women from professional and creative endeavors; equal pay; protective legislation for women; prostitution; reproductive rights; reform versus revolution; and the relationship of women's struggles to radical movements. In short, to paraphrase Georg Lukács, the present is itself a historical problem.

2

England

Feminism and Liberal Social Theory

The development of capitalism in England during the sixteenth and seventeenth centuries caused a transformation in the sexual division of labor. Among artisans, women were excluded from the most profitable trades, and because of increased agricultural productivity and a ready supply of cheap labor, the wives of successful yeoman farmers participated less than peasant women in direct economic production. The household dwelling was restructured to include separate bedrooms and dining rooms. The virtues of monogamy and chastity became standards of conduct for bourgeois men as well as for women. In short, the stable, monogamous, middle-class family was in place *before* the Industrial Revolution. Well-off farmers aped the upper classes by regarding the leisure of their wives as a symbol of status and by sending their children to boarding schools, where boys were given an academic education and girls learned "accomplishments." As historian Sheila Rowbotham has noted, these disparate sex roles, shaped by emerging capitalism, were the historical bases for nineteenth-century bourgeois-feminist attacks "on the exclusion of women from education, the professions," the middle- and upper-class world of work, and on the laws that upheld men's control of women's property. These themes recur in the writings of John Stuart Mill and Herbert Spencer about women. For peasant and poor women, lives of "ceaseless labor" in an essentially family-centered economy remained the norm. The silence of the historical record over the plight of these women is, in Rowbotham's words, "the silence of class and sex oppression."[1]

During the seventeenth century, Cromwell and his followers used the language and imagination of the Old Testament to make their revolution, which was associated with the emergence of bourgeois society in England. At the same time, the Puritan doctrine of the equality of the souls of men and women was used by radical or leftist sectarians, such as Quakers and "ranters," to draw feminist conclusions that would permit women to be preachers, that questioned monogamy, and that justified the participation of women in the politics of the Civil War. However, the spate of pro- and anti-feminist pamphleteering and the voices of women and children were silenced by the Restoration. Mainstream Puritanism abandoned the rule of king and priest but substituted for it patriarchal authority in the family; the Puritan bourgeois wife was given the role of an unequal partner whose soul might be equal in God's sight but whose place on earth was inferior to her husband's.[2]

During the eighteenth century, a "movement of resistance to patriarchy"[3] found expression in English novels, in proposals for new education for women, in calls for personal equality with men, and in criticism of the brutishness of men. Patriarchal responses were satirical, patronizing, and contemptuous. Coincidentally, there occurred a shift in conceptions of feminine nature: women were now considered sexually modest and passive; earlier they had been considered sexually insatiable. Already excluded from business and the professions and therefore economically dependent on men, and thought of as helpless by their very nature, women were divested of any legal personality in marriage by Blackstone's 1765 codification of common law. In similar circumstances in France, it required but a small step for Jean-Jacques Rousseau to justify the restriction of women to the domestic sphere by virtue of their "nature" and to develop "a natural female education" to fit them for the duties of chaste wives nobly taking care of and pleasing their husbands.[4]

Modern European feminism in general and the struggle for women's rights in nineteenth-century England in particular are usually dated to the publication in 1792 of Mary Wollstonecraft's *Vin-*

dication of the Rights of Women, a direct response to the French
Revolution. Citing Enlightenment ideas developed during the
revolution about the importance of environment and education and
using her own experience as an example, Wollstonecraft countered
Rousseau's proposals for feminine education, claiming that "the doll
will never excite attention unless confinement allows [the little girl]
no alternative." She observed the inconsistency of radical males
who fought for the freedom of individuals to determine their own
happiness and yet continued to subjugate women, leaving them "to
procreate and rot." Describing the ways in which sex roles set special limits on the freedom of women, she said, "There are some
loopholes out of which a man may creep, and dare to think and act
for himself, but for a woman it is a herculean task, because she has
difficulties peculiar to her sex to overcome which require almost
superhuman powers."[5]

Wollstonecraft's book and the liberation of women were cham-
pioned by a small intellectual circle that included the anarchist
William Godwin, with whom Wollstonecraft lived until her death
in childbirth. (They married when she became pregnant.) Other
members of the group were the poet William Blake, who could
imagine the disappearance of "A Religion of Chastity, forming a
Commerce to sell Loves"; Mary Hays, a feminist novelist and biographer of famous women; and, later, Percy Bysshe Shelley, who
married Wollstonecraft's daughter. Shelley showed awareness of the
constraints imposed on sexual love by marriage in his remark "Not
even the intercourse of the sexes is exempt from the despotism
of positive institution."[6] The feminist tradition was carried on by
the "free-thinking Christians," the Unitarians, clustered around
William J. Fox's *Monthly Repository,* with which John Stuart Mill
later became associated. However, as Rowbotham has noted, "The
English Jacobins were not primarily concerned with the rights of
women."[7] A signal and interesting exception was Thomas Spence,
"a poor schoolmaster from Newcastle" and a follower of Thomas
Paine. Spence, who was virtually alone in addressing Jacobin propaganda to working women, asked rhetorically, "What signifies Reforms of Government or Redress of Public Grievances, if people
cannot have their domestic grievances redressed?" In a dialogue
that he wrote, a woman character says to an aristocrat that husbands have been so negligent about "their own rights" that "we
women mean to take up the business ourselves."[8] For a time the
anti-Jacobin repression silenced the attempt to link the personal to

the political revolution. As E. P. Thompson has observed, "The war years saw a surfeit of sermonising and admonitory tracts limiting or refuting claims to women's rights which were associated with 'Jacobinism.'"[9]

The revival of the struggle for women's rights in England is associated with the effects of the Industrial Revolution, circa 1760 to 1840. The epoch was characterized by technological change in methods of production, the shift of the locus of industrial activity to urban settings, and the transformation of the organization, means, and authority relationships of work. The classic example is the introduction in the textile industry of first the water frame, then the self-acting mule, and finally the power loom.[10] The Industrial Revolution was, in Marx's periodization of the history of capitalism, the time of the replacement of manufacture based upon existing crafts by machine industry housed in factories.[11] It was the period of the emergence of new class relations and the transformation of the old, a time when master craftsmen, artisans, and domestic industry were being shoved aside by upstart, capitalist entrepreneurs; when the Luddite weavers attacked and destroyed the machines that threatened their very livelihood—in Thompson's conception, the age of "the making of the English working class."[12]

The effects of the Industrial Revolution on the work experience and lives of working-class women were not uniform. The evidence we have shows that women apparently continued to be employed primarily in their traditional occupations, single women in domestic service and retail distribution, married women in domestic manufacturing and agriculture (until its decline in England around 1850). Families persisted tenaciously as economic and social units. It was in the context of traditional relations of the sexes that change was occurring. Short of family financial crises, those women who were wives and mothers were least able to—and were not expected to—take advantage of opportunities for factory employment.[13] Rowbotham has commented: "The separation of family from work had occurred before capitalism, but as industry grew in scale it appeared in its most distinct and clear form."[14] As increasing numbers of women and children, as well as men, were employed in the factories, the social experience of some women changed, and therefore the conditions for the transformation in the relations of the sexes began to take shape.

In the first half of the nineteenth century, manufacturers introduced technical innovations that made it possible to replace adult male craftsmen with women and children who were paid lower wages. Employers and their apologists such as Andrew Ure justified the poor wages by saying they did not want to tempt women out of their homes. But the other motive behind the changed composition of the industrial labor force was the employers' interest in imposing discipline on their workers: children and unskilled women with no other sources of income were less likely to object to their employers' policies. By the early 1830s women made up more than half the adult labor force.[15] When Lord Ashley introduced the Ten Hours Bill in the House of Commons on 15 March 1844, he presented statistics to show that of the 419,560 factory workers in the British Empire in 1839, only 96,569, not one full quarter, were adult males; 80,695 were males under eighteen years of age, while 242,296 were females, of whom 112,192 were younger than eighteen.[16]

Speaking of some of the effects of the Industrial Revolution on the quality of women's lives, Thompson has pointed out: "It is here that it is most difficult to draw a balance. On the one hand, the claim that the Industrial Revolution raised the status of women would seem to have little meaning when set beside the record of excessive hours of labour, cramped housing, excessive child-bearing and terrifying rates of child mortality. On the other hand, the abundant opportunities for employment in the textile districts gave to women the status of independent wage-earners. The spinster or the widow was freed from the dependence upon relatives or upon parish relief. Even the unmarried mother might be able, through the laxness of 'moral discipline' in many mills, to achieve an independence unknown before."[17]

Thompson has observed that employment of women in the textile districts "gave rise to the earliest widespread participation by working women in political and social agitation." The first Female Reform Societies were formed in Lancashire about 1818–19, a possible indication of "a sudden leap forward in consciousness." The first independent trade-union action by women workers occurred in 1832 when fifteen hundred female card-cutters went out on strike in West-Riding. The event elicited John Wade's remark that "alarmists may view these indications of female independence as more menacing to established institutions than the 'education of the lower orders.'" Thompson has noted that "the coarse language and independent manners of Lancashire mill-girls shocked many witnesses." However, advances for women did not happen without a "paradox of feeling": "The Radicalism of northern working women was compounded of nostalgia for lost status [based upon successful management of a household economy] and the assertion of new-found rights."[18] Rowbotham adds that "conflict and competition between male and female workers was to continue to be an obstacle to joint unionisation," as in the case of the unsuccessful attempt to form a Grand National Consolidated Trades Union in 1834. Many workers (most men and some women) retained the traditional notions that women needed to be protected from the factory system and should not have to work, because a living wage should be one that would allow a man to support his family as well as himself.[19]

On the more private relationships of the sexes, it is difficult to assess the effects of the Industrial Revolution, as Thompson has noted:

> The evidence tells us so little about the essential relations . . .
> between . . . men and women. . . . But there is no evidence
> that a repressive sexual code and patriarchal family relations
> brought enhancement of either happiness or of love . . . while,
> as sexual conduct in the early 19th century became more in-
> hibited and secretive, so also, in the great towns, prostitution
> grew. . . .
>   But there is plenty of evidence as to the heroic family loy-
> alties which sustained many people in these years.[20]

The response of working people to changes in the family and in the economic system, Rowbotham has written, "was bound up with the desperate defence of a way of life, in which fear of the independence of wives and daughters working under another roof with other men, coming back with their own wages, mingled with a notion of the family as a producing unit and protest against the sheer brutality of conditions in the early factories."[21] Further, the contradiction between traditional roles and factory work for wages was most intensely experienced by women, as Thompson has noted:

> Each stage in industrial differentiation and specialisation
> struck also at the family economy, disturbing customary re-
> lations between man and wife, parents and children, and dif-
> ferentiating more sharply between "work" and "life." It was to
> be a full hundred years before this differentiation was to bring
> returns, in the form of labor-saving devices, back into the
> working woman's home. Meanwhile, the family was roughly

torn apart each morning by the factory bell, and the mother who was also a wage-earner often felt herself to have the worst of both the domestic and the industrial worlds.[22]

Commenting on the situation in the early 1840s of unemployed men who did "woman's work," young Friedrich Engels drew a perceptive conclusion:

> This condition, which unsexes the man and takes from the woman all womanliness without being able to bestow upon the man true womanliness, or the woman true manliness . . . degrades, in the most shameful way, both sexes, . . . we must admit that so total a reversal of the position of the sexes can have come to pass only because the sexes have been placed in a false position from the beginning. If the reign of the wife over the husband, as inevitably brought about by the factory system, is inhuman, the pristine rule of the husband over the wife must have been inhuman too.[23]

This development only proved to Engels that, at bottom, the traditional family was bound, not by affection, but by the economic power of the breadwinner. These disruptive effects on the working-class family are only dimly reflected, if at all, as we shall see, in what John Stuart Mill and Herbert Spencer wrote about women.

The liberating potentials of the French and Industrial revolutions began to come together in the 1820s and the 1830s in attempts by a vigorous minority to make a cultural revolution in the social position of women and in the relationships between men and women. Radical men and women included rationalists who subscribed to the ideas of Mary Wollstonecraft, followers of Great Britain's Robert Owen, France's Fourierist utopian socialists, and millenarian Saint-Simonians. The tradition was expressed in such publications as the *Black Dwarf*, for which John Stuart Mill wrote as a young man. Ideas for the liberation of women were not limited to middle-class and professional circles but were accepted and practiced by advanced artisans and by men and women working in the cities.[24]

During the 1820s, Francis Place, a tailor, advocated birth control for working-class women. He convinced Richard Carlile, editor of *The Republican* and a hero to feminist working women, of the necessary connection between sexual and reproductive rights. In an article entitled "What Is Love?" Carlile described extant methods: the vaginal sponge, the "skin" or glove, and withdrawal. While some radicals saw birth control as encouraging promiscuity, prostitution, and infidelity, the main issue of contention (as has continued to be the case even to the present) was the connection of birth control with the ideas of Malthus. Radical Malthusians regarded contraception as a strategy for maintaining population within the limits of the world's capacity to produce and distribute the means of subsistence; the radical opponents of Malthus believed that contraception was a tool that the upper classes used to interfere in the lives of the poor, to limit their numbers, and thus to put off needed reforms. In the years 1834 and 1835, several books that provided birth control information (one written by Robert Owen's son) sold hundreds of copies. The debate about contraception was clouded by the common prejudice that the economic independence women gained by working in factories was a cause of sexual promiscuity among them.[25]

Several proposals for the liberation of women were current in the first half of the nineteenth century. Charles Fourier's plans for great communes included communal responsibility for child care and the organization of work to fit individuals' interests. Owenites pioneered cooperative nursery schools, and classes of instruction held by Owen's followers were open to women. Owen believed that the nuclear family, because it promoted individualism and competition, was an obstacle to creation of a cooperative society. The Owenites believed in easy divorce. They also opposed celibacy and rejected the double standard in matters of sexual morality. Saint-Simonian "missionaries" arrived in Britain in 1833–34 and gave feminist and socialist lectures. One of the leaders, Barthélemy Prosper Enfantin, criticized what he saw as the oppressive nature of Christian marriage. He advocated the idea that God was both man and woman, from which premise he concluded that women and men are equal. The Saint-Simonians expected a female messiah who would usher in the new age.[26]

William Thompson, an Irish landowner, best summed up the currents of socialist feminism of the period. Against the utilitarian, middle-class radicalism of James Mill, which saw no need for separate legal interests for women, Thompson wrote his 1825 "Appeal of one half of the Human Race, Women, against the pretensions of the other Half, Men, to retain them in Civil and Domestic Slavery." Thompson used the analogy to slavery, which John Stuart Mill also

used: a woman's appearance was "indelible like the skin of the Black."
About the institution of marriage Thompson said, "Home . . . is
the external prison house of the wife." Without reforms, he said,
"to be a woman is to be an inferior animal." He also believed that
women must first respect themselves and exert their power before
they would be respected by men. Going further, he argued that a
competitive class society would keep women at a disadvantage and
would have to be replaced by a "positive" cooperative society in
which child care would be socialized. He was much influenced by
Anna Wheeler, "an important mediator between [these] several different tendencies in radical thought," to whom he dedicated his
"Appeal."[27]

International exchange of ideas among the utopians flourished
during the 1820s and 1830s. But some male radicals said sexual
equality had to wait for a change in the property system of society,
an argument that has recurred in our own time. Some feminists responded, then as now, that a cultural revolution in the relationships
between men and women is a precondition for a socialist society. As
Rowbotham has pointed out, with the defeat of Chartism in the
1840s and the resulting loss of hope for a new world, "these ideas
about transforming relations between the sexes and struggling in
the area of personal life faded in the working-class movement until
the socialist movement was reborn at the end of the century."[28]

Prosperity strengthened patriarchy and intensified the dependency of women of the Victorian middle class, who were considered part of their husbands' belongings; the wife's leisure was a
mark of the husband's success in the world.[29] Martha Vicinus has
suggested that there was a shift in models of femininity during the
Victorian period. Until the turn of the nineteenth century, the
ideal was that of the "perfect wife," whose first tasks were child-
bearing and child rearing, and who also contributed to the family
economy by managing the household. In the upper-middle class,
this notion was replaced by the ideal of the "perfect lady," a conspicuous consumer totally dependent economically on her father and
later on her husband. Her only roles were as wife and mother, incon-
gruously combined with "total sexual innocence." In Vicinus's words,
"Ruskin's vision of girls as flowers to be plucked is the norm, and Mill's
marriage between intellectual and emotional equals the aberra-
tion."[30] At the same time, however, as Rowbotham has noted, "A new
ideal of the relationship between men and women, reminiscent of
the puritans, and of Defoe's notion of wives as companions appeared

very clearly by the middle of the century."[31] It was precisely this ideal that Mill employed in his criticism of the subjection of women in bourgeois marriage. Further, the model of the "perfect lady" was challenged by yet another, that of the "perfect" or "'new woman,' who continued to hold chastity as an ideal, but made it equally applicable to men as to women. . . . The new woman worked, sought education, and fought for legal and political rights."[32] (This context must be recalled when Herbert Spencer's final position on equal rights for women is discussed later in this chapter.)

Correspondingly, legislation whittled away at patriarchy; in 1882, women gained the right to independent ownership of property. But from the late 1860s to the 1880s, bills to enfranchise women were defeated in Parliament even after male workers won the right to vote. The *Saturday Review* of 6 May 1871 opined that the vote for women would "endanger the institution of marriage and the family." Later, the militant feminist movement would rebound from these parliamentary defeats. In 1889, Emmeline Pankhurst helped found the Women's Franchise League, which took up the cause of the rights of married women in divorce, inheritance, and child custody. But on the question of women's sexual liberation, liberal feminists were "reticent."[33]

To be useful, middle-class women did charity work among the poor, and some argued that women should be educated in social science to promote reforms. Beatrice Potter (who later married Sidney Webb) was among the women radicalized by exposure to the conditions of working women.[34] By the 1860s, charitable work among the downtrodden was part of a movement to expand women's "proper sphere." Vicinus has pointed out that "activists . . . argued that just as women had an obligation to educate their children in morality, so too did they have the wider responsibility to educate society on moral issues." Women's special nurturing skills could be applied beyond the family and traditional philanthropy to help "eliminate the most grievous wrongs of society."[35]

Upper- and middle-class women were also motivated to fight against prostitution and venereal disease because they recognized that prostitutes were patronized by men of their own classes. A stratum of "kept women" was emerging in suburban villas along the new London rail lines. An 1864 bill to prevent contagious diseases allowed the physical examination of suspected prostitutes. In 1869, the Campaign against Contagious Diseases, led by Josephine Butler, made middle-class women aware of the hypocrisy of a male-defined and class-oriented sexual morality that worked with "murderous cruelty" on other women; even children were sold into white slavery. The reaction to this open discussion of one of Victorian culture's most taboo subjects is illustrated in a remark by a member of Parliament that the campaigners were "worse than prostitutes." While the campaign attracted working-class and union support, reformers revealed the gulf separating the classes by attempting to inculcate in workers the middle-class values of thrift, abstinence, good housekeeping, and proper child care.[36]

The liberal feminist attack on patriarchy did not immediately resonate in the working class, where such authority was already being shredded by capitalism. Lord Shaftesbury worried (as did Herbert Spencer) about the breakup of the family as a result of the factory system. "Domestic life and domestic discipline must soon be at an end," Shaftesbury said. The Trades Union Congress included such women as Emma Paterson in 1876 and supported women's suffrage in 1884. But male/female conflicts of interest were clearly evident in the workers' and socialist movements. Male trade unionists were suspicious of middle-class women reformers, and many also believed, as union leader Henry Broadhurst stated, that "wives should be in their proper place at home." During the depression of the 1870s and 1880s, men advocated legislation protecting working women, which working women viewed as "protecting" them out of jobs. During the last half of the 1880s and throughout the 1890s, a period of organizing noncraft unions and of a revival of socialism, there was heightened activity among working-class women. Radicals such as Eleanor Marx, Tom Maguire, and Tom Mann (who asked, "Who would choose to be a workman's wife?") supported strikes; and prominent women, such as Emmeline Pankhurst, joined the Independent Labour Party. During the 1890s different concepts of family, sexuality, and unconventional life-styles were subjects of intense discussion. In his *Love's Coming of Age* (1896), the cooperative-socialist Edward Carpenter attempted to link personal transformation and radical politics. Carpenter openly discussed in his pamphlets the sexual liberation of women and what he called the "intermediate sex" (homosexuals). He was told by Robert Blatchford, the non-Marxist socialist editor of *The Clarion*, to keep quiet until socialism was achieved; Blatchford assured the public that socialism had nothing to do with "Free Love" and the abolition of the family. Rowbotham has summarized this period: "Like the utopian socialists earlier, revolutionaries in the 1880s and 1890s tried to connect sexual subordination to property ownership, and to discover the relationship between the oppression of women and the exploitation of workers."[37]

In the last half of the nineteenth century, the debate about population continued to be cast in the mold of Malthus's "law" of population. Charles Bradlaugh and Annie Besant were arrested in 1877 for publishing a new edition of Charles Knowlton's book containing birth-control information, *Fruits of Philosophy,* first published in the 1860s. The solicitor general called it "a dirty, filthy book" that advocated the separation of sexual passion from its providentially ordained and only purpose, reproduction. (Besant lost custody of her child because of publishing an "obscene" book—the judge wished to prevent her daughter Jean from following in her footsteps.) The anti-Malthusians included the church, upper-class conservatives, moralists, and Marxists, an odd assortment. On the other side, as Rowbotham has remarked, there was an "uneasy relation between a section of the feminist movement in the nineteenth century and the Malthusian League." During the 1870s the Mensinga diaphragm was invented by a Dutch doctor; and economic depression provided an incentive to regulate family size, although the more effective methods of birth control were priced beyond the reach of working-class women. By 1880, the birth rate in England had dropped, and by 1900 survey evidence linked birth-control propaganda with the lower birth rate.[38]

This historical sketch ends at the turn of the century, because Mill died in 1873 and Spencer in 1903. The struggle for women's right to vote was a unifying issue, but the various radical and liberal movements were not without divisions. There were splits in Emmeline Pankhurst's Women's Social and Political Union (WSPU)—including a break with her more socialist daughter Sylvia—over which class to ally with and which tactics to adopt to win the battle for women's suffrage. Socialists and feminists parted company when some of the latter agreed with Hannah Mitchell's conclusion "that socialists are not necessarily feminists." Socialist women advocated the universal franchise and thus opposed the suffragists' position of electoral qualification. In 1904, after the Women's Enfranchisement Bill was voted down in Parliament, the WSPU became militant, engaging in strikes and violence. However, the death knell for militant liberal feminism came when the leaders of the WSPU supported the British government in World War I, and the extension of the franchise took away the single issue that unified feminists. The war also wore down the cutting edge of socialism's position on women's rights by integrating the workers' and radical movements into the emerging state capitalist order.[39]

The English Theorists

England is the *locus classicus* of the Industrial Revolution, which provided many of the themes of classical sociological theory—the industrial city, new forms of property, the condition of the working class, the factory system, and social legislation concerning female and child labor. Nevertheless, in Perry Anderson's words, England *"alone of major Western societies—never produced a classical sociology,"* in the continental sense.[40] Several historical conditions lay behind this anomaly. First, England had its bourgeois revolution in the seventeenth century. Its early transition to capitalism, dominance of the world market, and political institutions capable of encapsulating class conflicts had given it, to paraphrase Engels, not only a bourgeoisie but also a bourgeois aristocracy and a bourgeois proletariat. Second, England's tradition of philosophy is empiricism and its social theory utilitarianism.[41] As Robert Nisbet has argued, the paradox of the sociological tradition is that while it "falls, in its objectives and in the political and scientific values of its principal figures, in the mainstream of modernism, its essential concepts and its implicit perspectives place it much closer, generally speaking, to philosophical conservatism." The "conservative image of the good society" of the "Anti-Enlightenment" reasserted the values and ideas of community, authority, hierarchy, and the sacred, which came to constitute the "unit-ideas of Sociology." In England, in the absence of such a classical sociological tradition, we must look to the liberal social theory of John Stuart Mill and the writings of Herbert Spencer.[42]

John Stuart Mill
On *The Subjection of Women*

Strictly speaking, John Stuart Mill (1806–73) was not a classical sociological theorist.[43] His work is considered here because of its importance in the history of the literature on the subjection of women. As Susan Moller Okin has pointed out, he is "the only major liberal political philosopher to have set out explicitly to apply the principles of liberalism to women."[44] Since there are several excellent recent analyses of Mill's feminism, my examination of his treatment of the "woman question" can focus on its more sociological aspects.

Some facts of Mill's biography, particularly his relationship with Harriet Taylor, are pertinent to his thought. Mill was a member of the Philosophic Radicals (an intellectual-political society adhering to Bentham's utilitarianism), who were attempting to carry on the work of criticism and reform of traditional institutions in the manner of the French *philosophes*. In the late 1820s, Mill came into contact with a group of Unitarian radicals, free-thinking Christians, whose leader was the Reverend William J. Fox. "Concern for the status of women and the relations between the sexes," as Alice S. Rossi has pointed out, "was no new idea in the social circle of the Unitarian Radicals in the early 1830s."[45] It was in that social circle that Mill met Harriet Taylor in 1830. They developed a lifelong relationship and married in 1851, two years after her first husband's death freed her from that unhappy relationship.

Mill was a feminist before he met Harriet Taylor. At the age of seventeen he had been arrested for giving vaginal sponges to maidservants in public and to the wives and daughters of tradesmen and mechanics in marketplaces. For *The Black Dwarf* he wrote articles advocating birth control.[46] In 1824, he wrote a piece for the *Westminister Review* rejecting separate moral standards and sets of values for the two sexes and nicely describing the opposite and unequally valued character traits that society had prescribed for men and women. He observed that women who infringed on male prerogatives, showed independence, or tried to be useful "either to themselves or to the world, otherwise than as the slaves and drudges of their husbands, are called masculine, and other names intended to convey disapprobation."[47]

Although questions of the nature and extent of her influence and whether it was for good or ill continue to provoke controversy among Mill's biographers, there is no doubt that Harriet Taylor influenced Mill's ideas about the condition of women. Mill's testimony was that Taylor helped him transform what had been, in his words, "little more than an abstract principle" into a real grasp of the everyday lives of women denied equal rights and any prospects for self-advancement. However, it appears that many of Taylor's ideas, for example, about marriage laws, were more radical than Mill's. In the intellectual circles in which he moved, Mill had the opportunity to meet other educated, talented, and productive women, such as

Harriet Martineau and Jane Carlyle, who probably also contributed to his understanding of how women were treated in his society.[48] However, we must remember that Mill drafted *The Subjection of Women* in 1860 and 1861 (although it was not published until 1869) as a part of the larger context of "the great Victorian debate on Woman," taking the position of the democratic rationalist against sentimental, chivalrous romantics and reactionaries.[49]

Countering the argument that women voluntarily accept rule by men, Mill observed in *The Subjection of Women* that "an increasing number of them have recorded protests against their present social condition," that is, exclusion from suffrage, from equal education, and from the professions.[50] The protest was occurring, he noted, not only in England and the United States but also in France, Italy, Switzerland, and Russia (*SW*, 139–40). He asserted: "Through all the progressive period of human history, the condition of women has been approaching nearer to equality with men" (*SW*, 148). Further, the principle that distinguished the modern world, according to Mill, was that "human beings are no longer born to their place in life" (*SW*, 143; see also 147). "The disabilities of women are the only case, save one [royalty], in which laws and institutions take persons at their birth, and ordain that they shall never in all their lives be allowed to compete for certain things" (*SW*, 145). Sex roles, in short, were the sole remaining ascriptive adult status in the modern world.

Mill wrote that patriarchy as embodied in the marriage contract differed from other forms of rule of the stronger over the weaker in that it was "not confined to a limited class, but common to the whole male sex" (*SW*, 136). If the law of marriage is "a law of despotism," Mill observed, it is necessary to give women only Hobson's choice ("that or none") "lest all women of spirit and capacity should prefer doing almost anything else, not in their own eyes degrading, rather than marry, when marrying is giving themselves a master, and a master too of all their earthly possessions" (*SW*, 155–56)—and of their bodies as well. Wives may be treated better than slaves, Mill said, "but no slave is a slave to the same lengths, and in so full a sense of the word, as a wife is" (*SW*, 159; see also 160).

Employing an analogy commonly used by feminists of his own time, Mill described the condition of women:

What, in unenlightened societies, colour, race, religion, or in the case of a conquered country, nationality, are to some men,

sex is to all women; a peremptory exclusion from almost all
honourable occupations, . . . Sufferings arising from causes
of this nature usually meet with so little sympathy, that few
persons are aware of the great amount of unhappiness even
now produced by the feeling of a wasted life. The case will be
even more frequent, as increased cultivation creates a greater
and greater disproportion between the ideas and faculties of
women, and the scope which society allows to their activity.
(SW, 241–42)

It is with these general considerations that Mill justified the opening statement of his position:

That the principle which regulates the existing social relations
between the two sexes—the legal subordination of one sex to
the other—is wrong in itself, and now one of the chief hindrances to human improvement; and that it ought to be replaced by a principle of perfect equality, admitting no power or
privilege on the one side, nor disability on the other. (SW, 125)

The justification of the restriction of women to a separate domestic
sphere rested on a conception of "woman's nature." The strength of
Mill's analysis was in his strategy of logical-empirical argumentation
against the belief that inequality between the sexes is justified by
experience—"the feelings connected with this subject [are] the
most intense and most deeply-rooted of all those which gather round
and protect old institutions and customs" (SW, 126). Mill stated his
premise forcefully:

What is now called the nature of women is an eminently artificial thing—the result of forced repression in some directions, unnatural stimulation in others. (SW, 148)

To paraphrase Mill's argument: although there are dogmatic opinions on the subject of the seemingly ineradicable moral and rational
differences between men and women, the only inference that can
be made is the negative one, namely, that what is natural is what
would be left after eliminating every difference that could be accounted for by education or environment (SW, 149–50). Mill took a
swing at the prevailing weight of opinion when he said, "I do not
know a more signal instance of the blindness with which the world,

including the herd of studious men, ignore and pass over all the influences of social circumstances, than their silly depreciation of the intellectual, and silly panegyrics on the moral, nature of women" (*SW*, 213). Although physiologists and medical doctors may have had some knowledge about the differences in bodily constitution between the sexes, Mill considered that when it came to the mental characteristics of women, "their observations are of no more worth than those of common men." The opinions of common men about women, he observed, were based on single cases—their wives: "Accordingly one can, to an almost laughable degree, infer what a man's wife is like, from his opinions about women in general" (*SW*, 150–51). Inequality itself prevents men from having anything but incomplete and superficial knowledge of women, Mill believed, because "thorough knowledge of one another hardly ever exists, but between persons who, besides being intimates, are equals." According to Mill, men would have no sure knowledge of women "until women themselves have told all that they have to tell," and until a freely developed women's literature provided insight into what women think and feel (*SW*, 152–53).

Mill, like Wollstonecraft, pointed out how the socialization and education of women shaped their "nature." Unlike other subject classes, women were required not only to obey but also to *want* to obey. What men had done, Mill wrote, was to use the full force of education to enslave the minds of women:

> All women are brought up from the very earliest years in the belief that their ideal of character is the very opposite to that of men; not self-will, and government by self-control, but submission, and yielding to the control of others. All the moralities tell them that it is the duty of women, and all the current sentimentalities that it is their nature, to live for others; to make complete abnegation of themselves, and to have no life but in their affections. (*SW*, 141)

These affections were meant to be only for husbands and children. Given the complete dependence of women on their husbands, Mill noted, "It would be a miracle if the object of being attractive to men had not become the polar star of feminine education and formation of character" (*SW*, 141). Mill wrote that the condition of being "at the beck and call of somebody, generally of everybody," the restriction of ambition within narrow bounds, the infrequency of "eagerness for fame," and the condition of being recognized only as "an appendage to men"—all had contributed to prevent the occurrence of an original women's art and contributions to intellectual life equal to men's (*SW*, 211, 212, 203–13).

On the other side of the coin of sexual inequality are the character traits inequality produces in men. The absence of legal restraints on husbands brought out the worst in them, Mill wrote:

> If the family in its best forms is, as it is often said to be, a school of sympathy, tenderness, and loving forgetfulness of self, it is still oftener, as respects its chief, a school of wilfulness, overbearingness, unbounded self-indulgence, and a double-dyed and idealized selfishness. (*SW*, 165)

Clearly, Mill was debunking the mythic idealization of the Victorian family hearth put forward by John Ruskin and others who sought to keep women in their "true place" of "wifely subjection."[51] Mill also stated that the false sense of superiority men were taught could not but "pervert the whole manner of existence of the man, both as an individual and as a social being" (*SW*, 219, 218). Due to women's lack of legal rights and public power, he observed, the only restraints on the arrogance and brutishness of men toward women were "feminine blandishments" and "the shrewish sanction," the former working only while women were young, attractive, fresh with charm, and the latter working best on husbands who were of gentler natures (*SW*, 166–67). The unfortunate synthesis of the contradictions of inequality between men and women, Mill found, was the absence of intimacy and of "real agreement of tastes and wishes as to daily life" (*SW*, 232). Following Mill's argument to its conclusion, we find that for men and women to have different characters would require different—i.e., equal—relations between the sexes.

Much as a feminist would argue today, Mill argued that what we call sex discrimination in employment and high social functions occurred in order that they "be preserved for the exclusive benefit of males." Mill insinuated an even deeper level of the inequality between men and women: "I believe that their disabilities elsewhere [i.e., in occupations] are only clung to in order to maintain their subordination in domestic life; because the generality of the male sex cannot yet tolerate the idea of living with an equal" (*SW*, 181–82). Breaking down the barriers to women's participation in what is termed "men's business" would have as its effect the "consciousness a woman would then have of being a human being like any other, entitled to choose her pursuits . . . entitled to exert the share of influence on all human concerns which belongs to an individual opinion . . . this alone would effect an immense expansion of the faculties of women, as well as enlargement of the range of their moral sentiments" (*SW*, 222). The social good entailed, he maintained, "would be that of doubling the mass of mental faculties available for the higher service of humanity" (*SW*, 221). The foundation of domestic existence would no longer be "contradictory to the first principles of social justice" (*SW*, 220). He believed that "though the truth may not be felt or generally acknowledged for generations to come, the only school of genuine moral sentiment is society between equals" (*SW*, 173). In true utilitarian fashion, Mill rested his case on the greatest happiness for the greatest number, but especially "the unspeakable gain in private happiness to the liberated half of the species; the difference to them between a life of subjection to the will of others, and a life of rational freedom." Mill's firm belief was that the ideal marriage between "two persons of cultivated faculties, identical in opinions and purposes," with similar capacities, both of whom could contribute to each other's development with a kind of "reciprocal superiority," would commence the "moral regeneration of mankind," because the relation of men and women is "the most fundamental" in society (*SW*, 235–36).

Mill then turned his attention to the problem of how women could win equality, given the special nature of their oppression:

> Every one of the subjects lives under the very eye, and almost, it may be said, in the hands, of one of the masters—in closer intimacy with him than with any of her fellow-subjects; with no means of combining against him, no power of even locally overmastering him, and, on the other hand, with the strongest motives for seeking his favour and avoiding to give him offence. . . . In the case of women, each individual of the subject-class is in a chronic state of bribery and intimidation combined. (*SW*, 136–37)

Under such conditions of subjection, Mill believed, "Women cannot be expected to devote themselves to the emancipation of women, until men in considerable number are prepared to join with them in the undertaking" (*SW*, 215).

Evaluations of Mill from feminist perspectives have varied with the politics of the persons making the judgments. For example, from a liberal feminist viewpoint, Alice S. Rossi has asserted that Mill's essay surpassed anything written before and ranks in importance with Charlotte Perkins Gilman's *Women and Economics* (1898) and Simone de Beauvoir's *The Second Sex* (1953). However, Rossi omitted mention of Friedrich Engels's classic, and she dismissed the Marxist approach in an invidious comparison of it to Mill's.[52] From a Marxist perspective, Herman and Julia Schwendinger have criticized Mill for his laissez-faire, individualistic conception of women's rights, his emphasis on the family and the legal order as the major sources of the oppression of women, and the hidden functionalism in his notion of the complementarity of sex roles.[53]

From a feminist viewpoint in general, Mill's position is not without weakness. For example, in his discussion of the influence of women on public morality, Mill credited women with fostering "its aversion to war, and its addiction to philanthropy," but, like Spencer, he also stated that the directions women gave to these efforts were "at least as often mischievous as useful." Particularly in philanthropic activities, women's "religious proselytism" provoked animosity, Mill argued, and in charitable work, women concentrated on immediate rather than long-term effects, thus wasting resources and destroying attitudes of self-help among the persons meant to benefit (SW, 226–27). In these statements, Mill revealed that he shared some of the liberal, rationalist views about women that were current in his time. But he did recognize that women's approach to charity was conditioned by their own lack of independence.

As another and more telling example, Mill argued that women did not encourage devoting energy to purposes that promised no private advantages to their families. He observed that, in the upper classes,

> The wife's influence tends, as far as it goes, to prevent the husband from falling below the common standard of approbation of the country. It tends quite as strongly to hinder him from rising above it. The wife is the auxiliary of common public opinion. A man who is married to a woman his inferior in intelligence finds her a perpetual dead weight, or, worse than a dead weight, a drag, upon every aspiration of his to be better than public opinion requires him to be. It is hardly possible for one who is in these bonds, to attain exalted virtue. (SW, 228)

To keep the record straight, alongside these statements we must set Mill's observation in a letter to Thomas Carlyle in 1833 that the best persons of both sexes he had known combined the best of both masculine and feminine qualities.[54]

Mill's solution to the tensions and conflicts of existing private family life was to propose that women should have public rights and legal equality in marriage. Jean Bethke Elshtain has maintained, problematically, that Mill's liberal emphasis on law and his flat and "external" theory of human motivation caused him to miss the nonlegal dimensions, in particular the deep psychological dimensions, of men's power over women.[55] However, Mill's marriage pledge, in which he renounced the authority granted by the legal inequality of husband and wife, is evidence that he was aware of the interpersonal and private aspects of this problem. He had learned from his own family experience. His father was a domestic despot who encouraged in his children contempt for their mother. In his personal crises of the 1820s, Mill had to establish an identity separate from his father, and his attitude toward women seems to have served as his vehicle.[56]

However, Mill showed ambivalence "about thoroughgoing alterations in private social arrangements between the sexes." It appears that he held a traditional notion of true love, in which a wife was an educated but not quite equal companion whose ultimate purpose in life should be to support the public and creative pursuits of her husband by her private endeavors, providing the care for the disappointments, frustration, and exhaustion such pursuits inevitably entail. This contradiction is the major weakness of his work. In Elshtain's formulation: "His analysis runs ashoal on the rock of the traditionally structured family."[57] As Okin has pointed out, "It is striking that Mill chose not to question the family and the way it had developed, in any way, or to consider the relationship between the institution of the bourgeois family itself and the contemporary position of women in society."[58] Neither the family nor the legal order by themselves can explain the subjection of women. Mill accepted to a large extent the traditional division of labor in which "the man earns the income."

> When a woman marries, it may in general be understood that she makes choice of the management of a household, and the bringing up of a family, as the first call upon her exertions, during as many years of her life as may be required for the

purpose; and that she renounces, not all other objects and occupations, but all which are not consistent with the requirements of this. (SW, 178–79)

For Mill, a wife's role was analogous to a man's profession. He accepted "the immutability of the existing family structure."[59] His
consideration of the relationship of the family to the social order
was limited largely to the ways in which the public legal disabilities
of women interplayed with the private relationships of men and
women. He overlooked variations in the forms of the family as they
were conditioned by transformations of the economic structures of
society. Most striking in this regard is his failure to address the
changes in the status of women of different classes as they were
shaped by the development of industrial capitalism in England—
certainly crucial to the conditions against which he protested so
elegantly.

The major strengths of Mill's work are his indictment of the
existing relations of the sexes and his powerfully lucid exposition of
the problem of distinguishing nature from experience and education.[60] His approach is still the only way to arrive at a "sound psychology" of the sexes. However, Mill's focus on the family and the legal-
political order as major sources of women's oppression revealed the
class limitations of his perspective, for he was mainly concerned
with the equality of women from the middle and upper classes,
women of talent and property (see SW, 176, 194). He made clear his
acceptance of the existing class order when he stated that equality
in intellectual education would mean that "women in general would
be brought up equally capable of understanding business, public affairs, and the higher matters of speculation, with men in the *same
class* of society" (SW, 221; emphasis added).[61] Similarities between
Mill's ideas and Mary Wollstonecraft's in her *Vindication* are striking. "The *Vindication*," Rowbotham has written, "often taken as
the beginnings of feminism, was rather the important theoretical
summation of bourgeois radical feminism still in the phase of moral
exhortation, before there was either the possibility of a radical and
socialist movement from below, to which the revolutionary feminist
could relate, or a movement like that of suffragettes, of privileged
women for equal rights with bourgeois man."[62]

Although the young Mill credited the utopian socialists for their
stand on equality of the sexes,[63] Rowbotham maintains that, as a
middle-class radical, he was alienated by the Saint-Simonians' ap-

peal to workers. Further, when Mill became a member of Parliament, he introduced an amendment to Disraeli's Reform Bill of 1867 to substitute the word *person* for *man* in the language of the bill in order that women might also achieve the benefits of the extension of suffrage.[64] In conclusion, of the "two feminisms," Mill, as a middle-class reformer, clearly was allied throughout *The Subjection of Women* with the feminism "seeking acceptance from the bourgeois world, [not with] the other seeking another world altogether."[65]

Herbert Spencer
Determining Feminine Nature by
Evolutionary Functionalism

The work of Herbert Spencer (1820–1903), England's Auguste Comte in the history of sociological theory, was extremely influential in the nineteenth century and remains central to the legacy of contemporary evolutionary functionalism in academic sociology.[66] Spencer's thought is virtually synonymous with Social Darwinism, with its central theoretical tenet of the survival of the fittest in the struggle for existence as the motor and the outcome of social evolution and its political doctrine of noninterference by government in the workings of this "natural law" of progress. Spencer used this concept to explain and justify, as the final and best, or most ethical, stage of history, industrial capitalism with its class inequalities; its domination, through "industrial war," of "inferior races"; its racism; its domination of women by men and restriction of women to the functions of mothering and caring for the family. As Karen Sacks has stated, "Despite the lack of scientific method, social Darwinism has been the dominant anthropological approach to the woman question."[67] What Sacks missed in her otherwise excellent critique of Spencer's position is that his early views of women, published in his first book, *Social Statics* (1851), could easily be called feminist.

"Equity knows no difference of sex. . . . The law of equal freedom manifestly applies to the whole race—female as well as male," Spencer began the chapter of *Social Statics* entitled "The Rights of Women."[68] He found that opponents of women's rights could not show that "those trifling mental variations which distinguish female from male" should be the basis for denying women equal rights with men (SS, 155). Spencer maintained that "despotism in the state is necessarily associated with despotism in the family. . . . If injustice sways men's public acts, it will inevitably sway their private ones also" (SS, 161). He believed that male authority in marriage was incompatible with love and "connubial happiness" (SS, 166). To the argument "that 'woman's mission' is a domestic one,'" Spencer responded with historical and comparative evidence and asked the rhetorical question "Who will now tell us what woman's sphere really is?" (SS, 169). He continued, "However much, therefore, the giving of political power to women may disagree with our notions of propriety [which do not carry the weight of necessity], we must conclude that, being required by that first pre-requisite to greatest happiness—the law of equal freedom—such a concession is unquestionably right and good" (SS, 170–71). He summarized:

> Thus it has been shown that the rights of women must stand or fall with those of men; derived as they are from the same authority; . . . The idea that the rights of women are not equal to those of men, has been condemned [by Spencer] as akin to the Eastern dogma, that women have no souls. It has been argued that the position at present held by the weaker sex is of necessity a wrong one, seeing that the same selfishness which vitiates our political institutions, must inevitably vitiate our domestic ones also. Subordination of females to males has been also repudiated, because it implies the use of command, and thereby reveals its descent from barbarism. Proof has been given that the attitudes of mastery on the one side, and submission on the other, are essentially at variance with that refined sentiment which should subsist between husband and wife. The argument that married life would be impracticable under any other arrangement, has been met by pointing out how the relationship of equality must become possible as fast as its justness is recognised. And lastly, it has been shown that the objections commonly raised against giving political power to women, are founded on notions and prejudices that will not bear examination. (SS, 171)

Spencer's advocacy of equal rights for women (and children) in 1851 was grounded in the same utilitarianism adhered to by Mill.[69] But in a matter of years, Spencer began to change his mind about the "nature" of women. Already in 1855 in *The Principles of Psychology*, he held, in J. D. Y. Peel's summary, that "the women of his own day differ from men in the same way that savages do, similar in kind but less in degree, being fixed in their ideas and quick to draw conclusions."[70]

Matters became even clearer in 1865 when Spencer refused John Stuart Mill's invitation to join a society to promote women's admission to suffrage. Two months earlier he had refused Helen Taylor (Harriet Taylor's daughter and Mill's stepdaughter) permission to include the chapter on women's rights from *Social Statics* in a series of papers.[71] In a 9 August 1867 letter to Mill, Spencer explained that he no longer supported the *"immediate"* extension of suffrage to women. His reasons were as follows: Liberty would be diminished doubly because women more than men "habitually" side with authority, "both political and ecclesiastical," and, in the face of suffering, favor solutions involving legislation and increased state administration. Revealing his change of mind, Spencer added:

> Of course, whoever holds that the minds of men and women are alike will feel no difficulty of this kind. But I hold them to be unlike, both quantitatively and qualitatively. I believe the difference to result from a physiological necessity, and that no amount of culture can obliterate it. And I believe further that the relative deficiency of the female mind is in just those most complex faculties, intellectual and moral, which have political action for their sphere.[72]

Upon receiving a copy of *The Subjection of Women* from Mill, Spencer wrote to him (9 June 1869) that he felt the whole question was too much discussed on the assumption that the relations of the sexes were determined "mainly by law." He suggested that "a very trenchant essay might be written on the *Supremacy of Women* showing that, in present civilization, the concessions made voluntarily by men to women" have counterbalanced those enacted in law and that "throughout a large part of society the tyranny of the weak is as formidable as the tyranny of the strong." Mill agreed that women "in a great many cases tyrannize over men," usually the fate of the best men, he said, but he pointed out that "two contradictory tyrannies do not make liberty."[73] It is sufficient to mention at this point that prior to the construction of his sociology, in the early 1860s, just when "the woman question had become one of the most important topics of the day,"[74] Spencer had completed his study and writing of *The Principles of Biology*.[75] It is precisely a biological analogy that is the intellectual key to Spencer's sociology and to the changes in his position on the rights and "proper sphere" of women.

In 1873, four years after publication of Mill's *The Subjection of Women*, and responding to the same historical forces, Spencer published *The Study of Sociology*, in which the reversal in his position on the question of women's "nature" and women's rights is most apparent.[76] Spencer opened the discussion of the comparative psychology of the sexes by asking, "Are the mental natures of men and women the same?" His answer was completely opposite to the one he had given in *Social Statics* in 1851: "That men and women are mentally alike is as untrue as that they are alike bodily" (*SSoc*, 340). Spencer's new opinion was that the mental differences, like the physical, stemmed from the different shares men and women play in the perpetuation of the race, and that to suppose otherwise would be to believe that, unlike the rest of nature, there is no relationship between special powers and special functions (*SSoc*, 341).

Spencer listed the physical and psychic differences between men and women that he believed were adaptations to "paternal and maternal duties": First, that an individual woman's development began and ended more abruptly than a man's was a phenomenon Spencer supposed necessary for producing offspring; second, that women have comparatively smaller bodies, and so smaller brains, meant to Spencer that women's mental powers were also less than men's; and third, that women have a pronounced parental love of helplessness gives them "an adapted power of intuition and a fit adjustment of behaviour" to deal with "infantine life." Spencer elaborated his view of what he considered women's mental backwardness: "There is a perceptible falling-short in those two faculties, intellectual and emotional, which are the latest products of human evolution—the power of abstract reasoning and that most abstract of the emotions, the sentiment of justice" (*SSoc*, 341–42). Spencer believed women's adaptations to mothering determined their general conduct.

Spencer offered reasons why women should acquiesce to their secondary position. He said that the "remaining qualitative distinctions between the minds of men and women are those which have grown out of their mutual relation as stronger and weaker." He argued that since the barbaric tribes that survived and became civilized were those in which "the men were not only powerful and courageous but aggressive, unscrupulous, intensely egoistic," it followed that "necessarily the women of such races, having to deal with brutal men, prospered in proportion as they possessed, or acquired, fit adjustments of nature" (*SSoc*, 342). In the first instance, women developed the ability to please men in order to survive and reproduce, and in the second instance:

> The wives of merciless savages must, other things equal, have prospered in proportion to their powers of disguising their feelings. Women who betrayed the state of antagonism produced in them by ill-treatment, would be less likely to survive and leave offspring than those who concealed their antagonism; and hence, by inheritance and selection, a growth of this trait proportionate to the requirement. (*SSoc*, 343)

He added:

> One further ability may be named as likely to be cultivated and established—the ability to distinguish quickly the passing feelings of those around. In barbarous times, a woman who could from a movement, tone of voice, or expression of face, instantly detect in her savage husband the passion that was rising, would be likely to escape dangers run into by a woman less skilled in interpreting the natural language of feeling. Hence, from the perpetual exercise of this power, and the survival of those having most of it, we may infer its establishment as a feminine faculty. (*SSoc*, 343)

He admired an aspect of women's sensitivity:

> Ordinarily, this feminine faculty, showing itself in an aptitude for guessing the state of mind through the external signs, end[s] simply in intuitions formed without assignable reasons; but when, as happens in rare cases, there is joined with it skill in psychological analysis, there results an extremely remarkable ability to interpret the mental states of others. (*SSoc*, 343)

Spencer anticipated the sociobiologists[77] in finding that the women who seemed to prefer "the manifestation of power of every kind in men" were more likely to survive.

> Among women unlike in their tastes, those who were fasci-
> nated by power, bodily or mental, and who married men able
> to protect them and their children, were more likely to sur-
> vive in posterity than women to whom weaker men were pleas-
> ing. (SSoc, 344)

He observed further that some women preferred powerful men
even when that preference was detrimental.

> To this admiration for power, caused thus inevitably, is as-
> cribable the fact sometimes commented upon as strange, that
> women will continue attached to men who use them ill, but
> whose brutality goes along with power, more than they will
> continue attached to weaker men who use them well. (SSoc,
> 344)

His explanation is, of course, wrong, or at least problematic. That
women remain in brutal situations has also to do with fear, the lack
of legal recourse (as in the case of rape by a husband where that is
not a punishable offense), and the absence of economic alternatives.
    Although Spencer believed women's preference for powerful
men advantageous to men in marriage and for the survival of the
species, he thought it dangerous if transferred to public authorities.

> With this admiration of power . . . there goes the admiration
> of power in general; which is more marked in women than in
> men, and shows itself both theologically and politically. . . .
> And to this same cause ["natural character"] is in like manner
> to be ascribed the greater respect felt by women for all em-
> bodiments and symbols of authority, governmental and social.
> (SSoc, 344–45)

He implied that women should be excluded from participation in
public life; he thought their influence should be limited to the indi-
rect shaping of their husbands' and sons' characters (SSoc, 347–48)
    Spencer's work rested on ethnocentric and incomplete field-
work, as is characteristic of much nineteenth-century armchair anthropology, but his theory did allow the possibility of changes in sex
roles as society evolved.

It is inferable that as civilization readjusts men's natures to higher social requirements, there goes on a corresponding re-adjustment between the natures of men and women, tending in sundry respects to diminish their differences. Especially may we anticipate that those mental peculiarities developed in women as aids to defense against men in barbarous times, will diminish. (*SSoc*, 345)

Throughout Spencer's work there is the liberal ideal that scientific knowledge of the laws of social development should be the basis for intelligent social policy for "the furtherance of human welfare." One of the things he meant by this was that government must not interfere with the "natural" law of progress by protecting the unfit or promoting their survival. According to Spencer, a dangerous effect of feminine nature, what he considered to be its maternal instinct and less developed sense of abstract justice, was that women were more apt than men to be swayed by appeals to pity rather than equity and to support policies that gave aid to those whose suffering was conspicuous enough to excite commiseration, even if they had caused their own misery. He believed this an "unnatural" and "wrong-headed" policy to which women were especially vulnerable because of "the aptitude which the feminine intellect has to dwell on the concrete and proximate rather than on the abstract and remote" (*SSoc*, 346). Just as Spencer felt that women erred more in domestic affairs than men by thinking of their children's present rather than their future characters, so he believed "this difference between their ways of estimating consequences . . . makes women err still more than men do in seeking what seems an immediate public good without thought of distant public evils." He believed an awe of the symbols of power and a lack of "doubt, or criticism, or calling-in-question of things that are established" made women unfit for representation in a liberal democracy. He said, "Reverencing power more than men do, women, by implication, respect freedom less" (*SSoc*, 346–47). The effect of women's "nature," according to Spencer, was to contribute to the extension and consolidation of controlling agencies.

Spencer disingenuously refused to articulate an answer to the question of what roles should be open to women: "Whether it is desirable that the share already taken by women in determining social arrangements and actions should be increased, is a question we will leave undiscussed." He argued that any changes in the position of women must derive from his comparative psychology of the sexes, making clear he felt little need for change. He noted that advocates for equal rights for women would be unlikely to base their efforts on his work (*SSoc*, 348).

By the time Spencer had written *The Principles of Sociology*, published in three volumes in 1876 and reissued in nineteen editions, his opinion of women's rights was, as we have seen, the opposite of his early views.[78] The ideas that governed his treatment of women in this work were evolution, survival through fit adaptation, the idea that institutions "hang together," and that societies most evolved are, "ethically considered," the best. He viewed English industrial society as approaching the moral end of the historical progress of civilization (*PS*, 610–12, 615). In outline, because monogamy was the most developed form of marriage, Spencer thought it to be the best and the one that accorded to women the highest possible status. He believed that full-time mothers were necessary for the most improvement in the quality of offspring and, therefore, the species. As for the rights of women, Spencer maintained that biological and social evolution would eventually provide conditions in which women would approach equality with men and in which the rights of women would cease to be an issue.

Spencer engaged in a characteristically nineteenth-century search for the origins and evolution of the family, examining different forms particularly for their effects on the status of women, the education of children, and the relationship of the family to society. In the beginning, Spencer believed, there were no families, only promiscuous relationships between men and women. Among primitive tribes, men and women did not manifest "those ideas and feelings which among civilized nations give to marriage its sanctity" (*PS*, 616; and see 613–15, 643–44, 649–51).

Polyandry was the next step up from promiscuity, he thought; however, it was a form of the family oppressive to women—because having many husbands was synonymous with having many masters—and disconcerting to children because adult authority patterns were not stable (*PS*, 659).

Generally producing fewer offspring, weaker defense, and less family solidarity, polyandry gave way to polygyny in Spencer's anthropology; notions of property and women as property had developed at the same time. Spencer thought polygyny superior to polyandry in several ways: it promoted family cohesion, selected the wealthiest and strongest men for survival and reproduction, and resulted in better government because sons inherited from their fathers. However, polygyny was rejected in favor of monogamy, Spencer believed, because of the emotional and physical duress polygyny inflicted on women and children. Jealousy among wives, the use of wives as slaves, and inadequate paternal care for children were among the harmful effects that he noted (*PS*, 668–78).

Spencer believed that "the monogamic family is the most evolved" (*PS*, 681) and thus the standard by which relations between men and women must be judged. That he considered monogamy the most highly evolved form of marriage did not contradict its occasional appearance in more primitive societies. He considered the virtues of monogamy to be that it multiplied social relations, contributed to political stability, lengthened life, promoted the passions of romantic love, encouraged literature, and, in industrial societies, freed women to be full-time mothers, giving their children "constant maternal care," and beyond that "the children get the benefit of concentrated paternal interest" (*PS*, 684). Applying his Lamarckian conception of evolution, Spencer maintained that monogamy was becoming an *innate* characteristic "in the civilized man" (*PS*, 679–85).

In the chapter "The Family" in *The Principles of Sociology*, Spencer examined the relationship of family to society. He restated his theory of the correlation of militant or warlike societies with polygyny and of industrial society with monogamy. A plurality of wives captured in war or purchased "implies domestic rule of the compulsory type: the husband is tyrant and the wives are slaves." Industrialization brought about a balanced sex ratio, he asserted, and thereby compelled monogamy. With the decline in the practice of the bride price and with the advance in honoring women's choices of husbands, Spencer found, there was evolving "the voluntary cooperation which characterizes the marital relation in its highest form" (*PS*, 691).

Spencer believed that, politically, the "salvation" of all societies "depends on the maintenance of an absolute opposition between the regime of the family and the regime of the State," because the monogamous family operates on the principle of compassion for the weak whereas society works properly by rewarding the strongest and most competent (*PS*, 719–21). Therefore, according to Spencer, no society can progress if it allows family values to be the basis of the state. Contrarily, he raised "a question of great interest, which has immediate bearing on policy, . . . Is there any limit to the disintegration of the family?" The traditional functions of the family were being eroded, he believed, by poorhouses that provided care for children at public expense and public education that assumed the "paternal duty of the State" (*PS*, 717).

Feminist socialists alarmed Spencer; he asked:

> Are we on our way to a condition like that reached by sundry Socialist bodies in America and elsewhere? in these, along with community of property, and along with something approaching community of wives, there goes community in case of offspring: the family is entirely disintegrated. (*PS*, 718)

He answered his question by saying, "So far from expecting disintegration of the family to go further, we have reason to suspect that it has already gone too far." But, underneath it all, he believed, as did Talcott Parsons three generations later, in the emergence of a new type of family "composed of parents and offspring" (*PS*, 719), that is, the nuclear family.

The most important roles in maintenance of the nuclear family, Spencer asserted, were those of wife and mother. The chapter of *The Principles of Sociology* entitled "The *Status* of Women" reexamined treatment of women from primitive times to the time of industrial society. It may be interesting to look at his anthropological exposition in some detail. Spencer opened the chapter by stating a familiar nineteenth-century theme:

> Perhaps in no way is the moral progress of mankind more clearly shown, than by contrasting the position of women among savages with their position among the most advanced of the civilized. At one extreme a treatment of them cruel to the utmost degree bearable; and at the other extreme a treatment which, in some directions, gives them precedence over men. (*PS*, 725)

In the "lowest races," he said, the only limits to the sufferings of women were set by what they could endure and still survive. He was aware of "certain anomalies," namely, that "predominance of women is not unknown," as among the Fuegians, some Australian tribes, the Battas of Sumatra, the Dyaks, and the Haidahs, where matrilineality prevailed. Apparently he dismissed matrifocal societies as exceptions. The "average facts," he asserted, were that among most uncivilized, non-Western peoples, women were regarded as domestic cattle (*PS*, 726–28).

Regarding the travel literature that was part of the anthropology of his day, Spencer believed that "the only definite conclusion appears to be that men monopolize the occupations requiring both strength and agility always available—war and the chase." He noted that when women were pregnant and/or nursing infants, they were unfit for fighting and hunting. Contrary to his general theory of the natural division of labor between the sexes and the elevated treatment of women in industrial society, Spencer found that "women are better treated where circumstances lead to likeness of occupations between the sexes." He cited the Chippewa, Chinooks, and Cueba as examples and pointed out that among the Dahomans, with their Amazon army, "the participation of women with men in war goes along with a social *status* much higher than usual" (*PS*, 731–33).

Virtually the rest of the chapter Spencer devoted to sketches of the relationship between political structures and types of domestic arrangements in Egypt, the Roman Empire, China, Japan, prerevolutionary and Napoleonic France, contemporary Germany, England, and the United States. These comparisons were used to prove that political and patriarchal despotism occur together.

Spencer concluded that in monogamous families in industrial societies the condition of women was the best, the education of children was the best, and the degree of freedom was the highest. He stated his conclusions somewhat carefully. First, "monogamy [in contrast to polygyny], if it does not necessarily imply a high *status* [for women], is an essential condition to a high *status*." Second, like Mill in having a simplistic conception of the family and society, Spencer believed that "the freedom which characterizes public life in an industrial community [in contrast to a militant one, which is common to most savage life] naturally characterizes also the accompanying private life." The elevation of women in industrial societies resulted in the improved quality of offspring, accounting for their success in "the struggle for existence" around the globe (*PS*, 743). With the coming of industry, boys and girls were treated almost equally: "We thus find a series of changes in the *status* of children parallel to the series of changes in the *status* of women" (*PS*, 755; and see 747–55). These statements appear outrageous in light of the havoc wreaked on the lives of working-class women and children during the Industrial Revolution in his own country; Spencer failed to take into account any class but his own.

The final chapter of the first volume of *The Principles of Sociology* is called "Domestic Retrospect and Prospect." Coming full circle, Spencer said that monogamy "is manifestly the ultimate form" of the relationship between men and women; so future "changes to be anticipated must be in the direction of completion and extension of it" (*PS*, 764). Monogamous marriage had already been improved when industrial society's cooperative character and its practice of consulting the wills of others "outside the household" were brought "inside the household." Marriage had been transformed into an "approximately equal partnership" in which affection took precedence over legal authority (*PS*, 762). Spencer believed that the future would bring the extinction of promiscuity, the suppression of the crimes of adultery and bigamy, and the death of "the mercantile element in marriage." He felt that divorce would be facilitated but at the same time become rare because affection would be the primary and law the secondary basis for marriage (*PS*, 764–65). As for the status of women, he predicted that "further approach towards equality of position between the sexes will take place. . . . a diminution of the political and domestic disabilities of women [will occur], until there remain only such as differences of constitution entail" (*PS*, 767). This, as Sacks pointed out, is the biological key to Spencer's views of women,[79] for this was as far as he was willing to go for women's rights. Spencer thought that the unconscious sympathy of "the stronger sex for the weaker" would lead men to compensate women for their constitutional "disadvantages" (*PS*, 768).

In Spencer's judgment, "While in some directions the emancipation of women has to be carried further, we may suspect that in other directions their claims have already been pushed beyond the normal limits . . . from which there will be a recoil" (*PS*, 767). He cited an alleged lack of manners among American women as an example. Spencer wrote directly against the middle-class feminist demands of his time:

> In domestic life, the relative position of women will doubtless rise; but it seems improbable that absolute equality with men will be reached. . . . Evenly though law may balance claims, it will, as the least evil, continue to give, in case of need, supremacy to the husband, as being the more judicially-minded. And, similarly, in the moral relations of married life, the pre-

ponderance of power, resulting from greater massiveness of nature, must, however unobtrusive it may become, continue with the man.

. . .

When we remember that up from the lowest savagery, civilization has, among other results, caused an increasing exemption of women from bread-winning labour, and that in the highest societies they have become most restricted to domestic duties and the rearing of children; we may be struck by the anomaly that in our day restriction to indoor occupations has come to be regarded as a grievance, and a claim is made to free competition with men in all outdoor occupations. This anomaly is traceable in part to the abnormal excess of women; and obviously a state of things which excludes many women from those natural careers in which they are dependent on men for subsistence, justifies the demand for freedom to pursue independent careers. That hindrances standing in their way should be, and will be, abolished must be admitted. At the same time it must be concluded that no considerable alteration in the careers of women in general, can be, or should be, so produced; and further, that any extensive change in the education of women, made with the view of fitting them for businesses and professions, would be mischievous. If women comprehended all that is contained in the domestic sphere, they would ask no other. If they could see everything which is implied in the right education of children, to a full conception of which no man has yet risen, much less any woman, they would seek no higher function. (*PS*, 768–69)

On what grounds, then, did Spencer oppose the demands for equal rights of the feminists of his time? The answer, as was evident earlier in *The Study of Sociology*, is simple, namely, women's function was to reproduce the species and rear the young. If women were allowed influence in public life, Spencer feared that the political defects of "feminine nature"—too great a respect for authority and an inability to appreciate long-term results—would result in softheartedness toward the unfit, increased power for the state, and retarded progress toward justice in social arrangements. Only when the fully developed—i.e., nonmilitant—industrial society with complete voluntary cooperation and individual freedom was in place could women be granted political power without "evil" results, he said. He argued commonly that so long as war exists and is the responsibility of men, to grant women equal political power "would involve a serious inequality" and be "impracticable." In a final hedge, Spencer wrote that eventually the moral evolution toward the rights of individuals would render full equality for women "harmless and probably beneficial" (*PS*, 769–70).

Spencer moved from a position supporting women's rights in 1851 to the opposite position by the 1860s. In 1851, he believed that equity knew no difference of sex and that there were merely "trifling" mental differences in the natures of men and women; these ideas taken together provided justification for including women in all aspects of public life. By the 1860s, Spencer completely rejected claims for women's rights; his comparative psychology of the sexes and view of history at that time argued for such differences between men and women that he insisted women should stay in the home. What caused the radical change of mind from a progressive position to one staunchly supporting the status quo is a puzzle.[80]

Looking at Spencer's personal life offers few definitive clues to the transformation of his views. He never married and died a bachelor in his eighty-fourth year. The novelist Marian Evans (George Eliot) seemed to be romantically interested in Spencer for a brief time in the early 1850s. He rejected her offer of affection on the grounds that her physical appearance, which he considered somewhat masculine, did not match the beauty of her emotional and intellectual traits. Nevertheless, he kept a picture of her in his bedroom. Their friendship continued for the rest of his life, and Spencer enjoyed the companionship of this relationship in which there was no passion to hide or to confess. He tried to squelch rumors that there had ever been romance between them. In reply to a friend who urged him to marry for his health, he lamented that the educational system did not produce women who were morally and intellectually stimulating to him as well as good-looking.[81]

Spencer's intellectual mentor was his father; his mother had "little sympathy with his intellectual pursuits." He avoided her, not visiting home even during her serious illness.[82] (Spencer, like Weber, was afflicted with symptoms of "nervous disorder.") There is a suggestion in his autobiography that his mother was the source of his conception of feminine nature. However, in that same autobiography, Spencer printed, without comment, the remarks of a reviewer who took him to task for his advocacy of women's rights in *Social Statics*.[83]

Looking at Spencer's public life for answers puts us on more solid ground. E. L. Youmans, overseeing an American edition of *Social Statics*, wrote (12 April 1864) that Spencer's views, "considerably modified" in the direction of "divergence from the democratic views" expressed in his 1851 edition, would be less acceptable in the United States and requested that Spencer explain fully the reasons for his current views. Spencer replied in a letter dated 18 May 1864: "The parts which I had in view, when I spoke of having modified my opinions on some points, were chiefly the chapters on the rights of women and children." All Youmans got from Spencer was a vague disclaimer "not containing any specific explanations."[84] The second edition (1864) of *Social Statics* incorporated Spencer's rejection of equality for women and his developing biological views.[85]

The differences between Mill's and Spencer's responses to the scientific and intellectual currents of their time are revelatory of Spencer's rejection of his earlier views on women's rights. Mill did not become caught up in the "contemporary preoccupation . . . with the biological sciences." In his extensive correspondence with Auguste Comte during 1843, Mill rejected Comte's confident assertion that biology had already established "the hierarchy of the sexes, by demonstrating both anatomically and physiologically that, in almost the entire animal kingdom, and especially in our species, the female sex is formed for a state of essential childhood, which renders it necessarily inferior to the corresponding male organism." It followed that any change in social arrangements would be inexpedient and, more importantly, a biological absurdity. Mill, in the logico-empiricist tradition at its best, was skeptical that biologists had produced conclusive evidence. He was willing to accept the possibility that someday physiological data might show differences between the brains of men and women, but in the meantime he maintained that no precise relationship between, say, brain size and intellectual power could be stated. To do so, he wrote, would be to say that big men are more intelligent than small ones and elephants smarter than either.[86] Unlike Mill, Spencer not only did not question the contemporary popular and scientific belief that organic characteristics explained everything, but he also made it the centerpiece of all his mature work. The relevant influences in this regard were Karl Ernst von Baer's work in embryology (from which Spencer got the central propositions for "Progress: Its Law and Cause"),[87] Malthus's essay on population, Darwin's *The Descent of Man*, and other contemporary works in physiology, physical anthro-

pology, and historical geology—all linked together by a conception
of evolution in which survival of the fittest assured progressive development in all areas of human life, including morals and social
arrangements.[88]

It is important to recognize, as Robert Young has pointed out in
his brilliant essay "The Historiographic and Ideological Contexts of
the Nineteenth-Century Debate on Man's Place in Nature," that
Spencer was "perhaps the most influential of all the interpreters of
the philosophical, ethical, social and political meaning of Victorian
scientific naturalism."[89] Behind the popularity of the idea of evolution during the late 1840s and 1850s, among middle-class intellectuals like Harriet Martineau was the sense of a crisis of belief and a
loss of moral conviction associated in England with the decline of
Bentham's utilitarianism accompanied by its simplistic pleasure-
pain psychology, which the "plain man" simply refused to believe
was the basis of all human conduct.[90] Spencer's social theory from
beginning to end is a mixture of the water of utilitarian liberal individualism and the oil of evolutionary functionalism. To drop his
support of women's rights involved no more than working out consis-
tently the social implications of evolutionary functionalism; however, he retained a liberal individualism as a political ideology.
Spencer became interested in evolution when he failed to find a
sound intellectual basis in either utilitarianism or religious dogma
for social integration and progress. Biological evolutionism became
the contradictory basis for a liberal political economy.

Middle-class thinkers like Marian Evans, who introduced Spencer to Comte's writings (which exhibited similar concerns), told
workers to give up the notion of overthrowing class inequalities and
instead to turn "Class Interests into Class Functions or duties. The
nature of things in this world has been determined for us before-
hand," she said.[91] Spencer, as we have seen, had the same message
for women, also based on the "findings" of evolutionary biology.
Stanislav Andreski has pointed out that "Spencer's treatment of the
family shows him at his weakest. . . . He accepted as self-evident
that a rather idealised family pattern of Victorian England was the
resting point of human history."[92] In fact, this idealized and patriarchal family, not the adult individual, was fundamental to Spencer's
liberal political theory.[93] The highest evolution of nature resulted,
Spencer thought, in the English middle-class family and civilization.

It has often been noted how the struggle for the trough in
nineteenth-century England was projected onto nature in Darwin's

theory of evolution by natural selection. In the same way, Spencer may have transferred the conflicts of his own time, including the war between the sexes, onto his vision of the "primitive" relations of the sexes and family life in tribal societies while denying them in his own. At the end of the century, the world was not going according to the predictions of Spencer's theory. In 1893 Durkheim pointed out the inconsistencies in Spencer's use of the organismic analogy. Increasing social complexity brought about more not less governmental regulation. And toward the end of his life Spencer recognized that the militarization and centralization of European states preparing for war were leading to a reassertion of coercive forms of control.[94] At the age of twenty-three, he had noted the universal correlation "between great militant activity and the degradation of women."[95]

I have intended to show that behind his idealization of the Victorian bourgeois family and correlative repudiation of his earlier support for the rights of women was Spencer's adoption of a functionalist-evolutionary conception of social order and change. He used the organismic conception of society to justify the rights of men and to deny the rights of women by justifying theoretically the restriction of women to the domestic sphere. In this respect his work was close to French sociological theory.

3

France

Revolutionary Feminism and Sociological Moralism

"Women should learn to have influence as they have in France instead of trying to get votes."[1] That was the advice given to English feminist Sylvia Pankhurst by H. M. Hyndman, the leader of England's "Marxist" Social Democratic Federation, who disliked Engels and thought feminism irrelevant to socialism. His statement summarized the thrust of male antifeminism circa 1900, and it also reveals Hyndman's ignorance of the force of revolutionary feminism in French history. England's eighteenth- and nineteenth-century history seems staid when compared with the dramatic events in France. The French tradition of sociology was formed in the context of the ideals of the Enlightenment, the fervor of revolution, the vigor of feminists and socialists, and a marked rhythm of reaction and repression.

Feminist and antifeminist discourse on the "nature" and the "proper place" of women, on marriage, and on love has had a long history in France, beginning in the Middle Ages.[2] For our purposes, the appropriate starting point is the French Enlightenment. As Sheila Rowbotham has pointed out, unlike in England, "Feminism in France tried rather to apply reason to the advantage of women." With the increasing popularity of rational modes of analysis and demonstration, "new grounds for questioning the subordination of women appeared."[3] In eighteenth-century France, there was lively controversy over the position and education of women.

Émile Durkheim traced the heritage of the French sociological tradition to Jean-Jacques Rousseau and to Montesquieu, both of whom felt that men and women were by nature different. On Rousseau, Susan Moller Okin has written:

> Albeit in an exaggerated way and sometimes with almost hysterical fervor, Rousseau argues all the most commonly held assertions that have, as part of our patriarchal culture, rationalized the separation and oppression of women throughout the history of the Western world. He argues, to begin with, that woman's sharply distinct position and functions are those that are natural to her sex. It is interesting, since Rousseau was so much an advocate of the natural, to see how different his reasoning is about what is natural in and for women from about what is natural in and for "man.". . . Rousseau defines woman's nature, unlike man's, in terms of her function—that is, her sexual and procreative purpose in life.[4]

"Rousseau saw women as a major source of the world's evil," according to Okin, because their sexual power aroused "feelings of fear and guilt" in men. Therefore, he believed that women must be held in check—their fidelity and chastity must be assured to guarantee paternity and to prevent syphilis. However, he also wanted women to remain seductive to their husbands. Rousseau demanded, in effect, that a woman be "both virgin and prostitute." To this end, he designed a vastly different education for women than for his perfect man.[5] In her sensitive interpretation of Rousseau's portrayal of the complexities and dilemmas of being a woman, Jean Bethke Elshtain cites Judith Shklar's point that Rousseau believed that morally corrupt women in Paris deserved much of the blame for spoiling civilization. The private virtue of women devoted to husbands and children, he argued, was the foundation of civic virtue and the solution to the problem of decadence prevalent in his time.[6]

Rousseau's attitude toward women was the object of feminists' scorn; however, even feminists such as Mary Wollstonecraft were indebted to his ideas that children's education should emphasize simplicity and naturalness.[7] In private and public responses to the critics of his position regarding women's rights, Rousseau maintained that inequality between men and women, though expressed in tradition and law, "is not of man's making, or at any rate it is not the result of mere prejudice, but of reason."[8] The "romantic [and reactionary] woman cult" that started in the nineteenth century and appeared in caricatured form in the work of Auguste Comte owed much to Rousseau.[9]

Other male Enlightenment thinkers, however, did not exclude women from their ideas about the importance of environment and education. Claude Adrien Helvétius blamed poor education rather than nature for any disadvantages women might suffer. Citing examples of successful and famous women, he maintained that "if women be in general inferior, it is because in general they receive a still worse education." In a more thorough discussion found in the chapter on women in his book on the social system, Baron d'Holbach asserted, "From the way in which women in all countries are brought up, it seems that it is only intended to turn them into beings who retain the frivolity, fickleness, caprices and lack of reason of childhood, throughout their lives."[10] Holbach believed that the remedy for the universal enslavement of women was to give women a decent education. An especially persistent notion of their culture not overcome by these men's basically feminist attitudes was the idea that women are closer to nature than men, an idea expressed in La Mettrie's potentially liberating mechanistic physiology, Helvétius's sensationalism, and Denis Diderot's utopian portrait of Tahiti in *Supplement to the Journey of Bougainville*. Diderot felt that marriages could be happy if they occurred far from the inequities and artifices of society, but he also proposed that the "natural woman" should be shared by the men of the community in order to create solidarity among the men. Still, the *philosophes'* contrasting of nature and contract led many of them to favor the right to divorce, marriage being a man-made contract. As Maurice Bloch and Jean H. Bloch have written of eighteenth-century French thought, "The rhetoric of nature has some implication for the reform of the status of women."[11]

The eighteenth-century tradition of male advocacy of women's rights culminated in the writings of Marie-Jean-Antoine-Nicholas Caritat, Marquis de Condorcet, whose *Letters from a bourgeois of New Haven to a citizen of Virginia* (1787) comprised "the first text to demand political rights for women." He followed it in 1790 with *On the Admission of Women to Citizens' Rights* and in 1795 with his historical sketch of human progress. Already before this time, women of the *haute bourgeoisie* and the liberal wing of the aristocracy had organized salons in which intellectuals debated what was called feminine humanism and the extension of legal rights and education to women. However, as Elaine Marks and Isabelle de Courtivron have argued, "In a sense there is no history of feminism in France until the French Revolution of 1789 when feminist texts written by women and a feminist movement conscious of itself come together."[12]

In a January 1789 petition to the king prior to the outbreak of the revolution, women of the Third Estate implored him, not for a vote in the Estates-General, but for an improved free public education so that women might "be taught above all to practice the virtues of our sex: gentleness, modesty, patience, charity," in order that they might overcome the ambiguous position of being "the continual objects of the admiration and scorn of men." Accepting the traditional French conception of women, they claimed that they did not want a scientific education, which, they said, would go "against the desires of nature" and make women "mixed beings who are rarely faithful wives and still more rarely good mothers of families." However, as the crises of the revolution occurred, women's demands were not to remain so modest. Historical evidence reveals that "the majority of Parisian women . . . greeted the Revolution with enthusiasm." Prominent bourgeois women offered their jewels to help overcome the financial crisis. Poor and often illiterate women demonstrated "a sophisticated grasp of the implication of revolutionary events."[13] Sheila Rowbotham has described beautifully the character and complexities of women's participation in what seemed to contemporaries to be the greatest revolution in history:

> In the French Revolution the feminist aspirations of the privileged and the traditions of collective action of the unprivileged women encountered each other. They regarded each other uneasily and never really combined. But each emerged tinged with liberty, equality and fraternity and the memory of revolution. Things could never be quite the same again. Women rioting over prices in Normandy in 1789, women of the third estate in Grenoble taking action in favour of the States General, women demanding in the list of grievances presented better medical provision and improved education, protection

of trades from male competition, women marching to Versailles to confront the baker and the baker's wife, pamphlets and petitions about divorce, prostitution, are all indications of a great acceleration of activity and consciousness.[14]

In early October 1789, symbolically counterrevolutionary acts (e.g., the king and queen's insulting the tricolor) and concerns about bread and unemployment resulted in an increase of tensions in Paris. Parisian "women of the people," supported by radical National Guardsmen, marched on Versailles to insist that Louis XVI assure them of a regular supply of bread to Paris, accept the National Assembly's revolutionary legislation, and return to live in Paris under the popular eye. Feminist historians Levy, Applewhite, and Johnson have stated that "of all the popular insurrections during the Revolution, the October Days stand out as the women's insurrection." Radicalization of women was fostered by new revolutionary institutions, assemblies, a press, and political clubs. In 1791, the Marquis de Sade wrote *Justine*, and Olympe de Gouges set forth the *Declaration of the Rights of Woman*. In 1792, an attempt was made to organize "Amazons" to fight the Austrians. During 1793, *femmes sans-culottes* joined the Society of Revolutionary Republican Women, "the first political interest group for common women known in western history."[15] The group was headed by Pauline Léon and Claire Lacombe. That was also the year when Charlotte Corday assassinated Jean-Paul Marat and when the Convention declared that women were not citizens (April), moved against women's political clubs, and beheaded Gouges for "having forgotten the virtues which belong to her sex."[16] After Robespierre was deposed in July 1794 and the reactionary Thermidorians took power, "Women ceased political activity."[17] In 1795, women were prohibited from attending any political meetings.

For upper-class and middle-class refugees who returned after the Reign of Terror, Paris had become "a city of license." The family had apparently fallen apart: fathers abandoned their households; "free love" was apparently common; and the number of divorces, juvenile delinquents, and illegitimate children increased. "No country had up to this time seen such a transformation in familial habits," in J. M. Mogey's estimate.[18] Emperor Napoléon's Civil Code of 1804 attempted to reestablish patriarchal authority. Mme de Staël, "a woman Napoléon disliked with a special intensity, who combined everything he most detested in revolutionary intellectual women," waged "a personal literary guerrilla war against Bonaparte. . . . in such novels as *Delphine* and *Corinne* women with a high opinion of their own superiority conflicted with a society that would not allow them self-expression."[19] In 1816, after Bonaparte's abdication, divorce was abolished.

In 1808, Charles Fourier published *Theory of the Four Movements,* in which he presented his argument that the progress of civilization could be measured by the emancipation of women because the quality and equality of relationships between men and women reveal the extent to which human nature has triumphed over brutality, an idea that influenced Mill, Marx, and Spencer.[20]

Revolutionary feminism reemerged in the period between the revolutions of 1830 and 1848 along with the rise of utopian socialist and workers' movements. Central to the ideological climate of these movements were the ideas of Henri de Saint-Simon; around him gathered bright young graduates of the École Polytechnique, including Auguste Comte, who was his secretary for a number of years. On the basis of his contradictory synthesis of Enlightenment ideas and reactionary Romantic ideas, Saint-Simon can be classified as a utopian socialist or a prophet of authoritarian technocracy. From his work some of his disciples, especially Barthélemy Prosper Enfantin, drew feminist inspiration; they criticized sexual repression and argued for free love.[21] In the early 1830s, Enfantin preached—to the chagrin of other Saint-Simonians—a millenarian sexual mysticism to women and workers. Susanne Voilquin, a working woman who joined Enfantin's pilgrimage to Egypt in search of the female messiah, La Mère, was director of *La Tribune des femmes,* a feminist paper founded in 1832 and banned in 1834, which displayed a strong proletarian consciousness. In "Memories of a Girl of the People," Voilquin described how Enfantin's ideas awakened in her "the capacity for independent thought, feeling, and action." Claire Demar, another of Enfantin's disciples, linked the emancipation of women to that of the proletariat and imagined a law for the future that would permit complete sexual freedom for both women and men, collective child rearing, and the abolition of the family. Shortly thereafter, she committed suicide with her lover. In 1832, George Sand wrote a scathing attack on bourgeois marriage. Between 1836 and 1838, bourgeois women published *Gazette des femmes,* which focused on the right of women to petition the government for redress of their grievances.[22]

Also important to the decade of the 1830s were Fourier's rejections of the Saint-Simonians' "cult of Woman" and proposals for his own programs published in his newspaper, *Phalanx.* His historical/ anthropological theory of the development of society, as Rowbotham has observed, "was to have a lasting impression on revolutionary feminism." Fourier linked the phenomena of economic and sexual oppression and analyzed the social conditions that produced the supposed nature of women. He detected a "secret antipathy" behind the compliments paid to women by philosophers, pointing out that the same philosophers denied women access to intellectual training and then concluded that women were incapable of abstract thinking. He had little more regard for *femmes savantes*, who, having escaped the collective fate of their sex, closed their eyes to the misery of their sisters. In Fourier's phalansteries, men and women were completely equal, child rearing was a cooperative affair, and women were educated not for domesticity but for participation in the public life of the community.[23]

During 1843 Flora Tristan, often thought of as "the first French feminist," published *Workers' Union,* which contained one of the earliest conceptions of an international association of workers and an analysis of the double oppression of women, "the proletariat of the proletariat." In her depiction of working-class family life, she observed that working-class wives were brutalized and "few workers' homes . . . are happy," the husband ruling by law and economic power. She proposed a technical, intellectual, and moral education for women that would be available in workers' palaces, which she proposed for each town. Tristan appealed to male workers to grant the same rights to women—"the last slaves remaining in France"— that they had won as a result of the Declaration of the Rights of Man in 1791. Rowbotham has written of her: "Flora Tristan's own life followed the dramatic and tragic course which seemed to be the inevitable fate of the feminist socialist." Unable to gain a divorce from an unhappy marriage, in a legally weak position in the battle for custody of her child, ill, exhausted, and persecuted, she wrote to Victor Considerant (socialist political economist and follower of Fourier) just before her death in 1844: "I have nearly the whole world against me. Men because I demand the emancipation of women; the owners because I demand the emancipation of wage-earners." Workers carried her coffin to her grave, where a subscription was raised for a monument. On 23 October 1848, during the revolution, several thousand paid tribute at her grave.[24]

Other women made contributions not only to the preparation

for the Revolution of 1848 but also to the revolutionary process once it had begun. Jeanne Deroin, another self-educated working woman active in the early French trade-union movement, wrote about women's internalization of their oppression.[25] From March to June 1848, she, Susanne Voilquin, and Désirée Gay joined with Eugénie Niboyet in publishing *Women's Voice*, the "first feminist daily," which advocated women's suffrage.[26] Gay, a shirtmaker, represented the women of the National Workshops at the Provisional Government of 1848. During the Revolution of 1848 these working-class women were moving toward the idea of workers' control. They opposed middle-class philanthropy with their own plans for crèches (a new idea at the time, emerging from their needs as working women), socialized medicine, "enlightened care" and education for children, and, in the words of Henriette D., "equality between married couples."[27]

As in 1789, many women's political clubs were formed because only a few of the revolutionary clubs admitted women; the club of Étienne Cabet (utopian socialist and author of *Travels to Icaria*) was one. In April 1848, Deroin's attempt to run for the legislative assembly was ruled unconstitutional by the male representatives of the Second Republic. After the bloody suppression of the workers' insurrection of June, revolutionary women's clubs were shut down. This marked the beginning of a new period of reaction. Further, Rowbotham has written, the revolution was a fork in the road for French feminism: "After 1848 there is a clear division between the socialist and liberal feminist position."[28]

On 2 December 1851, the success of the counterrevolution was completed with the coup d'état by Louis-Napoléon Bonaparte.[29] Feminist-socialist leaders, including Deroin, Voilquin, and Pauline Roland, were jailed, deported, or escaped into exile.[30] Bonaparte, nephew of Napoléon I, became Emperor Napoléon III in 1852, and the Second Empire was born with a motto coined by Guizot: "Get rich." Paris was reconstructed so there would be no more revolutionary barricades; however, what remained in a new form was the gulf between rich and poor. And within the proletariat "women were the more exploited."[31]

Attitudes toward women during the authoritarian phase of the empire (to about 1860) might best be gauged by the violently anti-feminist book *Justice in the Revolution and in the Church*, published in 1858, by Pierre-Joseph Proudhon,[32] "the principal thinker" of the French working class during the period, who had made his peace with Bonaparte's protofascist regime. Earlier, in 1846, Proudhon had written, "For myself, the more I think of it, the less I am able to imagine woman outside the family and marriage. I see nothing between the state of courtesan and that of homemaker. . . . Mankind is created male and female: from this results the necessity of the ménage and of property."[33] He believed that a man's primary business in marriage was to dominate his wife, physically if necessary. For Proudhon, therefore, a woman had but two choices in life: to be a harlot or to be a wife.[34] In the First International Workingman's Association (created largely by Marx), the Proudhonians argued against women working at all, except as wives and mothers. Ironically, as Edith Thomas has pointed out, "Marriage in the eyes of the law and of God was not the rule in the working-class family. But . . . irregular unions were often of long duration, and displayed a much greater fidelity than legitimate marriages."[35]

During the liberal phase of the empire, Jenny d'Héricourt led the cause for "civic emancipation" of women. Juliette Lamber, a friend of George Sand, published *Anti-Proudhonian Ideas*, in which she opposed prostitution and advocated women's rights to work, education, divorce, and property. Victorine Brochon and Nathalie Lemel organized food cooperatives and joined the International. Marguerite Tinayre, a novelist whose pen name was Jules Paty, wanted to make women aware of the necessity of "physical harmony" in marriage, a subject approaching a taboo in 1860; she was also a member of the International.[36] Maria Deraismes argued, "The inferiority of women is not a fact of nature; it is a human invention and a social fiction."[37]

A common thread running through feminism in the 1860s was a passion for knowledge. Élisa Lemonnier, for example, founded professional schools for women. Louise Michel was a schoolteacher. She belonged to the opposition to Bonaparte and was a member of the International, and became involved in clashes with officials. Because she rejected marriage, she later became known as "the red virgin." Michel taught in one of Lemonnier's schools, at which time she also organized a society for short-term relief of the poverty of working women. Other liberal professions at the time were, of course, closed, even to young women of the bourgeoisie. In 1867, Julie Daubié won a prize from the Lyon Academy for her study "The Poor Woman in the Nineteenth Century," in which she described the economic necessity behind urban working-class prostitution, referred to as "the fifth quarter of the day." The rector at

Lyon opposed Daubié's taking the examination for her baccalaure-
ate; when she passed, the Minister of Public Education refused to
grant her her diploma, fearing he would be "forever holding up his
ministry to ridicule."[38]

In 1868, freedom of assembly was revived, and the feminist
movement burst forth, beginning with the famous conferences at
Vaux-Hall. The orators for women's rights included Maria Deraismes,
Paule Minck, a teacher and a linen draper, and André Léo, a novelist
and journalist. Léo's novels and sociopolitical writings were optimistic. She believed that happiness in marriage was possible when love
overcame considerations of money and age. She wrote about divorce; she examined current notions about women's nature and the
current belief that women's abilities were inferior to men's; she argued that such ideas were products of changing historical conditions. She commented on the prevalence of hysteria in women at
the time: "When nerves are no longer in style, they will be put
to much less use." She took democrats and socialists to task for
their hypocrisy about freedom for women, which they regarded
with "suspicion" and "terror." Socialist men claimed that women's
suffrage and the oppression of women were secondary to capitalist
exploitation and that since the subordination of women antedated
capitalism, there was no guarantee that the abolition of capitalism would end the oppression of women—an argument now used
more frequently by feminists arguing against the priorities of socialists. Reminiscent of Mary Wollstonecraft, the publicist Olympe
Audouard said: "For woman to succeed in any career whatever, she
must have ten times as much talent as a man, for he finds a spirit of
cooperation ready to aid and sustain him, while she has to struggle
against a stubborn attitude of ill will."[39]

The whole feminist movement and its leading participants came
together in 1869 to found the League for Women's Rights and the
feminist newspaper *Women's Rights*.[40] In August 1870, on the occasion of French military disaster in the war with Prussia, followers of
the French revolutionary Auguste Blanqui attempted to seize army
weapons to make revolution; they were arrested and condemned to
death. Louise Michel, André Léo, and Adèle Esquiros, "on behalf
of the people," took a petition with thousands of signatures to the
governor of Paris—"an extraordinary act, bordering on scandal." A
stay of execution was granted on 2 September; the republic was
proclaimed on 4 September. The workers felt that the victory was
theirs. As Edith Thomas has put it, "From that day on, an almost

unbridgeable gulf existed between the bourgeois and the socialist Republics."[41]

The essence of the relationship of women to French revolutions has been summed up by Thomas: "If women had participated in the great battles of the 1789 Revolution, they were even more caught up in the 1848 Revolution, from which they hoped for recognition of their rights. But the men of 1848 did not seem disposed to grant them these rights, any more than did their 'great forefathers' of 1789. The battle lines were drawn again in 1871, on the occasion of the Commune." She went on to observe: "Contemporaries were struck by the importance of women's participation in the 1871 Revolution."[42]

On the Right, Maxime du Camp said, "The weaker sex drew attention to itself during those deplorable days. . . . They bared their souls, and the amount of natural perversity revealed there was stupefying. . . . these bellicose viragos held out longer than the men did behind the barricades." Alexandre Dumas *fils* said, "We shall say nothing about their females, out of respect for women—whom these resemble once they are dead."[43]

On the Left, Benoît Malon (André Léo's husband) noted that "one important fact that the Paris Revolution brought to light is the entry of women into politics. . . . they felt . . . that woman and the proletariat, those ultimate victims of the old order, could not hope for their emancipation except by forming a strong union against all the forces of the past." Karl Marx, in *The Civil War in France*, contrasted the "tarts" whose "protectors" were "men of family, of religion, and especially of property" to "the real Parisian women [who] had come to the surface: heroic, noble, and devoted, like the women of Antiquity. . . . The women of Paris joyfully give up their lives on the barricades and execution grounds. What does this prove? It proves that the daemon of the Commune changed them into Megaeras and Hecates."[44]

Women took part in many political and military actions in Paris during the Franco-Prussian War and during the days of the Paris Commune. At the beginning of the Prussian siege of Paris, they worked to feed and find employment for poor women, and they assisted and accompanied the troops that defended Paris. Plans were again made to implement a women's battalion, Amazons; but the provisional government's military authorities squelched the idea. Women took initiative in the resistance to the Germans, demonstrating en masse at the Hotel de Ville against surrender, and they were fired upon by government troops. On 28 January 1871, Louis-Adolphe Thiers surrendered France, conceding territorial reparations to the Germans on 26 February. But the people had kept their cannons. The class war against the people of Paris was about to begin.[45]

On 18 March, Thiers ordered his troops into the working-class districts to retrieve the cannons and disarm the people. Parisian women formed a "veritable human barricade" between the National Guard of Paris and the Versailles troops. The latter refused the orders of General Lecomte and General Clément Thomas, the butcher of the June 1848 insurgents; they fraternized with the crowd and shot the generals instead. The treason (in the eyes of Parisians) of the Versailles government resulted in the declaration of the Commune on 26 March 1871. Béatrix Excoffon wrote about the public calls exhorting women to march to Versailles in an attempt at reconciliation following the tradition of October 1789, an attempt that failed.[46]

In early April, women participated in the ceremonies to dedicate the Commune, which had granted legal equality to common-law marriages and to their offspring. In the face of the bombardment of Paris by the bourgeois government at Versailles, on 11 April radical women called for revolutionary war in the style of 1792 to defend the Commune. But, as Thomas has noted, "Actually, the women were as much divided by their social origin as the men." Liberal bourgeois women proposed an armistice, while radical women responded with a call to social revolution.[47] The Commune was being pushed to the left by the pressure of its opponents in Versailles and in good measure by revolutionary women.

Central to this leftward rush of the Commune were women's political organizations. The Women's Union, part of the French section of the International, was organized by Elizabeth Dmitrieff (a friend of Karl Marx and an illegitimate child of a Russian noble). She proposed a plan for free productive associations of women workers, whose goals would be equal wages, jobs for those who wanted them, and maintenance of an ongoing political organization. The plan was approved by the Commune and later became a model for the organization of work in Yugoslavia. But its implementation in Paris was interrupted 21 May 1871 when the Versailles army invaded Paris. The Women's Vigilance Committees organized ambulance nurses, hunted draft evaders, and fed the poor; Excoffon, Sophie Poirier, and Anna Jaclard were prominent members. Poirier and Jaclard were sisters, children of the Russian intelligentsia. Jules Allix's Comité des Femmes was another women's political group. Discussion clubs thrived; the major topic was "Woman in the Church and Woman in the Revolution." A revolutionary paper declared, "It is time for us to halt the injustices and prejudices of which women are victims." Revolutionary leaders were from many countries: Fornarina de Fonseca was from Italy, Lodoyska Kawecka from Poland, and Mme Reidenreth from Austria. Reidenreth wore two American revolvers and discussed prostitution at a meeting in a church. The arrest of priests and the execution of draft dodgers were advocated in the Club des Prolétaires, of which Mme André, a laundress, was secretary. Nathalie Lemel urged women to armed defense of the Commune. In another church, an old woman coaxed the assembly to sing the "Marseillaise" in place of hymns, because "there is no more God," she said. [48]

Louise Michel often chaired the Club of the Revolution, an extremely anticlerical group. It advocated killing hostages one by one until the imprisoned Blanqui was freed by Versailles and returned to Paris. Michel refused to condemn prostitutes; she felt that they were "the saddest victims of the old world." Blanche Lefebvre, a dressmaker, tall and thin, wearing a red scarf and a revolver, spoke almost daily to the Club of the Social Revolution; she loved the revolutionary Commune "as others love a man" (in the words of one observer) and gave her life on the barricades. Women of the working class demanded revolutionary measures against the symbols of the old order and the counterrevolution. [49] They tore down, as Marx had predicted in *The Eighteenth Brumaire of Louis Bonaparte*, "that colossal symbol of martial glory, the Vendome Column." [50] The revolution spread beyond Paris to the departments.

Important in the plan of the Communards to organize a new world was the reform of secular education, reminiscent of the plans that Pauline Roland had drawn up in 1849. Technical and industrial schools were set up for girls so that they could earn a living and become self-governing citizens of the republic. Educational day nurseries were planned for the children of working women. On 20 May 1871, the Commune raised and equalized the salaries of men and women teachers. In its educational policies, the Third Republic followed the guidelines set forth during the all-too-brief two months of the Commune's existence. Revolutionary institutions also included art: Rosalie Bordas, a famous singer, performed *La Canaille* at the Tuilleries, and Agar (Mme Charvin) performed with the Comédie Française, for which she was eventually blacklisted after the fall of the Commune.[51]

Prominent women revolutionaries of this period included André Léo, who told General Dombrowski that he would not have been where he was were it not for women's support of the Commune. She suggested as a title for a book on the period since 1789 "A History of the Inconsistencies of the Revolutionary Party," a book that would focus on the question of women's rights and the treatment of women. (For example, women ambulance nurses encountered sexist attitudes in officers but acceptance by common soldiers, similar to Jeanne Deroin's experience during the Revolution of 1848.) An adherent of the beliefs of Bakunin, Léo defined the revolution as "the liberty and the responsibility of every human being, limited only by the rights of all, without privilege of race or of sex." In Thomas's judgment, she was "a great journalist." Victorine Louvet, the mistress of Blanquist General Eudes, impressed even reactionaries with her martial skills. Louise Michel was extremely active; in Thomas's words, "her great figure dominated them all." During the "bloody week" of 11 May 1871, when Parisian women constructed barricades, one of the combatants was Joséphine Courtois, a fifty-year-old seamstress who had fought in 1848 in Lyon, where she earned the sobriquet "Queen of the Barricades."[52]

Many Communards were from the provinces; they resisted the Versailles army, which marched into Paris, setting fires with kerosene and incendiary bombs. To the advancing troops, "every poor woman was suspect." The women of the Commune were assassinated, tortured, and raped. "Society women" beat the prisoners with parasols. Louise Michel turned herself in to save her mother from the firing squad. As a prisoner she remained defiant; to repeated threats that she would be shot, her reply was, "As you like."[53] *Les pétroleuses*, women accused of setting fires in order to prevent the capture of Paris by the Versailles troops, were predominantly working-class and poor women; whether they were justly accused remains a matter of controversy. However, the prosecution reacted to them with hysterical antifeminism, claiming they had repudiated "the great and magnificent role of women in society," thereby jeopardizing the continuation of civilization. The prosecutor, Captain Jouenne, "blushed" to give the defendants "the name of women." He thought they were misled by revolutionary intellectuals seeking recruits with their "dangerous utopias" namely, "the emancipation of women":

Have they not held out to all these wretched creatures bright prospects, incredible chimeras: women judges, women as members of the bar! Yes, women lawyers; deputies, perhaps and—for all we know—commandants? Generals of the Army? Certainly, faced with these miserable aberrations, we believe we are dreaming![54]

There were also trials in mid-1872 for the summary executions carried out by the Commune, including that of the Archbishop of Paris. In these trials, women were blamed for inciting men to their "crimes." A parliamentary enquiry, surprisingly, pointed out that women had supported the Commune because of the misery they had had to endure under the old order. Louise Michel had appeared before the Sixth Council of War on 16 December 1871, accused of a long list of crimes resulting from her participation in the Commune. She refused to defend herself but fully, proudly, and defiantly assumed responsibility for her acts in support of the Commune because "the Social Revolution is the dearest of my desires."[55] Michel was banished to a fortress in New Caledonia along with Sophie Poirier and Nathalie Lemel. Anna Jaclard, Paule Minck, André Léo, and Elizabeth Dmitrieff escaped to Switzerland, where they continued to defend and support the Communards. Béatrix Excoffon repented and recanted, and her sentence was reduced because she returned to "the duty of women in society." Thomas has observed that in prison "the characters of this story retain their individuality. The women of the Commune were of every description." While serving her sentence, Michel studied science and fought for prisoners' rights and against racism.[56]

A partial amnesty was granted to the Communards in 1879 and full amnesty in 1880. The actions of women in the Commune were memorialized by Eugène Pottier, composer of *L'Internationale*, and in the poetry of Rimbaud and of Victor Hugo. Hugo never gave up interceding on behalf of Communards under sentence of death. He also exposed the hypocrisy of the politicians who condemned the supporters of the Commune as common criminals. This morality of the victorious was a lie flying in the face of the whole of French revolutionary history since 1789, a betrayal of the very basis of the legitimacy of their own authority, he said. Verlaine wrote in a ballad:

Heavenly name and heart, exiled
By bourgeois France of supple spine:

Listen, good-for-nothing wretches,
Louise Michel is doing fine.[57]

Marx, in *The Civil War in France*, contrasted two Parises:

The Paris of M. Thiers was not the real Paris of the "vile multitude," but a phantom Paris, the Paris of the *francs-fileurs*,
the Paris of the Boulevards, male and female—the rich, the
capitalist, the gilded, the idle Paris, now thronging with its
lackeys, its blacklegs, its literary bohème, and its cocottes at
Versailles, Saint-Denis, Rueil, and Saint-Germain; considering the civil war but an agreeable diversion, eyeing the battle
going on through telescopes, counting the rounds of cannon,
and swearing by their own honour and that of their prostitutes, that the performance was far better got up than it used
to be at the Porte St. Martin. The men who fell were really
dead; the cries of the wounded were cries in good earnest;
and, besides, the whole thing was so intensely historical.[58]

He was even more stinging than Hugo in his denunciation of the
bourgeoisie.

The civilisation and justice of bourgeois order comes out in its
lurid light whenever the slaves and drudges of that order rise
against their masters. Then this civilisation and justice stand
forth as undisguised savagery and lawless revenge. Each new
crisis in the class struggle between the appropriator and the
producer brings out this fact more glaringly. Even the atroci-
ties of the bourgeois in June 1848 vanish before the ineffable
infamy of 1871. The self-sacrificing heroism with which the
population of Paris—men, women and children—fought for
eight days after the entrance of the Versaillese, reflects as
much the grandeur of their cause, as the infernal deeds of the
soldiery reflect the innate spirit of that civilisation of which
they are the mercenary vindicators. A glorious civilisation indeed, the great problem of which is how to get rid of the
heaps of corpses it made after the battle was over![59]

During the years following the Commune came "the despair
that swept France after the debacle of the Franco-Prussian war."[60]
Émile Durkheim, born in 1858, was in his teens during this period

of war, revolution, reaction, and malaise. As historian James F. McMillan has pointed out, "It is one of the little recorded facts of the Third Republic's history that the inequalities of sex became a matter for widespread public discussion in the years before 1914." We have seen in our sketch of the history of French feminism its close connection with the fortunes and failures of revolutionary republicanism. What distinguished mainstream feminism during the Third Republic, McMillan has suggested, was its "conscious reaction to what had gone before. . . . Now, just as the Third Republic's new breed of moderate politicians wished to obliterate the connotations of republicanism with the violence and disorder of the Commune, the June Days [of 1848] and the Terror [during the Great Revolution], so too the feminists were equally anxious to dispel memories of previous links between feminism and political and sexual radicalism. Intent on living down the past, republicans and feminists alike sought above all to establish their respectability." The two most important figures of this modern French feminism were Maria Deraismes and Léon Richer. Their anticlericalism led them to ally with antifeminist politicians in order to save the republic from its reactionary enemies. Richer even believed that to give women the vote would be to give power to the "clericals." Suffrage was not as important to French feminists as it was to English women at the turn of the century because of the relatively stronger current in France of "social feminism," with its concern for philanthropy and moral reform. McMillan has characterized French feminism in the Third Republic thus: "Indeed, if mainstream feminism can be said to have had any one overriding goal, it was to obtain a single standard of morality by abolishing the regulated system of prostitution and by making men conform to the standards of sexual respectability demanded of girls and women. Feminism in France was very largely a 'purity crusade.'"[61]

Women achieved some successes in the decade following the Commune. In 1878, Deraismes and Richer organized the First International Congress for Women's Rights. During the conservative presidency of Jules Grévy (1879–85), the Camille Sée Law (1880) was enacted, extending to young women the right to attend secondary schools. During 1880 and 1881, normal schools for women were established. In 1882, Hubertine Auclert, more radical than Deraismes and Richer, founded *The Woman Citizen*, which advocated women's suffrage. (A year earlier, she had refused to pay taxes, saying, "I don't vote, I don't pay.") During 1882 at Rouanne, an amendment demanding "the abolition of all paragraphs of law which . . . put women in a subordinate position to men" was attached to the Marxist French Workers' Party's "minimum programme" for women's emancipation. In 1884, divorce was once again possible, but the law favored husbands.[62]

Just as liberal feminism avoided contact with Catholic women's associations, so it steered clear of alliances with the Left and with workers' movements, which themselves were divided on the issue of feminism. McMillan has observed that "solidarity with the bourgeois Republic kept feminism isolated from the socialist movement, despite socialism's theoretical commitment to the cause of women's emancipation." Socialist feminists themselves disagreed about the issue of class conflict and collaboration, and they faced the chauvinism of male socialists. The result was that "feminism and socialism ultimately went their separate ways."[63]

In 1892, for the first time an international congress of women called itself "feminist." Aline Valette published *Socialism and Sexualism* in 1893; she focused on the double oppression of women at home and at work, and she held maternity in high regard. *La Fronde,* the "first feminist daily" to be written, managed, and printed by women exclusively, was established by Marguerite Durand in 1897. In 1904, Paul Lafargue, leader of the Marxist French Labor Party and husband of Marx's daughter Laura, set forth the Marxist theory of the oppression of women in *The Question of Women.* Three years later, in *Socialism and Feminism,* Lydia Pissarjevsky rejected the Marxist equation of the oppression of women and the exploitation of workers, expressing skepticism that socialism would result in different treatment of women by men. Also in 1907, married women won the right to control their own incomes. In 1910, Auclert and Durand tried for legislative office, without success. Six years later, during the Great War, socialist and workers' organizations were taken to task for their lack of sensitivity to the problems of women. Anticipating the future, Hélène Brion entitled her criticism *The Feminist Way: Women, Dare to Be!* She was sentenced to prison in 1918 for spreading pacifist propaganda. In 1917, the year of Durkheim's death, *Women's Voices* was begun by Colette Reynaud. Nelly Roussel described the paper as "feminist, socialist, pacifist and internationalist."[64]

From a contemporary feminist perspective, nonrevolutionary French feminism and French sociology shared a common weakness. By the early twentieth century, it was clear that French feminists had not continued the project begun by their revolutionary sisters of earlier times, namely, "to develop a new consciousness of themselves as women." McMillan has described them as confined in "their aspirations to institutional reform and shackled to conventional ideas about femininity and the family."[65] Like the French sociologists, as we will see, they were ideologically limited by deeply rooted traditions concerning the "second sex," as well as by the relative backwardness and uneven development of French capitalism. For the French tradition of sociology, from Montesquieu in the eighteenth century to Durkheim and his disciples in the twentieth, the social order was also the moral order. In this sense, much of French sociology can be located in "the intellectual tradition of the French *moralistes,* most specifically those who wrote about political and religious matters with an eye to the 'decadence' of existing society."[66] Durkheim's description of the nineteenth century as an age of "moral mediocrity" is indicative of the moralistic conception of society in French social theory. In this, as in any other conservative view of society, the family plays a crucial role in the maintenance of society's morality.[67] As a consequence, French social theory was quite sensitive to the "woman question": the position of women in the structure of the family and in society, and the role of women in the division of labor. This stands to reason: French feminism, as we have seen, originated with the French Enlightenment and developed in the revolutionary tradition to which French sociology—reaffirming the traditional doctrine of separate spheres for men and women—was a conservative response.

The French Theorists

Nowhere are the characteristics of French sociology more evident than in the writings of Frédéric Le Play (1806–82). Le Play was not a classical theorist but rather a classical sociological empiricist,[68] whose work can be characterized as sociological familialism. For Le Play, the working-class family, not the individual, was the bedrock of society.[69] In contrast with the stability of the patriarchal family of nomadic shepherd societies and the stem or stock family based on primogeniture of coastal fishing communities, the working-class family of industrial society approximated an "unstable" type, he believed. According to Le Play, industrial work and democratic laws that weakened patriarchal authority concerning women and family property were destroying the family, which in turn meant a degeneration of values and morality and, in Fletcher's summary, "an instability and malaise in the whole nature of modern society."[70] As Nisbet has observed, Le Play "made the conservative trinity of family-work-community into a methodological framework."[71] Variations on this theme are played throughout French social theory.

Alexis de Tocqueville
The Impact of Democracy on the Position of Women

The contribution of Alexis de Tocqueville (1805–59) to a sociology of women is to be found in the context of his observations of the effects of democracy on the family, observations made by comparing different kinds of families in democratic and aristocratic societies in his classic work, *Democracy in America*.[72] Tocqueville asserted that "in America the family, if one takes the word in its Roman and aristocratic sense, no longer exists" (*DA*, 560); he noted that "in aristocracies . . . the father is not only the political head of the family but also the instrument of tradition, the interpreter of custom, and the arbiter of mores" (*DA*, 562). Children and women listened to him with deference, spoke to him with respect, and feared as well as felt affection for him, Tocqueville said; democracy, with its attention to the present, weakened paternal authority. "So at the same time as aristocracy loses its power, all that was austere, conventional, and legal in parental power also disappears and a sort of equality reigns around the domestic hearth" (*DA*, 562). He concluded that "democracy loosens social ties, but it tightens natural ones. At the same time as it separates citizens, it brings kindred closer together" (*DA*, 564). In the tradition of French classical liberalism, he argued that women shaped the mores of a free society: "Therefore, everything which has a bearing on the status of women, their habits, and their thoughts is, in my view, of great political importance" (*DA*, 565).

Tocqueville believed that in Protestant nations, in contrast with Catholic countries, "girls are much more in control of their own behavior"—especially in the United States, where the young woman "thinks for herself, speaks freely, and acts on her own." Young American women were taught self-control to preserve chastity; they were not cloistered. He felt this approach had its drawbacks because it developed in women "judgment at the cost of imagination" and made them "chaste and cold rather than tender and loving companions of men," thus reducing "the charms of private life." Nevertheless, he averred, "A democratic education is necessary to protect women against the dangers with which the institutions and mores of democracy surround them" (DA, 565–67).

Young American women may have had a certain degree of independence, but it only lasted until marriage, Tocqueville discovered:

> In America a woman loses her independence forever in the bonds of matrimony. While there is less constraint on girls there than anywhere else, a wife submits to stricter obligations. For the former, her father's house is a home of freedom and pleasure; for the latter, her husband's is almost a cloister. (DA, 568)

America's Puritan beliefs and trading habits were the cause, Tocqueville claimed: "Inexorable public opinion carefully keeps woman within the little sphere of domestic interests and duties and will not let her go beyond them" (DA, 568). The young woman found "these ideas firmly established" and could not depart from them without threatening her personal and social survival; knowing the sacrifices expected, American women did not enter into marriage lightly (DA, 568–69).

Historical changes in the economic and social structures of societies determined, from Tocqueville's perspective, variations in the "intensity" of the "reciprocal attractions of the sexes" and the character of sexual morality. His view of relationships between the sexes in aristocratic societies was as follows:

> Among aristocratic peoples birth and fortune often make a man and a woman such different creatures that they would never be able to unite with one another. Their passions draw them together, but the social conditions and the thoughts that spring from them prevent them from uniting in a permanent and open way. The necessary result of that is a great number of ephemeral and clandestine connections. Nature secretly gets her own back for the restraint imposed by laws. (DA, 571)

In aristocratic societies, the major purpose of marriage was to combine property, not persons, and once the fortunes were united, such an arrangement left "their hearts to rove at large" (DA, 572). Those who attempted to cross the barriers of aristocratic inequalities

and defy the tyranny of custom and the wishes of family found themselves without family and friends. In Tocqueville's words, "The prejudice which they have defied separates them. This situation soon
wears down their courage and embitters their hearts" (DA, 572).

In democratic societies, social barriers between men and women
were swept aside, Tocqueville found. Thus "when each chooses his
companion for himself without any external interference or even
prompting, it is usually nothing but similar tastes and thoughts that
bring a man and woman together, and these similarities hold and
keep them by each other's side" (DA, 572). So love became the basis
of marriage and rendered "irregular morals before marriage very
difficult," he wrote, because it was difficult, the passions notwithstanding, for a man to convince a woman that he loved her when he
was completely free to marry her but would not (DA, 571). After
marriage, he believed, men diverted their attention from love-
making to business. What did not change in a democracy was the
economics of sex roles: "Limited incomes oblige the wives to stay at
home and watch in person very closely over the details of domestic
economy" (DA, 573).

Tocqueville concluded his discussion of the impact of democracy on the family and women in the United States with a chapter
entitled "How the American Views the Equality of the Sexes." Believing that democracy destroys or modifies social inequalities, he
posed the question: "May it not ultimately come to change the
great inequality between man and woman which has up till now
seemed based on the eternal foundations of nature?" He answered
in two parts: first, he agreed that democracy "does raise the status
of women and should make them more and more nearly equal to
men" (DA, 576); but, second, he dissociated himself from the license that "the crude, disorderly fancy of our age" took with the
subject of sexual equality:

> In Europe there are people who, confusing the divergent at-
> tributes of the sexes, claim to make of man and woman crea-
> tures who are, not equal only, but actually similar. They would
> attribute the same functions to both, impose the same duties,
> and grant the same rights; they would have them share every-
> thing—work, pleasure, public affairs. It is easy to see that the
> sort of equality forced on both sexes degrades them both, and
> that so coarse a jumble of nature's works could produce nothing
> but feeble men and unseemly women. (DA, 576)

Tocqueville believed Americans had quite a different, and correct, view of equality of the sexes: "In America, more than anywhere else in the world, care has been taken constantly to trace distinct spheres of action for the two sexes" (DA, 577). He thought Americans had applied to this realm the "great principle of political economy which now dominates industry," namely, the division of labor and specialization of functions based on the belief in "great differences between the physical and moral constitution of men and women." He noted in particular that in America women were never found "interfering in politics," "managing a business," or doing a man's "rough" job. "Nor have the Americans ever supposed that democratic principles should undermine the husband's authority and make it doubtful who is in charge of the family." American women, he claimed, accepted their subordination (DA, 576–77).

In Europe, according to Tocqueville, "a certain contempt lurks in the flattery men lavish on women," and while men made themselves women's slaves, they never sincerely thought women their equals. American men, in contrast, thought "that woman's mind is just as capable as man's of discovering the naked truth, and her heart as firm to face it" (DA, 577). He warned of the consequences of European male chauvinism:

> It would seem that in Europe, where men so easily submit to the despotic sway of women, they are nevertheless denied some of the greatest attributes of humanity, and they are regarded as seductive but incomplete beings. *The most astonishing thing of all is that women end by looking at themselves in the same light and that they almost think it a privilege to be able to appear futile, weak, and timid.* The women of America never lay claim to rights of that sort. (DA, 577–78; emphasis added)

Tocqueville believed that the double standard for sexual behavior was more prevalent in Europe than in America, and he found that rape was treated more seriously in America than in Europe. Rape was punishable by death in the United States, and no crime was judged more heinous by public opinion, since Americans "think nothing more precious than a woman's honor." However, in France, penalties for rape were less severe and conviction more difficult to win from a jury. Tocqueville asked, "Is the reason scorn of chastity or scorn of woman? I cannot rid myself of the feeling that it is both" (*DA*, 578).

Tocqueville summed up by saying, "The Americans do not think that man and woman have the duty or the right to do the same things, but they show an equal regard for the part played by both and think of them as beings of equal worth, though their fates are different" (*DA*, 578). Then came the rub: "Thus, then, while [Americans] have allowed the social inferiority of woman to continue, they have done everything to raise her morally and intellectually to the level of man. In this I think they have wonderfully understood the true conception of democratic progress." So, although the American woman was restricted to the domestic sphere, and further restricted within it, the compensations were, in Tocqueville's judgment, that "nowhere does she enjoy a higher station." In true French fashion, Tocqueville attributed "the chief cause of the extraordinary prosperity and growing power" of Americans "to the superiority of their women" (*DA*, 578–79).

Whatever one may think of Tocqueville's attitudes toward women's position in the social order, I think his conception of the laws of motion of democratic society and the dialectic of the past and present can describe the emergence of the women's liberation movement. A theme that pervaded Tocqueville's work on democratic society was that equality cannot be restricted to one sphere. He argued that "by no possibility could equality ultimately fail to penetrate into the sphere of politics as everywhere else. One cannot imagine that men should remain perpetually unequal in just one respect though equal in all others; within a certain time they are bound to become equal in all respects" (*DA*, 49). Later he argued, "There are certain great social principles [equality and inequality] which a people either introduces everywhere or tolerates nowhere" (*DA*, 561). The contradictions that emerge in historical processes give rise to social movements for extending equality to oppressed groups.

In the chapter "Why Great Revolutions Will Become Rare," Tocqueville, following Aristotle, postulated that revolutions are always about the issue of equality, arising from a real and felt sense of injustice. Tocqueville foresaw the likelihood of a revolution by blacks if slavery were abolished but full civil rights denied by a competitive society in which money and status were precarious—a society in which majority opinion could seize upon differences that appeared to be rooted in nature, namely skin color, to justify the exclusion of blacks and thereby protect the stake in the social order of white men of middling property (*DA*, 610–20, 313–33).[73] Such an analysis could be extended to women, if, after being granted political equality by law, they were still denied their full civil rights; Tocqueville could have as easily predicted a women's liberation movement.

Tocqueville's descriptions of the effects of revolutionary tumult—when equality is penetrating a society and "still fights painfully against prejudice and mores"—on the relations of master and servant (as a microcosm) could be used as an apt characterization of the contemporary war between the sexes. Law and custom clash, and traditional subordination becomes degradation because it is no longer accepted as natural or divinely ordained. Men cease to entertain those sentiments of protective kindness that are the product of "long and uncontested power," and women see the men who give them orders as unjust usurpers of their own rights; in such times every home becomes a scene of internecine war. Things become "so jumbled and confused that no one knows exactly what he is, what he can do, and what he should do" (*DA*, 533–54).

In my judgment, Tocqueville's observations, from his value-laden aristocratic perspective, can be employed to provide a clear picture of the limits and contradictions of the position of women in bourgeois, democratic societies; his theory has more heuristic value than does liberal social theory. On the other hand, the limits of his perspective on the condition of American women can be readily grasped by comparing his analysis with that of Harriet Martineau in *Society in America* (1837). She observed American society at the same time, covered the same ground, and arrived at many of the same conclusions that Tocqueville reached. However, despite her judgment that American marriage laws were more favorable to women than England's, her assessment of the condition of American women was quite different from his. She stated, "The Americans have, in the treatment of women, fallen below, not only their own democratic principles, but the practice of some parts of the Old World." She added, in contrast to Tocqueville's moralizing, "While woman's intellect is confined, her morals crushed, her health ruined, her weaknesses encouraged, and her strength punished, she is told that her lot is cast in the paradise of women: and there is no country in the world where there is so much boasting of the 'chivalrous' treatment she enjoys." She pointed out the similarity of the condition of women to slavery. She mentioned the role of women in the abolitionist movement, expressed concern for working-class women, and cited the Declaration of Independence as a basis for a feminist movement.[74]

Auguste Comte
Scientific Sociological Positivism on the Nature of Women

There is probably no better place to witness sociology's conservative underpinnings than in the work of Auguste Comte (1798–1857), who coined the very name of the discipline. His purpose was to use scientific sociological knowledge to help end the political upheavals of his time, which he felt stemmed from moral and intellectual anarchy. To this end he offered his "positive philosophy" as an alternative to the negative, that is to say critical, philosophy of the Enlightenment, with its belief in human perfectability, inalienable rights, and natural equality.[75]

Comte's first major work, *Cours de philosophie positive*, was published in Paris between 1830 and 1842. In volume 4 (1839), he argued that society's "true social unit is certainly the family." He believed that the family had two relational dimensions, "namely the subordination of the sexes, which institutes the family, and that of ages, which maintains it." The "revolutionary spirit" of the eighteenth century had attacked marriage, he thought, because marriage was infused with theology, like everything else at the time.[76] However, Comte's assurances reveal his awareness of the revolutionary criticisms of the patriarchal family in his own time:

> When the positive philosophy shall have established the subordination of the sexes, and in that, the principle of marriage and of the family, it will take its stand on an exact knowledge of human nature, followed by an appreciation of social development as a whole . . . and in doing this it will extinguish the fancies by which the institution is at present discredited and betrayed.

Contemporary philosophical fancies, Comte noted, mistook the current phase of the family "for an overthrow of the institution."[77]

Comte offered the belief that the future conditions of marriage "will be consonant with the fundamental principle of the institution—the natural subordination of the woman, which has reappeared under all forms of marriage, in all ages." He believed the principle was scientifically confirmed:

> Biological philosophy teaches us that, through the whole ani-mal scale . . . radical differences, physical and moral, distin-guish the sexes. Comparing sex with age, biological analysis presents the female sex, in the human species especially, as constitutionally in a state of perpetual infancy, in comparison with the other.

Women were inferior to men intellectually, Comte wrote, but supe-rior in their natural social sympathies. Women's "nature" made them unfit for politics and extradomestic pursuits but fit them exactly for the moderating function in the moral economy of the family and so-ciety. Sociology would settle scientifically the debate over the equality of women, according to Comte.

> Sociology will prove that the equality of the sexes, of which so much is said, is incompatible with all social existence, by show-ing that each sex has special and permanent functions which it must fulfil in the natural economy of the human family, and which concur in a common end by different ways, the welfare which results being in no degree injured by the necessary subordination, since the happiness of every being depends on the wise development of its proper nature.[78]

Such statements earned Comte the disapproval of his English correspondents. In a letter (4 March 1844) to Mrs. Austin, a trans-lator whose husband was legal philosopher John Austin, Comte wrote to clear himself

> of a charge which would distress me much, and which I be-lieve I have never deserved, namely, the imputation of a ten-dency to an insufficient appreciation of the worth of women in general and your worth in particular. Though I am deeply convinced that the social office of your sex must remain essen-tially distinct from that of ours, in order to [secure] the hap-piness of both, yet I think I have rendered to the moral and even the intellectual qualities which belong to women an exact fundamental justice, which will naturally be more ex-

plicit in the great special treatise on philosophy which I am to
commence this year.[79]

In that work, *System of Positive Polity; or, Treatise on Sociol-*
ogy, Instituting the Religion of Humanity, the first volume of which
was published in 1851, Comte argued that the restoration of orderly
progress required that the "proletaries" renounce violence in order
to improve their condition and that the positivist philosophers be
given control of (*and* adequate compensation for overseeing) formal
education in Europe.[80] For the positivist program of regeneration
to be successful, Comte said, the cooperation of women was required. Comte's "new religion" of "Humanity" would only be complete when all three elements of human nature were represented,
namely, reason (responsible for progress and represented by philosophers), activity (responsible for order and represented by the
working classes), and feeling (responsible for love and morality and
represented by women, the "sympathetic sex") (*SPP*, 164–66, 168,
208). The first and third of these three elements, in Comte's view,
could only preserve their respective powers in this trinity by "keeping clear of all positions of political authority" (*SPP*, 218); generally,
politics had to take second place to morality (*SPP*, 166).

He believed it would not be difficult to get women to join his
movement because "the social mission of Woman in the Positive
system follows as a natural consequence from the qualities peculiar
to her nature" (*SPP*, 169). Positivism would attract women, he felt,
because of its emphasis on the emotion of love; and, "happily,
women, like the people, judge . . . by the heart rather than by the
head" (*SPP*, 185). He viewed women as "less capable than men of
abstract intellectual exertion" (*SPP*, 180) and believed that prac-
ticality was what women had in common with the working classes.
"In the most essential attribute of the human race, the tendency to
place social above personal feeling, she is undoubtedly superior to
man" (*SPP*, 169). The "Positive principles" that rested "on scientific
laws of human nature or of society" demonstrated that the nature of
woman found its "highest and most distinctive sphere of work" in
the family (*SPP*, 187). In the family, the woman was the spiritual
power and the moral educator of her children and her husband,
who voluntarily submitted to her superior altruism and thus completed his moral education (*SPP*, 194–96); persuasion, not command, was appropriate to her role. Comte emphasized the role of
woman as wife and companion over her functions of procreation

and maternity (*SPP*, 188). In Comte's summation, "Her function in society is determined by the constitution of her nature"—that is, as "the spontaneous organ of Feeling" (*SPP*, 204).

Comte argued against those who advocated equality for women, especially "the Communists" (*SPP*, 184). He stated, "In all ages of transition, as in our own, there have been false and sophistical views of the social position of Woman" (*SPP*, 196). Comte's authoritarianism showed clearly in his belief that his views would find the greatest sympathy among the working class, "the very class where the preservation of the institution of the family is of the greatest importance" (*SPP*, 197). To allow women to compete with men in the occupational division of labor would subject "every occupation to a degree of competition which they [women] would not be able to sustain," and competition would destroy the affection between the sexes. Men should provide for women and preserve "the essentially domestic character of female life" (*SPP*, 199). Comte opposed divorce and polygamy, the inheritance of wealth by women, and professional education for women, although he was in favor of equalization of noncoeducational secondary-school instruction. He preferred that widows remain unmarried, and he accepted the possibility of platonic marriages because he felt that women were by nature less sexual than men and that abstinence was character-building for men (*SPP*, 198–202). He was sure that women found contemporary proposals attacking marriage repugnant (*SPP*, 184–85). He felt that history supported his views:

> The continuous progress of Humanity in this respect, as in every other, is but a more complete development of the pre-existing order. Equality in the position of the two sexes is contrary to their nature, and no tendency to it has at any time been exhibited. All history assures us that with the growth of society the peculiar features of each sex have become not less but more distinct. (*SPP*, 198)

Capping off Comte's positivist utopia was the private and public worship of "Woman . . . the spontaneous priestess of Humanity." In his conclusion, he maintained he had put the best of chivalry and Catholicism on a scientific foundation appropriate for restoring social order to the modern world (*SPP*, 183, 205–11).

Raymond Aron's statement in *Main Currents of Sociological Thought* coincides with the view Comte expressed in his letter to

Mrs. Austin, but it is difficult to find the basis for it in the foregoing quotations from Comte's work.

> Auguste Comte had, if you will, a sense of the equality of be-
> ings, but it was an equality based on the radical differentiation
> of functions and natures. When he said that woman is intellec-
> tually inferior to man, he was ready to see this as a superiority
> of woman, because by the same token woman is the spiritual
> power, the power of love, which to the Comte of the *Système*
> was far more important than the futile superiority of intelli-
> gence. At the same time, in the family it is the men who have
> the experience of historical continuity, who learn what is the
> condition of civilization, who control the transmission of civi-
> lization from generation to generation.[81]

Some insight into Comte's position on "woman's proper place" and his eccentric proposals may be gleaned from his personal rela-tionships with women. His first wife, Caroline Massin, was an erst-while prostitute on whom he vented his rage in recurrent psychic breakdowns, during which he had to be physically restrained from such acts of violence as throwing knives. For twenty years, Massin stuck by him, finally leaving him after he completed his *Cours de philosophie positive* in 1842; even later, however, she assisted him with his personal difficulties by intervening with the Ministry of Education, which allowed him to continue to lecture. In 1844, he met a younger woman, Clothilde de Vaux, at the home of a disciple and at once fell in love. She was an upper-class woman who had been deserted by her husband, a petty official. The affair never went beyond the platonic level (despite Comte's wishes). After her death, Comte devoted his life to "his angel"; the *System of Positive Polity,* which he worked on in the second half of the 1840s, is a long memorial to his beloved. In that work, as described by Lewis A. Coser, Comte "proclaimed over and over again the healing powers of warm femininity for a humanity too long dominated by the harsh-ness of masculine intellect."[82] In the end, Comte in effect pro-claimed himself the High Priest of the Religion of Humanity, the Pope of the Church of Class Peace, and Clothilde its Madonna and object of ritual worship of woman. In Comte's positivist utopia, there would be no work, no aggression, and no sex. Birth would be virgin, a curious intellectual projection of Comte's unrequited and sublimated love for Clothilde.[83] He may have learned more from the relationship than he realized: a former teacher of mine pointed out, half seriously, that their correspondence revealed Mme de Vaux to be the better sociologist.

Émile Durkheim
Suicide and the War between the Sexes

Émile Durkheim (1858–1917) developed the Comtean project of establishing scientifically a new secular morality in conflict-ridden nineteenth-century France. He considered sociology and education the major tools with which to accomplish this purpose. Although a Dreyfusard, Durkheim steered a middle course between the anti-clerical left and the clerical and monarchist right during the Third "Republic of Professors."[84] His work contains the first truly modern statement of sociological functionalism.[85] The political ideology implicit in his functionalist perspective is plain in *The Division of Labor in Society* (1893).[86] Yet we shall also see that his writings about the position of women took a course exactly the opposite of Spencer's—a fact not given sufficient attention by Durkheim's commentators.

Durkheim's discussion of sex roles and sex differences occurred in the context of his attempt to assess the function and the moral value of the division of labor in society. The division of labor, he wrote, "is more and more becoming one of the fundamental bases of the social order," and "the categorical imperative" of the collective moral conscience is: "*Make yourself usefully fulfill a determinate function*" (*DLS*, 41, 43). Durkheim felt that growing specialization of functions in the economy, politics, administration, and other areas of life met with resistance and criticism from those who believed that the division of labor inevitably produced economic crises, class conflicts, and the warping of individuality. He conceived of his work as a way to settle these issues—by treating "facts of the moral life according to the method of the positive sciences," thereby reconciling science and morality by establishing a science of ethics, which would contribute to the reform of society through moral education (*DLS*, 32).

Durkheim sought to establish "the function of the division of labor," that is, "the need which it supplies" (*DLS*, 49). He rejected out of hand the idea that material and intellectual progress enhanced personal happiness, because an increase in the number of suicides accompanied modern progress (*DLS*, 50–51; see also 233–

55). Understanding the moral effects of the division of labor seemed to Durkheim more important than focusing on its economic aspects. After a brief consideration of friendship, a phenomenon of undisputed moral quality, he concluded that "the economic services that it can render are picayune compared to the moral effect that it produces, and its true function is to create in two or more persons a feeling of solidarity." Further, Durkheim stated, "The history of conjugal society offers us an even more striking example of the same phenomenon." He said that "the sexual division of labor is the source of conjugal solidarity" and has developed concomitantly with it (DLS, 56–57). In Durkheim's argument, then, the sexual division of labor in marriage became the paradigm, the basis for understanding the whole society.

Durkheim attempted to demonstrate a pattern of increasing physical and cultural differentiation between men and women. The general conclusion at which he arrived was that "the further we look into the past, the smaller becomes the difference between man and woman"—with respect to general appearance, strength, brain size, and social roles and functions. He believed that "the two sexes lead almost the same existence" in contemporary tribal societies. Following the developmental anthropology of his time, he accepted "that there was an epoch in the history of the family when there was no such thing as marriage"; there was, rather, a kind of primitive promiscuity combined with a matriarchal family. In general, "the state of marriage in societies where the two sexes are only weakly differentiated thus evinces conjugal solidarity which is itself very weak" (DLS, 57–59).

Conversely, Durkheim felt that as marriage developed and became characterized by more complex rules, men and women became more differentiated. He thought that women became "weak creature[s] . . . with the progress of morality"; they acquired the quality of gentility, and he believed there was anthropological evidence that women's brains became relatively smaller than men's. With the development of marriage, he continued, citing Spencer among others, women retired from warfare and public affairs and consecrated their entire lives to the family, until finally they had come to lead completely different lives from those of men. He added, à la Comte and Tocqueville, "One might say that the two great functions of the psychic life are thus dissociated, that one of the sexes takes care of the affective functions and the other of intellectual functions" (DLS, 60). His argument was, in short, that the division of labor in sexual roles made domestic solidarity possible. From this history of conjugal solidarity, Durkheim set out to prove the hypothesis that the larger social division of labor produced not disagreement and conflict but consensus and solidarity (*DLS*, 57–63). That during his lifetime the division of labor was causing intellectual anarchy, economic crises, and class conflict Durkheim attributed to its "abnormal forms," "forced" and "anomic" (see *DLS*, book 3).

The serious flaw in Durkheim's analysis of conjugal solidarity is that it leaves out the roles of coercion, repression, and unequal exchange in its concern with the technical complementarity of specialized functions institutionalized in sex roles in the family. In what must be taken as understatement, Durkheim admitted the hidden hand of "economic utility" in the sexual division of labor, but he denied the importance of economic interests because the division of labor also constituted "the establishment of a social and moral order *sui generis*. Through it, individuals are linked to one another" (*DLS*, 61).

These social relations had their psychological correlates: "The image of the one who completes us becomes inseparable from ours . . . [and] thus becomes an integral and permanent part of our conscience" (*DLS*, 61). Yet one might turn Durkheim's argument to other conclusions than support for the differentiation of sex roles as a basis for conjugal solidarity (see discussion of Parsons in chapter 6). Durkheim believed, "Permit the sexual division of labor to recede below a certain level and conjugal society would eventually subsist in sexual relations preeminently ephemeral." Without the sexual division of labor, women "would be independent" of men (*DLS*, 61). In other words, to the extent that women become equal to men politically, socially, and economically, the solidarity of the patriarchal family would weaken, and relations between the sexes would be of shorter duration. To a certain degree, this has been happening in contemporary North American society.

Often neglected in references to Durkheim's work is the fact that his ideas about the relations of men and women changed between the time he wrote *The Division of Labor* and the publication of *Suicide*.[87] Throughout *Suicide*, his "methodological classic," Durkheim discussed the position of women in nineteenth-century European societies.[88] Arguing against the theory that suicide results from psychopathic states, Durkheim pointed out that while there were greater numbers of women than men in insane asylums (possibly due to their greater longevity), "suicide happens to be an essentially male phenomenon"; he wrote that there were on average four male suicides to each female suicide (S, 70–72). All European countries except Spain had lower suicide rates for women than men. The differences in motives for the suicides of men and women, as recorded in the official records of France and Saxony, showed "poverty and losses" were more characteristic of men and "mental troubles" of women (S, 150).

Leaving aside questions of the theoretical and empirical or scientific adequacy of Durkheim's work,[89] in the following discussion I focus on how Durkheim explained sex differences in suicide statistics and the conclusions his data forced upon him. He pointed out that, in general, while suicide rates for men and women increased with age, the difference between their respective rates remained. Ruling out heredity as an explanation (since an inherited trait would be expected to afflict men and women equally), Durkheim took the position that any tendency to suicide by women "is usually offset by the *social* conditions peculiar to the female sex" (S, 99–101; emphasis added).

He accounted for some of the difference in male and female suicide rates by the second-class status of women in society: where women were less educated, were restricted from the professions, and had no property of their own, their suicide rates were lower. In general, suicide "is undeniably exceptionally frequent in the highest classes of society" and specifically among the liberal professions (S, 165–66). In England, where the illiteracy rate for women was lower than in France, the sex differences with respect to suicide were reduced. In the United States, in places where black women were equally or more highly educated than their husbands, their suicide rate surpassed that of black men and that of white women (S, 166–67). In addition, "Industrial and commercial functions [in contrast to agricultural occupations] are really among the occupations which furnish the greatest numbers of suicides. The enormous rate of those with independent means (720 per million) sufficiently shows that the possessors of most comfort suffer most" (S, 257). Obviously, since most women were excluded from the world of industry and trade and lacked independent means, their suicide rate was lower. One might say that lower suicide rates for women were a backhanded benefit of sexism.

In his theoretical explanation, Durkheim argued that suicide varied inversely with the degree of integration in religious societies and within the family. Thus, since members of Catholic and Jewish religious congregations were more integrated within their fellowships, they had lower suicide rates than Protestants, whose values dictated a more individual relationship with their God (S, 152–216, especially 158–59, 168). He argued further that the higher the degree of integration within the family (as measured by marital status and family size), the lower the rate of suicide. Therefore, married persons over 20 years of age killed themselves less frequently than unmarried persons. However, this relationship varied with the sexes between societies. In France, men were favored; in Oldenburg, women (S, 179). But, in general, suicide statistics led Durkheim to conclude that "the wife profits less from family life than the husband" (see S, 171–188). And since childless women in France committed suicide "*half again as often as unmarried women of the same age,*" it was clear to Durkheim that marriage was harmful to women and aggravated any other tendency to suicide they might have. What he wished to establish was that the "immunity of married persons in general is thus due, wholly for one sex and largely for the other, to the influence not of conjugal society but of the family society" (S, 188–89). Summing up, he remarked that "conjugal society, so disadvantageous for women, must, even in the absence of children, be admitted to be advantageous for men" (S, 193). Put in plain language, what made marriage tolerable for women was having children.

The suicides of Protestants, intellectuals, and unmarried persons Durkheim termed "egoistic"—suicides of "excessive individualism." Durkheim believed life meaningful only when one is attached to others, not merely to abstractions. It would appear, then, that egoistic suicides by definition could not have been the suicides of women in a patriarchal society. Yet, to avoid a possible contradiction—that, since women were less integrated in society, they should have a *higher* suicide rate[90]—he drew a quaint conclusion about the desires of women, in which he repeated a Victorian prejudice about the "nature" of women:

As she lives outside of community more than man, she is less penetrated by it; society is less necessary to her because she is less impregnated with sociability. She has few needs in this direction and satisfies them easily. With a few devotional practices and some animals, the old unmarried woman's life is full. (S, 215)

Men, Durkheim thought, were "more complex social being[s]," whose moral and psychological balance was more precarious and who therefore benefited more from marriage and family life (S, 216). Up to this point in Durkheim's argument we can say, if we ignore his language, that the explanation is sociological in that it rests on the restriction of women within the bounds of domestic life.

If society is *nomic* or rule-bound life—"the spirit of discipline"—then it follows that *anomie*—the breakdown of discipline due to rapid change or the presence in society of conflicting norms—has negative social-psychological effects, in particular an increase in suicides.[91] Underpinning Durkheim's putative sociological explanation for anomic suicide was the psychological assertion that "no living being can be happy or even exist unless his needs are sufficiently proportioned to his means" (S, 246). This proposition accounted for the increase in suicides in times of rapidly increasing prosperity as well as during economic collapse and also explained why poverty was a protection from suicide.[92]

Likewise, Durkheim considered the suicides that occurred after divorce and widowhood a result of what he referred to as conjugal anomie. Statistics proved that "throughout Europe the number of suicides varies with that of divorces and separations" (S, 260). Further, "divorced persons of both sexes kill themselves between three and four times as often as married persons" (S, 262). However, the impact of sex roles on self was illustrated strikingly by the differential effects of divorce on the suicide rates of men and women: "It appears that, in countries where divorce does not exist or has only been recently instituted, woman's share is greater in the suicides of married than of unmarried persons. This means that marriage favors the husband rather than the wife. . . . [In contrast,] her profit is greatest in the country [Saxony] where divorces also are greatest." Durkheim stated the statistical law as follows: "*From the standpoint of suicide, marriage is more favorable to the wife the more widely practical divorce is; and vice versa*" (Durkheim's emphasis). The thrust of his argument was that "marriage may very possibly act in an opposite way on husband and wife. For though they have the same object as parents, as partners their interests are different and often hostile" (S, 268–69).

For Durkheim, monogamous marriage was no more than a "regulation of sexual relations" not only in their physical aspects but also in "the feelings of every sort gradually engrafted by civilization on the foundations of physical desire." But this state of "moral equilibrium" solely benefited the husband. The unmarried man was, of course, in a different position: he had the right to form attachments wherever inclination led him. His sexual desires and fantasies were like that "longing for infinity" endemic to modern economic life. Durkheim suggested that "the result of it all is a state of disturbance, agitation and discontent which inevitably increases the possibilities of suicide." The frequency of divorce "implies a weakening of matrimonial regulation," putting a man in the position of a bachelor, thus increasing his chances for voluntary death (S, 270–71).

However, Durkheim pointed out, "This consequence of divorce is peculiar to the man and does not affect the wife" (S, 272). Why is this the case? The reasons Durkheim offered reveal his conflating biological stereotypes about women with his inconsistent recognition of the social subordination of women:[93]

> Woman's sexual needs have less of a mental character because, generally speaking, her mental life is less developed. . . . Being a more instinctive creature than man, woman has only to follow her instincts to find calmness and peace. She thus does not require so strict a social regulation as marriage, and particularly as monogamic marriage. . . . By limiting the horizon, it closes all egress and forbids even legitimate hope. . . . it prevents her from changing it if it becomes intolerable. The regulation therefore is a restraint to her without any great advantages. Consequently, everything that makes it more flexible and lighter can only better the wife's situation. So divorce protects her and she has frequent recourse to it. (S, 272)

To buttress his argument, he presented evidence that unmarried women were immune to the form of anomie that afflicted unmarried men (S, 274), again not fully recognizing that what we would term sexism in socialization was crucial. Durkheim summarized:

> Speaking generally, we now have the cause of that antagonism of the sexes which prevents marriage favoring them equally: their interests are contrary; one needs restraint and the other liberty. (S, 274)

He added that a "woman can suffer more from marriage if it is unfavorable to her than she can benefit by it if it conforms to her inter-

est. This is because she has less need of it. This is the assumption of
the theory just set forth" (S, 275). Durkheim's analysis could be restated thus: Society's arrangements for control and discipline of
male sexuality are at the expense of women and their sexuality.
With some modification such a formulation could include prostitution. The problem with Durkheim's formulation of the theory is
that the purpose of his work as a whole and of *Suicide* in particular
was to establish the validity of strictly sociological explanations of
human behavior. Employing sexist biological notions to account for
unusual data thwarted his purpose. A social explanation would have
produced the theoretical consistency he so valued.[94]

In his quest for theoretical completeness, Durkheim delineated
two more types of suicide. Altruistic suicide, the polar opposite of
egoistic suicide, he defined as the suicide caused by overintegration
of individuals in societies, most commonly, in traditional societies,
where life lost its meaning apart from the individual's membership
in a group. He cited the example of the "suicides of women on their
husbands' deaths" (S, 219; see also 217–40). Finally, fatalistic suicide, the polar opposite of anomic suicide, Durkheim described as
follows:

> It is the suicide deriving from excessive regulation, that of
> persons with futures pitilessly blocked and passions violently
> choked by oppressive discipline. It is the suicide of very young
> husbands, and of the married woman who is childless. (S,
> 276n.25)

A rather damning indictment of patriarchal marriage. (See also S,
176–79.)

In his discussion of the "practical consequences" of his work on
suicide, Durkheim faced squarely the issue of sexism and women's
equality. Stating that "the only way to reduce the number of suicides due to conjugal anomie is to make marriage more indissoluble," he went on to say:

> What makes the problem especially disturbing and lends it an
> almost dramatic interest is that the suicides of husbands can-
> not be diminished . . . without increasing those of wives.
> Must one of the sexes necessarily be sacrificed, and is the
> solution only to choose the lesser of the two evils? Nothing

else seems possible as long as the interests of husband and wife in marriage are so obviously opposed. As long as the latter requires above all, liberty, and the former, discipline, the institution of matrimony cannot be of equal benefit to both. But this antagonism which just now makes the solution impossible is not without remedy, and it may be hoped that it will disappear.

It originates in fact because the two sexes do not share equally in social life. Man is actively involved in it, while woman does little more than look on from a distance. Consequently man is much more highly socialized than woman. . . . But it is by no means certain that this opposition must necessarily be maintained. . . . To be sure, we have no reason to suppose that woman may ever be able to fulfill the same functions in society as man; but she will be able to play a part in society which, while peculiarly her own, may yet be more active and important than that of today. The female sex will not again become more similar to the male; on the contrary, we may foresee that it will become more different. . . . Both sexes would thus approximate each other by their very differences. They would be socially equalized, but in different ways. And evolution does seem to be taking place in this direction. Woman differs from man much more in cities than in the country; and yet her intellectual and moral constitution is most impregnated with social life in cities.

In any case, this is the only way to reduce the unhappy moral conflict actually dividing the sexes, *definite proof of which the statistics of suicide have given us*. Only when the difference between husband and wife becomes less, will marriage no longer be thought, so to speak, necessarily to favor one to the detriment of the other. As for the champions today of equal rights for woman with those of man, they forget that the work of centuries cannot be instantly abolished; that juridical equality cannot be legitimate so long as psychological inequality is so flagrant. Our efforts must be bent to reduce the latter. For man and woman to be equally protected by the same institution they must first of all be creatures of the same nature. Only then will the indissolubility of the conjugal bond no longer be accused of serving only one of the two parties pleading. (S, 384–86)

This passage reveals the way in which his support of greater equality for women was limited by the functionalism of the intellectual tradition that he had inherited.

But it is an oversimplification of Durkheim's position for L. J. Jordanova to say that in *Suicide* Durkheim was "able to conjure up a set of biological assumptions which added to the woman = nature stereotype, conveying a degree of biological determinism for women which far exceeded that for men."[95] In their brief discussion of Durkheim's work, Richard A. Cloward and Frances Fox Piven have also oversimplified in asserting that Durkheim's explanation of women's lower suicide rate—namely, that women participate less in collective life and therefore experience less stress—"may well be absurd."[96] They have overlooked Durkheim's recurrent theme that women benefit less than men from marriage and experience more stress from it. However, it is true that Durkheim opposed divorce by mutual consent (a woman's issue widely discussed at the time) as a threat to marriage and family life and all their functions, especially the regulation of individual desire and sexual passion. In addition, he claimed that his research had shown him the "obscure, mysterious, forbidding character of the sexual act," which led him to oppose national sex education. Yet is is also the case that Durkheim's work responded to feminist concerns, and his respect for the facts is demonstrated by the greater sympathy for the plight of women in *Suicide* as compared with his earlier book, *The Division of Labor in Society.* This is the aspect of Durkheim that many writers overlook in their effort to document sexism in the history of classical sociology. I think Steven Lukes has captured the essential contradiction of Durkheim's position, characterizing it as "an alliance of sociological acumen with strict Victorian morality."[97]

Whatever radical feminists may think of Durkheim's gradualist and reformist position on sexism, he saw clearly its curious and multiple effects in nineteenth-century suicide rates. He saw even further, although dimly, that social equality of the sexes could mean that women might have to pay equally "the ransom money of civilization"—an increased rate of suicides. It would appear, logically speaking, that the only ways out, given his analysis, are the feminization of society or the transformation of marriage and sex roles in an androgynous socialism. For it seems clear to me that equality of the sexes in a capitalist society can only mean for most women, i.e., working-class women, equality in being exploited.

4

Germany

Die Frauenfrage and Historical Sociology

Capitalist industrialization began later but developed more rapidly in Germany than in England or in France. However, bourgeois democracy never did quite take hold in Germany, in part as a result of unsuccessful revolutions—one coming too early (at the time of the early sixteenth-century Reformation in Germany), and the other too late (as part of the revolutions of 1848). Fascism and imperialist war "solved" the problem of the modern class struggle after the suppression of yet a third revolution (that of workers, soldiers, and socialist intellectuals in November 1918) and after the failure of the Weimar Republic.[1] In Germany, as in England and in France, there were two feminisms, liberal and socialist. But in Germany there was also a third feminism; associated with the erotic movement, it was bohemian and cultural, overlapping anarchism.

As a result of the political, social, and economic changes that accompanied the beginnings of industrial capitalism, the number of legally free industrial workers in Germany increased from between fifty and one hundred thousand in 1800 to nearly a million by 1848. The number and proportion of women who worked in factories also rose. The percentage of women in the total labor force rose from about 16 percent in 1816 to 25 percent in 1846.[2] Many women continued to work in the deteriorating home industry (including Luise Zietz, who later became a prominent socialist-feminist).[3] In general, trade associations forbade male/female cooperation. Prior to 1848, little was heard of what later was termed the "woman question" except among communist workers and such revolutionary intellectuals as Karl Marx and Friedrich Engels.

Industrial capitalism got into high gear between 1851 and 1870, drawing more women into new occupations as manual and day laborers. During the 1860s, the controversy over whether women should work outside the home first occurred in German workers' organizations, and what Werner Thönnessen has called "proletarian antifeminism" was first expressed.[4] In the Saxon textile-workers movement, however, the many women members had equal rights with men within an organization that advocated equal pay for equal work. German socialist women traced their heritage to this organization.[5]

Socialist Feminism

Women's rights became a widespread issue in Germany in the mid-1860s. In 1865, Luise Otto-Peters, a novelist and a proponent of women's rights during the Revolution of 1848, helped establish the General German Women's Association (Allgemeiner Deutscher Frauenverein, or ADF), which advocated civil equality for women. It was the first organization of liberal feminists (see "Liberal Feminism," below). Otto-Peters criticized the antifeminism of the General German Workers' Association, founded by Ferdinand Lassalle, who was Marx's great ideological and personal rival in the German working-class movement. The Lassalleans opposed female labor because they thought it depressed wages and harmed the working-class family; they thought women should be restricted to the domestic sphere until after the emancipation of male workers. At the Third Congress of the Federation of German Workers' Associations, held at Stuttgart in 1865, Moritz Müller, an enlightened manufacturer from Frankfurt, advocated the rights of women to develop their talents and interests, to work at any occupation of which they were capable, and to carry out independent action as workers; surprisingly, the majority of those in attendance agreed with him.

More characteristically, the German section of the First International Workingmen's Association distinguished between the "solemn" duties of fathers in public and family life and the duties of mothers, who should stand for "the coziness and poetry of domestic life." During the first two Congresses of the International, 1866 and 1867, two main positions on the "woman question" were in evidence: The General Council of the International (of which Marx was a leading light) approved of women working but disapproved of the poor conditions under which they worked in the capitalist system; however, German and French followers of Proudhon argued that women's working outside the home violated their "naturally determined role." Marx's other great rival for control of the International was the anarchist Mikhail Bakunin, who supported a third position—equality in all spheres for both sexes.[6]

In 1869, when the General Congress of German Social Democratic Workers met at Eisenach, two positions, one traditional and the other more feminist, were again presented. The program adopted called for restriction of women workers and abolition of child labor. The demand for equal pay for both sexes was voiced. A drive to organize working-class women began during the period 1869–71, but the Combination Law that governed political association in Germany proscribed organizations of men and women and barred women from political parties. During 1872–73, the Erfurt Workers' Congress and *Der Volksstaat*, the Social Democratic organ, opposed female labor because of the terrible conditions in the factories.[7]

At the famous Unification Conference at Gotha in May 1875, the United Social Democratic Workers' Party, later known as the Social Democratic Party (Sozialdemokratische Partei Deutschlands, or SPD), was formed. The compromise on women's rights worked out between Lassalle's adherents and Marx's followers (the Eisenachers, led by Wilhelm Liebknecht and August Bebel) called for suffrage for all citizens (but without specifically mentioning women) and for restriction of women to jobs that were not considered morally or physically detrimental. As Thönnessen has pointed out, even radicals such as Bebel and Marx accepted the bourgeois notion of femininity. Social Democratic deputies in the Reichstag did not demand protection for women workers until 1877, and they did not demand women's suffrage until 1894–1895. The party's position on these two issues remained unchanged until the Erfurt Program of

1891. In the 1880s, there were few debates about women's rights because discussions of Bismarck's Anti-Socialist Law (Exceptional Law) of 1878–90 dominated party conferences.[8] It should be noted that the stock market crash of 1873 ended rapid growth and set off more than two decades of depressed prices. Protectionism inaugurated the fateful alliance of industrialists and large landowners, preserving their power and protecting Imperial Germany from the threat of socialism—and of feminism.[9]

August Bebel's *Woman and Socialism* (*Die Frau und der Sozialismus*) was originally published in 1878 as *Woman in the Past, Present and Future*. Thönnessen has described it as "the first book to attempt to investigate the question as a whole from a socialist viewpoint."[10] It went through fifty-eight printings in German alone, fifty of which were published between 1879 and 1909. Bebel took the position that "the so-called women's question is . . . only one side of the whole social question" and that both could be solved only by a socialist reorganization of society that would abolish the double exploitation of women. Bebel recognized that woman was "a slave before the slave existed," that the oppression of women antedated capitalism, and that the social subordination of women had become internalized. Further, he realized that women must take charge of their own emancipation; men, in his words, "are like all rulers well nigh inaccessible to reason." Bebel did not stop there but brought the argument home: "There are socialists who are not less opposed to the emancipation of women than the capitalist to socialism." The significance of Bebel's book was that it posed the problem of the formulation of a feminist socialism.

> The question as to what position in our social organization will enable woman to become a useful member of the community, will put her in possession of the same rights as its other members enjoy, and ensure the full development of her powers and faculties in every direction, coincides with the question as to the form and organization which the entire community must receive, if oppression, exploitation, want and misery in a hundred shapes are to be replaced by a free humanity.[11]

Bebel believed that a system needed to be created that would make possible certain changes in human relations, such as eliminating sex-linked roles, removing barriers that separated family and public life, and communalizing some human activities.

The influence of *Woman and Socialism* was great: "Numerous personal testimonies, such as those of Rosa Luxemburg, Clara Zetkin, Marie Juchacz, Ottilie Baader, and Luise Zietz, give evidence of the enduring effect that Bebel's book had on women. It prepared the ground for the achievements of the Social Democratic women's movement after 1890 in the realms of education, agitation and organization."[12] The following testimonies give a sense of the effect of Bebel's book on socialist feminists. Baader described her encounter with the book as having the character of a "religious rebirth." She saw in it "my own fate and that of thousands of my sisters. . . . I read the book not once, but ten times. . . . I had to break with so many things that I previously regarded as correct." Zietz claimed Bebel's book removed the "blinders" from her eyes and helped her understand her "disgraceful" and "humiliating" position as a proletarian woman. Helene Grünberg, a trade unionist of working-class origin, said Bebel explained why "we [women] were burdened under capitalism." In Wilhelmine Kähler's words, Bebel's book "forged the most unshakable belief that tomorrow's dawn would also bring women deliverance." Middle-class women also read *Woman and Socialism* and were encouraged by it.[13] However, more important for subsequent theoretical controversy over the causes of the oppression of women and their liberation was Friedrich Engels's *The Origin of the Family, Private Property, and the State*, which was published in 1884, six years after Bebel's book. (See discussion of Engels's work in chapter 7.)

In 1889, Clara Eissner Zetkin published "The Question of Women Workers and Women at the Present Time," a pamphlet that became the basis for the Social Democrats' policy until the outbreak of the war. Zetkin, having broken with the bourgeois world in which she had been raised, was, in Jean Quataert's characterization, "the leading theoretician and school mistress of the socialist women's movement."[14] Zetkin connected the emancipation of women and the achievement of socialism. She believed that under capitalism it was inevitable that women work, that trying to abolish female labor under capitalism was like trying to destroy machine industry. She believed the task was to educate and organize women workers to achieve solidarity with the men of their class. For Zetkin, the freedom of women was an economic and a class problem.[15] She described herself as an "inveterate Marxist," relying more heavily on Engels and Marx than on Bebel. To her mind, *Woman and Socialism* was too feminist; she felt that it minimized class struggle, glossed over class differences between women, and criticized too harshly the sexism of working-class men.[16]

At the Paris International Workers' Congress in 1889, Zetkin argued that women should join the struggle of the working class to overthrow capitalism; she also argued (unsuccessfully, however) against special protections for women workers on the grounds that work was necessary to enable women to be economically independent of men. Zetkin pointed out that it was not women who depressed wages but rather capitalists, who determined wages by deciding what portion of a family's income they thought a woman, a man, or a child should earn; believing that women were not supporting families, employers therefore did not pay a woman a living wage. The congress adopted a stand for protection but also took positions in favor of equal rights for women in the ranks of labor and equal pay regardless of sex or nationality. Since women were more vulnerable than male workers under existing conditions, Zetkin's position (which was in this regard close to the position of bourgeois feminists against special privileges) was rejected as untenable because the Social Democrats hoped to improve the conditions of all workers by first gaining protection for women workers.[17]

Emma Ihrer, a shoemaker's daughter, was, along with Zetkin, a leading figure in the formation of the SPD's program for the emancipation of women. She arrived in Berlin from Schleswig in 1881 to work in the garment industry and became active in the organization of women's clubs that had moral and financial backing from the SPD. Ihrer recalled that life under Bismarck had not only politicized women but had created class solidarity between men and women workers through the sharing of repression in what was termed "the community of defeat." The Halle Party Congress of 1890 agreed with the theory expressed in Zetkin's position and reveled in the SPD's electoral successes following the abolition of Bismarck's Anti-Socialist Law.[18]

The SPD program authored by Karl Kautsky and adopted at the Erfurt Conference (1891) called for universal suffrage for all citizens over twenty without regard to sex, for the removal of all laws that discriminated against women in private and public life, and for the establishing of local "agitation commissions" for women. Subsequently, national and international meetings of socialists adopted similar programs. The Berlin Party Conference of 1892 set up a system of "spokespersons," substituting the word *Vertrauensperson* for *Vertrauensmann* in order to evade the Combination Law prohibitions against membership of women in political organizations but still represent women's interests in the SPD. Ottilie Baader presided over the spokespersons' hierarchy from 1899 to 1908. Between 1901 and 1907, the number of female spokespersons increased from 25 to 407. With the abolition of the Combination Law in 1908, the SPD executive committee made a place for a women's representative. A woman also took a place on the executive committee of the General Commission of Trade Unions, which had been formed in 1890. A magazine for the interests of women workers, *Die Gleichheit* (*Equality*), edited by Ihrer and Zetkin, was first published in Stuttgart in 1891. Between 1900 and 1913, *Die Neue Zeit*, the official organ of the SPD, published more articles on the "woman question" than it had ever published before.[19]

At national conferences and international congresses in the early 1890s and among the public at large, the issues of protection, women's and children's legal rights, and the appointment of women factory inspectors were debated. In 1894 and 1895, SPD deputies introduced bills for women's suffrage. At the London International Congress of 1896, resolutions were passed obliging unions to accept women workers as members and demanding equal pay for equal work and paid leave for postnatal recovery. That year at the Party Conference at Gotha, Zetkin once again put forth a straightforward class analysis of the "woman question," distinguishing the individualistic struggles of bourgeois women from the class struggles of proletarian women. The conference adopted an advanced program on all issues concerning women. For example, in order to resolve the conflict between the position advocating equal pay for women and the position advocating protection for women, Gertrud Hanna, the trade unions' women's secretary, proposed the concept of "equivalent efficiency" (similar to today's "comparable worth," or "pay equity") as a standard by which different jobs for men and women could be compared. (The negative aspect of protection, of course, was that, in order to excuse superexploitation of women, employers inferred that women workers were less efficient than their male counterparts.) Since her teens, Hanna had worked and gained leadership experience in the largely female Printers' Aides Union.[20]

Between 1900 and 1913, there was "phenomenal growth in the strength of the women's movement." Thönnessen has suggested that three factors were most responsible: the increase in the number of women workers, the expiration of the old Combination Law in

1908, and the effectiveness of SPD agitation and organizational activity. In 1895, there were around five million women workers, about 20 percent of the total work force. By 1907, the number was about eight million, between 25 percent and 30 percent of the work force. Between 1900 and 1910, membership of women in the trade unions increased sharply from 23,000 to 190,000, and to 223,000 in 1912. By comparison, during the period from 1900 to 1913 subscriptions to *Gleichheit*, increased from approximately 4,000 to approximately 112,000.[21]

In September 1900, German Social Democratic women held their first conference at Mainz. Socialist women were becoming embroiled in the revisionist controversy that had been given open theoretical expression with the publication of Eduard Bernstein's *Evolutionary Socialism* in 1899 (foreshadowed in his letter to the Stuttgart Conference of 1898). Bernstein suggested that Marx's notions of the breakdown of capitalism and of increasing class polarization were apocalyptic, not factual. He advocated a critical reappraisal, in the spirit of Kant, of the rhetoric of violent struggle and materialist historical necessity, and, observing the reformist *practice* of the SPD, he provided a theoretical, moral, and political basis for gradualist reformism. In *Gleichheit*, Zetkin and Baader argued against attempts to modify the class-struggle perspective and opposed Lily Braun, who wrote *The Women's Question* in 1901. Braun (whose first husband was Georg von Gizycki, a professor of philosophy in Berlin, and whose second husband was Heinrich Braun, a writer) sided with the revisionists and urged cooperation with the middle-class women's movement. Zetkin characterized middle-class feminists as "bourgeois women's libbers," who, by the use of vague "humanitarian phrases" and small reforms for women workers, sought to draw workers away from commitment to the class struggle. In 1902, the government's policies to increase the birthrate (after a small decline) prompted proposals for a "birth-strike" to extract concessions for women's rights. Social Democrats split: the reformists supported contraception to improve the lot of women, and the centrists and leftists (including Kautsky, Zetkin, and Rosa Luxemburg) opposed it because it smacked of Malthusianism and they feared it would detract from the class struggle.[22] Among women, and in the SPD as a whole, theoretical radicalism existed side by side with quotidian economic and legal political struggles. Thönnessen summarizes: "Electoral assistance to the Party, therefore, became the most important task for the women's movement."[23]

This process of the displacement of ends (socialism) by means (the SPD party apparatus) received its classic sociological analysis in Robert Michels's *Political Parties*.

An article published in 1905 in *Sozialistische Monatshefte* by the reformist SPD Reichstag deputy Edmund Fischer provoked intense responses from leading Social Democratic women. He wrote that the "so-called emancipation of women . . . is unnatural, and hence impossible to achieve."[24] His Proudhonian position was that socialism's purpose was to restore the sex roles of the traditional family—just what capitalism had destroyed. Ihrer exposed Fischer's traditional assumptions when she said, "To be a mother is as little a life's goal as to be a father." Her ideal was that "the woman of the future will choose one occupation according to her capabilities and inclinations: she will be either working woman or educator of children or housekeeper, but not all three, as today's proletarian woman." Zetkin, closely following Engels's thought, argued against Fischer that capitalism was pushing the working-class marriage to a higher form of monogamous union, with men sharing more household tasks. Braun's contribution to the debate was less optimistic about the prospects for happy marriages between equals. She believed that the pressures of modern life and greater sexual freedom challenged the adequacy of monogamy. She wrote, "On the corpse[s] of the martyrs of marriage speaks the priest of the religion of love with the words, 'faithful spouse.'" Braun understood clearly one of the effects of contemporary feminism: "Since the women's movement has loosened our tongues, we see that the sexual drive is as strong in women as in men." Although she accepted premarital sex, she did not consider free love or common-law marriages as liberating alternatives for women. For Braun, motherhood was a woman's true mission in life.[25]

Prior to 1908, women had gained autonomy in the SPD through a system whereby women could elect women to its national congresses if the men failed to do so. In 1900, to the charge that the women's organization would become a "state within a state," Zietz replied forcefully, "I do not want anything exceptional or even special rights but—as we are already second-class citizens—we refuse to be degraded to second-class comrades." After 1908, when the new Law of Association replaced the old Combination Law, women could participate legally in political parties. At the 1908 Nuremberg conference of the SPD, female separatism in the party was voted down resoundingly. Only one woman was elected to the national

executive committee; Zietz replaced Baader, who had been the
women's national leader from 1899 to 1908. Women leaders in the
party were given a mandate to increase female membership in the
SPD, and from 1908 to 1914, the women's movement of the SPD became a mass organization, whose membership grew from more than
29,000 to almost 175,000. German Social Democratic women demonstrated in all provinces in Germany in 1911 on the occasion of the
first international conference to promote women's suffrage.[26]

The price of full membership for women in the SPD was high—
the autonomous decision-making power of the women's bureau was
now subordinate to the party executive committee. As Zietz characterized the situation, local women leaders felt "hemmed in" by
party directives. As a member of the national executive committee,
she was herself caught in the middle of feminist criticisms of the
party and the desires of its national leadership, especially in the
controversy over the failure of the executive committee to call a
women's conference in 1910. Despite (or because of?) the success of
women, there was a male backlash against women in the party.
Male leaders met radical feminist arguments and criticisms with
jokes—the intended effect was to put the "women comrades" back
in "their place." There was also conflict between some feminists
and the party leadership over the increasingly reformist drift of the
party. In particular, relations cooled between, on one side, Zetkin
and her close personal friend Luxemburg, and, on the other, Kautsky
and Bebel—both of whom believed women should be supportive
companions of men. The general trend was toward a sex-linked division of labor within the SPD, with women assigned to municipal
welfare and child-labor committees.[27]

Alongside this reactionary turn were the emerging hegemony
of the trade unions in the German working-class movement and the
trade unions' rejection of revolutionary Marxism as mere idealism
that was irrelevant to the day-to-day economic and social struggles
of workers. The emerging conflict between the party and the trade
unions was dividing the socialist feminists: radicals Zetkin, Baader,
and Zietz were challenged by revisionists Ihrer, Hanna, and Helene
Grünberg (who had been influenced by the reformism of the Bavarian SPD). Michels characterized revisionism as the "theoretical
expression of the scepticism of the disappointed, the weary, and
those who no longer believed; it was the socialism of non-socialists
with a socialist past."[28]

Nevertheless, an assessment of equality within the SPD must

recognize all of its dimensions for, as Quataert has written, "the socialist subculture provided . . . the most supportive milieu in Imperial Germany for women seeking to improve their economic, social, and political position." Quataert also has suggested that the Marxist ideology of socialist feminists "interfered with a thorough critique of family life, since the activists expected women's economic independence to be translated into more equitable family relations, beginning first in the working class. . . . Socialist women underestimated the degree to which male comrades, even those supporting the women's struggle, had retained bourgeois expectations of sex roles."[29]

In summary, "Women's liberation was a live and explosive issue in the emerging socialist movements at the end of the century."[30] The SPD was the leading party in regard to socialist feminism as it was in the Second International in general. But then with the rejection of what Lenin called the "revolutionary soul" of Marxism by the German socialists, women's emancipation was put off until "the next world." Even women adherents of revisionism in the SPD found themselves caught between radicals, revisionists unsympathetic to women, and "proletarian antifeminists" in the trade unions.[31] On the plus side of the feminist ledger, the SPD was a source of strength for socialist feminists. What brought radical women into and kept them in the SPD was that, in Quataert's words, it was perceived as "the most forceful advocate of women's equality in Imperial Germany."[32] Its position was far advanced over all the other parties when it came to the central demand for women's suffrage. Therefore, when compared to bourgeois parties in Germany, the record of the SPD would have to be judged exemplary.[33]

Liberal Feminism

The debates within the Social Democratic Party over the nature of women, work, family, class, and sex in some ways paralleled those in the bourgeois feminist movement between the last half of the 1890s and World War I. Discussions among socialist feminists, like those among bourgeois feminists, responded to literature depicting emancipated women. Lily Braun criticized the character of Nora in Henrik Ibsen's *A Doll's House* for lacking "heart and femininity"; Braun preferred an ideal that combined strength and softness in women, allowed for individuality and choice of occupation, and included a relationship to a man involving friendship, love, and comradeship. Clara Zetkin, too, maintained that a woman should stand by the man of her choice. Likewise, she attempted a synthesis of the traditional conception of a woman as solely a sexual being with the feminist idea of a woman as solely a person. The weakness of the latter notion, she felt, was to make of woman nothing but "a superficial copy of man." In Zetkin's formulation, women are female human beings—no more, no less. Emma Ihrer pointed out that women were "intellectually crippled" by their education and their dependent positions in the house and at work. Helene Grünberg scoffed at the stereotype that woman's place was within the family, supported by a man; she noted that "million[s of] working women are torn from their homes and families and work for the capitalist state."[34] In contrast, the politics of liberal feminism reflected the class situation of bourgeois women in the latter part of the nineteenth century.

Middle-class, liberal feminism in Germany got its impetus from the Revolution of 1848. The organized middle-class feminist movement in Germany began in Leipzig in October 1865 with the formation of the General German Women's Association (Allgemeiner Deutscher Frauenverein, or ADF). The association maintained friendly contacts with the labor movement in Saxony until the late 1860s. But in the 1870s and 1880s, in the face of the consolidation of Prussian rule and the Anti-Socialist Law, the association retreated from its early position and turned its attention to educational reform of curricula and to the establishment of schools to prepare girls for admission to universities. In fact, during this period, women teachers provided the main support of the middle-class feminist movement. The movement's watchwords were motherhood, morality, charity, and social welfare for wayward girls. Auguste Schmidt, a foremost leader of education in the ADF, claimed that the purpose of female education was to develop the qualities of "true womanhood." Helene Lange, who later became a prominent leader of moderate feminists in Berlin in the 1890s, accepted the authoritarian and conservative-evangelical conception of women she had learned as a child. She believed that girls must be taught the precepts of "morality, love, fear of God" in order to fulfill to the best of their abilities the duties of womanhood.[35]

Liberal feminism was limited by the forces that shaped the position of middle-class women in German society. In Evans's words, "The family, the school, the State and the nation, it was felt, were analogous institutions all based upon the same aims and principles, and in each case the role of each sex was clearly defined; men were to rule, women were to obey." As one Reichstag deputy put it, to give women political rights would transform the peaceful haven of the family into a "living hell." In 1910, toward the end of this period, Kaiser Wilhelm II admonished that

> our women . . . should learn that the principal task of the German woman lies not in the field of assemblies and associations, nor in the achievement of supposed rights, with which they can do the same things as men, but in quiet work in the house and in the family. They should bring up the younger generation above all else to obedience and respect for their elders. They should make it clear to their children and their children's children that what matters today is . . . solely and exclusively committing all one's mind and strength to the good of the Fatherland.[36]

The weakness of middle-class feminism was inextricably linked to the weakness of German liberalism, which had been mortally wounded by the failure of the Revolution of 1848 and by Germany's subsequent revolution "from above"—capitalist industrialization without bourgeois democracy. The unification of Germany by military victories resulted in the notion that rights were dependent upon military service (which women did not perform) rather than upon a conception of natural law (as in France or the United States, for example). Women, therefore, had to demand rights on the basis of moral and social service to the nation. The model held up to unmarried women was that of the officer's wife. As could be expected in a society in which military values were held supreme, the state opposed abortion but supported prostitution. Evans has described German liberal feminism prior to 1890:

> The German women's movement, then, was in a state of stagnation and decay by the late 1880s. It was numerically weak, fragmented, timid and conservative. Like the liberalism which inspired it, it had been bludgeoned into submission by the successive defeats of 1848, 1866, 1871, and 1878. It avoided public controversy, it fully accepted the role of housewife and mother laid down for women by society. . . . Feminism of the classical liberal individualist type had no place in the German women's movement before the 1890s.[37]

In contrast to the repressive period of the Anti-Socialist Law (1878–90), the 1890s were, as Evans has noted, "a decade of social and political ferment in Germany." The processes of economic change and urbanization brought with them social problems and various proposals or programs to solve them. Liberal reform associations, such as the German Society for Ethical Culture, were founded, as were associations for women professionals, white-collar workers, teachers, and salaried employees. Liberals came into conflict with the policies of the Wilhelmine ruling classes. It was in this context that by the middle of the decade something like a left-liberal feminist movement emerged, and on 29 March 1894 a national council to coordinate local efforts by German women, the Federation of German Women's Associations (Bund Deutscher Frauenvereine, or BDF) was formed. By 1901, it comprised 137 member-associations with 70,000 members. In contrast to this growth, membership in the General German Women's Association (ADF) had remained at approximately 13,000 members for twenty years.[38]

Radicals in the bourgeois feminist movement came into collision with traditionalists in the last half of the 1890s. Minna Cauer, leader of the Women's Welfare Association (Verein Frauenwohl), formerly the German Academic Alliance (Deutsche Akademische Vereinigung), established *Frauenbewegung* (*Women's Movement*) as the organ for radical middle-class women. Along with Anita Augspurg and Marie Stritt, Cauer began to persuade the BDF to adopt the Frauenwohl's positions for women's suffrage and against state-supported prostitution and the new Civil Code, which they called "an expression of one-sided men's law (Männerrecht)." In opposition to Hanna Bieber-Böhm's ideas (which were similar to those of antisocialist Pastor Weber and anti-Semitic Adolf Stöcker) about the suppression of obscenity and immorality and the punishment of prostitutes, leaders of the Frauenwohl (called abolitionists after Josephine Butler's campaign in England) opposed state-supported prostitution because of its double standard of morality and on the feminist grounds of the individual woman's dignity and right to self-determination. Cauer referred to prostitution as "the most important women's question, the morality problem." Lida Gustava Heymann, whose father was a rich Hamburg merchant, organized many practical feminist projects. From 1898 to 1907 in Hamburg, in opposition to the conservatism of local ADF leaders, Heymann led a campaign against state-regulated prostitution that also attracted Social Democratic women. Although police could legally ban abolitionist meetings before 1908 and despite the failure of the abolitionist campaign, in Evans's words, "the Hamburg Abolitionist crusade made it clear that by adopting Abolitionism, the women's movement as a whole was placing itself firmly in the camp of those who opposed the existing structure of the Wilhelmine State." The success of the moderate old guard in resisting the radicalization of the BDF program in 1898 led the frustrated Augspurg and Cauer to set up a rival organization, the Union of Progressive Women's Associations (Verband fortschrittlicher Frauenvereine) for the dissemination of radical propaganda to expand the rights of women.[39]

In the battle between the traditionalists and the progressives, the meeting of the General Assembly of the BDF in October 1902 was a turning point. Not only did the radicals achieve a vote in favor of abolition of the section of the Civil Code (361/6) that was the basis for state control of prostitution, but they also persuaded the assembly to pass by a large majority a resolution to promote women's suffrage to help achieve the aims of the federation. Heading the opposition to these efforts by Cauer, Augspurg, Pappritz, Stritt (who became the new BDF president), and others was Helene Lange, the leader of the traditionalists, who was also associated with Max Weber's circle.[40]

On 1 January 1902 in Hamburg, Augspurg and twelve other middle-class, radical feminists, most of whom were also abolitionists, founded the German Union for Women's Suffrage (Deutsches Verband für Frauenstimmsrecht), as an offshoot of the Frauenwohl association. Heymann later wrote that radicals were embarrassed because German feminists were not represented at the first international congress for women's suffrage held in Washington in February 1902. The liberal press was beginning to give some support to the feminist cause by publicizing feminist ideas; in fact, by middecade most of the national newspapers ran a regular column on the women's movement. In Berlin in 1904, the International Woman Suffrage Alliance was founded. Although the literature of the German Union for Women's Suffrage spoke of the vote in terms of the personhood of individual women, the purpose of the radicals' campaign was the moral regeneration of German society and its political system. As Cauer put it, "We believe it to be our duty to educate State and society so that a recognition of our equal rights is not only (seen as) a necessity, but also as desirable for the maintenance of order, manners, and morality." Therefore, German suffragists, in Evans's characterization, "felt it was necessary to employ the tactics of a moral crusade rather than the quiet, steady pressure that had been usual in the women's movement before the turn of the century."[41]

Despite the efforts of the radicals during the liberal phase of bourgeois feminism between 1902 and 1908, they failed to win support for women's suffrage from even the left-liberal parties. Disillusioned, Augspurg urged feminists to independent militancy. In 1907, she and Heymann moved to Munich, "which now became a third centre [after Hamburg and Berlin] of the female suffrage movement." Probably even more than they feared the meetings and demonstrations of the German suffragists, the established authorities feared that German women would be inspired to bring the militant tactics of English feminists outside the House of Commons to the Reichstag. However, even the BDF condemned the tactics of their English sisters.[42]

The event that was most crucial to the German feminist movement, liberal as well as socialist, was the passage in 1908 of the Law of Association, which permitted women to belong to political parties. As Evans has noted, "The Suffrage Union no longer had a monopoly in the political field as far as middle-class women were concerned." Despite the proliferation of suffrage organizations in Germany, the increasing participation of men in support of women's suffrage, and a membership of 10,000 in the Suffrage Union on the eve of World War I, for radical feminists the issue of independence from or cooperation with liberal parties was never resolved. Radical feminists were caught in a dilemma: they needed liberals as a source of political support, but the liberal parties were moving to the right and abandoning even their half-hearted support of women's rights. In Evans's description, "In the growing atmosphere of conservatism among the middle classes after 1907–08, the radical politics of the suffrage movement appeared increasingly out of date. Under these circumstances voices were soon raised within the suffrage movement calling for the abandonment of its radical stance."[43]

The radicals launched one more effort to transform the character of the middle-class feminist movement. From 1905 to 1910, moral and cultural issues were again debated. The abolitionists of 1898–1902 had held that men had to learn to discipline their sexual instincts so that there would be a single, repressive standard of sexual morality for both sexes. As Evans has pointed out, "Some Abolitionists began to question the validity of this outlook and the assumptions that lay behind it, and they developed by 1905 a new and radically libertarian set of ideas about sexual morality. In effect, they began to preach a gospel of free love, and to argue that the prostitution problem and other connected social evils could be solved not by moral repression but by moral libertarianism."[44]

The most important person in formulating this new morality was Helene Stöcker. Born in 1869 in Elberfeld, by the 1890s she had rejected the repressive Calvinism of her parents. She had become a schoolteacher in order to gain entrance to the university. In the late 1890s, she worked as a research assistant for the philosopher Wilhelm Dilthey in Berlin, where she was active as a feminist writer and in the most liberal of the existing feminist organizations. She received her Ph.D. from Bern in 1901. The chief influence on Stöcker's radical feminism was the work of Friedrich Nietzsche, specifically his endorsement of the life-affirming morality of the heroic individual in opposition to the self-denying, guilt-inducing morality of Christianity and the stultifying confines of bourgeois custom.

Stöcker's early view was that a married woman with children could also have a profession. After the turn of the century, an unhappy affair with a married man caused her to be more critical of patriarchal marriage and the whole notion that women were by nature less sexual than men. Speaking in 1903 to the General Assembly of the Union of Progressive Women's Associations, Stöcker observed that "the women's movement has ignored all problems of love, marriage and motherhood for decades. But today it is recognised that emancipation from economic subjection also involves emancipation from sexual subjection." Sexual love—not just mutual respect, as the traditional abolitionists believed—should be part of the basis of marital partnership, according to Stöcker. Patriarchal attitudes and laws were responsible for prostitution and for the stigma attached to illegitimate children and unmarried mothers (who were, as a consequence, driven to prostitution), Stöcker believed. Making contraceptives universally available would solve this problem, she argued to the abolitionists in Berlin in 1903. She was opposed by Pappritz, who accused her of advocating a male viewpoint, and, further, one that would result in sexual immorality. An organizational vehicle for Stöcker's ideas appeared with the formation in late 1904 in Leipzig of a society to improve the condition of unwed mothers, the League for the Protection of Motherhood and Sexual Reform (Bund für Mutterschutz und Sexualreform).[45]

The Mutterschutz League was founded by Ruth Bré, a struggling feminist poet. Her plan was to set up "mother-colonies" in rural areas where unwed mothers and their children would be supported by the state. The purpose of the league was the improvement of the nation's "racial health" by allowing only healthy mothers to breed. As Evans has pointed out, Bré's scheme, "with its Social Darwinist and racialist overtones and its anti-urban philosophy, was very similar to the many *völkisch* Utopias being mooted by groups on the extreme right at this time." When Walter Borgius, leader of liberal industrialists, found out about Bré's project, he offered to set up a Berlin branch. She agreed, and Borgius obtained pledges of support from prominent male intellectuals and politicians: Friedrich Naumann, a leader of the National Social Association (a liberal organization); Werner Sombart, the *Kathedersozialist* (socialist of the chair, or academic socialist); Eduard David and Heinrich Braun, revisionist SPD deputies; Max Weber; and also Sigmund Freud, who was affiliated with the league's sister branches in Austria. Some of the feminist supporters of the league were Cauer, Lily Braun, Adele Schreiber, Heymann, Augspurg, and Stöcker, who became president after Bré was ousted.[46]

The league eventually shifted its emphasis to propaganda for its feminist sexual ideology, and its attention to the welfare of unmarried mothers in the cities. The league's principles rejected the "traditional clerical-ascetic moral teaching, which condemns extramarital sexual intercourse" and opposed it with the "modern, individualist, scientific moral teaching" that proclaimed sexual intercourse to be a natural activity that is moral when based on love. Ernst Kromayer, professor of medicine at Berlin, drew out the feminist implications of the New Morality (Die Neue Ethik): by arguing that marriage should be a free contract based on sexual love between equal partners, the league was not only encouraging "the liberation of human society from an unnatural and harmful sexual morality" but also advocating "the liberation of woman." Stöcker answered her critics' charge that the New Morality would destroy marriage by saying that she was for a higher form of marriage in which women could freely develop their personalities. She reminded liberal feminists, "One sex should never dispose over the other to so great an extent as it does in our society, in its social life, its legislation, and in its sexual and love-life."[47]

Between 1904 and 1908, the women's movement split over the issues raised by the New Morality. Lange, leader of the traditionalist feminists, declared that advocates of the New Morality had no place in the women's movement. Coincident with the move of the radicals from abolitionism to sexual reform came their program of legislative reform based upon the application of the principles of liberal individualism. They argued for legal equality in marriage, legal equality of both parents with regard to their children, and legal recognition of "free marriages" and of the offspring of such unions. When the BDF set up a legal commission to recommend changes in the Criminal Code, the abolition of Section 218 of the code, which provided for imprisonment of women who had deliberately obtained abortions, became a dividing issue for moderates and radicals. In 1908, Stöcker exposed the ideological underpinning of section 218 of the code when she said that the state's view of a woman was that "of a childbearing machine, her children regarded as the property of the State while still in the womb." Stritt, president of the BDF, wrote in favor of the deletion of Section 218: "If we women do not take a stand for our own responsibility for ourselves here, in the most female of all tasks in life, in that of 'giving life', if we do not take a stand here against our being regarded merely as the involuntary producers of cannon-fodder—then in my opinion we do not deserve to be regarded as anything else!"[48]

In 1908 the BDF General Assembly rejected its commission's recommendation that the organization come out for the deletion of Section 218. As a result, members of the Mutterschutz League resigned from the BDF, and there was a split within the league itself over the issue of how much of its resources should be devoted to practical work as opposed to propaganda. As Evans has observed, the Mutterschutz League's "demands outraged respectable society in Wilhelmine Germany. In many ways they were more akin to the demands of the Women's Liberation Movement of the 1960s and 1970s than to those of the feminism of pre-1914 days. . . . the feminist movement in Germany was, at its most radical point, more advanced than any other feminist movement." However, most of the members of the organized women's movement were comfortable neither with radical feminism in general nor with the New Morality in particular. Evans has summarized the conflicts within German feminism thus: "The collapse of the Suffrage Union and the New Morality movement was in fact part of a general process in which the women's movement as a whole, after becoming steadily more radical from 1898 onwards, began in 1908 to move rapidly to the right, away from the liberal individualism that had been its most marked feature in the first half of the 1900s."[49]

The Erotic Movement

The dark shadow of Otto von Bismarck and his policy of "blood and iron" dominated Germany in the last third of the nineteenth century. The "iron chancellor" unified Germany "from above" (after the failure of the Revolution of 1848 to do so "from below") under the domination of Prussia by successful wars against Denmark for Schleswig-Holstein (1864), against Austrian pretensions to unify Germany (1866), and against France's imperial caricature in the person of Louis-Napoléon Bonaparte, Napoléon III (1870). Following these wars and the continued development of advanced capitalism from 1870 to 1890, Germany became the most powerful state on the continent, ruled by the old Junker aristocracy represented by Bismarck and allied with the big-industrial bourgeoisie against the threat of the working-class and socialist movements.[50] The apparatus of Bismarck's domination was Prussia's bureaucratic and military state organization. Bismarck's regime was given legitimacy by a population whose Lutheranism influenced them to view politics as an irredeemable vale of woe best left to state authorities. Interestingly, this state Lutheranism was viewed at the time as a "religion for women." Bismarck "created a [nationalized and imperialized] Germany whose imagination was in thrall to him, and therefore to Junkerism, to Prussianism, and to a rankly masculine mode of being," Martin Green has written. "He created a country which intensified, exaggerated, all the patriarchal elements in Western European culture, which made itself a caricature of the patriarchal male." That German world of "ultramanly men" was in essence the "institutionalization of [Bismarck] himself."[51]

Bismarck's character and powerfully corpulent physique were "legendary in Germany." At his home he kept "wild dogs who terrified all his visitors." In the Reichstag he drank steaming punch in great gulps from a giant glass. The following anecdote was related by Max Weber's friend Heinrich Rickert, a philosophy professor at Heidelberg. While outlining a policy to the Reichstag, Bismarck thought he heard one of the deputies call out in protest, *"Feigheit"* (cowardice). Glaring at the deputies, Bismarck demanded to know who had spoken. When not a soul said a word, he proceeded to shake by the shoulders those he suspected, repeating his interrogation. Not one man protested. When Bismarck returned to the podium, he remained silent for some time and then quietly said, "Give thanks to God that nobody *did* say anything." Green has observed that "a society in which such anecdotes are current is one obsessed with power, patriarchal power. And this anecdote was current in liberal academic Heidelberg, where even the professors were affected by the example of Bismarck and inspired to a kind of imitation. As Alfred Weber, Max's brother, put it, Bismarck infected them with the 'power-virus.'"[52]

There was an affinity between German university life and Bismarckian Germany. German academic tradition was intellectually "massive" in style. And academia was predominantly a male world: the relations of professors to students were "autocratic, patriarchal"; professors' wives were addressed as *Frau Professor*; and in 1900, for example, only four young women matriculated at Heidelberg. Most important for our concern—the treatment of women in classical sociological theory—was "the patriarchal mode in the intellectual Germany of that time—the mode of which the greatest, though most self-divided, representative was Max Weber."[53]

Against the "new breed" of "ultramanly man" in Germany, against a "haughty . . . race of masters in whom all the dominant male traits were exaggerated," some women "rebelled and determined to themselves [to] embody other human possibilities—to embody an idea of Woman." "Du bist Erotik" was the slogan of the third type of German feminism, which reached its high point around 1906. Members of this movement, which was both aristocratic and bohemian, believed in "eroticism as a philosophical and metaphysical value, as, above all, a life-creating value." Green has argued that "only in extreme crisis will a group try to make the values of Woman [life and love] prevail over those of men [law and order]." Such a crisis existed in Bismarck-dominated Germany, for Bismarck "had made a country in which the matriarchal values were almost completely ineffective, a country whose values were based almost entirely on those of the Prussian officer." In particular, this penchant for discipline and hierarchy was manifested in the authoritarian German family, in which fathers and husbands were much more dominant than in Anglo-Saxon cultures. Lest we attribute too much to Bismarck, however, it should be made clear that the matriarchal rebellion of women was part of "an ideological revolution that seems to have occurred all over Europe between 1890 and 1910, and to have been the major hope of the resistance to patriarchal civilization." This antimaterialist current, in England as well as in Germany, contributed to the "relaxation of the patriarchal grip on life." Green has commented: "Most notably in Bavaria and Munich, there arose a matriarchal rebellion which expressed itself in behavioral terms by idealizing the Magna Mater or Hetaera role, a role in which a woman felt herself 'religiously' called to take many lovers and bear many children without submitting to a husband/father/ master. This matriarchal rebellion was one of the most sharply characterized forms of the erotic movement, which was in turn an off-shoot of the *Lebensphilosophie* movement, the devotion to life-values, to intuition and instinct, which all across Europe then was rebelling against scientific materialism and positivism. In Germany all these movements were unusually active, just because what they were reacting against was unusually solid."[54]

Bismarck's patriarchal society was centered in Berlin; Max Weber's liberal, rationalist opposition to Bismarck was centered in Heidelberg; and the erotic movement was centered in Munich. The three cities with their three movements formed the "apices of the German triangle." In Schwabing, "the Greenwich Village of Munich," lived the leading exponent of the erotic movement, Fanny zu Reventlow (1871–1918), whom Green considered "the most remarkable free woman of her time." A tomboy daughter of the aristocracy, she was an Ibsenite and a saint of the new paganism, "of sensuality, pride, power, life-worship, and self-assertion." She rebelled against hypocrisy and demanded equal rights for women in social and sexual but not political matters; she practiced free love and raised her illegitimate child by herself. (Her brother Ernst led a pan-German anticommunist study group in 1933 with the blessing of the Nazis.)[55]

The center of the intellectual and artistic life of Schwabing was the Cosmic Circle (*die Kosmische Rūnde*), which met from 1897 until 1903 and developed a weltanschauung based on "the primacy of the female mode of being." The inspiration for their world view came from J. J. Bachofen's book, *Das Mutterrecht* (1861), which argues by inference from Greek myths and Roman antiquities that a society based on "Mother-Right" had preceded each patriarchal civilization. For Bachofen, all of history was explained by a dialectic of masculine and feminine principles.

Ludwig Klages, a member of the Cosmic Circle, believed that using abstract mind and exercising intellectual will were crimes against life, against body and soul. He attacked the ideas of technological progress and industrial civilization because he thought they were destructive of nature and had a withering effect on the soul. These evils Klages attributed to the hypermasculine rationality of Western culture. For Klages, "The oldest wisdom of Humanity was the possession and privilege of Woman." He believed this wisdom was needed to save people from what Weber would refer to as "the disenchantment of the world" and the "parceling out of the soul" brought about by the rationalization and specialization of social and cultural life along with the development of the "iron cage" of bureaucratic high capitalism. Other leading members of the Cosmic Circle were Stefan George, Professor Karl Wolfskehl, and Alfred Schuler. Schuler (characterized by Green as a do-nothing) identified the fully healthy person as androgynous and transvestite; he placed positive value on "sexual inverts" (the analytic term for homosexuals). The Cosmic Circle broke up early in 1904 because of anti-Semitism on the part of Klages and Schuler and possibly because of a disruption caused when Fanny zu Reventlow transferred her affections from Klages to Wolfskehl.[56]

Members of the erotic movement believed in matriarchy, feeling, blood, life instinct, women as initiators of sexual activity—values found in D. H. Lawrence's novels and also in the work and life of Otto Gross, a brilliant young psychoanalytic rebel. Gross typified the anti-Bismarckian Schwabingite adherent of the erotic movement and greatly influenced the lives of the von Richthofen sisters, Else and Frieda. He rebelled against his father, Hanns, who was the founder of Austrian criminalistics and might be characterized as the Bismarck of the penal aspect of patriarchal culture. Hanns Gross studied the relationship of psychosexual abnormality and crime and, in 1913, explored the idea of castration and sterilization as crime-prevention measures. Otto Gross countered his father's concern with the "criminal type" with "an equally profound *but sympathetic* knowledge of antisocial types," as Green has put it. Indeed, he himself became one: "Otto Gross made himself a living antithesis to his father. He came to stand for total freedom and for the repudiation of patriarchal authority in every possible way." However, he was very close to his mother, who, according to Green, "seems to have been completely her husband's victim, in the sense that many German wives then were."[57]

A psychoanalyst who had studied with Gabriel Anton (director of the psychiatric-neurological clinic at the University of Graz where Hanns Gross had also studied and later taught), Otto Gross began his career by making admired and influential contributions to the psychiatric and psychoanalytic literature. His first book, *The Secondary Function of the Brain*, was published in 1902. From Freud

he borrowed analytic technique; however, the substance of his insights and feminist ideology were drawn from Nietzsche and later
from Bachofen and anarchists Peter Kropotkin and Max Stirner.
Gross's departures from Freud's ideas are evident in a 1908 paper, in
which he argued for a social-cultural perspective on neuroses and
asserted that psychoanalysts should be revolutionaries as well as
doctors. In his clinical work, he acted on the belief that trans-
ference was a symbolic approval of monogamy and that his patients
needed sexual freedom instead. Gross felt that society's power
structure repressed and distorted sexuality, resulting in many instances of hysteria in females and pathological cowardice in males.
He also believed that erotic homosexuality was necessary to mental
health. Anticipating Wilhelm Reich and Herbert Marcuse, Gross
perceived the revolutionary implications of Freud's ideas, the connection between the liberation of sexuality and the revolt against
authority in all forms, but especially against the authority of the
father in the monogamous family. He felt that the original sin of
society was the oppression of women and that the approaching
revolution would restore *Mutterrecht* on a higher level. Gross came
to the conclusion that Freud, betraying the true direction of his
own doctrines, "had gone over to the fathers." For Gross, Freud's
ideas became the weapons of antipatriarchal, anarchist-communist
revolution. He lived out his beliefs in Ascona, Switzerland—"the
Schwabing of Schwabing"—among bohemian, anarchist, and criminal types.

By 1909, Freud deemed Gross a heretic, and orthodox analysts
in Switzerland are said to have complained to the police about
Gross because of what they considered his scandalous conduct (i.e.,
his heterodox ideas and practices). Freud remarked once that every
man has two fathers. Freud was Gross's second, symbolic father.
Against him too Gross rebelled through his support of matriarchal
values and in his antipatriarchal relationships with women. Gross's
ethic of sexual freedom rejected chastity, fidelity, jealousy, and pos-
sessiveness as moralistic distortions of the authentic self. He was
married to Frieda Schloffer and had affairs with Else Jaffe (née von
Richthofen) and Frieda Weekley (née von Richthofen), whom he
revered as "woman triumphant," the type of woman he endeavored
to help other women become.[58]

Else and Frieda von Richthofen are striking examples of participants in two divergent rebellions against the strictures of Bismarck-
dominated, patriarchal Germany. Else became a part of the liberal,

rationalist circle gathered around Max Weber, although in her affair with Gross, she came in contact with the erotic movement. But Frieda, her younger sister, immersed herself fully in the life and ideas of the erotic movement. Their father, Baron Friedrich von Richthofen, was a Prussian military officer. Their mother, the former Anna Marquier, whose personality and background were opposed to the "ultramanly" Bismarckian world of her husband, raised and educated the girls in her matriarchal world. The marriage was held together by convention. Frieda von Richthofen described the effects of the "fierce hatred" between her parents in the home of her childhood as follows: "The children vaguely felt the atmosphere of strife without understanding; there is something frightening to children in the war of the sexes. Sex, that thing not understood by children, hidden from them, yet constantly in the air, warps and tortures the life of children." Green has written that Frieda was "determined to prove herself . . . a significant *woman*, even in patriarchal Germany. . . . She did so mainly, of course, by means of the brilliant men who made her the emblematic source of all life within matriarchal or anti-patriarchal *Weltanschauungen*."[59]

Frieda von Richthofen had an affair with Otto Gross while she was married to Ernest Weekley, an Englishman and a professor. Then in 1912 she left her husband and children to live with D. H. Lawrence, whom she married in 1914. To Weekley, she sent letters of Gross's that she felt explained her actions. To Lawrence, she brought an "ideological dowry," to which Gross had contributed and which later appeared in Lawrence's writings. In *Fantasia of the Unconscious*, published in 1922, Lawrence asked:

> Was man, the eternal protagonist, born of woman, with her womb of fathomless emotion? Or was woman, with her deep womb of emotion, born from the rib of active man, the first created? Man, the doer, the knower, the original in *being*, is he lord of life? Or is woman, the great Mother, who bore us from the womb of love, is she the Supreme Goddess?
> This is the question of all time.

But in the foreword to *Sons and Lovers* published in 1913, he had already given his answer: "For in the flesh of the woman does God exact Himself." Frieda von Richthofen rejected the "outer" world of men for "a deeper one, where life itself flows, there I am at home!" she declared. This world of feeling and emotion toward which she had guided Lawrence was one which he could not fully join because he was a male writer, therefore a part of that "outer" world.[60]

Else von Richthofen rebelled against the patriarchalism of Wilhelmine Germany in a different way—by participating in the world of men. She earned a doctorate in economics at the University of Heidelberg in 1901; she had taught school since she was seventeen in order to pay for her university studies. She was Max Weber's "first woman student," and he helped her get an appointment in 1900 to a position as the first woman factory inspector, responsible for the protection of women workers in the state of Badenia, even though she was not at ease with working-class women. It was at Weber's home that Else became acquainted with the liberal feminist movement, of which she was, for a brief time, the heroine. Helene Lange, Gertrud Bäumer, Gertrud Simmel, Gertrud Jaspers, Alice Solomon, Marie Baum, and Marianne Weber, Max's wife—all moderate feminists—were members of this group. Marianne Weber, in Else von Richthofen's words, had a "dominating influence" on her by exemplifying a woman who could be part of the man's world of intellectual and political activity. Although Alfred Weber, Max's brother, fell in love with her when they met in Berlin in 1899, in 1902 Else von Richthofen married Edgar Jaffe, also a student of Weber's, who was an instructor in political economy and who became a leader in the Bavarian Soviet Republic (a short-lived attempt at a communist regime at the time of the German Revolution of 1918–19). Jaffe's friends included Otto Gross and Fanny zu Reventlow. With inherited wealth, Jaffe built his wife a beautiful villa overlooking Heidelberg, where she became "one of the social foci of its intellectual life," as well as a link between Heidelberg and the Stefan George circle in Munich, where she lived from 1911 to 1925.[61]

One might say that for a fleeting moment Else von Richthofen was part of the other pole of antipatriarchal revolt—the erotic movement—when she had an affair with Otto Gross, at his home, probably in 1906, with the knowledge of his wife, Frieda, who was a friend of Else's. A son, Peter, was born to Else and Otto in 1907, the same year that Otto's other son, also named Peter, was born to his wife, Frieda. Although Else von Richthofen felt she was in touch with her true self when she was with Gross, finally she rejected him and the values of the erotic movement for the man who "remained her master," Max Weber—and the liberal, rationalist values of Heidelberg. What Heidelberg represented at the time was, as Green has stated, "the active center of liberal, reformist, resistance Germany, one of the two great nodes of the anti-Bismarck movement." It was, even, "one of the centers of liberalism for the whole world," through which many radicals passed, of whom probably the most intellectually powerful was Georg Lukács.[62]

The other great node of the anti-Bismarck movement (for Green, who does not take into account the socialist resistance of the Social Democratic Party) was Munich, the center of the erotic movement. But, as Green has observed, in that movement's ideas resided "those hideous political possibilities—for there is an undeniable link between Schwabing and the Nazi ideology—which justify the revulsion of such observers as Else Jaffe and Max Weber." The attack on the bourgeois world by the "true Schwabingites" did not leave intact what Lenin once referred to as the "best of bourgeois thought," with its commitments to reason, rationality, knowledge, and democracy, nor any of the bourgeois virtues. Not only were Klages and Schuler anti-Semitic, but it is no large leap to go from the Cosmic Circle's emphasis on life and feeling to the Nazi conception of "thinking with one's blood." For the Schwabingites, socialism offered no alternative to the ruin of the world—it, too, was "patriarchal" and "old hat."[63]

The end of the first decade of the twentieth century was a turning point in the struggles against patriarchy by the erotic and the feminist movements. The curious crisscrossing of eugenics, feminism, and antifeminism that occurred in English history also appeared in Germany. In 1909, Grete Meisel-Hess, an advocate of free love, published *The Sexual Crisis*, in which she argued that with the development of feminist awareness, the most intelligent women would refuse to marry until the conditions of motherhood were improved.[64] In 1910, Lou Andreas-Salomé, mistress of Rainer Maria Rilke (who was fourteen years her junior) and characterized as "intellectual and seductress" by Green, published *Die Erotik*, "the book of a high priestess of Eros."[65] In 1911–12, Elly Heuss-Knapp helped to organize an ideologically moderate feminist exhibition in Berlin on the subject "The Woman at Home and at Work." Heuss-Knapp was inspired by the social work with the poor that Max Weber's mother did. Heuss-Knapp's husband was Theodor Heuss, a follower of the liberal Friedrich Naumann, a friend of Max Weber.[66]

The elections of January 1912 resulted in the Social Democratic Party's having the largest representation of any single party in the

Reichstag, an event that shook the confidence of the ruling classes. In response, in June of the same year reactionaries founded the League for the Prevention of the Emancipation of Women. The main supporters have been characterized by some writers as racists, anti-Semites, and militaristic imperialists.[67] In 1913, Hanns Gross had the Berlin authorities arrest his son Otto on the grounds that he was "a dangerous psychopath" (and clinically certified as such by Carl G. Jung); he was confined to an Austrian asylum for the insane. Hanns also sued to get Otto's son Peter taken away from Frieda Gross, an advocate of sexual liberation who was living with another man. Weber supported Frieda Gross in her fight for legal custody; Green has referred to it as a "classic case of patriarchal tyranny."[68]

Otto Gross's arrest made of him a martyr in the struggle of the "Sons against the Fathers," a theme in expressionist art and one connected with the erotic movement. Franz Jung, a follower of Gross, wrote in the Munich magazine *Revolution:* "He destroys himself—as long as his father lives. The father, on the other hand, destroys himself by taking up these weapons. . . . He gorges himself on brutality; he sends his son to prison." The outcry from his followers contributed to Otto's release in 1914. But this victory in the battle of the son who was the prophet of matriarchal rebellion was swallowed by the war toward which, to use Engels's image, Europe had been sliding as if on an inclined plane since Bismarck's victory in the Franco-Prussian War. The First World War, as Green concisely put it, "called all the patriarchal virtues back to life." Green quotes a letter that D. H. Lawrence wrote about the war: "The world of men is dreaming, it has gone mad in its sleep, and a snake is strangling it, but it can't wake up."[69] The war divided the middle-class feminist movement. The majority, led by Lange and Bäumer, saw the war as an opportunity to gain concessions by serving the government's mobilization. A minority, led by Augspurg and Heymann of the Women's Suffrage League, took a pacifist position against the "men's war."[70]

The struggle between feminism and patriarchy had been going on for more than fifty years in Germany when the First World War broke out. Between 1911 and 1914, the Federation of German Women's Associations campaigned against the New Morality, and by the outbreak of the war, the suffrage movement was, in Evans's words, "in total disarray."[71] By 1914, the lines had been drawn for the post-1918 war between the sexes. *Population and Birth Con-*

trol, a collection of essays edited by Eden Paul and Cedar Paul, was published in 1917. In one of those essays, "Women and Birth Control," Stella Browne (described by Margaret Sanger in 1915 as "an ardent feminist") predicted a postwar reaction against feminism and the advances women had won, which would have the following features: "A specialised education for girls, concentrating on the sentimental and the domestic, and a fevered propaganda in favour of what some reactionaries already term 'the normal family,' a propaganda in which the licensed imbecilities of the pulpit are backed up by the venal and impertinent irrelevancies of the press and the pomposities of the debating platforms and stiffened by determined efforts to penalise (or at least to restrict) the sale of contraceptives to the poor."[72]

The antifeminists did not succeed immediately. With the defeat of Germany and the establishment of the Weimar Republic, German women got the vote in November 1918, and in 1919 Marianne Weber became the first woman member of the parliament of Badenia. Two years earlier she had written an essay about "The Personality Change in the Woman Student" wrought by the erotic movement. The students were no longer militant about women's rights, Weber found, but instead were hyperfeminine "romantic types," concerned about love and sex above all else. The change in attitude was reflected in a change in the style of dress, away from the "masculine," practical style of earlier feminists. Weber saw these young women as very vulnerable as a result of their dropping the fight for women's rights.[73]

The deaths of major pre–World War I figures mark the immediate postwar years. Fanny zu Reventlow died in Ascona in 1918; Otto Gross died in Berlin in 1920 (from debilitation due to drug addiction). At least one version of Schwabing's world of women died with them: the era of the erotic movement had ended. The People's Republic of Bavaria, centered in Munich, was crushed in 1919. Edgar Jaffe died in 1921, broken by the defeat of the socialist revolution, a defeat that ended efforts to smash the old German state. Also, Max Weber had died in 1920. In Green's interpretation, Germany's experiment in democracy, the Weimar Republic, might better have been called the "Heidelberg Republic," and Heidelberg from 1900 to 1933 could have been called "Max Weber's Town," an intellectually exciting world that included "the active participation of so many clever and educated women."[74] However, Green, captivated—as are so many academic intellectuals—by Weber's life and work and also fascinated by the lives of the Von Richthofen sisters, has told only part of the story. In some ways, the Weimar Republic might have been called the "Republic of Revisionism," with right-wing social democrats helping the bourgeois state to remain intact.[75]

Socialism, Feminism, and the Fate of the Weimar Republic

The fate of socialist feminism is the story to which I now return. The German Social Democratic Party failed to make good on its revolutionary promise to the men and women of the German working class; in the end, the socialists were unwilling to wager on revolution (to borrow a phrase from Lukács). The Second International of 1889–1914, led by the SPD, had been committed programmatically to turn the anticipated war into the occasion for socialist revolution. In practice, the majority representatives of the workers' movements of the various European countries acquiesced in their governments' imperialist war—which an already disillusioned Robert Michels saw as a confirmation of his analysis of the oligarchical and conservative tendencies of modern socialist political parties.[76] The world war divided the German party; most of the important women leaders, Rosa Luxemburg, Clara Zetkin, Luise Zietz, and Käthe Dunker went over to the minority left-wing opposition to the war, as did Karl Liebknecht and Franz Mehring, Marx's biographer. Despite censorship and the party's truce with the government, there is evidence that a majority of readers of *Gleichheit* were opposed to the war and to the party's policy.

In 1915, Zetkin was active in organizing the International Women's Conference in Bern. During the same year she was arrested for antiwar activities. Later the party chose Marie Juchacz to replace Zetkin as editor of *Gleichheit*. Zietz was expelled from the SPD executive committee in 1916, and Baader's position in the women's bureau was weakened. The subtitle of *Gleichheit* was changed to "Magazine for the interests of workers' wives and women workers" for the 1916–17 volume, and it announced an editorial policy of "political education, simple teaching and valuable entertainment." In that paper and at National Conferences of Social Democratic Women, Zetkin was vilified indirectly by criticisms of past "radical verbiage" and her failure to edit the paper in a way that could be understood by the masses of people without political or intellectual training.

The campaign against Zetkin masked deeper theoretical and political differences going back to the revisionist controversy in Social Democracy, which did not become the source of a clear ideological divide until working-class revolutions broke out in Russia and Germany. Nevertheless, the fate of the "woman question" was inextricably linked with the struggle between the reformist social democratic tendency and the revolutionary Marxist tendency. The appearance in 1916 of *Gewerkschaftliche Frauenzeitung* (*Women's Trade Union Paper*), edited by Gertrud Hanna, was yet another evidence of this conflict. It focused on trade-union issues, and its circulation far outstripped that of *Gleichheit* at the same time that the SPD lost female membership (more than 50 percent, by one estimate). As Thönnessen has pointed out, "The Party split weakened the Social Democratic women's movement considerably." Wilhelmine Kähler stated in 1919 that women "have increasingly moved to the left-wing of the Party" or to the opposition United Social Democratic Party. The increasingly reformist and trade-union consciousness of the SPD and of working-class women can be explained not only by revisionism, the predominance of the trade unions in the party structure, and the integration of the SPD into the state capitalist order, but also by the fact that the number of women working during the war increased to approximately 15 million from the 1913 level of 9.5 million. The large number of women workers and the prosperity caused by the war economy led some wishful thinkers (for example, Wally Zepler, "a leading woman Social Democrat") to see the German political economy as "war socialism."[77]

When the socialists took over the government in November 1918, women got the right to vote. But the socialist parties failed to gain a majority of the 421 seats in the Reichstag, and of the 36 women deputies, only 18 were Social Democrats. Soon after came the shocking realization that the vote and equal rights in the family did not change the fact, as Juchacz put it, that "the economic dependence of women still exists as previously." Thönnessen commented, "The Socialist women's forty years' experience in organizing the female proletariat crumbled before the demands of parliamentary practice. . . . The achievement of women's suffrage signaled the end of the heroic epoch of the Socialist women's movement."[78]

When the war was over, women workers were laid off almost immediately, bringing the proportion of women in the labor force back to its March 1914 level. The postwar economy pitted the sexes against one another in competition for jobs. At the Weimar Party Conference of 1919, Hanna posed the question, "What is the lesser evil, female or male unemployment?" It was clear that the official

Social Democrats had no answer. The achievement of bourgeois equality of rights by women meant little in the face of the conditions of the economy and the failure of the SPD to get control of the state power structures. The policy of employers was to lay off married women first, which, as Grünberg argued at Kassel in 1920, only caused more misery for working-class families. Hanna said, "The campaign being waged against female labour exceeds anything known for years in the working-class movement." There was, in short, a resurgence of what Thönnessen called "proletarian antifeminism" and corresponding attacks on the "old theory" of women's emancipation.[79]

In 1917, Edmund Fischer reiterated his 1905 position that "the so-called emancipation of women . . . is unnatural, and hence impossible to achieve." But unlike the spate of refutations of his 1905 article by leading Social Democratic women in *Gleichheit*, this time, as Thönnessen notes, "there was hardly any protest." Fischer maintained that with postwar prosperity there would come "a movement towards the disappearance of wage-labour for married women since wage-labour cannot enrich their lives more than housework can." According to Fischer, the purpose of socialism in this area was to restore the traditional sex roles of family members. But in *Sozialismus und Frauenfrage*, published in 1919, Wally Zepler offered an alternative explanation for why women appeared as Fischer described them: it was a consequence of the drudgery of motherhood, she said, and of the fact that their "lives were dried up by the women's need to accommodate themselves to the male circle of life and ideas." For women to compete equally with men required the sharing of the duties of child rearing, she asserted. Nevertheless, Zepler's book did not lead to renewed discussion of the contemporary situation in terms of the classical theory of women's emancipation.[80] Party theory and policy had cut off that possibility.

At the party conferences at Görlitz (1921) and Heidelberg (1925), programs supporting equal rights for women were adopted. Discussion revealed "a series of constantly recurring themes: the distribution of women's votes over the various parties, the number of women Party members, criticism of the women's papers, discrimination against women in the Party, and the importance of women's involvement in social work."[81] On the last point, socialist women had moved into municipal administration during the war. In the postwar period, SPD women were increasingly turning to municipal welfare work. This second generation had become "social feminists" with their own functional sphere.[82]

Antifeminists blamed women's suffrage for the party's electoral failure in June 1920. At Görlitz, a woman delegate responded that "if there had been more practical socialism in families" in the preceding generation, then women would have voted for socialism: "It is the big brother who is to blame" for denying women political education, she said. Also at Görlitz, Juchacz tried to explain away the party's failure of nerve and lack of decisiveness, claiming that many women who "had joined the Party purely on the strength of their emotions amidst the turbulence of the revolutionary atmosphere felt cheated of their hopes, for they had not had any political education." At the Berlin National Women's Conference in 1924, Juchacz, who was the theorist for second-generation women party functionaries, again concluded that women had voted wrongly (that is, not overwhelmingly for the SPD), but she blamed "the bad state of the economy." In his study of church-influenced Cologne, where the Socialists got one-third of the women's vote, Max Schneider pointed out that it had taken thirty years for the SPD to get that many male votes in 1912. The evidence showed that in general throughout the 1920s fewer women than men voted, except in the case of the Centre Party; until 1928 there was a decline in women's votes for the SPD, and after 1930 an increase of women's votes for parties of the Right. From a leftist, feminist-socialist perspective, one could argue that the SPD had nobody but itself to blame for the disappointing results of women's suffrage, for it had not broken emphatically either with sexism or with other institutions of the old order.[83]

The pattern of the number of women members of the party is clear: there was a tremendous increase in female membership between 1908 and 1914 (from about 29,500 to almost 175,000), a decline during the war years to around 67,000 in 1917, an increase from 1918 to 1921 (up from over 70,000 in 1918 to around 207,000 in 1920), another decline between 1921 and 1923 to about 130,000, and then another increase from 165,000 in 1926 to 230,000 in 1931. Male membership increased again during the period of inflationary crisis (1920 to 1923), whereas, conversely, the number of female members increased in the period of stabilization (1924 to about 1930). Juchacz hypothesized that work was the key to increases in female party membership, and unemployment to female exodus, because "restriction to the narrow confines of the household results in narrow-mindedness and the suppression of class consciousness." Women with jobs seemed to be the key to the health of the SPD women's movement.[84]

Propaganda in party newspapers directed toward women was affected by swings in the political economy and by the party's response to them. Circulation figures for *Gleichheit* declined from 124,000 in July 1914 to 25,000 in September 1921; *Gleichheit* ceased publication in the fall of 1922 after having been turned into "a family paper" with the subtitle "Magazine for women and girls of the working people." Its successor was *Die Frauenwelt* (*Women's World*), modeled after bourgeois leisure magazines and edited by a man. The party organ for women party officials was *Die Genossin* (*The Comrade*). At the Berlin Conference of 1925 and the Women's Conference of Kiel in 1927, a minority of women critical of the SPD executive committee's press policy called for the revival of *Gleichheit*; they argued that *Gleichheit* had been responsible for nearly all the intellectual education about socialism that women had had. The party responded that *Gleichheit* was unnecessary because in *Frauenwelt* the party employed scientific mass propaganda—in effect popularizing socialism by appealing to the lowest common denominator. Even by 1929, out of four hundred to five hundred editors of party papers, there were only one or two women.[85]

At the party conferences in Berlin (1924) and Heidelberg (1925), women protested their loss of jobs to male trade unionists and violations of the Constitution's provisions for equal rights for women (drafted in part by the SPD); they demanded that the party return in practice to its "old" position on the "woman question." The proceedings of the Berlin meetings record the complaint of women who said that measures against women were taken "without any real signs of the strong protest which this should have aroused in the ranks of Social Democracy. We are merely the advance guard for the huge army of women who are fighting for equal economic status, economic freedom and intellectual liberty." And at Heidelberg, radical women demanded that "the liberation of women . . . must be carried out by the Party and not evaded by every possible means." These words did not move the men to action. The words that did rouse them unfortunately came too late.

In 1931 at the Leipzig Conference of the SPD, a resolution was adopted that said: "Our demand is not 'struggle against jobs for women' but 'struggle against the capitalist system,' which is alone to blame for the increasing unemployment." This position, which contained the traditional party principle of equal rights to jobs, was in the party's interest, for membership of women in the SPD increased as employment of women increased. Nevertheless, the revisionist policy of the SPD was largely responsible for the fact that the party never gained control over the levers of power in the Weimar Republic. In Thönnessen's formulation, "Capitalism continued to emerge the winner in all the important political conflicts."[86]

The struggle against sexist attitudes within the party continued from 1919 throughout the 1920s. In Berlin in 1924, the essence of the complaint was recorded in the Proceedings: "Male comrades today still treat us with a sort of irrelevant benevolence, and we ought to change this into due confidence in our achievements." The response of party delegates and the party executive committee was to stonewall the women. At the 1929 Magdeburg Conference, women noted that men "debate for hours about the most trivial matters. But if we want to discuss things that concern women, then time suddenly runs out and the comrades have to go home." Juchacz complained about the bad state of affairs with regard to women's influence in the party: "The forms of chivalry and deference, which are actually borrowed from feudalism, inevitably turn into brutality and a sort of sexist contempt when the women become independent and express their own political opinions." Another woman delegate pointed out that there existed in most men an "instinctive inclination" to reinforce "the woman's feeling of inferiority . . . regardless of the splendour of her achievements." That the percentage of SPD women in elected positions, from municipal positions to seats in the Reichstag, was always considerably less than the percentage of female membership in the party is suggestive of the discrimination existing within the party. In contrast, although it was smaller, the German Communist Party (Kommunistische Partei Deutschlands, or KPD) apparently helped elect more women members, proportionally, to the Reichstag, despite being labeled a "male" party.

The SPD reacted to women's demands for useful participation with a bourgeois solution: they channeled them into social work in cooperation with the government. This position was defended, illogically and through appeal to the bourgeois idea of thrift, by Frau Dr. Schöfer. While the SPD's effort in this area was considerable, it boiled down to socialist home economics. Its consequence, if not its purpose, was to maintain the sexual division of labor within the party.[87]

Toward the end of the 1920s there was, however, increasing radicalization. The economic crisis of 1929 provoked even Lily Braun to refer to the "old literature"—meaning *Gleichheit*, Bebel's work, and other socialist-feminist publications about women. Interestingly, as the number of women increased in the SPD, there was a corresponding decrease in the number of women in the trade unions, possibly indicating that women understood that their struggles for equality and against the emerging crisis were more complex than what the trade unions stood for. At the 1927 national women's conference at Kiel, where the main topic was housing, there were also discussions about party recruitment, education, women's newspapers, and opposition to laws that were punitive to women (for example, the law against abortion). German Social Democratic women also struggled actively against fascism. In 1931, the International Women's Conference adopted the motto "Against war and Nazi terrorism, for socialism and peace." At the meeting of the World League for Women's Suffrage held in Paris in 1926, the issue of special protection for women workers was again debated; the German SPD delegates voted for special protection, and the Scandinavians and English voted against (with similar lineups in 1927 and 1929). The Social Democrats continued to advocate special protection for women workers (despite declining wages for women between 1926 and 1932) on the grounds that removing protection would only worsen the conditions of women workers and intensify competition between women and men workers. As Thönnessen observed: "The Social Democratic women's movement after 1929 rediscovered its former theory of women's emancipation."[88]

The old theory, formulated most purely by Zetkin, held that the path to the emancipation of women cut through the "wilderness of exploitation." It maintained that work was the key to legal equality but that legal equality by itself was not the key to women's emancipation. In 1892 Zetkin had written, "The liberation of women workers does not consist merely in obtaining equality with the male world within the present society. Rather, the existing social order must be abolished in its entirety, for the economic and property relations of this society are at the root of both class and sexual slavery." When this theory was the reigning one in the SPD, there occurred "a vast growth in the women's movement." When it was given up by the SPD, coincident with the party's revisionism, not only did the party suffer political losses but socialist feminism suffered as well. The communists then began to advocate the "old theory," that is, the Marxist theory, of women's emancipation.[89] But the Nazis took over the even older theory, that of justifying women's subjection.

The cause of equal rights for women shared the fate of the Weimar Republic. As Renate Bridenthal and Claudia Koonz have pointed out, "The 'woman question' continued to be one of the most controversial topics of the 1920s, but the economic and legal status of women did not improve."[90] A reading of the period gives one the sense that the middle-class feminist movement was neither strident nor independent. As we have seen, suffrage weakened the radicals. Under the guidance of Bäumer, at the end of the war, the Federation of German Women's Associations (BDF) abandoned its 1907 feminist goals for the nationalist politics that had consolidated its ranks just before and during the war. This stance was coupled with an ideology of familism: the federation members espoused self-sacrifice by women, whose traditional feminine virtues, they believed, would bring a motherly influence that would moderate political conflicts. Marianne Weber succeeded Bäumer as BDF president in 1919; from 1924 to 1931, Emma Ender, a conservative, was president. The BDF increasingly lost its autonomy in the 1920s and in 1932 favored a corporate state—with one corporation for women—modeled after Mussolini's fascist Italy.[91] In cultural terms, whereas the earlier "Revolt of the Sons" had been waged partly on behalf of mothers, sisters, and daughters, the election of Hindenburg as president in 1925 marked the beginning of the era of the "Revenge of the Father," as Peter Gay characterized it.[92]

Anti-Semitism had become more apparent in Germany. Sociology had already been considered "the Jewish science," as Marxism has been called a Jewish doctrine. Georg Simmel's Jewish background and Robert Michels's socialist affiliations were in part responsible for their problems with the academic world.[93] Otto Weininger published a book, *Sex and Character*, often republished, "declaring the emancipation of women to be a Jewish plot."[94] All this reminds one of Bebel's remark that anti-Semitism is the "socialism of fools." Germany had an extremely solid tradition of misogyny. For example, Heinrich von Treitschke opposed the entrance of women to universities as a "shameful display of moral weakness";[95] and Nietzsche, in *Beyond Good and Evil*, correctly associated feminism with pacifism, democracy, and socialism and approved of Napoléon's infamous outburst to Mme de Staël: "Woman, shut up about matters of state! Woman, shut up about women!"[96] As we have seen, there was an ideological affinity between Nazism and the Lebensphilosophie of Munich/Schwabing. One might argue that Alfred Weber tried to formulate a patriarchal version of eroticism and life philosophy.[97] At any rate, when the National Socialists received 6.5 million votes in the 1930 elections for the Reichstag, "it was a sign of the end of the Weimar period."[98] What this meant for women was a return to *Kinder, Küche, und Kirche*. In Adolf Hitler's view, "Equal rights for women means that they experience the esteem that they deserve in the areas for which nature has intended them."[99] Where cultural historians and critics go wrong—and this is the central theoretical and practical issue in the oppression of women in Germany—is in failing to realize that the fate of Weimar was, in good measure, an outcome of the class struggle. The fate of feminism was reflected in and inextricably bound to the decline of socialist consciousness among the working class. In addition, many middle-class feminists, caught between the hammer of antifeminist and antisocialist nationalist liberalism and the anvil of socialist feminism, took up the hammer and contributed to the defeat of feminism as well as socialism.[100]

These events and historical processes affected the writings on the "woman question" of Tönnies and Mannheim, as well as those of Simmel and Weber. Tönnies' early romanticism about women was altered by the facts that socialist theory emphasized, the increasing employment under capitalism of women with the consequent weakening of patriarchal authority and the growth of women's trade-union and feminist movements. Mannheim witnessed and participated in the political upheavals and intellectual ferment of the 1920s, 1930s, and 1940s. All the tensions between feminism and patriarchy, between Marxism and bourgeois thought are manifest and wrenching in Max Weber's work.

The German Theorists
Max Weber
Oedipus, Personal Values, and Historical Sociology

Max Weber (1864–1920) is the central figure of German classical sociology. In addition to the obvious intellectual quality, range, and power he demonstrated in his work, Weber is important because he stood "at more decisive meeting points [on intellectual and political issues] than any other thinker" of the social theorists writing between 1890 and 1930, as H. Stuart Hughes has put it. Many of these meeting points involved what Albert Salomon termed Weber's "debate with Marx's ghost." As Hughes characterizes Weber: "He was both a democrat in his personal convictions and a contributor to that radical critique of democracy which Pareto and Mosca had launched. He was skeptical about the viability of the Enlightenment under twentieth-century conditions, yet his temperamental reaction to events was more often than not of an 'enlightened' character."[101]

H. H. Gerth and C. Wright Mills have described Weber's demeanor and his attitude toward women's equality: "A model of the self-conscious masculinity of Imperial Germany, he nevertheless encouraged the first woman labor official in Germany and made vital speeches to members of the woman's emancipation movement of the early twentieth century."[102]

Further, as Julien Freund has pointed out, Weber "gave a prominent part in his sociological expositions to sexuality, as one of the most irrational forces in life," especially in its connection with magic, symbolic phenomena, and ecstatic rites. He considered the tension between sexuality and religious asceticism and major world religions particularly important. The problems central to Weber's sociology of religion, in Freund's words, "clearly affect the always controverted position of woman in society."[103]

Untangling the contradictions of Weber's life and work with respect to the "woman question" entails two interrelated exercises: to establish the linkage of Weber's character to his family life and German social structure and to explore the connections between his biography and the history of his intellectual production and political life. Generally, Weber's life and work mirrored the contradictions of Germany in the nineteenth century, particularly the dramatic tension between industrial, scientific rationality and romanticism, on the one hand, and between humanistic high culture and irrational authoritarianism, on the other.

As Hughes has described him, Weber was "for all the intemperance of his polemical style, . . . hesitant, self-divided, and enormously troubled."[104] He was the prototype of the lone, brilliant, torn, and neurotic intellectual, "the critical intelligence of our century."[105] In answer to a question about what his scholarship meant to him, Weber responded tersely, "I want to see how much I can endure." His disciple, Karl Jaspers, the psychiatrist turned existential philosopher, said that one could view in Weber's life what is humanly possible, "catch sight of what a human being actually is." A newspaper report of Weber's lectures in Vienna in the spring of 1918 described his charisma:

> It is by no means . . . rhetorical mastery . . . alone that calls forth this extraordinary power of attraction . . . but rather . . . the ability to awaken feelings that slumber in the souls of others. From each and every word it is clearly apparent that he feels himself to be the heir of the German past and that he is governed by the consciousness of his responsibility toward posterity.[106]

"Men are not open books," Weber himself said.[107] To read between the lines and get beneath the text of Weber's life, biographers and commentators have worn both strong and weak analytic glasses.[108] For their data about Weber's personal life, they have relied primarily on *Max Weber: Ein Lebensbild* (1927), by Marianne Weber; Weber's own *Jugendbriefe*; and works by several of his relatives, the Baumgartens. The following discussion relies on the major interpretations in English of those biographical texts and also on Weber's own method of *Verstehen*. The purpose of this discussion is to illuminate the connections of Weber's biography to his work on the "woman question." In such an enterprise, it is necessary to guard against a crude, psychologically reductionist perspective on ideas. Consequently, it must be remembered that Weber's character and biography were shaped not only by his family life but also by the historical changes and debates about ideas in German society. Guenther Roth has pointed out that Max Weber was the spokesman for the new generation that was rebelling against the previous one that had united Germany. But Weber lived with the feeling that by comparison his generation could be no more than a mere epigone of the generation that had founded the modern German state in all of its glory.[109]

Weber's early years were spent in the Bismarck-dominated atmosphere of Berlin. His father, Max Weber, Sr., came from a prosperous, though not wealthy, family and was successful as a politician in Berlin, Prussia, and the Reichstag. Among his friends were major figures in the National Liberal Party, and the Weber home was visited by such influential intellectuals and political figures as Heinrich von Treitschke, Theodor Mommsen, and Wilhelm Dilthey. Max Weber, Sr., was a National Liberal, one of Bismarck's "eunuchs" (in Martin Green's reading), but he made up for it at home, where "he played the part of a stupid domestic tyrant, a minor Bismarck." Helene Weber, Max's mother, was born to a well-to-do Heidelberg family, the Fallensteins, a family of professors connected with the nationalism of the anti-Napoleonic resistance. Helene Weber was "a woman for intellectuals." She faithfully lived out a life of Calvinist-derived ethical and spiritual values and in 1904 was honored for her social work with poor women. However, in the fashion of a true mother-wife-martyr, she suffered in silence the petty tyranny of her husband, whom the children resented. The characters and concerns of the Webers were simply in contradiction. Max, Sr., rejected Helene's moral concerns and her "effeminate" world.[110] Typical of such alienated marital relationships, Helene Weber lived devotedly and vicariously through her precious eldest son, whom she once referred to as "an older daughter."[111] One cannot resist the conclusion that she tried to get from Max the son part of what she failed to achieve from Max the father. The victim of this unsuccessful marriage, Max Weber, Jr., was sickly, uncommunicative, and filled with self-reproach, fears, and feelings of inadequacy. As Green puts it, "All his life he was in a state of apology, first to his mother, then to his wife."[112]

Young Weber later compensated for his physical weakness by engaging in exaggeratedly masculine activities: as a university student in Heidelberg, he joined a dueling fraternity, drank, and got into debt; later he served in the army. Weber himself noted that being trained for "haughty aggression" during these years developed his physique and "removed the shyness and insecurity of my adolescence." His dress and physical appearance earned him a slap in the face from his mother when he visited home in Berlin.[113] As Green has noted, "He was in his early twenties, very unlike the forceful tragic hero of later years, and unlike the handsome boy he had been."[114] This phase ended when he returned to his earlier, studious posture, first as a diligent law student and then as a brilliant doctoral candidate on the road to a successful academic career. He remained in his parents' home until he was almost thirty years old.[115]

The tragic manifestation of Weber's oedipal situation, those internal contradictions presented by his mother and father, occurred in a dramatic and catastrophic way. In 1897, four years after Weber had married, his mother planned a visit to her son in Heidelberg unaccompanied by her husband, but he insisted on joining her. On this occasion in July, years of resentment boiled over, and young

Max, in front of his wife and mother, sat in judgment of his father's treatment of his mother, "a lifetime's brutal selfishness," in Green's summary. Young Max threatened to sever relations with his father if deterred from seeing his mother alone. He ended by ordering his father out of his house. Seven weeks later, in August, his father died, at age sixty-one, without having reconciled with either wife or son. Shortly thereafter, in early 1898, Weber suffered an emotional collapse, which lasted with intermittent intensity for at least five years and recurred and threatened him for the rest of his life. He had to take leaves of absence and finally had to resign his professorship at Heidelberg; he was unable to write (or even to read) and was totally dependent on his uncritical wife, Marianne. Throughout these years, Marianne Weber gave lectures supporting the women's movement.[116]

The European family structure of the period was characterized by the Hamlet complex, in the sense that male children were emotionally paralyzed by the conflicts presented by their mothers and fathers. Green has suggested that "an important clue to Weber's development lies in the fact that this [close but smothering] relationship with his mother persisted so long." It may have been no coincidence that Weber outlived his mother by only a year. The scene with his father may have been so explosive because Weber also blamed his mother for tolerating her husband's tyrannical behavior. Green has argued (correctly, I think) that although Weber punished himself for wishing his father dead, it was his mother "he wished to destroy"—evidenced by the hostility he expressed toward her. Her constant demands that he meet her needs and assuage her sense of failure sapped him of energy, preventing him from responding to his healthier passions. Weber revenged himself by not speaking to his mother when she visited him during the years of his depression, and he was the only son who did not attend her gala seventieth birthday celebration. In mythical terms, he wanted to be Orestes but believed himself to be Oedipus. It is no wonder he was an advocate of the reform (rather than the abolition) of the then-existing patriarchal form of marriage. He never really resolved his inner conflict between mother and father. He may have been a model of "the self-conscious masculinity of Imperial Germany"; but it was a masculinity that he always doubted, and he is believed to have been impotent with his wife.[117]

Extended families were the norm during the period; significant in Weber's life were aunts, uncles, and cousins as well as sisters and brothers. In particular, Weber was influenced by the Baumgartens. His aunt Ida Baumgarten was even more extreme in her Christian, social piety than his mother, her sister. Her husband, Professor Hermann Baumgarten was an uncompromising liberal critic of Bismarck and his ideological henchman Treitschke. Their son Otto, forced by his mother into the study of theology, began as a Christian socialist and became friends with Weber in college. Weber credited his aunt with influencing his choice of moral loyalty to his mother over his father. Weber later reflected, however, that the Baumgartens made matters "desperate" by always asking "Who is morally right and who is morally wrong?" to the exclusion of any other consideration. Weber preferred an ethic of responsibility to their ethic of absolute ends (see his "Politics as a Vocation"). He was engaged to be married to his cousin, Emmy Baumgarten, who was a frail and emotionally disturbed young woman. He broke off the engagement to marry a distant cousin, Marianne Schnitger, who became his wife in the fall of 1893. Weber's guilt about breaking off with Emmy Baumgarten was perhaps compounded because a friend of his had also been courting Marianne Schnitger. Gerth and Mills have observed that Weber's "proposal letter to his wife, dealing with this situation, seems as much a confession of guilt as a love letter. And later letters to his wife are apologetic for sacrificing his marriage with her by allowing his energies to be used up on the 'inner treadmill' of his intellectual life," that is, his endeavor to be a successful professor and his devotion to writing books.[118] He attributed his "*need* to feel submerged under a load of work" to his fear of "deep depression."[119] Later, he realized that the years of depression cured him of that need and taught him the value of escape, reopening to him "the human side of life, which mama used to miss in me."[120]

Max Weber's relationships with his siblings were also troubled. According to his uncle, during Weber's student phase of exaggerated masculinity, his mother sent his sister Lily away from home out of apprehension that his affections for Lily might cross the boundary of incest. In addition, Max felt a keen rivalry with his younger brother Alfred, who also became a sociologist. Several anecdotes are indicative of the destructive nature of their competition. On his deathbed, Max is reported to have said as he groped for a glass of milk, "Give it to me quickly, or Alfred will suck it all away." For his part, Alfred tried to keep apart from "der grosse Max," who recommended Georg Simmel over him for a teaching post; a generation

later, some of Alfred's students referred to him as "Minimax," and
he had to lecture in a room that contained a bust of his brother.
Alfred never escaped, not even in his eighties, the identity of the
younger brother. Else von Richthofen was the object of one of their
most passionate competitions. Alfred had wanted to become engaged to her in 1900, without success. As noted earlier, she married
Edgar Jaffe, but by 1910 she was estranged from him. In 1910, in
Venice, Max declared his love to Else—causing "a revolution in
Weber's life" by giving him "a vision of erotic happiness." But she
would not betray Marianne and instead had an affair with Alfred.
The conditions which allowed her to do this were orchestrated by
Marianne and Max. Given the emotional load of the situation, it is
not surprising that Else and Max quarreled, and she stayed away
from him until 1917, when, it is believed, they finally became lovers.
In 1913, Weber is believed to have had an affair with Mina Tobler, a
pianist and member of his circle. After Max's death, Else devoted
the rest of her life to Alfred, despite his neurotic personality, but he
never married her.[121]

In a letter to Ferdinand Tönnies, Weber described himself as "a
cripple, a mutilated being," at best like a tree stump, able to grow
buds but not able to become a whole tree. He was a son of a generation of nation-building founding fathers and took on the male role
his culture prescribed, but he struggled to get out of the "strong
house" Bismarck and men like his father had built. His brother
Alfred described these post-1848 men as *"kurzgeschorene"*—"the
physically and psychically crewcut" in Green's rendition, the ener-
getic realists of Bismarck's Germany. Weber styled himself in appearance after Bismarck, and his effect on women was derived from
expressing with every move, as Marianne Weber said, that he was
"a powerful *man*"—in the world of men, political and intellectual.
He held a "fearful fascination" for some women.[122] The interpersonal costs of this posture were linked to his inability to open up
emotionally and sexually. Obviously, for Weber, there was considerable ambivalence and ambiguity in becoming a man in the German
patriarchal context.

Weber married a woman who resembled his mother "in the lofti-
ness of her ethical goals and the strength of her will," in Hughes's
words. "Reading between the lines of . . . [Marianne Weber's]
vastly informative and sensitive biography of her husband," Hughes
has written, "we may surmise that the two women early struck up a
tacit alliance directed toward the goal of making a great man out of

the individual they cherished in common." He entered this marriage with a feeling of vulnerability about his masculinity and, in his wife's description, with the "enigmatic feeling that he did not have it in him . . . to make a woman happy."[123] Perhaps this feeling paralleled his conviction that no matter what he did, he could not succeed in making his mother happy.

A closer look at Marianne Weber will allow us to cut through some mythology about Weber's feminist views. As a young woman she, like Else von Richthofen, rebelled against the domestic life of her class. She went to Berlin to study for a profession and moved into the Weber's house—"a bold step for a young girl" in 1892, as Green has pointed out. Weber's mother encouraged her aspirations, and her marriage to Weber meant that she could have an intellectual career and a role in political life as a leader of the liberal women's movement rather than being confined to the role of *Hausfrau*.

In 1904, she wrote an essay on *Mutterrecht*, sarcastically noting that many considered matriarchy "a kind of Paradise Lost." Her attack on the theory might have been directed at Engels or Bachofen. Criticizing Engels's popular reconstruction of evolution, she offered her own: despite its excesses, *Vaterrecht* was necessary for individualism to develop, she believed. In her 1907 essay "The Principal Questions of Sexual Ethics," she denied that perfect happiness and harmony could be realistic criteria of marriage and downplayed the importance of eroticism in marriage. She also argued that women must be educated to a calling in order to achieve autonomy. The essence of her position was: "Not, then, a substitute *for* marriage, but a reform *of* marriage." In a 1913 essay on women and objective culture, she wrote that when a woman chose a profession, it did not relieve her of the traditional duties of a wife. Although a feminist, Marianne Weber, like her husband, held to what Green aptly characterized as "a patriarchal romanticism, fixed principally on *power* in a man."[124]

For Max Weber, who shared the same view of the world, Marianne Schnitger was certainly his soul mate on the level of his superego. Arthur Mitzman has pointed out that, despite Weber's opposition to "authoritarian patriarchalism" in private life and in the public domain,

Feminism was not, for the Webers, a vehicle to emancipate women altogether from the bonds of matrimony, but only from its authoritarian side, which subjugated wives to their hus-

bands, and from that middle-class Puritanism which equated
morality exclusively with sexual ethics (or, more precisely,
an ethic of sexual unhappiness). Beyond this they refused
to go.[125]

When student feminists whom Weber supported were receptive to
arguments advocating free love, Weber, sounding like Lenin speaking to Russian youth years later on the same topic, responded:
"Crude hedonism and an ethic which would only benefit the man as
goal of the woman! . . . it is simply nonsense."[126]

"Weber often said that a wife *must* resist her husband, or else
she is partly guilty of his brutality towards her," Green has written,
adding, "This exemplifies his reformist resistance to patriarchy as
a whole." The alternative to Bismarck's version of manhood was
Weber's mother's liberal humanitarianism, which Weber translated
into advocacy of a "better" patriarchy. He was still fascinated by
Bismarck—who turned the men who served him into children, to
paraphrase Otto Gross. Weber's contradictions are well portrayed in
Green's image: Weber cultivated a Bismarckian "root in himself
even as he clipped its thorns." Weber's relationship with his wife
was a teacher-student relationship, "with Max expounding, in-
structing, correcting her." In their relationship, he gave her intellect, and she returned "total devotion, a kind of worship," which
contributed to his public accomplishments. As Green has pointed
out, during his life she "was his spokeswoman. His ideas and even
his phrases are discernible in her work." Weber was "always the
Brutus of patriarchy."[127]

I think the evidence lends itself to a somewhat different, but
not contradictory, interpretation. In good part as a response to his
father's treatment of his mother, Weber had a "strong sense of chivalry."[128] He also exhibited a related cultural form: he was a patron of
intelligent women. But because of the effects of German patriarchalism on himself and on the women he knew, I believe he was
incapable of treating women as equals.

The First World War yanked Weber out of his ever-threatening
depressiveness. In 1917, he associated with revolutionaries and
members of the erotic movement in Munich. He told Frieda Gross
in 1919 that he was in sympathy with her mission of sexual liberation, but publicly he argued against the attractions of cults of experience. It was in Munich that he resumed his relationship with Else
Jaffe and is believed to have become her lover. He characterized his

experience with Else with the words "my mother, my sister, my unutterable happiness." He also cherished his relationship with her as a retreat from the cruelties of war and counterrevolution. He spoke of himself using images of revolution and war: barricades, "rubble," "abandoned and collapsed houses"; and an image to express his frustration with the patriarchal, prisonlike families of Bismarck's Germany: the bolted gates of his "committed desire." To Else he wrote, "There is very little love in the world, Else—a cold wind—people who love each other must be very good to each other nowadays."

His wife wrote to him that she understood there were things only Else could give him, and to Else (who was ashamed of her betrayal of Marianne's friendship and of her affair with Gross) she wrote, in effect, that she would share her husband with her. Green has described Weber's death: "He died in the presence of his wife and Frau Jaffe, both of whom had joined in caring for him at the end, and it seemed, to those intimate with the whole situation, that his divided love for the two was tearing him apart. . . . It was an agonizing and embittered death, despite the elements of harmony and nobility which made it tragic. In its private aspect as well as its public, it corresponded to the agony of German culture as a whole. . . . The hopefulness of 1910, the hopes of renewal, of the erotic movement, seemed very remote."[129]

Weber died as he had lived, surrounded by women devoted to him but feeling torn down the middle. He barely outlived his mother, who died in 1919 at the age of seventy-five. On the political level, neither Otto Gross nor Kurt Eisner nor the Social Democrats nor Max Weber had been able to shatter the foundation of the house that Bismarck built. It was left for Hitler to put new walls on the foundation and then lock people inside them. In his speech "Politics as a Vocation" at Munich University in 1919, Weber said that he feared that in "ten years . . . the period of reaction will have long since broken over us. . . . Not summer's bloom lies ahead of us, but rather a polar night of icy darkness and hardness, no matter which group may triumph externally now."[130]

To analyze the connections between Weber's relationships with women and the shifts in his opinions on the "woman question," let us first look at his response to Freud's ideas, specifically Otto Gross's interpretation of them. It can be argued that Freud's work was a response to the felt need to analyze the psychic conflicts of Victorian society as a whole and of Germanic patriarchy in particular.[131]

These conflicts were destroying the lives of some people; and others—in the erotic movement, led in theory and practice by Freud's disciple, Otto Gross—were in open rebellion against patriarchy.

One of Weber's initial responses to this situation appears in his evaluation of an article submitted by Gross for publication in *Archiv für Sozialwissenschaft und Sozialpolitik*, which Weber coedited with Edgar Jaffe. In Weber's letter to Jaffe (13 September 1907) recommending rejection of Gross's article (sent along with a letter to Else Jaffe), Weber conceded the heuristic value of Freud's work for the interpretation of cultural phenomena, especially morality and religion, but considered its support by historical and cross-cultural evidence "alarmingly thin." In Weber's view, "Freud's discoveries, if they are ultimately confirmed, I consider to be certainly of scientific importance." However, he observed, "Freud's revelations from the Unconscious have *nothing* particularly 'terrible' to add" to what Christianity or Kantian ethics taught about the average person. For Weber, it followed that Freudian analysis was not much more than "a revival of *confession*." Weber recommended rejection of Gross's paper because he felt it contained the common and "childish" mistake of attempting to derive ethical consequences, a world view, a new morality, from a scientific discovery. The idea that an ethic could be based on gratification of appetites ("the 'new' sexuality") or that actions should be based solely on one's feelings on the grounds that to repress or inhibit them would be against one's "*nervous hygiene*" Weber sarcastically pronounced absurd; that is the attitude of the "medical philistine," he said. Given Weber's insistence on the separateness of the realms of facts and values, he and Gross did not speak the same language. In Weber's reading, Gross's article was "absolutely bursting with noisy value-judgments," and his moralizing about sexual liberation had no place in a scientific journal.[132]

Weber's grounds for rejection are most certainly convincing if one accepts certain conventions of scientific and moral discourse. If one were to take Gross's point of view, however, one would have to say that Weber, at that point in his life, was unwilling to reflect upon the harm to his own nerves caused by the inhibitions and repressions of German patriarchal culture. One could also say that Freud eventually sided with Weber's ideas and not with the radical conclusions Gross drew from Freud's theory of repressed sexual energy as the basis of human striving and psychic tension.

Mitzman and Green both view the period around 1910, when

Weber professed his love for Else Jaffe, as a turning point in his life and work. Nonetheless, feminist concerns are only implicit in the section titled "The Household Community" in *Wirtschaft und Gesellschaft (Economy and Society)*, probably written between 1910 and 1913 but not published until 1920. It is "value free," as Weber believed scholarly work should be. In the letter to Jaffe, Weber defined a value-free work as work that satisfies "the requirement of sobriety and respect for facts."[133] In *Wirtschaft und Gesellschaft*, Weber presented a clear exposition of his anthropology.[134] He wrote that "what appear to us today as particularly fundamental relationships," the "stable sexual grouping" of father and mother, and their children—the nuclear family—are historically "wholly unstable and tenuous" when "separated from the extended kinship household as a producing unit." Biologically and sexually based relationships were insufficient as a basis for continuing communal action, he believed. Further, he denied "that there ever were human forms of existence in which maternal groupings were the only communities"; maternal groupings appeared where the "men's house," a concomitant of militaristic development, existed, but such groupings did not preclude sexual and economic relationships between men and women ("HC," 296–97).

Historically, concepts of the family varied; "marriage as a social institution comes into existence everywhere only as an antithesis to sexual relationships which are *not* regarded as marriage," especially those not tolerated by kinship groups. Weber asserted that it was the regulation by other communal groupings and not just the otherwise unstable biological and sexual grouping and the common experiences of father, mother, and children that endowed marriage with its institutional quality. In short, marriage and family relationships "can engender communal action only by becoming the normal, though not the only, bases of a specific economic corporate group: the household community"—which, Weber pointed out, seemed not to have existed in the primitive economies of hunters and nomads. The prerequisite of the household community did not imply a household in a contemporary European sense "but rather a certain degree of organized cultivation of the soil." Prior to modern European history, he wrote, the household community was often subordinate to more inclusive communal—kinship and local—groups which in turn provided more freedom for the individual vis-a-vis parents, siblings, and close blood relatives. This condition was indicated by the separation of the husband's and wife's belongings

and the existence of "independent organizations of women with female chieftains alongside the men's organizations" within the political corporate group ("HC," 297–98).

Weber examined the emergence of sex-role differentiation and
household authority. Household management by women came
about, he wrote, when men were away from the house performing military service, as in Sparta. The household economic unit
was "the most widespread" and "continuous" basis "of intensive
communal action" ("HC," 298). In Weber's words, the household
community

> is the fundamental basis of loyalty and authority, which in turn
> is the basis of many other human communal groups. This "au-
> thority" is of two kinds; (1) the authority derived from supe-
> rior strength; and (2) the authority derived from practical
> knowledge and experience. It is, thus, the authority of men as
> against women and children; of the able-bodied and brave
> against those of lesser capability; of the adult as against the
> child; of the old as against the young. The "loyalty" again
> unites those who are subjected to an authority against those
> who [w]ield authority, but it also binds one to the other.
> ("HC," 298)

How males gained the authority derived from practical knowledge and experience was not explained by Weber. He accepted the
idea that the household community implied common ownership of
property and solidarity against the outside world but believed that
"household communism" was disrupted in several ways. Increase in
household size brought about creation of separate communities,
which involved granting special privileges to some ("HC," 298), and
(I would add) some incipient social stratification. In addition, "The
earliest decline of the continuous household authority evidently
does not stem directly from economic motives but from the development of exclusive sexual claims of the household partners on the
women who are subject to the common household jurisdiction"
("HC," 299).

Yet, in Weber's words, "economic realities intervene in a compelling manner." First, there was the development of *oikos*, which
"refers to the authoritatively governed, expanded household of a
prince, great landowner, or a patrician, the principle of which is not
to earn money but to produce enough to satisfy the needs of the

master through income received in kind." Such forms involved male dominance, patriarchy, and production by slaves or serfs. Second, there was the dissolution of the household community and shifts in authority due to "exchange with the outside world," the path that led to capitalistic enterprise. Two factors were crucial, Weber thought: inheritance or the marriage of children often divided household communities, and outside employment made the household an economic unit of consumption only, not production. Desires and abilities expanded with the development of a money economy and an increase in economic means and resources, and life chances multiplied and improved, Weber wrote. Under such circumstances, individuals became "less and less content with being bound to rigid and undifferentiated forms of life prescribed by the community" ("HC," 300–305). Presumably women were affected by this great transformation, when "continuous capitalistic enterprise became a regular occupation," although Weber did not mention women in this context.

In the sections on religion in *Wirtschaft und Gesellschaft*, sometimes published separately as *The Sociology of Religion*, Weber did mention women—in his discussion of sexuality and of the attitudes of world religions toward women.[135] (Curiously, he did not mention women in "Class, Status, and Party," the section on stratification.) He wrote that "one of the most powerful components of eroticism, namely sexual love . . . along with the 'true' or economic interest, and the social drives toward power and prestige, is among the most fundamental and universal components of the actual course of interpersonal behavior" (*SR*, 236). Like Durkheim in *The Elementary Forms of Religious Life*, Weber observed that "totemism has frequently been very influential in producing a division of labor between the sexes which is guaranteed and enforced by magical motivations" (*SR*, 40).

However, the heart of Weber's treatment has to do with the tensions between salvation religions and sexuality. Showing that he may have taken some of his reading of Freud seriously, Weber asserted, "The specifically anti-erotic religions, both mystical and ascetic, represent substitute satisfactions of sexually conditioned psychological needs." For the mystic, sexuality may interfere with the goal of flight from this world of flesh and animality, he pointed out. For rational ascetics and for certain Puritan denominations, "self-control, and methodical planning of life are seriously threatened by the peculiar irrationality of the sexual act, which is ultimately and uniquely unsusceptible to rational organization" (*SR*, 237, 238). This idea, of course, sounds quite Victorian—odd in a time when the topic of sex was beginning to be subjected to rational scrutiny and control—and it reminds one of Durkheim's similar attitude.

Major world religions outlawed the sexual orgy, "orgiastic temple prostitution," which in practice serviced traveling traders (*SR*, 158, 237). Weber added, "But an additional effort is made by religion to eliminate all free sexual relationships in the interest of the religious regulation and legitimation of marriage" (*SR*, 238). After noting similarities and differences between Islam, Hinduism, and Confucianism (in the last of which it is taught that irregularity in matters of sex throws off a man's equilibrium, partly because a woman is "viewed as an irrational creature difficult to control"), Weber pointed out that "the religious preaching of Jesus, with its demand of absolute and indissoluble monogamy, went beyond all other religions in the limitations imposed upon permissible and legitimate sexuality." Early Christianity, he wrote, regarded only adultery and prostitution as "absolute mortal sins" (*SR*, 239). Legal marriage in both prophetic and priestly ethical systems as well as among tribal peoples was "simply an economic institution for the production and rearing of children as a labor force and subsequently as carriers of the cult of the dead" (*SR*, 240). Weber, with some humor, described Luther as one who "construed marriage as a legitimate sin which God was constrained not to notice, so to speak, and which of [c]ourse was a consequence of the ineluctable concupiscence resulting from original sin" (*SR*, 241). Luther accepted the view that there will be "no sexuality in Jesus' kingdom to come," but Muhammad promised the feudal warriors of his faith a veritable sensual paradise as their reward in the world to come (*SR*, 238). Islam's view in this regard corresponded to its worldly acceptance of polygamy and its "disesteem for and subjection of women" (*SR*, 264). Weber emphasized that all salvation religions except Islam had an attitude of hostility toward sexuality. Further, in contrast with the natural sexuality of the peasant, the rationalization of social life of the middle and upper classes and the increasing impediments to sexual intercourse due to clan and class interests were "the most important factors favoring this sublimation of sexuality into eroticism." Weber denied that these conventions were responsible for prostitution by observing that "the absolute proscription of prostitution dates only from the end of the fifteenth century" (*SR*, 242).

With regard to the position of women, Weber stated, "The religion of the disprivileged classes, in contrast to the aristocratic cults of the martial nobles, is characterized by a tendency to allot equality to women. . . . But the presence of priestesses, the prestige of female soothsayers or witches, and the most extreme devotion to individual women, to whom supernatural powers and charisma may be attributed, does not by any means imply that women have equal privileges in the cult." Further, equality in relationship to God, as in Christianity, went along with monopoly by men of priestly functions, professional religious training, and participation in the religious community (*SR*, 104). Generalizing, Weber concluded that "practically all orgiastic and mystagogic religious propagandizing, including that of the cult of Dionysos, called for at least a temporary and relative emancipation of women. . . . Women are accorded the greatest importance in sectarian spiritualist cults, be they hysterical or sacramental, of which there are numerous instances in China" [as well as in Europe] (*SR*, 239–40). But once the routinization of charisma sets in, a "reaction takes place against pneumatic manifestations among women, which come to be regarded as dishonorable and morbid"—as early as the time of Saint Paul in the history of Christianity (*SR*, 104). Weber denied, however, that the origins of brotherly love and the command "love thine enemy" were influenced by women but believed that women intensified the "emotional or hysterical" aspects of religion, as in India. Pacifist teachings "must have been quite close to the interests of the disprivileged classes" as well as to those of women (*SR*, 106).

Weber described some of the consequences of the Calvinist ethic of innerworldly asceticism, which was an aspect of his own background: "This religion demanded of the believer, not celibacy, . . . but the avoidance of all erotic pleasure . . . not the ascetic death-in-life of the cloister, but an alert, rationally controlled patterning of life, and the avoidance of all surrender to the beauty of the world, to art, or to one's own moods and emotions." Its typical representative was the "man of a vocation" (*SR*, 183). Weber wrote, "Above all, Puritanism limits the legitimation of sexual expression to the aforementioned rational goal of reproduction" (*SR*, 240). Weber knew firsthand the moral and psychological dimensions of this kind of piety concerning sex and work, which Freud had designated the two poles of human misery in his theory about the human condition. Weber had assured his mother that she had saved him from "*schlechten Streiche*"—fornication. In his wife's analysis, Weber's mother, by her "saintly purity of being, not by anything she said . . . had developed in him indestructible barriers against yielding to the passions."[136] And as we have seen, with regard to his scholarship he was possessed by a calling.

It is difficult for me to avoid the interpretation that in his discourse about the tension between religion and sexuality, Weber was coming to terms with the repression of his own sexual passions occasioned by his extramarital affairs and the influence on him of the erotic movement. This speculation gains support from his November 1915 article in the *Archiv*, "Religious Rejections of the World and Their Directions."[137]

In one section of this essay, "The Erotic Sphere," Weber began by repeating, "The brotherly ethic of salvation religion is in profound tension with the greatest irrational force of life: sexual love." Weber believed that the tension was not removed but instead was intensified by the sublimation of sexuality into a consciously cultivated eroticism of rationalized and intellectualized culture. Why? Because sexuality was raised to the "sublime" level of "conscious enjoyment"—in contrast to "the sober naturalism of the peasant." Some pages later he wrote, "Eroticism appeared to be like a gate into the most irrational and thereby real kernel of life, as compared with the mechanisms of rationalization" ("RR," 343–45). The implicit evaluation of the erotic movement here was much more sympathetic than in his 1907 letter on Gross's paper.

Weber proceeded to sketch the variations in value-emphasis placed upon the erotic sphere of life in Western history. During the preclassic Hellenic period, "the capture of a woman could be considered the incomparable incident of a heroic war," equaling the conquest of power and treasure. The myths lingered on in Greek tragedy: however, as Weber noted, "a woman, Sappho, remained unequaled by man in the capacity for erotic feeling." The classic Hellenic epoch was a "masculine" democracy but still knew "the deadly earnestness of sexual love." The "'comrade,' the boy, was the object demanded with all the ceremony of love." Platonic eros was "a strongly tempered feeling"; it did not know the "beauty of Bacchian passion." Significantly, as Weber pointed out, "The possibility of problems and of tragedy of a principled character came about in the erotical sphere, at first, through certain demands for responsibility, which, in the Occident, stem from Christianity" ("RR," 345).

Weber noted that enhancement of the value of erotically sublimated sexuality occurred within the context of the feudal system of honor and knightly vassalship. Troubadour love was "an erotic service of vassals" directed not toward young, unmarried women, "but exclusively towards the wives of other men." The eroticism of the Middle Ages involved the conception of the "lady," who, "by virtue of her judging function," made the man go through a probation at the bench of her erotic interest. (The similarity of the Renaissance to antiquity in this regard was in its basically masculine and combative character.) The "salon culture" of the Enlightenment, in Weber's words, "rested upon the conviction that intersexual conversation is valuable as a creative power." In this period, "the actual love problems of women became a specific intellectual market value, and feminine love correspondence became 'literature'" ("RR," 346).

Weber's central concern, however, was other than historical. Contemporary intellectual accentuations of the erotic sphere involved a collision "with the unavoidably ascetic trait of the vocational specialist type of man." He noted that "under this tension between the erotic sphere and rational everyday life, *specifically extramarital sexual life*, which had been removed from everyday affairs, could appear as the only tie which still linked man with the natural fountain of all life" ("RR," 346; emphasis added). From at least this point on in his essay, there is no doubt about the influence of the erotic movement on his intellectual interests, and the conclusion is unavoidable that he himself experienced these tensions in his personal life. He wrote that eroticism resulted in a "sensation of an inner-worldly salvation from rationalization. . . . A joyous triumph over rationality," and at the same time a rejection of any kind of salvation ethics by its systematic glorification of the "animality" of sexual life ("RR," 346–47). The following passage contains some of his description of the erotic experience:

> [It] seems to offer the unsurpassable peak of the fulfillment of the request for love in the direct fusion of the souls of one to the other. . . . The lover realizes himself to be rooted in the kernel of the truly living, which is eternally inaccessible to any rational endeavor. He knows himself to be freed from the cold skeleton hands of rational orders, just as completely as from the banality of everyday routine. This consciousness of the lover rests upon the ineffaceability and inexhaustibleness of his own experience. ("RR," 347)

Summarizing the central theme of the essay, Weber noted the radical antagonism of the "religious brotherhood" (the World of Man) toward the erotic sphere (the World of Woman) because the latter diverted devotion away from a supramundane God and adherence to his "ethically rational order" ("RR," 347–48).

Weber then turned to a discussion of the physiological and psychological basis for this conflict of values between eroticism and "heroic piety": they stand in a "mutually substitutive" relationship, he wrote. Employing images of combat and violence, he described asceticism as "a powerful and deadly enemy" of eroticism; for the mystic, sex is "irrational" and a "constant threat of a deadly sophisticated revenge of animality." Weber thought that any "religious ethic of brotherhood" considered sexual relationships to be relationships of conflict and brutality: the former involved "jealousy and the will to possession," and the latter, unbeknownst to the partners and "pretending to be the most humane devotion" was "a sophisticated enjoyment of oneself in the other" or, put more strongly, "the most intimate coercion of the soul of the less brutal partner." According to the erotic ethic, such relationships were determined by destiny, producing the "euphoria of the happy lover [which] is felt to be 'goodness,'" and "genuine 'passion'" looked at as "the type of *beauty*." These were the claims to legitimacy of the erotic, although "in an entirely amoral sense," Weber qualified. The ethic of "the most sublimated eroticism is the counter-pole of all religiously oriented brotherliness." By salvation religion, eroticism was considered "the most complete denial of all brotherly love and of bondage to God," in addition to "an undignified loss of self-control." There was one exception to the constant tension between the two: "The erotic frenzy stands in unison only with the orgiastic and charismatic form of religiosity." The Roman Catholic Church's sacrament of marriage was thought by Weber to be a concession and an attempt to regulate innerworldly sexual sentiments ("RR," 348–49).

Weber described the Protestant ethic that had governed his life and that lay at the heart of the tensions in, relations between, and directions of his psychological and intellectual biographies:

Inner-worldly and rational asceticism (vocational asceticism) can accept only the rationally regulated marriage. This type of marriage is accepted as one of the divine ordinations given to man as a creature who is hopelessly wretched by virtue of his "concupiscence." Within this divine order it is given to men to live according to the rational purposes laid down by it and only according to them: to procreate and to rear children, and mutually to further one another in the state of grace. This inner-worldly rational asceticism must reject every sophistication of the sexual into eroticism as idolatry of the worst kind. . . . All elements of "passion," however, are then considered as residues of the Fall. . . . The ethic of the Quakers (as it is displayed in William Penn's letters to his wife) may well have achieved a genuinely humane interpretation of the inner and religious values of marriage. In this respect the Quaker ethic went beyond the rather gross Lutheran interpretation of the meaning of marriage. ("RR," 349–50)

Weber concluded this section of his essay with what can be interpreted as a comment on his own marriage:

From a purely inner-worldly point of view, only the linkage of marriage with the thought of ethical responsibility for one another—hence a category heterogeneous to the purely erotic sphere—can carry the sentiment that something unique and supreme might be embodied in marriage; that it might be the transformation of the feeling of a love which is conscious of a responsibility throughout all the nuances of the organic life process, "up to the pianissimo of old age," and a mutual granting of oneself to another and the becoming indebted to each other (in Goethe's sense). Rarely does life grant value in pure form. He to whom it is given may speak of fate's fortune and grace—not of his own "merit." ("RR," 350)

To support the interpretation of the influences suggested above, one can compare these writings on religion with Weber's classic, *The Protestant Ethic and the Spirit of Capitalism*, first published in 1904–5 in the *Archiv*, which was a celebration, in a sense, of the world-transforming role of the ethics of rational asceticism and contained little and very restrained mention of the conflict of inner-worldly asceticism and sexuality, except to note the Puritan view that sex is a threat to religious discipline and that hard work is the means of resisting sexual temptation. Women were mentioned in the context of the Protestant conception of work as a calling, where Weber noted that women workers with a pietistic upbringing were not tradition-bound or resistant to new methods of work as were those without such a religious background.[138] There was no intellectual or logical reason—given the relationships of capitalist industrialization, the channeling of sexual energy, and changes in the family and the position of women—for Weber to have excluded an analysis of those aspects of the Protestant ethic. His conception of the world as one of "warring gods" (values) was exemplified in his discussion of sexuality and religion, which in turn reflected the warring demons within himself. He attempted to manage his intellectual and personal conflicts by compartmentalizing them.

Weber's final position on the "woman question" appeared in his *General Economic History,* which exhibited a less personal tone than "Religious Rejections" but was not without polemical overtones (although Weber believed vehemently that a professor must not use the podium of the classroom as a soapbox).[139] This work was compiled by editors from Weber's lecture notes and from notes taken by students during a course given in the winter semester 1919–20 at Munich. I think Weber's arguments can best be read as sophisticated critiques of nineteenth-century evolutionary theory—especially its Marxist versions—which posited a stage of matriarchy. Following is a summary of the general points in part one, "Household, Clan, Village and Manor (Agrarian Organization)," bearing on the status of women.[140] In chapter 1, "The Agricultural Organization and the Problems of Agrarian Communism," Weber observed that among some southern European groups (Croatian) and eastern European groups (Slavic), an economically communistic household was under male leadership (*GEH*, 11–12). Further, he gave the example of the Iroquois, possibly in argument against Lewis Henry Morgan's *Ancient Society* in which the Iroquois were presented as a matriarchal tribe, among whom a head woman supervised women in the long house and men were warriors, hunters, housebuilders, and cattle herders. Cattle herding had the status of an "exalted occupation because taming required strength and skill," esteem for which later became conventional (*GEH*, 25).

In his discussion of "Property Systems and Social Groups," chapter 2, Weber distinguished two bases of appropriation:

> Either the physical means of labor, especially the soil, are treated as implements, in which case they frequently appertain to the woman and her kindred; or, the land is treated as "spear land," territory which has been conquered and is protected by the man; in this case it belongs to an agnatic clan or

some other masculine group. In any case purely economic considerations do not uniquely determine the form of primitive appropriation and division of labor, but military, religious, and magical motives also enter. (*GEH*, 26)

This passage (like Weber's famous trichotomization of inequality—class, status, and party) illustrated his loosening up of the Marxian approach to the issues of women's place and power or lack thereof in societies.

Household structures are universally consumption groups but are anthropologically diverse in masculine and feminine modes of inheritance, Weber wrote. Clans may assert property rights over and against the household, including, commonly, "joint proprietorship over women belonging to the clan, hence, a share in bride purchase money. The clan may be masculine or feminine in constitution" (*GEH*, 27). All of this led up to the central concern in Weber's lectures, a critique of the socialistic version of the theory of mother-right found in the works of Bebel, Engels, and Heinrich Cunow. In this context Weber cited his wife's 1907 book on the subject, *Ehefrau und Mutter in der Rechtsentwicklung*, as "indicating the present state of knowledge, and in general free from bias" (*GEH*, 372n. 2). After a summary of his reading of the mother-right literature, Weber presented an assessment of the theory: "Although it is untenable in detail it forms, taken as a whole, a valuable contribution to the solution of the problem. Here again is the old truth exemplified that an ingenious error is more fruitful than stupid accuracy" (*GEH*, 28–30). Weber criticized the notion that prostitution is a consequence, an obverse, of monogamy, which in turn is connected with the origin of private property. Prophets and priests opposed orgies, such as those associated with fertility rites, and police suppressed them, because "the state feared the rise of revolutionary movements of the lower classes out of the emotional excitement connected with orgiastic phenomena" (*GEH*, 32). Weber wrote that prostitution as an income-producing profession "is of immemorial age. There is no historical period and no stage of evolution in which it is not to be found" (*GEH*, 31). Usually an outcast occupation with the exception of sacerdotal prostitution, it survived as an illicit profession and was an officially recognized guild in Europe during the Middle Ages, despite the church's opposition. However, a serious outbreak of venereal diseases that occurred during the late-fifteenth-century campaign of Charles VIII against Naples provoked severe condemnation of prostitution, an attitude continued and reinforced by ascetic Protestantism, especially Calvinism (*GEH*, 33).

Weber maintained that "an analysis of sex relations outside of marriage must distinguish between prostitution and the sexual freedom of women. Sexual freedom for the man was always taken for granted, being first condemned by the three great monotheistic religions, and in fact not by Judaism until the Talmud." Weber inferred from the practice of "trial marriages" among Arabs at the time of Mohammed and in Egypt that originally women had "equal sexual freedom. . . . Girls of upper-class families were especially reluctant to submit to the harsh domestic confinement of the patriarchal marriage, but clung to their sexual liberty, remaining in their parental homes and entering into contracts with men to whatever extent they pleased." There was also the "possibility" of the sexual exploitation of women, for example, in customs of "sex hospitality" and the exchange of sexual favors for provisions. In passing, Weber mentioned that the legally recognized institution of concubinage permitted sexual relationships across class barriers, as for senators during the time of the Roman Empire (*GEH*, 33–34).

In his discussion of the different forms of marriage, again Weber made evident his central purpose: "Further investigation of the socialistic theory of mother-right shows that none of the stages of sexual life which it asserts can be shown to exist as steps in a general evolutionary sequence. Where they are met with, it is always under quite special circumstances." For example, an alleged stage of "primitive promiscuity" was in reality associated only with orgiastic cultural phenomena. A point for socialism: mother-right existed in cases where the father was not known (*GEH*, 34).

Endogamy, Weber wrote, was found in the marriages of brothers and sisters in aristocracies; citing the Ptolemys as an example, he described endogamy as "an aristocratic institution for maintaining the purity of royal blood." In other cases, male clan members were preferred as husbands in order to prevent dissipation of wealth; after "social stratification has appeared . . . daughters must be reserved for the members of a particular political or economic group," as in Greek democracy, Weber wrote. Hypergamy characterized India's caste system: "While the man of a higher caste can enter into sex relations or marry below his level at will, this is forbidden to the woman." Thus, lower-caste women might be sold for money, while higher-caste women had marriage services purchased for them, through arrangements made in their childhoods. Weber found that "exogamy with regard to the household has obtained everywhere and always, with few exceptions"; he speculated that "it arises from the effort to forestall jealousy of the men within the household" and—in a truly pre-Freudian remark—"out of the recognition that growing up together does not permit a strong development of the sexual impulse." Noting the ambiguities where gender is thicker than blood but not material interests, Weber wrote, "Marriage by capture is always regarded as illegal by the kindred affected, justifying blood revenge or exaction of head money, but at the same time is also treated as a knightly adventure." The kinds of kinship arrangements other than patriarchal marriage were distinguished by the reckoning of the lineage of children through the mother or her clan. Weber pointed out that patriarchal marriage developed out of a condition in which all children of a father have equal standing regardless of the legal status of their mother and in which "both children and women are subject to his unrestrained authority" (*GEH*, 35–37).

In a discussion of "the evolution of the family as conditioned by economic and non-economic factors," Weber argued, contrary to the conventional wisdom of the time, that the "primitive condition" of agriculture was nomadic and usually associated with hunting. Technologically, it was "hoe-culture," that is, "husbandry without domestic animals." Later, the plow drawn by beasts of burden represented "the transition to agriculture in our sense" (*GEH*, 37–38). This hypothesis provides a context for understanding some of Weber's views on the status of women:

> Cutting across these distinctions in the mode of husbandry [individual, family, and socialized] is the form of the division of labor between the sexes. Originally, the tilling of the soil and the harvesting fell mainly to the woman. Only when heavy labor, with the plow instead of the hoe, was required, the man had to participate. In the house work proper, in which textiles take the leading place, the woman alone was involved. Man's work included also hunting, tending domestic animals as far as cattle were concerned—while the small animals were again the woman's province—wood and metal working, and finally and before all, war. The woman was a continuous worker, the man an occasional one; only very gradually, with the increasing difficulty and intensity of work, was he led on to continuous labor.

Out of the interaction of these conditions arise two types of communalization, on the one hand that of house and field work, and on the other that of hunting and fighting. The first centers around the woman and on the basis of it she often occupies a dominant social position; not infrequently she was in complete control. The women's house was originally the workhouse, while the socialization of hunting and fighting gave rise to the men's society. But whether the head of the household was a man or, as among the Indians, a woman, there was always a traditional bondage and a corresponding patriarchal position within the house. In contrast, the socialization of hunting and fighting was carried out under the leadership based on merit or charism of a chieftain chosen for this purpose. Not his kinship connections but his warlike and other personal qualities are decisive; he is the freely chosen leader with a freely chosen following. (*GEH*, 38–39)

Here again Weber described the men's house, a kind of clubhouse in which men lived apart from their families. In the house, the men made weapons; carried out magical rituals, such as rites of passage; and planned hunting and war activities—including the capture of wives. Weber noted that "women are forbidden to enter the men's house, in order to guard its character of secrecy" (*GEH*, 39–40). The custom of men's houses deteriorated due to innovations in military technology, especially horse and chariot fighting; after those developments, men lived with their families, ties of blood became more significant, and special rights to the land were given to individual warriors (*GEH*, 40–41). Weber considered the custom significant because of its influence on the structure of sex roles and power in tribal societies:

In the institution of the man's house is apparently to be sought the origin of totemism, resting on animistic grounds, although later it becomes independent of the latter. . . . Those belonging to a totem form a culture union, a peace group, whose members must not fight among themselves. They practice exogamy, marriage between members of the totem being considered incestuous and expiated by terrible punishment. Thus one totem stands over against others as a marriage group. In this regard the totemic group is a ritualistic conception which often cuts through household and political groupings. Although the individual father lives in domestic communion with his wife and children, maternal succession is rather generally the rule, the children belonging to the mother's clan and being ceremonially alien to the father. This is the factual basis of the so-called matriarchate which is thus, along with totemism, a survival from the period of the men's house. Where totemism is absent we find a patriarchate, or paternal dominance with paternal inheritance. (*GEH*, 41)

In Weber's formulation, "The struggle of the growing tendency toward the patriarchate with an older maternal system" was settled in several ways, in terms of economic or military principles of land tenure (*GEH*, 41–42). If a woman tilled the land, it was inherited by the maternal uncle of her children (the avunculate). If land was militarized ("spear land"), the children were reckoned in the lineage of the father; the land was controlled by the paternal clan, and the woman had no right to the land. (Associated with this historical alternative is the levirate.) Concerning the relationship of property and women, Weber wrote:

The other possibility was that individual property relations were decided between the patriarchate and a maternal organization. Between economic equals the older form of marriage was apparently exchange of wives; especially as between households, youths exchanged their sisters. With differentiation in economic status, the woman is regarded as labor power and is bought as an object of value, as a work animal. The men who cannot buy a wife serve for her or live permanently in her house. Marriage by purchase and marriage through service, the one with patriarchal law and the other with maternal, may exist side by side and even in the same household; hence, neither is a universal institution. The woman always remains under the authority of a man, either in her own house community or in that of the man who has bought her. The marriage by purchase, like marriage through service, may be either polyandrous or polygamous. While the well-to-do buy wives at will, the propertyless, especially brothers, often club together for the purchase of a common wife. (*GEH*, 42)

Up to this point, Weber appears to have been offering a refinement of Engels's theory of the relationship of private property and the family. But he went on to conjecture that these relations implied "group marriage," which he denied held the scientific status of "a general stage in the evolution of marriage" because he thought it probably occurred only sporadically, between totem groups whose collective exchange of women had magical significance. Reminiscent of Spencer, Weber emphasized, "The wife obtained by purchase is regularly subject to the absolute patriarchal authority of the man. This supreme power is a primitive fact. It was always present in principle, as a characteristic of primitive peoples" (*GEH*, 43).

In his discussion of "the evolution of the clan," meaning "blood kindred," Weber pointed to variations in the social structural conditions and the patterns of historical change. One of his observations shows how sexism is embedded in language and practice: a man who did not meet the tests for initiation into military clans (phratries) was called a "woman" and was not permitted to enjoy the political and economic privileges of clan membership. The main focus of Weber's discussion was the agnatic clan, which was in effect "a privilege of property owners." In the Occident, he wrote, the agnatic clan "has completely disappeared, and in the Orient been just as completely maintained." Two factors favoring dissolution of the agnatic clan in the West were religious prophecy and political bureaucracy. Weber quoted Christ: "If any man come to me and hate not his father, and mother, and wife, and children, and brethren and sisters—he cannot be my disciple" (Luke 14:26). He noted also that during the medieval period in Europe the church tried to abolish clan inheritance so that it could keep property willed to the clan. The other force in antiquity that opposed the clan, he wrote, was "the political bureaucracy," especially under the New Empire in Egypt: "In consequence, there is equality between man and woman and sexual freedom of contract; children receive as a rule the name of their mother." In China, however, the state did not have sufficient power to break the hold of the clan (*GEH*, 43–46).

Emphasis on the independent effects of factors other than economic continued to be a theme in Weber's analysis of the household. Weber opened his discussion of the evolution of the household community with the argument that its primitive condition "is not necessarily a pure communism" in regard to property but only in regard to consumption. As a result, according to Weber, "There is frequently a considerable development of proprietorship, even over the children, and further especially over iron tools, and textile products. There is also a special right of inheritance of the woman from the woman and of the man from the man. Again we may find the absolute *patria potestas* as the normal condition, or it may be weakened by other organizations as for example the totemic group or the maternal clan" (*GEH*, 46–47). Where centralization of work for economic reasons occurred, the "small family" developed into an expanded household in a free community. Where political-military motives prevailed, it became part of a manorial household of the landed nobility:

> The typical form of the seigniorial development is the patriarchate. Its distinguishing characteristics are the vesting of property rights exclusively in an individual, the head of the household, from whom no one has a right to demand an accounting, and further the despotic position inherited and held for life by the patriarch. This despotism extends over wife, children, slaves, stock, and implements, the *familia pecuniaque* of the Roman Law, which shows this type in its classical perfection. This *dominium* is absolute and it is a deviation from principle to speak in connection with the woman of *manus* or in connection with the children of *potestas*. The power of the house father extends with only ritualistic limitations to the execution, or sale of the wife, and to the sale of the children or to leasing them out to labor. According to Babylonian, Roman, and ancient German law, the father can adopt other children in addition to his own and into full equality with them. There is no distinction between female slave and wife or between wife and concubine, or between acknowledged children and slaves. The former are called *liberi* only because of the one distinction between them and slaves, that they have a chance sometime to become heads of families themselves. In short, the system is that of a pure agnatic clan. It is found in connection with pastoral economy, also in cases where a knighthood fighting as individuals forms the military class, or finally, in connection with ancestor worship. . . . Ancestor worship involves . . . a union of worship of the dead with clan membership; on this union rested in China and Rome, for example, the invulnerable position of the paternal *dominium*. (*GEH*, 47–48)

Contrary to Engels's position, Weber argued that the introduction of class endogamy weakened the patriarchal extended house-

hold and improved the condition of some women—those who were
wives (*GEH*, 48). Parents in upper-class clans married their daughters to men in clans of the same class only, he wrote. When wives
ceased to be bought for their labor power, the dowry appeared to
ensure that when daughters of the upper class married they could
continue to live in the style to which they were accustomed.

> The operation of the class principle gave rise to the distinc-
> tion between legitimate, monogamous marriage, and the pa-
> triarchal *potestas*. Marriage with dowry became the normal
> marriage, the woman's clan stipulating that she was to be the
> head wife and that only her children could succeed as heirs. It
> is not true, as the socialistic theory has assumed, that the in-
> terests of the man in legitimate heirs for his property opened
> the way to the development of marriage. The man's desire for
> heirs could have been secured in numerous ways. It was the
> interest of the woman in having assured to her children the
> property of the man that was decisive. This development,
> however, by no means involved by absolute necessity, monog-
> amous marriage. In general, partial polygamy persisted; in
> addition to a head wife secondary wives were kept, whose
> children possessed limited rights of inheritance or none at all.
> (*GEH*, 49)

Weber observed that the Greek attitude toward monogamy was
one of flexibility, while "Romans maintained [monogamy] rigorously." Christians did not rigorously practice monogamy "until the
time of the Carolingians." In Rome, the female clan was able to protect "the interests of the woman" in that it "carried through complete economic and personal emancipation of the woman from the
man, in establishing the so-called free marriage, which could be
terminated at will by either party, and which gave the woman complete control over her own property, although she lost all right over
the children if the marriage was dissolved" (*GEH*, 49–50). Weber
added that even the Emperor Justinian was unable to get rid of this
institution.

In conclusion, it may be argued that Weber did not refute a
Marxist approach to the question of women's rights but only improved upon the theory of mother-right by specifying its historical-
structural conditions. In addition, as Gerth and Mills have interpreted his work, Weber augmented historical materialism with a

political and military materialism and a notion of the ideal interests of world religions, specifically of prophets and theologians.[141] The strength of Weber's approach to the "woman question," linked as it is with sexuality and the family, was that he placed the question in the historical and comparative context of economy and society. What he omitted was an analysis—or even the conception of the possibility—of the historical conditions surrounding women's challenges to patriarchal authority.

Although Weber believed that scholarly work must be value free, he maintained that "an *attitude of moral indifference* has no connection with *scientific* 'objectivity.'"[142] However, he also felt that passionate concerns over values threatened objective evaluation of evidence by social scientists. For Weber, there was no mechanical solution to this tension (such as simply to follow the rules of the scientific method); only an effort of will on the part of the scholar would do.[143] In a discussion of masculine and feminine imagery in Weber's work, Mitzman considers Weber's concept of charisma to be infused with "a number of rather archaic feminine characteristics":

> In point of fact, his extended celebration of charisma as an "emotional life force" antagonistic to the dreary construction of the "iron cage" coincided with his coming to terms with his own emotional life-force: his erotic faculties. Through his surrender to "animality" Weber was at last able to obtain from a woman he loved the grace of sexual release. What charisma represented then, in Weber as in German culture, was the resurrection of the long-suppressed deities of the libido, of femininity, Eros, and community, of blind passion as well as compassion. The gift of grace was the grace that comes from accepting, rather than mutilating, one's nature.[144]

Despite his rejection of Gross's article in 1907, from 1910 to 1920 Weber's work was "infused" with Gross's values, according to Mitzman, and in his life he engaged in a "desperate effort" to achieve "harmony between libidinal drives and rational ethics which he had earlier seen as weakness."[145] Weber may have succeeded in arguing for a picture of the world as one of conflicting values in which science offered no basis for choice, but on the personal level his attempt to deal with the conflict of the demons within himself by compartmentalizing them resulted in failure—in the form of psychic collapse. Weber's scholarly interests shifted in his last decade, associated, as he would have put it, with a shift in value-emphasis and his passionate concerns.

Green has judged that "Weber's life was, in one important respect, hypocritical. His love story is a Victorian drama of renunciation and of involuntary, ethically noble hypocrisy." In contrast, D. H. Lawrence's hypocrisy was more of the twentieth century, in Green's description, "the erotic movement hypocrisy, of sexual heroics in a drama of fulfillment." Lawrence "got himself into the position of having to claim more sexual prowess, more masculine desire, than he had, whereas Max Weber had to claim the opposite." (Gross was "guilty of neither" but was rejected by the Von Richthofen sisters because he was so at variance with the world as it was or could be.)[146] To avoid misunderstanding, Karl Marx's remark on humor might be modified to say that hypocrisy is not in persons but in circumstances.

Weber can at best be classified as a liberal feminist, in the sense given the term by his contemporaries; "patriarchal romantic" might be an equally accurate characterization. Those scholars, male and female, who try to portray Weber's feminism as more than this seem to me to commit the error of making Weber seem larger than life and to misread the evidence and context of his biography.[147] Weber's intellectual style was "masculine"—which is not to deny his sociological and personal contributions to feminist scholarship. However, it was left to Georg Simmel, Weber's friend and respected colleague, to point out the male bias built into so-called objective culture and reason and logic, a bias Weber himself did not publicly take into account.

Georg Simmel
Male Culture and the Social Psychology of Sex Roles

German sociology as an independent academic discipline was reputed to be the creation of Georg Simmel (1858–1918). Nevertheless, the variety of fields to which Simmel made contributions (philosophy, aesthetics, psychology, as well as sociology) and his intellectual style as a master of the essay—full of brilliant insights on apparently unrelated, esoteric, and taken-for-granted matters but without the scholarly apparatus to identify his intellectual parentage—all make it difficult to place him neatly in the sociological tradition.[148] However, in Lewis Coser's words, he maintained a "commanding position" in the German intellectual world of his time.

Currently, there is a revival of interest in his work. It is curious, as Coser has pointed out, that "his seminal insights into the social position of women have been totally neglected until recently."[149]

Before turning to a presentation of Simmel's contributions to analysis of the "woman question," some relevant facts about his personal and public lives should be considered. Simmel's wife, Gertrud, was prominent in Weber's Heidelberg circle. Coser wrote: "In the Berlin years Simmel and his wife Gertrud, whom he had married in 1890, lived a comfortable and fairly sheltered bourgeois life. His wife was a philosopher in her own right who, using the pseudonym Marie-Luise Enckendorf, published on such diverse topics as the philosophy of religion and of sexuality; she made his home a place for cultivated gatherings where the sociability about which Simmel wrote so perceptively found a perfect setting."[150] In that salon-like setting, one could meet not only some of the most important artists and academics of the period but also important figures in the feminist and erotic movements, such as Elly Heuss-Knapp and Lou Andreas-Salomé.

Berlin was one of the most important centers of feminist agitation and organization, both bourgeois and working-class. At the turn of the century, Berlin epitomized the culture of the modern metropolis. Simmel later reflected, "Perhaps I could have achieved something that was also valuable in another city; but this specific achievement, that I have in fact brought to fruition in these decades, is undoubtedly bound up with the Berlin milieu." As David Frisby has pointed out, Simmel's contemporaries saw as his special competence his ability to capture and analyze the distinctiveness of the social experience of modern life.[151] I will argue that he was equally attuned to the special quality of female experience in a male-dominated culture and to the female side as well as the male side of social relations and interactions between the sexes.

Between 1891 and 1894 Simmel was the only academic social scientist who wrote (anonymously) for "the official Socialist press," Weber recalled in 1905. In the 1890s, Simmel was a part of what Paul Honigsheim had called "the unofficial Berlin culture" of anti-Bismarckian socialists and the liberal left. Simmel's work was also influenced by the emerging antimodernism and cultural and intellectual ferment in Europe around the turn of the century. Young, previously modernist intellectuals devoted their energies to apolitical aesthetic and philosophical concerns. After 1900, Simmel associated himself with "the circle of modernity-hating poet-seers around

Stefan George." As a result of his participation in the George circle, according to Arthur Mitzman, "Simmel developed a prolonged extramarital intimacy with Gertrude Kantorowicz, the only woman whose poetry George published in his journal, and had an illegitimate child by her." [152]

Although, as Coser has stated, Simmel was a "stranger in the academy" (at Strasbourg he was not given the title of associate professor until he was forty-three, and the title of professor at fifty-six, only four years before his death), his intellectual work was considered brilliant by his most important German contemporaries—Max Weber, Ferdinand Tönnies, and Leopold von Weise—and elicited favorable responses in France and in the United States. [153] Weber's critique of the antisexual, mechanistic culture of ascetic rationalism was indebted to Simmel's notion of the tragedy of modern culture, that individuals become prisoners of the very cultural forms they have created to express themselves. [154] Simmel's influence was even greater in the twenties. His insights into the situation of women may in part be accounted for by his marginality (he was at once inside and outside of German culture), by his wife's influence on him, and by the erotic and feminist movements, liberal and socialist, of his times. Simmel's writings that touch on women's rights extend from the beginning of the 1890s to the year of his death, including an 1899 article on the admission of women to the University of Berlin. (He was one of the first German professors to allow women to audit his courses, well before 1908 when they were allowed entrance to Prussian universities.) [155] Simmel's works are presented here not in chronological order but by topic.

Simmel was concerned with the subjection of women, and he emphasized the ways in which a male-dominated culture hinders autonomy in female identity and prevents women from contributing to the common culture. [156] He penetratingly observed that the standards by which achievements are measured "are formally generically human, but are in fact masculine in terms of their actual historical formation" ("SNC," 872). The human species, he wrote, historically operates with the equation "objective = male." As in the case of master/slave relations, as a consequence of their position of power men appear to "think in terms of purely factual categories without their sense of maleness coming into play; by contrast it seems as if women never lose the sense, be it clearly felt or only subjacent, that they are in fact women" ("SNC," 872).

In an analysis reminiscent of that of Marx and Engels about the ruling ideas of any epoch, Simmel pointed out that male domination was naively perceived by men to be rooted in the objective and eternal moral order of things; for example, the will of the paterfamilias was not conceived as arbitrary power but as the exercise of authority in the suprapersonal interest of the family as a whole. Simmel observed that, as a consequence, "the psychological superiority granted male behavior through the domination of man over woman, is transformed into a logical superiority; this state of affairs is given normative significance and claims a trans-sexual validity as the yardstick of truth and justice," and, as a consequence, Coser summarized, Simmel recognized that "women are judged in terms of criteria that were created for the male sex" ("SNC," 872–73).

The roles to which women were restricted provided no basis for female autonomy, and the male criteria by which they were judged prevented an independent assessment of a woman's moral worth, Simmel wrote. Given the division of labor implicit in sex roles, women were seen only in relationship to men. Not only were they subjected to male criteria of value, but they were also denied by their social position the opportunity to live up to the performances required by those criteria. By themselves women were assumed to be "nothing" because their roles did not allow them to be themselves either, that is to say, to act out specifically female qualities. From a Kantian perspective, women in male culture were treated and valued solely as means, and "women tend to evaluate themselves in these terms: as means for the man, for the home, for the child." This completed the circle: women lived in a world "that is full of 'otherness.'" Simmel concluded, "The fact that women are existentially placed in a natural and historical world that is governed by a dualism of expectations is at the source of the typical tragedy of femininity" ("SNC," 873–74).

There was, as Coser pointed out, another side to Simmel's views of feminine nature: he observed that apart from all the "contempt and mistreatment of women, one notices in all cultures" that women were believed to have special powers, for example, as witches. Simmel himself held such a view. He stated that women "are indeed closer to the dark primitive forces of nature, . . . their most essential and personal characteristics are more strongly rooted in the most natural, most universal, most biologically important functions. . . . This unity of womankind, in which there is less than in men a distinction between universal and individual elements, must be reflected in the greater homogeneity of each woman's nature" ("SNC," 874). Simmel's analysis in this instance focused not on male strength and brutality but on male culture and female nature.

There are additional materials in Simmel's works (not discussed by Coser) that consider variations in male-female relations. The question of "the nature of woman" occurred again in the context of a 1908 discussion of "adornment." Simmel observed that historically women became owners of private property later than men did; and usually women's property consisted of personal adornments—in contrast to men's ownership of weapons.[157] He inferred that

> this reveals his active and more aggressive nature: the male enlarges his personality sphere without waiting for the will of others. In the case of the more passive female nature, this result—although formally the same in spite of all external differences—depends more on the others' good will. (SGS, 344)

Thus, women extended their personalities "under primitive conditions" and expressed their egos by possessing adornments "which can intensify the value and significance of [their] wearer only through the recognition that flows back to her from these others" (SGS, 344). In his discussion of the superpersonal or social-cultural character of marriage, Simmel referred to marriage as a "close union" formed of "two fundamentally different beings, man and woman" (SGS, 129). In the context of a 1902 discussion of dyadic relationships, he stated, "Now women are the less individualized sex; variation of individual women from the general class type is less great than is true, in general, of men. This explains the very widespread opinion that, ordinarily, women are less susceptible to friendship than men" (since friendship is based on individuality). He observed, however, that "the modern, highly differentiated woman shows a strikingly increased capacity for friendship and an inclination toward it, both with men and with women" (SGS, 138). Thus Simmel recognized the historical variability of personality in women.

Simmel used his discussions of the relations of the sexes, especially in marriage, to illustrate his broader sociological concepts—for example, the dialectics of sociation and individuation. Of the socially and legally coercive aspects of marriage, he noted in 1906 that while they often preserved bad marriages, making "the common life utterly unbearable," they also preserved good ones from fits of anger and separation which "would impoverish or destroy [people's] lives irreparably" (SGS, 299). This socially regulated sub-ordination of individuals was the advantage Simmel believed mar-riage to have over free love—given the weaknesses of human na-ture. The generality and uniformity of the ideal form of marriage in his day, he wrote, "certainly leaves more room for individual artic-ulations than do a larger number of socially pre-determined forms" (SGS, 131). Contemporary marriage, he wrote, ideally differed from marriage in other cultures and from those in previous civiliza-tions in that its basis was erotic, not social and economic. On the other hand, he found that the Greek conception of marriage as stated by Demosthenes—namely, providing men with legitimate children, clean houses, and the sexual license they found in the double standard—could also be observed "of actual contemporary marriages." The fourth Greek component, "the hetaerae [compan-ion] for pleasure," Simmel wrote, had been recently added. In pre-vious forms of marriage it was hoped that the feelings of love would follow the marriage arrangement; in the modern form it was hoped that the feelings would last (SGS, 327–28).

Simmel was at his best in his descriptions of the subtle interac-tions of men and women in love and marriage. The very nature of the intimacy of modern marriage, he wrote, was at the core of its weaknesses and traps. Spouses shared the trivial, indifferent, and unpleasant intimacies of everyday life; some inevitably defined their relationships in terms of these intimacies, he said, which "leads them to consider what they share with others and what is perhaps the most important part of their personalities—objective, intellectual, generally interesting, generous features—as lying out-side the marital relation; and thus they gradually eliminate it from their marriage" (SGS, 127). He suggested, about the tendency to give of oneself totally in the first stages of love, that "this abandon probably threatens the future of the relationship seriously." Psycho-logical exhaustion sets in: "It is highly probable that many marriages founder on this lack of reciprocal discretion—discretion both in taking and giving. They lapse into a trivial habituation without charm, into a matter-of-factness which has no longer any room for surprises." To remedy this, each participant, "even in the most in-timate relation that comprises the total individual, respects his [mate's] inner private property, and allows the right to question to be limited by the right to secrecy" (SGS, 328–29).

Finally, on equal rights in marriage, Simmel wrote:

Probably, what is called the "equal rights" of man and wife in marriage—as a fact or as a pious wish—is actually to a large extent . . . an alternating superordination and subordination. At least, this alternation would result in a more organic relationship than would mechanical equality in the literal sense of the term, especially if one recalls the thousand subtle relations of daily life which cannot be cast in the form of principles. The alternation also would make sure that momentary superordination does not appear as brute command. (SGS, 288)

Whether one takes Simmel's position as self-serving to males is a matter of judgment. Nevertheless, one may infer from this discussion that romantic love gave women power they did not have earlier. The influence of the feminist movement in Germany was clearly evident in Simmel's writings.

Simmel's style of sociological work was to illustrate abstract concepts and properties of culture and society by concrete examples and to try to understand them through analogies. For example, in a 1908 discussion of conflict,[158] he explained the "disproportionate violence" of conflicts in relationships with those closest to us, in marriage and family life, by the fact that they involve us "*as whole persons*"; thus the "slightest antagonism" between persons who are in virtually total agreement takes on a significance it would not have with a stranger with whom we already differ on many points. In intimate relations, conflict often occurs, Simmel believed, as a phase prior to passionate love—"a step back before running as it were." He observed that "the inverse phenomenon shows the same form: the deepest hatred grows out of broken love" (*SISF*, 91–93).

To have to recognize that a deep love—and not only a sexual love—was an error, a failure of intuition [*Instinkt*], so compromises us before ourselves, so splits the security and unity of our self-conception, that we unavoidably make the object of this intolerable feeling pay for it. We cover our secret awareness of our own responsibility for it by hatred which makes it easy for us to pass all responsibility on to the other. (*SISF*, 93)

He also noted in this context the "untruthfulness" of "affectionate, moral, and loyal" behavior to one's spouse when "unconditional emotional devotion" was not there. In erotic relationships, "feelings are involved which are not accessible to the will but, like fate itself, exist or do not exist" (*SISF*, 93–94). Such comments seem to fit the Webers' and the Jaffes' marriages.

In 1908, Simmel appeared to accept that "the rise of masculine force" was responsible for the displacement of "the matriarchal family." The extended patriarchal family was then supplanted by "the more recent family" living in "an autonomous household" (*SISF*, 264), which, in contrast to earlier family groups, allowed for the development of individuality. The processes of individuation and of socialization were insightfully and dialectically formulated by Simmel. In more traditional societies, less differentiated individuals and relationships allowed "the individual male" to choose "almost any girl from the appropriate circle"; however, in the modern world "the circle of potential marriage partners" was "vastly expanded" due to breaking down of cultural barriers, and to social and geographic mobility. "But for all that," Simmel pointed out, "individual selection is far more stern, a fact and a right of wholly personal inclination. The conviction that out of all mankind, two and only two people are 'meant' for each other has now reached a stage of development that was still unheard of by the bourgeoisie of the eighteenth century." Thus, "individual freedom is freedom that is limited by individuality" (*SISF*, 269–70). In "Eros, Platonic and Modern" (published posthumously in 1921), Simmel returned to this theme, suggesting that, except for Platonic love, "perhaps the most neglected [by philosophers] of all the great vital issues has been love" (*SISF*, 235). For Plato, love arose by necessity from the perception of beauty, which involved the experience of bringing together the realm of ideas and the realm of earthly phenomena. But, as Simmel reminded us, "The object of Platonic love was not woman, but male youth." Plato's metaphysical conception of love made it "equivalent with the yearning for a purely suprasensual, only-intellectual [love]—precisely this conception must have the man appear as the appropriate object in love. . . . For the higher intellectual development was considered peculiar to the male." The bonds of Greek men were characterized by "their equality of being." The Greeks' notion of friendship presumed equality and was similar in some ways to "our idea of love." He summed up his discussion of Plato and the Greeks by saying: "The thought that friendship could encompass both masculine and feminine structures is remote from them." Since Plato's conception of love was supraindividual—individuality had "negative significance"—it followed that it was "slavish and foolish to bind one's feelings exclusively to a single beautiful person." Simmel contrasted Plato's thought with Goethe's confession that for every struggling and toiling man, a woman was "the only vessel into which he could pour his idealism." For Simmel, what separated the modern view of love from Plato's was that, in the modern view, individuality of beauty and the beauty of individuality formed a dialectical totality (*SISF*, 236–45). In addition, "the real goal of modern love is reciprocal love," and

> modern love is the first to recognize that there is something unattainable in the other: that the absoluteness of the individual self erects a wall between two human beings which even the most passionate willing of both cannot remove and that renders illusory any actual "possession" that would be anything more than the fact and consciousness of being loved back . . . a becoming rooted in oneself and an isolation within oneself which turns the wish to "possess" into a contradiction and a grasping into the void. (*SISF*, 245–46)

What Platonic doctrine missed, Simmel concluded, was "the irrational dimension which we feel in individuality as the ultimate element of Eros" (*SISF*, 247). However, one of its advantages is that in some ways Platonic love is not prey to unrequited love, the tragedy of modern love: to paraphrase the young Marx, if you love without evoking love in return—if through a living expression of yourself as loving person, you do not receive love from the object of your love—your love is impotent, a misfortune. In many ways, Otto Gross's erotic ideology and practice signaled a return to Platonism.

Simmel's view of women was subtle, multifaceted, ideologically contradictory, sometimes flawed. In a 1910 article entitled "Sociability," Simmel argued that not only are social games played "*in* a society" but that people also "actually 'play' 'society'" (*SISF*, 134). He continued, in a penetrating social-psychological description of flirtation:

> Further, in the sociology of the sexes, eroticism has elaborated a form of play: *coquetry*, which finds in sociability its lightest, most playful, and yet its widest realization. . . . The coquette brings her attractiveness to its climax by letting the man hang on the verge of getting what he wants without letting it become too serious for herself; her conduct swings be-

tween yes and no, without stopping at one or the other. . . .
the fundamental condition of sociability . . . appears only
when the man desires nothing more than this free moving
play, in which something definitely erotic lurks only as a remote symbol, and when he does not get his pleasure in these
gestures and preliminaries from erotic desire or fear of it. Coquetry . . . becomes a play of shadow pictures of these serious
matters. Where the latter enter or lurk, the whole process becomes a private affair of the two persons, played out on the
level of reality; under the sociological sign of sociability, however, in which the essential orientation of the person to the
fulness of life does not enter, coquetry is the teasing or even
ironic play with which eroticism has distilled the pure essence
of its interaction out from its substantive or individual content. As sociability plays at the forms of society, so coquetry
plays out the forms of eroticism. (*SISF*, 134–35)

One can infer the influences of the erotic movement and feminism in other papers by Simmel. In a long paper, "Fashion" (1904),
Simmel discussed the dialectics of fashion as consisting of equalization and individuation on one level and imitation and conspicuousness on the other. These explained "why it is that women, broadly
speaking, are its staunchest adherents" (*SISF*, 308). Simmel's contradictions became evident in the following warning:

Scientific discretion should caution us against forming judgments about woman "in the plural." At the same time it may
be said of woman in a general way, whether the statements be
justified in every case or not, that her psychological characteristic in so far as it differs from that of man, consists in a lack of
differentiation, in a greater similarity among the different
members of her sex, in a stricter adherence to the social average. Whether on the final heights of modern culture, the facts
of which have not yet furnished a contribution to the formation of this general conviction, there will be a change in the
relation between men and women, a change that may result in
a complete reversal of the above distinction, I do not care to
discuss, inasmuch as we are concerned here with more comprehensive historical averages. The relation and the weakness
of her social position, to which woman has been doomed dur-

ing the far greater portion of history, however, explains her strict regard for custom, for the generally accepted and approved forms of life, for all that is proper. (*SISF*, 308)

It was precisely this condition that made women more fashion-conscious than men, because "it seems as though fashion were the valve through which woman's craving for some measure of conspicuousness and individual prominence finds vent, when its satisfaction is denied her in other fields." Simmel presented some historical examples of fashion as an indicator of the degree of the emancipation of women. Women did not take part in "an unusually strong development of individuality" that took place in Germany between 1300 and 1500, he wrote; in that period, women adopted "the most extravagant and hypertrophic styles in dress." In contrast, during the same epoch, "the woman of the [Italian] Renaissance possessed opportunities of culture, of external activity, of personal differentiation such as were not offered her for many centuries thereafter. In the upper classes, especially, education and freedom of action were almost identical for both sexes." Therefore, he asserted, it was no surprise "that no particularly extravagant Italian female fashions should have come down to us from that period." Women of that time, he argued, were more like men—many-sided creatures—and thus felt no need to express their individuality through fashion (*SISF*, 309).

Fashion functioned as a compensation for women denied status based on a profession, Simmel concluded. "Therefore, the emancipated woman of the present, who seeks to imitate in the good as well as perhaps also in the bad sense the whole differentiation, personality and activity of the male sex, lays particular stress on her indifference to fashion" (*SISF*, 310). In the context of the relationship of fashion to the "natural," he provided the interesting example of Elizabeth Charlotte, who was related by marriage to Louis XIV: "Exceedingly masculine in her ways, [she] inspired the fashion at the French Court of women acting like men and being addressed as such, whereas the men conducted themselves like women" (*SISF*, 322). However, Simmel did not draw out the relationship of fashion and power at which his example hints.

Simmel's blind spots are as striking as his seminal insights. For example, in "Adventurer" (1911), he noted the discontinuous and dreamlike qualities of the adventure and how closely it is associated with the erotic in our linguistic convention (*SISF*, 188). Next he discussed the sex-role dimension:

A love affair contains in clear association the two elements which the form of the adventure characteristically conjoins, conquering force and unextortable concession, winning by one's own abilities and dependence on the luck which something incalculable outside ourselves bestows on us. A degree of balance between these forces, gained by virtue of his sense of their sharp differentiation, can, perhaps, be found only in the man. Perhaps for this reason, it is of compelling significance that as a rule, a love affair is an "adventure" only for men; for women it usually falls into other categories. In the novels of love, the activity of woman is typically permeated by the passivity which either nature or history has imparted to her character; on the other hand, her acceptance of happiness is at the same time a concession and a gift. (*SISF*, 195)

Of course, *Lady Chatterley's Lover* was written many years later (1928), but Simmel must certainly have known at least secondhand of the adventures of the women prominent in the erotic movement.

As Richard Evans has written, "One of the most distinctive features of the urban culture of the nineteenth century . . . was the existence of prostitution on a scale so widespread and so obvious as to cause considerable alarm to contemporaries."[159] In his neglected book, *Philosophy of Money* (expanded in 1907), Simmel took up this issue of concern to Victorian socialist and liberal feminists. He began his analysis by noting the equivalences of money and prostitution (sounding like the Marx of the Paris Manuscripts): "In prostitution the relation of the sexes is reduced to its generic content because it is perfectly unambiguous and limited to the sensual act. . . . the nature of money resembles the nature of prostitution. The indifference with which it lends itself to any use, the infidelity with which it leaves everyone, its lack of ties to anyone, its complete objectification that excludes any attachment and makes it suitable as a pure means—all this suggests a portentous analogy between it and prostitution." Writing from a Kantian point of view, he stated that the intimate historical relationship of the money economy and prostitution was understandable because prostitution violated the categorical imperative that every person should be treated as an end in herself or himself. He believed that this was true *"for both parties involved.* Of all human relationships, it is perhaps the most significant case of the mutual reduction of two persons to the status of mere means." However, he thought that women suffered more from prostitution than men because "the debasement of prostitution lies in the fact that the most personal possession of a woman, her area of greatest reserve, is considered equivalent to the most neutral value of all, one which is most remote from anything that is personal" (*SISF*, 121–22).

Simmel commented on sexism: "If men are inclined to lump all women together and to judge them collectively, surely one reason for this is that the feature which men—particularly the coarser sort of men—find particularly attractive in women is shared by the seamstress and the princess." Simmel himself commits this error by treating female sexuality as a possession of a woman rather than as a varying quality of persons. Men may view women as sex objects, but women, he wrote view the sexual act "as supremely personal, as involving the innermost self." Like Durkheim in *Suicide,* Simmel resorted to "nature" rather than to the social-cultural dominance of men in his explanation of why women view this universal act so subjectively: "This can be understood if one assumes that women in general are more deeply embedded in the species type than are men, who emerge from the species type more differentiated and individualized. . . . If this is indeed so, then perhaps there is some truth in the assumption that for a woman, this single, vital function, with its contribution of one part of her self, involves more fully and unreservedly her entire person than is true for the more differentiated man in a sexual situation" (*SISF*, 123–24). He then described the social consequences—differential sanctions by sex—of this assumption:

> Therefore a girl who has gone astray only once loses her reputation entirely, a woman's infidelity is more harshly judged than a man's (of whom it seems to be believed that an occasional purely sensual indulgence is compatible with loyalty to his wife in every spiritual and essential respect), and prostitutes become irredeemably déclassé; but the worst rake can still rise from the mire by virtue of other facets of his personality and no social status is closed to him. (*SISF*, 124)

Simmel's description of the double standard would do justice to Mary Wollstonecraft.

Simmel's analysis of money and prostitution had some interesting sidelights. Given the depersonalization that prostitution involves for the female prostitute, "the institution of the pimp and the alleged frequency of lesbianism among prostitutes become comprehensible, for in her contacts with men who are never involved as real and whole persons, the prostitute must feel a terrible loneliness and dissatisfaction which she seeks to diminish by relationships which involve at least some further aspects of the persons." Because he thought, incorrectly, that the woman, more than her customer, involved her whole self in prostitution, Simmel felt that "money is the most inappropriate and inadequate remuneration, whose offer and acceptance is the greatest possible suppression of the woman's personality." In general, Simmel overlooked the power relationships, the brutality, and the causal economic factors of prostitution, but he did provide a few cross-cultural comparisons that illustrated the power aspects of prostitution. Contrasting polyandry in India, which provided high-caste women with superior status, to prostitution in Europe, he correctly asserted that the key feature of prostitution was "not polyandry, but polygyny; . . . the advantage of the buyer over the seller means the polygynous features, which give the man a vast superiority, determine the character of prostitution." (In the case of the gigolo, the man is dependent—once again revealing the power of money.) Simmel pointed to "the striking fact that in many primitive cultures, prostitution is not considered humiliating, nor does it lead to outcast status"; in Asian antiquity and among the daughters of sovereigns in some African tribes, there was a different relationship between money and a woman's honor than obtained in Simmel's modern European culture. "Explorers report that among a great many savage tribes, women are remarkably similar to men physically and frequently also mentally," he wrote; women there lived in societies in which money was rare and individualized. Unlike women in tribal societies, modern cultivated women, although less individualized than men, nevertheless had a personal sexual honor that money, as a universal equivalent, could not match, he argued. The style and subtlety of Simmel's thought was revealed in his view that prostitution was an example of the imbalance in modern culture between "the service and the payment," or, on another level, individuality and money. When an equivalence existed between money and individuality, as in prostitution, it led to "a terrible suppression of personal dignity" (*SISF*, 124–26). Put in the language of Marx, a society in which individuals without property are forced to sell their lives for wages and thus become alienated and estranged from themselves in their most basic activity—producing a world—is one in which prostitution is general.[160]

Simmel characterized the historic war between the sexes as follows:

> Among the extremely complex elements that make up the over-all relation between men and women, there is a typical hostility which derives from two sources. As the physically weaker sex, women are always in danger of economic and personal exploitation and legal powerlessness; and as objects of the sensuous desire of men, they must always always hold themselves on the defensive against the other sex. This fight, which pervades the inner and personal history of mankind, has rarely led to the direct cooperation of women against men.[161]

This passage occurs in the context of Simmel's discussion of rigidity and elasticity of groups and the role of custom in conditions of conflict. Women more than men adhere to custom, "the super-personal form which serves as a protection," because of the threats men pose. Custom equalizes the weak and the strong and may, according to Simmel, even favor the weak (as in chivalry). It is, therefore, in the interest of women to defend custom, given "the creeping conflict" with the stronger and more aggressive sex. Men are aware of this "sex-linked solidarity" of women in their commitment to the complete and detailed upholding of custom. Interestingly, Simmel said, "The contrast between the sexes fully has the character of a *party* contrast" (*CW*, 95). He followed out this last line of thought by observing that because custom is the common weapon in their defense against men, women do not tolerate breach of custom by other women: "Their party, in principle, knows no compromise but only absolute acceptance of the individual woman into the ideal totality of 'decent woman' or her equally absolute exclusion from it" (*CW*, 96). Such unity is imposed and required by the common enemy. Simmel has offered at least a partial explanation of the reactionary backlash by some antifeminist women against women's liberation. Women who are excluded from their sex's "party" as a consequence of violating custom also face sanctions for trying to participate in the world of men, especially if they play by the rules of that world. Women who do not "know their place" in a male-dominated world face double jeopardy.

In "The Web of Group-Affiliations" (published posthumously in 1922), under the heading "The Significance of Concepts in the Formation of Groups," Simmel provided examples of social solidarity in groups of workers and in groups of employers. He noted the emergence of women as "a new social group" out of a somewhat abstract group or, better, aggregate, based on the separate affiliations of individual women. He observed that women "now stand at the 'crossroads' between this new affiliation and the old ties." In short, his concern was with "the social development of the concept of 'woman' in recent times" (*CW*, 179–80).

He took a line of reasoning reminiscent of Marx's analysis of the French peasantry in 1848, in which Marx stated that peasantry constituted a class *in* itself in that they lived in identical conditions different from other classes, but did not constitute a class *for* itself because they lacked the consciousness of their condition as a common one (*The Eighteenth Brumaire of Louis Bonaparte*).

> The most general of her qualities, the fact that she was a woman and as such served the functions proper to her sex, caused her to be classified with all other women under one general concept. It was exactly this circumstance which removed her from the processes of group-formation in their strict sense, as well as from all actual solidarity with other women. Because of her peculiar functions she was relegated to activities within the limits of her home, confined to devote herself to a single individual, and prevented from transcending the group-relations established by marriage, family, social life, and perhaps charity and religion. The parallelism in the way of life and the activities of women is of such a nature as to effectively prevent the development of associations on the basis of this equality. (*CW*, 180)

Simmel asserted that "in very primitive ethnological conditions," however, "women appear to be less dissociated and act on occasion as a unified party in opposition to the men." He hypothesized that under the conditions of tribal life, the family is less differentiated from other aspects of life than it is in modern societies, and, there-

fore, women do not lose connection with "the general feminine interests" (*CW*, 180–81).

Simmel's characterization of the changes in the position of
women in his time is worth quoting at length:

> In our time it is sociologically very characteristic that this net-
> work of obligations has become less stringent and the problem
> of the emancipation of women has arisen. This problem has
> become a common concern of women as a group which has led
> to all sorts of actions, changes of conditions, and to the forma-
> tion of groups. Isolation of women from one another, caused
> by the integration of each into an entirely individual sphere,
> was based upon the complete differentiation of women from
> men. As a result of our culture, man appears on the whole to
> be the higher type in terms of the training of the intellect and
> the development of activity, in terms of self-assertion and the
> ability to relate to the environment. Even apart from ques-
> tions of ranking, the two sexes appear to be so essentially dif-
> ferent, that they can only be destined to complement one an-
> other. The meaning of feminine existence lies exclusively in
> what the man cannot be or do, or does not want to be or do.
> Consequently, this meaning of the life of women does not re-
> fer to a relation on equal, but on unequal, terms, and it is in
> this relation that women are almost completely absorbed.
> (*CW*, 181)

He observed, as Tocqueville did, the conflicts engendered by the
processes of democratization:

> In recent years, women have placed themselves in direct op-
> position to men in aiming at equalization . . . and occasionally
> they have succeeded, in such matters as personal position and
> economic independence, intellectual attainment and con-
> sciousness of self, in their freedom in society, and in their role
> in public life. A differentiation from men along party-lines,
> which emphasizes the solidarity of interests among women
> becomes noticeable as soon as their basic dissimilarity as over
> against men decreases with regard to their ways of life, their
> interest-orientation, and in terms of the law. These party-
> alignments [of women against men] are both cause and conse-
> quence of this development. (*CW*, 181)

More concretely, Simmel observed, on the way to bringing his analysis full circle:

> Very often it is in those comic figures of the emancipation, in those women whose ambition it is to be entirely masculine in their personality and their appearance, that we find the most passionate antagonism against men. This pattern is easily understood. The independence of women will develop to the same extent that their position, their value, and their qualities become equal to those of men, to whom women had stood either in a relation of inferiority or, at any rate, of dissimilarity and, consequently, in a relation of dependence. It is apparent that this partial freedom makes those qualities more conspicuous and effective which women have in common with men, and which had to be suppressed previously in a relationship which confined the woman to a subordinate and complementary role. This is, then, an extraordinarily clear-cut case of group-formation on a higher level, which is based on the fact that members are brought together by a general concept. Previously, each of the members had been confined to a single group; now the new group emancipates them from this confining relationship. (CW, 182)

That Simmel had not forgotten his left-wing past is evident in his statements about the effects of industrial capitalism on women of different classes: "The movement for the emancipation of women goes in one direction with regard to working-class, and in an opposite direction with regard to middle-class women." He explained:

> The development of industry has given economic and social freedom to the proletarian woman—no matter how scanty her individual freedom may be. The girl works in a factory at an age at which she would still require the protected atmosphere of the parental home. The married woman works away from home, and this forces her to neglect her duties toward home, husband, and children. In this case, the woman is in fact released from this all-embracing tie which had been tantamount to her total subordination to the man, or to a complete separation of activities between them. This sociological fact is indeed undesirable and pernicious. But that does not change it, nor is it changed by the desire of the proletarian woman

to have that "freedom" limited, and to have the possibility of again devoting herself to a greater extent to her family as a wife and mother. The same economic development has also affected women of the middle-class by separating from the home a great many domestic activities, both service and productive activities. Consequently, a very large number of women have been deprived of an adequate outlet for their energy, while they remain restricted in the main to the tasks of the home. These women long to have the freedom to engage in economic or other activities; in an emotional sense they feel just as removed from the special sphere of the home as the proletarian woman is externally. . . . One class of women wants to return to the home, the other wants to escape it. These discrepancies are, nevertheless, compatible with interests which all women have in common: the rights of women with regard to marital laws, property laws, custody of children, etc., are of equal concern to both classes. (CW, 182–83)

Simmel summarized his discussion of group formation by women, noting the effects of women's release from restriction to the home:

The general concept [of women] has become the guiding purpose of a cohesive group which is manifest in such details as charitable clubs organized exclusively by women and for women, leagues for the attainment of the rights of women, associations of women-students, women's congresses, and the organization of women for the realization of political and social goals. (CW, 183–84).

He concluded with a note of caution: Since the traditional role of women is more restrictive than the roles of traders and workers, he felt that "today no one can predict either direction or limitation of the movement for the emancipation of women" (CW, 184).

Other manifestations of the strong influence of feminism and the erotic movement on Simmel's work are the examples he used from the realm of the relations of the sexes to illustrate his assertions about abstract properties of social groups. In 1918, in "The Conflict of Modern Culture." he gave as an example of conflict a trend in "a specialized area of ethics":

A systematic critique of existing sexual relationships has been named "the new morality." It is propagated by a small group, but its aims are shared by a large one. Its criticism is directed mainly against two elements of the contemporary scene: marriage and prostitution. Its basic theme can be expressed as follows: the most personal and intimate meaning of erotic life is destroyed by the forms in which our culture has reified and trapped it. Marriage, which is entered for a thousand non-erotic reasons, is destroyed from within by a thousand unyielding traditions and legalized cruelties; where it is not wrecked, it loses all individuality and leads to stagnation. Prostitution has almost turned into a legal institution which forces the erotic life of young people into a dishonorable direction which contradicts and caricatures its innermost nature. Marriage and prostitution alike appear as oppressive forms which thwart immediate and genuine life. (*SISF*, 388–89)

Simmel declined, however, to propose an amelioration of these problems. In his judgment, "These reformers are not really interested in working out an adequate replacement for the forms which they condemn. The destructive force of their criticism impedes the cultural process of obsolescence and reconstruction which would normally take place" (*SISF*, 389). Here he returned to the stance of the deterministic sociological rationalist.

A dominant theme running through Simmel's work is the dialectic of life and form. Human beings create suprapersonal (objective) cultural forms to express their lives and in turn live under, as well as through, these forms. As we have seen at the outset of this exposition of Simmel's work, male culture confronts women in a reified form, an objective reality not of women's making. Guy Oakes, a Simmel scholar, has argued (on the basis of his 1984 translation of Simmel's essays "Female Culture," "Love," "Flirtation," and "The Relative and the Absolute in the Problem of the Sexes") that what he terms the "Simmelian problem of feminism" hinges implicitly on the issue of "a feminist politics of culture." That is, how and in what ways can women objectify female life in culture? and can culture be feminized?[162]

According to Oakes, Simmel rejected the ideological models about women current in his time: The traditionalist defense of a separate sphere for women, the liberal model of the extension of male rights to women, and the socialist model that accepted liberal aims but denied the possibility of their realization in a liberal, capitalist order. He did so because none of these models accepted the autonomy of women. For Simmel, a woman's life is different in content from a man's, and it is not reducible to or expressible by male cultural forms. The female mode of being can express itself only in the home as a cultural form, because, in Oakes's words, "As Simmel conceives it, the problem of feminism is a consequence of this intractability of the female character to the the division of labor and the [cultural] process of objectification . . . [that is,] the uniformity, integration, personalization, and immediacy of the woman's being and its resistance to any force that threatens its self-contained existence." (The male character stands at the opposite pole of each of these aspects of woman's nature.) Putting it a bit too simply, he believed that women, unlike men, live in a world of subjectivity.[163] In sum, Simmel, like Freud, saw female life as radically opposed to culture, male culture, that is.

The easiest way to deal with Simmel's analysis of women in culture and society would be simply to dismiss it as sexist, as a number of feminist writers have done. Keeping in mind the multifaceted character of Simmel's writings, I would argue, however, that regardless of the flaws in his explanation, he was fully aware of the existence of a relatively autonomous female world constituted by distinct social and psychological experiences. As Oakes has pointed out, Simmel's approach to female culture raises the issue of whether the feminization of culture would interrupt the tragedy of modern culture, its reified and instrumentalized forms.[164] Answers in the affirmative have been given in the antinuclear and peace movements. The issue had been raised before, by the persons in the erotic movement and by some feminists on the eve of the First World War, regrettably without success.

As we have seen, the problem of women and culture does not exhaust everything Simmel had to say about women, nor would we expect him, because of his style and range of interests, to have been consistent in his views. Although the sensitively dualistic perspective with which he described the relations of the sexes is marred by the sexist cultural categories he used, there are ways in which Simmel's analysis of women and Durkheim's in *Suicide* are the best analyses of the conflictful and double-bound position of women in patriarchal society and culture that the male-dominated sociological tradition has to offer. I concur with Coser's judgment that

Simmel's work ranks "among the few major analyses not only of women's position in society, but of the male-dominated culture which over the ages has been a powerful obstacle to women's ability to make contributions to the common culture." I also agree that Simmel's notions of "woman's nature" show how deeply he was bound to the cultural assumptions of his time. His remedy for the plight of women was a separate but equal "female culture" expressed in the theater and in the home as a work of art and civilization, realms in tune with traditional notions about women. Coser summed it up well: Simmel's "female culture of the future, it turns out upon inspection, has a close family resemblance to the world of cultivated women in his Berlin. His diagnosis was resplendently modern, his cure was Wilhelminian." [165]

Ferdinand Tönnies
Womanly *Gemeinschaft* and Liberating *Gesellschaft*

Ferdinand Tönnies (1855–1936) is famous for two concepts that every sociology student knows: *Gemeinschaft* and *Gesellschaft*, or community and association. He conceived of his work as speaking to the political conflicts of his time, the struggle between capitalism and socialism. The subtitle of the first edition of his magnum opus, *Gemeinschaft und Gesellschaft*, was *A Treatise of Communism and Socialism as Empirical Forms of Culture*. In the prefaces to the 1887 and 1912 editions, he explicitly acknowledged the influence of Marx on his work,[166] later recalling that he had been "fervently devoted to socialism," and that the "most favorable" outcome of Western civilization would be for it to be "gradually transformed into a socialistic organization of society" (*OS*, 4, 11). However, Tönnies also noted that "the great sociological works of Comte and Spencer have accompanied me on my way" (*OS*, 21). He was influenced by Comte's "critical position toward progress, modernity, and liberalism" and viewed Comte's and Saint-Simon's positive position toward the organic order of the Middle Ages (combined as it was with a belief in science and modernity) as "also the inevitable position of socialist theories toward the problem of culture" (*OS*, 29). Werner J. Cahnman and Rudolf Heberle aptly characterized Tönnies' politics as follows:

Tönnies was not a liberal in the sense of the Manchester liberalism of the nineteenth century. . . . He was a democrat, a

republican, a freethinker, a socialist of a kind, and a devoted
supporter of the labor movement; he was intensely interested
in trade unions, consumer cooperatives, and adult education,
especially workers' education. One can say that he was conservative in temperament but radical in conviction.[167]

His temperamental conservatism pervades his sociological work,
especially about the position of women in society. Tönnies' position
on the status of women was influenced by the works of Comte, and
especially by J. J. Bachofen's *Mutterrecht* and Lewis Henry Morgan's
Ancient Society. Interestingly, his conception of *Gemeinschaft* as
feminine contrasts with Weber's early conception of it as masculine.

Arthur Mitzman has characterized Tönnies as "a lonely and sensitive" person. Not much is known about any influence of women in
his mature life. In 1881, he had an affair he hoped would turn into
marriage but was disappointed. In 1883, he was in competition
with two other men for the favors of Lou Andreas-Salomé, but that
relationship didn't last. Around the time of the death of poet Theodor Storm in 1888, Storm's daughter Gertrud "was in love with
Tönnies, but it is unclear whether this love was reciprocated." According to Mitzman, early romance, if there was any, must have
been conducted at a distance: "Thus, with three possible exceptions, there were no women in Tönnies' life until his marriage in
1894 at the age of thirty-eight. This highlights the significance of
anyone to whom Tönnies did feel particularly close. Certainly one
such person was [Friedrich] Paulsen [his professor]. Theodor Storm
was another."[168]

Tönnies argued that "social entities" resulting from "a together-
willing" must be "analyzed from the inside out" (*OS*, 8). The psychological concepts of "essential will" and "arbitrary will" parallel
and underpin the concepts of *Gemeinschaft* and *Gesellschaft*. "The
sharpest contrast, then, arises if affirmation of a social entity for its
own sake is distinguished from an affirmation of such an entity because of an end, or purpose, which is extraneous to it" (*OS*, 35, 65).
Such a conception—in spite of Tönnies' recognition of the ways in
which social order shaped willing—led him into consideration of
the natures of men and women in his "youthful work of genius,"
Gemeinschaft und Gesellschaft.[169]

Tönnies argued that the social differences between men and
women "follow a pattern of nature, however often these inherent
regular tendencies, like all others, may be interrupted, counter-

balanced, or reversed."[170] That women are "weaker by nature" than men accounted for the original "one-sided subjugation of the woman." He went on: "Relevant to the sex difference, the difference in natural strength becomes evident in the division of labor" (*CA*, 43, 45). The man's field was fighting and the teaching of sons, whereas the woman's was "the inner circle of home life" and attachment to male children (*CA*, 46). Tönnies obviously used well-worn ideas to "distinguish in general features the psychological contrast between the sexes"; he believed that "women are usually led by feelings, men more by intellect" and that women "lack the necessary requirement of rational will." He wrote, "Because the male must make provision for food, his life is more active," whereas the female must spend the greater part of her time caring for offspring. Tönnies also believed that men are less dependent and passive with respect to organizing their perceptions of the world, that they are more clever, pugnacious, nimble, and faster than women; and finally that it is only where intellectual power is more synthetic that the female mind excels (*CA*, 174–79). Like Simmel, Tönnies believed that "natural will" characterizes women. The genius of women expresses itself in such arts and crafts as music, dance, and textiles (*CA*, 189). Also like Simmel, Tönnies maintained that women are more natural, and thus passionate, beings than men: "Passion, because it belongs to vegetative life and the force of reproduction, prevails more in feminine nature; courage, which belongs to animal life and irritability, is stronger in the man" (*CA*, 179). He believed that "women and children belong together as they have the same mentality and understand each other," and that the differences between the sexes are "lasting and inflexible" but not always completely developed (*CA*, 179, 181–89).[171]

From all this it followed—Tönnies' protestations to the contrary notwithstanding—that Gemeinschaft was the most natural form of society. Early in the text of *Community and Association*, Tönnies asserted that "the authority of the father is the prototype of all Gemeinschaft-like authority" (*CA*, 22, 45). The kinds of authority based on age, force, and wisdom "are united in the authority belonging to the father engaged in protecting, assisting, and guiding his family" (*CA*, 47). The point of his argument was that "the study of the house (home) is the study of the Gemeinschaft as the organic cell is the study of life itself" (*CA*, 60). Gemeinschaft was not just family-based society but society qua family: "The prototype of all unions of Gemeinschaft is the family" (*CA*, 223). "The great main laws of Gemeinschaft" were that relatives and married couples loved each other, understood each other, and remained together to organize their common life in "concord" or "family spirit" (CA, 55). Marriage, the free union of a man and a woman, was the basis of the family, and "in its moral sense, . . . [monogamy] can be defined as a perfect neighborhood" (CA, 223). Only where "mutual furtherance and affirmation predominate can a relationship really be considered Gemeinschaft" (CA, 50). However, coercion and conflict in the family were given short shrift by Tönnies (see CA, 44, 46, 195, 241). He recognized that "all superiority carries with it the danger of haughtiness and cruelty," if not accompanied by a desire to benefit the dominated, which, he found, was fortunately a natural tendency (CA, 47). When conflict occurred in the family, it eventually submitted to "the natural authority of the family head" (CA, 241).

The basis of social structures, in Tönnies' view, was rooted in psychobiology—that is, sex differences. In 1925, Tönnies wrote in "The Concept of Gemeinschaft":

> With respect to being together, the deepest contrast among human beings, especially with respect to its psychological consequences, is the biological difference of sex; as a consequence, men and women always part with each other while at the same time they are attracted to each other; the principle of what is eternally feminine (das Ewig-weibliche) or the principle of motherliness, is the root of all being together. Men depart more readily and farther from the natural foundation of essential will and Gemeinschaft. Correspondingly, women persist more readily in the forms of understanding, custom, and faith, which are the simplest forms of communal will; men find it easier to pass on to those of contract, statute, doctrine as the simple forms of societal will. As men and women live together, so is the same kind of interdependence required for all forms of communal will [city and country, ruling and ruled classes, etc.] (OS, 69–70)

In the historical development from Gemeinschaft to Gesellschaft, this unity of opposites becomes confused, and "tragic conflict necessarily evolves," Tönnies wrote (CA, 186). The destruction of "natural relations" led the women to "use cunning against the men, the young against the old, and the lower classes against the higher"

(*CA*, 195). This historical change and conflict was caused by the economic factor of trade, which "in its development is nothing but the capitalistic system." Trade connected peoples, promoted science (which fought ignorance and superstition), and liberated "the individual forces of will and mind" (*OS*, 10). Trade, the basis of capitalistic *Gesellschaft*, Tönnies argued, was opposed to "organic-living, feminine-natural labor and Gemeinschaft-like labor" (*CA*, 189). He concluded, therefore, that anyone could see "how averse to the feminine mind and nature trade must be." Although the facts contradicted him, he observed that "the tradeswoman, not an infrequent phenomenon in early town life, left her natural sphere to become the first emancipated woman" (*CA*, 189).

Tönnies pointed out that although the *Gemeinschaft*-like character of women and children made them more easily exploitable factory hands than men, the entrance of women into the labor market contributed to the liberation and cultural transformation of women and of society as a whole (*CA*, 190–92).

As woman enters into the struggle of earning a living, it is evident that trading and the freedom and independence of the female factory worker as contracting party and possessor of money will develop her rational will, enabling her to think in a calculating way, even though, in the case of factory work, the tasks themselves may not lead in this direction. The woman becomes enlightened, coldhearted, conscious. Nothing is more foreign and terrible to her original inborn nature, in spite of all later modifications. Possibly nothing is more characteristic and important in the process of formation of the Gesellschaft and destruction of Gemeinschaft. Through this development the "individualism" which is the prerequisite of Gesellschaft comes to its own. However, the possibility of overcoming this individualism and arriving at a reconstruction of Gemeinschaft exists. The analogy of the fate of women with the fate of the proletariat has been recognized and outlined long ago. Their growing group consciousness, like that of the isolated thinker, can develop and rise to a moral-humane consciousness. (*CA*, 191)

Following Tocqueville, Tönnies viewed capitalistic individuation as the basis for the struggle of the labor movement for equality of rights of workers.

Besides the labor movement there is the feminist movement, another struggle for emancipation, for private and political rights; the struggles for private rights, too, are essentially political struggles. The emergence of women as individuals surely is a giant final step in the disintegration of age-old communal ties (*Gemeinschafts-Zusammenhang*); it decomposes what had remained an authoritative core in domestic relations. . . . it is not even women's own will and endeavor so much as life itself, that is, the national economy, capitalism and commercialism, communication, and the need to earn a living. Women already are individuals in economic life, and we see them become more and more so; the fact that they become political individuals as well is a consequence that may, like other consequences, bear within itself the seeds of a sound restoration on a new basis. (*OS*, 306)[172]

The merits of Tönnies' analysis are his criticism of capitalism as the force breaking up community in the modern world and his recognition that the liberation of women from the domestic sphere is crucial to the breakdown of the traditional authority of patriarchy and the restoration of community on a higher level. The demerits of his analysis are equal to its merits. Despite his pretensions to a socialist, dialectical, and critical perspective on the liberal social order and its dominant philosophy (see *OS*, 18–19), there is a vicious circularity to his positivistic, psychological view of society. In effect, his method was to take existing manifestations of sex-role behavior as expressions of types of "willing" and then attempt to explain those social/cultural entities by the wills they manifested. Finally, his writing has a certain tone that romanticizes the past, glorifying what Marx characterized as those feudal castles, estates, and patriarchal relations that were the workshops of cruelty, subjugation, inefficiency, and narrowness.[173] In this regard I characterize Tönnies as the Proudhon of *Katheder-Sozialismus*. Similarly, following this line of allusions to the Marxist heritage, Karl Mannheim might be characterized as the Hungarian Saint-Simon.

Karl Mannheim
A Return to Enlightenment

Karl Mannheim (1893–1947) is significant because his work is the European culmination of the classical sociological tradition. He was influenced as a student at Berlin, Heidelberg, and Freiberg by Simmel, Max Weber, Alfred Weber, and Georg Lukács. Mannheim's work reflected diverse and contradictory political and intellectual currents in central Europe from the First World War through the 1930s.[174]

Mannheim was the only son born to middle-class Hungarian-German-Jewish parents in Budapest. As a young leftist intellectual, Mannheim was caught up in what Trotsky later called one of those mad inspirations of history, the revolutionary attempt to create a Hungarian Soviet Republic. He also experienced the counter-revolutionary White Terror.[175] A friend of Mannheim's, the progressive social scientist Oscar Jaszi, characterized the situation thus: "The old order had been caught between the millstones of the animal appetite of the mob and the transcendental enthusiasms of the young men."[176] In general, Mannheim's work signified the departure from the Enlightenment characteristic of non-Marxist sociological theory.[177] However, when it came to the "woman question," Mannheim maintained an enlightened attitude. In one discussion of perceptions and personality, he took a straightforward sociological perspective on so-called character traits. He believed the structure of marriage created a "functional polarity" of behaviors: "The man's free and easy approach to pecuniary matters and the woman's acceptance of the compensatory restraint are merely the economic aspects of a complex division of roles: the man uses prerogatives which reaffirm the woman's subordination and her restricted choices in the marital situation."[178]

A second example of Mannheim's approach to the relations of the sexes is provided by his discussion of sexuality and marriage in the West. He noted that the companionate marriage, fashionable at the time, might involve in the long run "successive polygamy" (or serial monogamy, as it is now termed) and had the "characteristics of a genuine partnership based on a multitude of joint interests of which the sexual is but one." He believed that sexual love had taken two forms since the emergence of prostitution in the West: "tender and individualized *eros*" and the "unsublimated and aggressive" type associated with prostitution. In Greece, he wrote, the former was often lavished on the boy hetaera, not the man's own wife. Women of different strata, Mannheim believed, played two roles corresponding to two types of male sexual drives (sometimes evident in the same man): the middle-class woman "responds to the sublime form of the male *eros*," and the prostitute is the caretaker of the "polygamous and despiritualized drives of men." He concluded: "It is clear that what may appear to be a masculine trait is actually the personal manifestation of a structural cleavage in a historical society" (*ESC*, 49–50).

Mannheim saw the evolving eros manifested in the companionate (democratized?) marriage as a middle solution to these two extremes, affecting not only women but gradually also modifying "the dichotomous approach of men to women." In the past, the biological sexual differences between men and women imposed a burden that fell mostly on prostitutes, he stated, "commercialized sex [being] a brutalization of the female partner." But with "the declining polarization of the feminine role," he thought that a majority of women were sharing the "burden" of male sexuality, because the romantic, highly repressed, sublimated form of love was being challenged by that of the emerging companionate marriage with its weakened spirituality (*ESC*, 50–51).

In 1925, Mannheim married the psychologist Juliska Lang, who had similar origins and was also a student at Budapest and Heidelberg. Coser has commented: "Mannheim's interest in psychology and psychoanalysis, especially in his later years, was mainly inspired by his wife, with whom he collaborated intimately."[179] In his English years, having fled the Nazis in 1933, Mannheim became obsessed with social reconstruction through a kind of Comtean sociological engineering. For example, in the essay "On the Diagnosis of Our Time," about the crises associated with the aftermath of World War I, Mannheim wrote: "Even the layman has been able to see clearly that the family is losing its inner consistency, and this in proportion to the social dissolution of a given country. . . . Psychoanalysis with its revelations of the psychic mechanisms which, full of resentment, dominate family life is only one of the forms in which we become aware of this conflict between home and world."[180] He felt that the solution to these problems would be found in the ideas of the "free-floating intelligentsia"—the sociologists.

What can be concluded about Mannheim's analysis of the "woman question"? First, I would expect his position to have been more advanced than his teachers' because he wrote later than the other classical theorists. He had read Margaret Mead's *Sex and Temperament in Three Primitive Societies* (1935) (see *ESC*, 50n.2). As for providing tools for analysis of the social position of women and conflicts between men and women, Mannheim introduced the extremely useful concept of "generations," which helps account for historical experiences contributing to or hindering feminist movements.[181] The concepts of his most well-known book, *Ideology and Utopia*, could be applied to complexes of notions about biology, family, and personality, ranging from conscious lies to unwitting deceptions, ideas bound up with maintaining male domination and privilege in society. Equally relevant is his conception of utopian mentality as comprising those reality-transcending orientations that, "when they pass over into conduct, tend to shatter, either partially or wholly, the order of things prevailing of the time."[182] In the light of the feminist movement, we would have to add to Mannheim's list of utopias those of radical feminism, Amazonia, the lesbian alternative, an androgynous future, feminist socialism, all of which have had their advocates in the United States.[183]

German classical sociological theory is the centerpiece of my story, as Weber is of its history. The case of Germany is important because of the range of political and intellectual phenomena it encompasses: Marxist, non-Marxist, and anti-Marxist theory; Freudianism; liberal and socialist feminism; reactionary antifeminism; an organized socialist working-class movement; conservative bourgeois politics; and fascism. The history of Germany reveals the costs— fascism, repression, and war—of the inability and/or unwillingness of socialists and socialist feminists to transform an authoritarian, capitalist society in crisis.

Within the confines of German domestic life, the psychic price exacted by patriarchy was made painfully clear, as was the political price exacted by the confines of the German state. In Germany were revealed the dangers—the ugliness, viciousness, and anti-intellectualism—of an ideology focused on the traditional family, including the nation as one big family, under siege from without and from feminists and socialists within. The parallels between Germany in this period and the United States of the last two decades are disturbing, as a reading of Weber's "Science as a Vocation" and "Politics as a Vocation" reminds us. We may not have had to worry about what Gloria Steinem has called the "Nazi Connection,"[184] however, unfriendly fascism and a reinvigorated sexism could be on the agenda. The historical comparison of Italy with Germany is much less speculative.

5

Italy

Women, Sexuality, and the

Tradition of Machiavelli

Women in Italy were "far behind [women in] France and England,"
John Stuart Mill observed in 1869, because they were "very little
educated." Nevertheless, he acknowledged that women in Italy as
elsewhere were "beginning to protest, more or less collectively,
against the disabilities under which they labour."[1] Sheila Ryan
Johansson has pointed out that "modern nationalism in Italy was
first promoted in early nineteenth-century salons, by aristocratic
women who refused to recognize Napoléon as a liberator."[2] However, the slow start of the Italian women's-emancipation movement
may be attributed partly to the following: the bourgeois national
revolution occurred later in Italy than in other European countries;
the development of capitalism between the North and the South
was uneven;[3] and the Roman Catholic Church exerted a strong influence on Italy's specific pattern of male dominance. The historical
context might explain why references to women's emancipation in
the work of Vilfredo Pareto—one of the Italian theorists who will

be considered here—were not about Italy. Some Italian women, however, were participants in the revolutionary struggles of other nations. For example, a frequent speaker in the revolutionary clubs during the Paris Commune was Fornarina de Fonseca, whose grandmother Eleonora (once a lady-in-waiting to Marie Caroline, queen of Naples) had founded *Il Monitore Republicano*, a newspaper that advocated the ideas of the French Revolution. Eleonora de Fonseca had been arrested, freed by the French, and eventually executed after the restoration of Ferdinand IV. Edith Thomas has noted that "her granddaughter proudly revived this heritage, and never failed to invoke her grandmother's memory whenever she spoke in a Commune Club."[4]

In nineteenth-century Italy, the roles open to women of the middle class were traditional family roles: mother, daughter, sister, and wife. The strength of the family's control was evidenced by its power to dictate marital choice. However, women saw in the family their only hope for security. In backward Sicily, "the most sacred thing on earth was a woman's chastity—a value that [was] not just hers but belong[ed] to the entire family"; when violated, it had to be avenged by her male relatives. According to Tullio Tentori, women were considered vulnerable to seduction and thus weak. Sisters were considered valuable only for giving their brothers a sense of responsibility; otherwise they were felt to be a liability. For women of the middle class, the convent was the only alternative to the security of the family. Young women of this class lived lives filled with leisure time, boredom, uselessness, and romantic fantasy, according to Tentori; at best, they attended private schools. Women of the upper and middle classes were not permitted even to attend Mass unchaperoned. Tentori has pointed out, however, that "it was among the urban poor that exceptions to this rule were found, because poverty forced them to live practically in the street." The Italian Constitution of 1865 mimicked the Napoleonic Code in legitimating the second-class treatment of women.[5]

Improvements in the education laws made possible greater freedom for Italian women. A compulsory-education law passed in late 1859 called for two-year schools for boys and girls (the latter taught by women); and the Casati Law of 1860 introduced educational reform for middle-class women. Upper-class and middle-class girls were sent to private schools or the better *licei*. Normal schools were set up to train teachers. Lower-middle-class and middle-class women were permitted to become elementary-school teachers.

Noblewomen who were the wives and mothers of patriots of the Risorgimento during the first half of the nineteenth century later achieved recognition through philanthropy, which, from about 1850, was the one acceptable sphere of activity outside the family for high-status women. Princess Filangeri, for example, founded hospitals and shelters for orphans. Between 1850 and 1900, new religious orders for women dedicated to social work, such as Sisters of the Poor, were formed.[6]

The relatively slow pace of industrialization in Italy played a role in the slow development of feminist consciousness and the struggle for women's rights. In 1867, 90 percent of all working women were employed in agriculture, and there was little change in the domestic status of peasant women. In the North especially, urban industry offered work to lower-class women and children. Slightly more than 12,000 women were employed in the silk-textile industry in 1890, and in 1901 approximately 83,000 women were employed in the cotton industry. In that year, the total number of women in the labor force was only 354,732.[7]

The central issue of nineteenth-century Italian political history was the movement for national unification and independence—the Risorgimento. These goals were achieved in 1871 when Rome became the capital of the United Kingdom of Italy. Writing of the connection between the Risorgimento and feminism, Claire La Vigna has stated:

> The leading theorists of the great Italian movement for national revitalization, the Risorgimento, showed little or no inclination to revive in the nineteenth century the active role Italian women had played in the Renaissance. As Eugenio Garin has noted, even those who during and immediately after Unification looked favorably upon women's liberation— Melchiorre Gioia, Giuseppe Mazzini, Salvatore Morelli— leaned more toward "empty rhetoric" than toward a profound discussion of the woman question. Others, especially those of a neo-Guelph (Papal) persuasion—Antonio Rosmini, Caterina Franceschi-Ferrucci, Vincenzo Gioberti—were decidedly opposed to equality between the sexes. Gioberti even concluded, "In short, in a sense, a woman in relation to a man is like a vegetable in relation to an animal or like a parasitic plant in relation to one which is self-sustaining." Likewise, the feminist movement in post-Risorgimento Italy could expect little

intellectual guidance from its two dominant philosophical schools—the positivists and the Crocean idealists. The positivist criminologist Cesare Lombrose [*sic*] cited woman's small head and lack of beard as positive indicators that the female was merely an underdeveloped male; *ergo* inferior to him in body and mind. Women's limited mental capacity, though precluding genius in every field, had, however, one positive aspect for him; women lacked the necessary intellect to be as criminal as men. Benedetto Croce, unlike Lombroso, recognized the significant contribution that women had made to Italian culture. Notwithstanding this sympathy, Croce was hardly a candidate for the position of Italian philosopher of feminism. Early in his distinguished career, Croce denied the very validity of the woman question, asserting in response to a survey on feminism that "feminism is a movement which to me seems to stand condemned by its very name. It is a feminine idea in the bad sense of the word. Even males have their particular problems, but they have not yet invented masculinism."[8]

One can infer that the Risorgimento overshadowed and overwhelmed an incipient feminism, explaining why, in La Vigna's words, "feminist ideology was particularly retrograde" in the post-Unification period.[9]

Since so few women were feminists, the traditional Italian feminist movement was, according to Tentori, "represented in Italy by eccentric and isolated individuals." Nevertheless, some feminist organizations were formed. The National Council of Italian Women was founded in 1900 as an affiliate of the International Council of Women established in Washington in 1888. Founding members of the Italian group included the Duchess of Aosta, Princess Letizia of Savoia, and the intellectual Ada Negri. Countess Ruspoli Spalletti was president of the group for many years; she was assisted by Dr. Teresita Sandewski Scelba. The council "defended the role of the family according to the Italian tradition which held that the real duty of women was to bear children and educate the men."[10]

Italy's "foremost feminist in the nineteenth century" was Anna Maria Mozzoni (1833–1920), who wrote *Woman and Her Social Relationships* in 1864 and translated Mill's *Subjection of Women* into Italian. Mozzoni's major contribution was in the area of raising the consciousness of Italians by her intellectual work; she was not involved in political organizations. She opposed special protections for women workers because she believed they perpetuated sex inequality.[11]

In opposition to the feminists of the middle class, socialist women founded the Socialist League for the Protection of Women's Rights in 1906. Its concerns were feminist: protection of mothers and children; otherwise, it was politically reformist rather than radical.[12] The central personage of Italian socialist feminism was Anna Kuliscioff (1854–1925), a native of Russia and cofounder, with Filippo Turati, of the Italian Socialist Party (Partito Socialista Italiano, or PSI). Kuliscioff was a gynecologist who practiced in a working-class neighborhood of Milan. Influenced by Bakuninism, she lived for a time in a free union with anarchist Andrea Costa, with whom she had a child. Later she became a student of Marx, Engels, and Bebel. Milanese socialist Carlo Tanzi reportedly referred to Kuliscioff as "the most intelligent man in Italian Socialism." La Vigna has observed that "when Kuliscioff, who was a political activist and not a philosopher, sought an ideological guide for her life's work, the more developed Marxism held more attraction than the still embryonic feminism."[13] For Kuliscioff, class and socialism took precedence over sex and feminism.

In 1908, the National Council of Italian Women held its first important national conference in Rome. Many delegates were disappointed. Anna Kuliscioff wrote in her social review, *La Critica Sociale*, that the conference omitted "the overall declaration of the rights of women to economic and spiritual independence which necessarily depends on the question of work."[14] Similarly, Angelica Balabanov, a socialist feminist of international renown, criticized the abstract approach of the conference to the problem of the status of women in major institutions of Italian society.[15] Catholic women left the council in disagreements over secular schools and curricula and in July 1908 established the Union of Italian Catholic Women. The inspiration for the Christian Democrat feminist movement came from Pope Leo XIII's 1891 encyclical, *Rerum Novarum*, which called for the establishment of Catholic associations to guide workers back from Marxism to Christianity. Between 1910 and 1912, Kuliscioff pressed hard for female suffrage—with the argument that it would give new life to the PSI, a party suffering from the doldrums. She became, in La Vigna's words, "the Clara Zetkin of Italian socialism," heading up the National Union of Female Socialists, the women's auxiliary of the PSI.[16]

The issue of the vote for women was brought up in Parliament for the first time in 1873; it was introduced again in 1880, 1884, 1900, and 1907, "always in vain." It was again defeated in the vote on the 1908 election law. In 1919, Deputy Gasparatto introduced a bill for women's suffrage in the Chamber of Deputies, but it never reached the Senate.[17]

After the achievement of unification, the mood in the country changed. Croce described it in his *A History of Italy: 1871–1915*:

> No more trembling hopes, as in 1848 and 1859; no more gener- ous rivalries and renunciations of individual ideas in order to unite in a common purpose; no more understandings, whether tacit or avowed, between republicans and monarchists, Catho- lics and free-thinkers, ministers and revolutionaries, kings and conspirators, all alike being dominated and inspired by devo- tion to the patriotic cause.[18]

The élan and esprit of the national movement was followed by the normal routines of corrupt government, broken promises to im- prove the national well-being, repression of discontent, and failed colonial adventures. As Francesco Crispi (one of the heads of the several left governments after 1876) put it: "From 1878 on, there have been no political parties in Italy, but only politicians."[19]

The chronic crises of Italian politics became acute during and after the First World War and were exploited by Benito Mussolini in his rise to power. A delinquent boy and decadent young man, Mussolini first flirted with revolutionary socialism and then gave it up—in the wake of the dashed expectations of Italian nationalism and the militance of workers following the war—to become a strident Italian nationalist. He organized the fascist, blackshirted *squadistri*. On 28 October 1922, the fascists marched on Rome, and three days later King Victor Emmanuel III granted Mussolini dictatorial pow- ers. In a search for intellectual legitimacy for his politics, Mussolini referred to Pareto's theory of the elite as "probably the most ex- traordinary sociological conception of modern times."[20]

The "woman question" was also trampled by the march on Rome. The fascists took over the National Council of Italian Women in 1924. Even among women Mussolini was able to find apologists for his sexism and fascism.[21] Only after his execution in 1945 did Italian women get the vote, and they used it: 81 percent of eligible women voted in the 1946 elections. The 1948 constitution gave to Italian women equal rights with men.[22]

The Italian Theorists

In the 1917 introduction to his essays on historical materialism, *Materialismo storico ed economia marxistica*, Benedetto Croce declared that studying Marxism—as he had done in the 1890s, a period he referred to as the "Marxist parenthesis" in his life—had actually pulled him back

> to the best traditions of Italian political science, thanks to the firm assertion of the principle of force, of struggle, of power, and the satirical and caustic opposition to the anti-historical and democratic insipidities of natural law doctrine—to the so-called ideals of 1789.[23]

Other famous nineteenth- and twentieth-century representatives of Italian social thought were Gaetano Mosca and Vilfredo Pareto, "the heirs of Machiavelli," in H. Stuart Hughes's characterization. Pareto, Mosca, and their pupil, Robert Michels, asserted "the necessary role of force and fraud in government, and . . . the inevitable degeneration of all political groups and institutions."[24] Their central contribution to political science and sociology was the theory of elites: that all societies, regardless of political, legal, or economic forms, are sharply divided into two strata, a ruling political elite (a fraction of the nongoverning elite) and a ruled majority (the masses), and that all large-scale societies necessarily must be divided in this way. These assertions "formed part of a political doctrine which was opposed to, or critical of, modern democracy, and still more opposed to modern socialism."[25] For Pareto, history was, and would continue to be, in his famous phrase, "a graveyard of aristocracies." And Pareto, "thoroughly steeped in Italian intellectual tradition," was an heir of Machiavelli in another way: he believed that the task of the social theorist was to grasp the unchanging features of human nature as the true cause of human behavior in the way that the natural scientist must understand the elements in order to explain the physical world. The emphasis of Italian theory was on the state in contrast to society. The tradition that considers human conduct to be the product of social relations was foreign to this theory. Social order was not considered an emergent property of group life but rather an order imposed upon an intractable nature. This, in Lewis A. Coser's words, "is the central theoretical focus of Italian social thought from Machiavelli to the days of Pareto." Upon the tradition of Machiavelli, Pareto grafted the positivistic belief in social laws that he had acquired from his reading of Saint-Simon, Comte, and Spencer. But, as Coser has pointed out, "Like Machiavelli, he wanted to construct a science that would lay bare the springs of human action rooted in man's fundamental nature, a science of power that would explain how the few manage to rule over the many."[26]

Vilfredo Pareto
Misanthrope and Misogynist

Vilfredo Pareto (1848–1923) was born to a noble Genovese family. His father, a republican supporter of Mazzini, was forced to emigrate to France in the 1830s to avoid persecution by the House of Savoy for his liberal political views. The son, like the father, was educated as a civil engineer. Upon completion of his studies at the Turin Polytechnical School in 1870, he began a career in business management. Despite his left-liberal political leanings, he moved in the society of the haute bourgeoisie. After the 1876 fall of the rightist regime that was committed to free trade, Pareto publicly opposed the policies of state intervention in the economy by the succeeding, moderately left governments. He ran as an opposition candidate in Florence in the 1882 elections and was defeated by a government-supported candidate. Pareto's love affair with the Mazzinian ideals of his father ended, and he became increasingly bitter about the direction of Italian politics. In 1889, he resigned his directorship of an iron-products company and began making vitriolic attacks on government policy, continuing from that year to 1893. During this period, he studied economics seriously. His work won him an appointment in 1893 at the University of Lausanne as the successor to mathematical economist Leon Walras. In 1902, he published *Les systemes socialistes*, a critique of socialist and state-interventionist doctrines. In 1906, he published his *Manual of Political Economy*. In both of these works, Pareto criticized the rationalistic assumptions of classical economics about human nature, because he concluded that the behavior of most people is governed by nonrational beliefs, not by rational argument.[27]

There are several features of Pareto's life that seem to account for the antidemocratic tone and substance of his major work, *The Treatise on General Sociology* (1916). He came to view most men as "imbeciles" and "scoundrels." He became increasingly isolated from even his academic colleagues when an inheritance allowed him to retire almost completely from his academic duties in a university that was itself in the backwaters of Europe. Like Comte, his work and behavior became more eccentric and idiosyncratic, and less and less governed by socially grounded norms of discourse. Surrounded by his Angora cats, suffering from insomnia and heart disease, he lived a life of epicurean tastes. In addition to his isolation, Pareto was affected by the corrosive political climate of Italy, which, according to Coser, by the turn of the twentieth century had spawned "several generations of disillusioned cynics or decadent irrationalists. . . . intellectual decadence became a pervasive mark of the time. Only the saving remnant of rational and liberal philosophers around Benedetto Croce and the growing phalanx of Marxist intellectuals around Antonio Labriola upheld libertarian ideals and clung to rational standards." Coser summarizes: "Much of what Pareto wrote is only the fruit of the labors of an embittered, disillusioned, and resentful man who felt that his times had let him down."[28] Presciently, Pareto wrote in his *Treatise on General Sociology*, "Just as Roman society was saved from ruin by the legions of Caesar and Octavius, it may be that one day our society will be saved from decadence by those who will then be the heirs of our syndicalists and anarchists."[29]

Without rehashing the controversy over Pareto's relationship to fascism—whether he was "the Karl Marx of Fascism" or just "an old man who aspired to be the Machiavelli of the middle classes"—I will mention that he accepted two positions offered him by Mussolini: senator (which he had refused from the previous government) and delegate to the Geneva Disarmament Conference. Pareto publicly welcomed fascism, and his work was praised by Mussolini. Only when fascism interfered with academic freedom did he oppose it.[30]

Werner Stark has suggested that Pareto's personality revealed "the psychology of the disappointed lover." He received a severe blow when his new, very young wife, whom he had married at forty-one, left with the cook and Pareto's possessions. Pareto declared that even if he returned to earth for another life, he would not marry again. However, sixty-one days before his death, he married Jane Regis, who had lived with him in his later years.[31] His unhappy first marriage may help to explain the misanthropy and misogyny evident in his work, its scornful and mocking tone, in evidence particularly when women were the subject of discussion.

Close to the end of his life, Pareto wrote of his *Treatise* that its "sole purpose" was "to seek experimental reality, by the application to the social sciences of the methods which have proved themselves in physics, in chemistry, in astronomy, in biology, and in other such sciences."[32] The starting point of Pareto's analytical sociology is the distinction between logical and nonlogical action. He considered logical action to be that which employs appropriate and logically linked means to the achievement of given ends. Logical action, he believed, is based on scientific knowledge and exhibited in the model of human action postulated by classical political economy (which he later rejected as an inadequate explanation of human behavior); nonlogical action describes the rest of human action. Pareto thought motives for nonlogical action are sentiments, or what he termed unchanging *residues*, such as those having to do with sex, sociality, self-expression, and individual integrity. Pareto termed *derivations* people's attempts to rationalize their actions. He used a debunking mode of analysis to expose what he considered the falseness of the beliefs by which people justify their actions and to demonstrate that their real motives lie elsewhere, in unchanging elements of human nature, the residues.

Pareto's political sociology focused on his hypothesis of the cycles of mutual dependence between two types of residues: one, the "instinct for combinations," and the other, "group persistences," or "persistence of aggregates." Pareto offered an example from the economic sphere that illustrated the dynamics of the relationships of the two types. When dominated by speculators, who represent the first type, the economy is characterized by change and threatened by instability; when dominated by rentiers, who represent the second group, the economy is characterized by stability and threatened with stagnation. Machiavelli's foxes and lions fit Pareto's theory in the political sphere, he asserted. The foxes, the group with "instinct for combinations," are innovators, builders of systems, and manipulators ungoverned by scruples; and the lions, representative of "group persistences," are loyal to tradition, deeply committed to stability, and willing to use force to maintain it. Pareto believed that most people of most times and places belong to the second group.

Pareto's focus on these two types was linked to the third element of his political sociology: his theory of the circulation of elites.

He believed there are dangers to the equilibrium of the polity when either type of residues overwhelmingly dominates the governing elite. Coser has summarized his views:

> In the world of his day, more particularly in Italy and France, Pareto believed that the foxes were in ascendancy. The political and economic scene was dominated by political wheelers and dealers, by unscrupulous lawyers and intellectual sophists, by speculators and manipulators of men. Pareto's concern was that if this condition were to remain unchecked, social equilibrium would be fundamentally upset and the social order would totter.[33]

Pareto anticipated that a new group of lions would throw out the foxes by force. But the foxes would return because the residues they carried were necessary to maintain the moving equilibrium of the social system. Quoting Coser:

> They [the foxes] will slowly undermine the certainties that the lions uphold, and their corrosive intelligence will undermine the uncomplicated faith of the militant lions. As a result, the wheel will come full circle and a new age of deceit and manipulation will dawn.[34]

For Pareto, history was an endless process of the circulation of elites. Progress, he argued, like justice and liberty, was an unscientific illusion. Pareto was a man of the Enlightenment but without its faith that reason and equality are rooted in the natural order of things. Given the antihumanistic cast of neo-Machiavellian social theory, we should not expect Pareto to have had an enlightened view of the "woman question." A passage from his *Manual of Political Economy* (1906) is revelatory of his attitude toward feminism.

> Among the very poor peoples the woman is treated with less consideration than the house pets; among the civilized peoples (especially among the very rich population of the United States of America) she has become a luxury object that consumes without producing. Obviously, in order for anything of this sort to be possible, the wealth of the country must be very great. These living conditions affect morals immediately. Feminism is a disease that can occur only among rich people or

among the rich portion of a poor people. With the increase of wealth in ancient Rome women's lives grew more depraved. If modern women did not have the money necessary to place their idleness and greed on exhibition, the gynecologists wouldn't be so busy.[35]

Although Pareto did little analysis of the social role of women, references to women appear throughout his four-volume *Trattato di sociologica generale* (1916), translated as *The Treatise on General Sociology*, or *The Mind and Society*.[36] He included much material about conceptions of women in Greek mythology, Roman civic law, medieval Christian theology, and witchcraft. In the first reference to women, in a discussion of the synthetic character of most human thinking, Pareto stated, "Women especially, and the less-educated among men, often experience an insurmountable difficulty in considering the different aspects of a thing separately, one by one" (*MS* 1:18). The reader was advised to provide his or her own empirical proof: "Read a newspaper article before a *mixed social gathering*" (*MS* 1:18; emphasis added). Sounding superficially like Weber, Pareto professed that scholarly work should be value-free. He advised his readers that there were no "personal sentiments" in his work (*MS* 1:39n. 75), because "sentiments are the worst enemies the scientific study of sociology has to fear" (*MS* 1:112n. 186). He hammered at the distinction between facts and values. Science, he wrote, has no knowledge of what ought to be. However, he presented the following as a description of fact (deeming it "superfluous to note similar contrasts in the case of my own country, Italy"):

One may note the licentiousness of certain emancipated women in the United States and still cherish the deepest reverence for the many admirable wives and mothers who are to be found in that country. Finally, to point the finger of scorn at the hypocrisies of German sex-reformers is not inconsistent with admiration for their mighty nation and reverence for German scholarship. (*MS* 1:39n. 75)

According to Pareto, patriarchy is universal and rooted in unchanging human nature. He pointed out that in Western theogonies sexual unions of male gods with women were the rule "because the myths were composed chiefly by men among peoples where the patriarchal family prevailed" (*MS* 2:545–46). He also noted that "the

only literature we have comes from peoples who have had a patriarchal family system—and they, after all, are the civilized peoples."
In fact, the only residues we know, Pareto claimed, are of the "patriarchal type." The discovery of other family forms "among uncivilized or barbarous peoples," which may have influenced the
family organization of the West, came as an "extreme astonishment"
to "the learned world." Pareto thought Engels's views on the family
were false; the only merit he saw in them was that Engels "brought
the infamy and hypocrisy of the *bourgeoisie* to clearer light" (*MS*
2:612–14). Pareto felt that women naturally submitted to the authority of their husbands (see the section entitled "Sentiments of
Inferiors," *MS* 2:687).

Although Pareto had no interest in the equality of women, he
used the "woman question" to expose and rail at the main object of
his wrath—democratic humanitarianism (*MS* 2:973–74).[37] He was
fond of pointing out the contradictions and hypocrisy of democrats
on the issue of equality for women:

Both European and American democracies profess to be
founded on principles of thorough-going equality between
human beings. . . . There must be perfect equality, because
all human beings are equal. But that fine principle is forgotten
when it is a question of women. By a neat trick of sleight-of-
hand, equality of human beings . . . is of certain males. The
very persons who regard the principle of universal suffrage
as a dogma above discussion, superior to every consideration
of expediency or convenience, deny suffrage to women on
grounds of expediency and convenience; because, they say,
votes for women would strengthen the clerical or conservative
parties. (*MS* 2:735)

Pareto was not in favor of universal suffrage and equality; he commented on "the absurdity not only of electoral inequality between
men and women, but of the very principle of universal suffrage"
(*MS* 2:559). He identified with "the bitter resentment in the public
at large" over the "outrages" of the suffragists in England in 1913
and worried that "to grant the right of disturbing the peace to anyone desirous of using force would sooner or later bring about the
dissolution of society" (*MS* 2:731n.217). Pareto believed that "the
so-called feminist is often just a hysterical woman in want of a mate"
and that "forced chastity" accounted for all religious, charitable,

and agitational activities among women (*MS* 2:841, 840). Similarly, "Many feminists hate men and persecute women who have lovers simply because they have been unable to find men of their own" (*MS* 2:696).

Many of Pareto's barbs were reserved for upper-class women. He stated that the contemporary "pest of 'psychological' studies of writers . . . [were] so especially dear to ladies of fashion who imagine they are following the scientific movement in devouring them" (*MS* 1:324). He wrote that "society women and wealthy members of the French *bourgeoisie* . . . dally as a sport with Tolstoian or some similar brand of pity" for allegedly revolutionary prisoners, who to Pareto were all thieves, panderers, murderers, bandits, or "exploiters of female vice" (*MS* 2:671–72, 2:673n. 1136). Certain women, he wrote, were fascinated by such prisoners and gathered at their trials.[38] In the same vein, he argued that "anybody willing to go to the trouble of reading the newspapers and following cases in the courts" would find that it was not men who misled and seduced women into committing crimes but often just the reverse (MS 3:1318n. 1890).

> If there must be this craze for protection [the crusade against white slavery], why worry so much about the seduction of women and so little about the seduction of men? . . . Only a sick or childish mind can imagine that it is just the material requirements of getting a living that drive women to prostitution. With many women it is a case of vanity and love of extravagance. Not a few others turn to the occupation out of indolence; and, in higher social circles, there are those who like this profession the way a hunter likes hunting and the fisherman fishing. (*MS* 3:319n. 1890)

Drawing upon the character of Fortunata in Petronius's *Satyricon*, Pareto wrote about what he considered the hedonism of bourgeois women, contrasting it with his view of the proper role of wives:

> From the economic standpoint of the husband, Trimalchio's wife is far superior to the women of our plutocracy. Our modern wives, when they get rich or even reach moderately easy circumstances, disdain the cares of the home and become mere luxuries, devourers of wealth and savings. The good Fortunata devotes herself in all earnestness to domestic economy,

and once when her husband had been ruined she gave him
her jewels—in that too differing, quite, from many women in
our plutocracy, who make haste to divorce men who cease to
be able to keep them in luxury. (*MS* 4:1894)[39]

Pareto argued against what he called the "article of faith—that
if there were no capitalism all women would be chaste and prostitution would be abolished" (*MS* 3:1317–18).

The woman of the petty *bourgeoisie* sells herself to get a stylish
hat; the society woman sells herself to get a string of pearls—
but they both sell themselves. The conclusion has to be that if
all individuals in a given community had exactly the same income, there would still be women ready to give themselves to
the men who were disposed to supply them with the things
they want. (*MS* 3:1318n. 1890)

Contemporary prostitution cannot be explained by capitalism, he
argued, on the grounds that a variable—income—cannot explain a
constant—prostitution. To the objection that the political economy
produced its own brand of immorality—the self as commodity[40] and
the social psychology of utility (see Marx and Engels, *The German
Ideology*)—Pareto responded that it "is an article of faith and faith
transcends experience" (*MS* 3:1318n. 1890).

As is evident from the preceding quotations, the sexual residue
figured heavily in Pareto's schema (as a kind of external Freudianism). He stated that the cult of woman in myths and genealogies
"goes to show how at all times thoughts of sex crowd into the human
mind" (*MS* 2:840). Sexual residues and sentiments are so powerful,
according to Pareto, that they override the prescriptions of faith,
are unaffected by laws and measures against sexual immorality, and
play a part in "nearly all judgments" of pity on crimes of passion
(*MS* 2:674). He asserted, "Whenever war is declared on Cythera,
Sodom, Lesbos, and Onan gain in vogue. In the countries where
public women are hunted down under the pretext of suppressing
the 'white-slave trade,' adultery and annual marriages dissolved by
easy divorce flourish and prosper" (*MS* 3:1282). Pareto believed a
condition something like this—that is, sexual immorality is most
widespread where it is most harshly condemned by law and morality—existed in several American states (*MS* 2:813). Comparing

the morality of the matrons of the Roman republic favorably with the morality of the emancipated women of the United States, Pareto termed the latter country "the paradise of sex hypocrisy" (*MS* 2:833).

Pareto's *Treatise on General Sociology* is permeated with considerations of sex. For example, he referred to sex reformers as "the professional prudes of our day"; he discussed birth control, religious views about sexuality, "the sex heretic," fetishism of genitalia, sex in literature, the conflict over pornography, and evidence of the "human hankering to dwell on procreative [*sic*] acts" (*MS* 2:807–84). If this is not a sociology of prurience, then it is a prurient sociology.

Despite his hostility to women, Pareto is worth reading, not because he made a positive contribution but because his work reveals how much sexism can exist in an allegedly value-free positivistic version of sociological theory. Pareto articulated feelings about women's rights, birth control, sexual morality, and sexual freedom that constituted a reaction against women's emancipation, a reaction subscribed to by a vocal faction today. In that sense, the *Trattato* is strikingly pertinent to contemporary affairs. In addition, conservative elite theory has been of recurrent interest to intellectuals and academic sociologists searching for a theoretical defense against Marxism and, in some cases, a defense of their own class. This was the case with the "Pareto circle" at Harvard in the 1930s, which included biologist L. J. Henderson, sociologists Talcott Parsons and George Homans, and historian Crane Brinton.[41]

Robert Michels
Socialism, Disillusionment, and Sexuality

The stature of Robert Michels (1876–1936) in sociological tradition is rightly based on his classic *Political Parties*, in which he posited the "iron law of oligarchy," namely, that all large-scale organizations eventually come to be dominated by a small group of self-perpetuating leaders: "It is organization which gives birth to the domination of the elected over the electors, of the mandataries over the mandators, of the delegates over the delegators. Who says organization says oligarchy."[42] Maintenance of the organization, originally the means, becomes an end, and original aims are displaced. The organization generates new interests, and the leaders

become a ruling political class within the party, committed to preserving the party organization above all else. In this way Michels
explained the drift toward reformism in nominally revolutionary
Marxist parties in turn-of-the-century Europe. In addition to his
writings on political movements, Marxism, elites, and intellectuals,
Michels also wrote on issues that little interested sociologists of his
generation: "eugenics, feminism, sex, and morality."[43]

Michels was born in Cologne to a patrician family of French,
Belgian, and German heritage; he was an Italophile by inclination.
The latter part of his life displayed the transformation of his political views from "international socialism to Italian nationalism." In
1900, he received his doctorate from the University of Halle, married Gisela Lindner, whose father was a history professor there,
and moved to Turin, where he joined the Italian Socialist Party
(which, along with the French Socialist Party, he held up as a model
in his criticism of the opportunism of the leaders of the German
Social Democratic Party in the prewar years).[44] In the 1920s and
1930s, he taught at the University of Perugia. He died in Rome. As
Juan Linz has commented, "His life was that of a romantic, a frustrated politician, a patriot of an adopted country, and a scholar; it
reflected as have few others the conflicts of loyalty and intellectual
ambivalences of the first decades of the twentieth century."[45] What
makes Michels interesting and important is that he linked many of
the French, German, and Italian political and intellectual currents
of the period. He was originally a Marxist socialist under the influence of Syndicalism. He was a protégé of Max Weber, a friend
of Georges Sorel in Paris, a student of Mosca, and a houseguest of
Pareto in his isolated and eccentric years.[46] Michels said of Mosca
that he was "the most distinguished living advocate of this sociological conception [the circulation of elites] and that Pareto was "its
ablest and most authoritative exponent" (PP, 344).

Political Parties is not concerned with feminist issues per se.
But Michels employed sexual imagery to describe how the bureaucratic oligarchy of the German Social Democratic Party watered
down socialist ideals by concentrating on mass appeal.

By such methods, not merely does the party sacrifice its political virginity, by entering into promiscuous relationships
with the most heterogeneous [impure] political elements, relationships which in many cases have disastrous and enduring

consequences, but it exposes itself in addition to the risk of losing its essential character [purity] as a party. (*PP*, 341)

In her study of German socialist feminists of the turn of the century. Jean H. Quataert found *Political Parties* useful in illuminating the careers and conflicts of women leaders. Michels also analyzed the factors restricting participation of wives of members of the German Social Democratic Party.[47]

In some respects, Michels's writings between 1903 and 1913 on the relations of the sexes parallel the development of his political views, including his emerging disillusionment with the conduct and policies of social democratic parties in the years preceding World War I. In an article published in 1903, in the spirit of revolutionary romanticism, Michels celebrated proletarian over bourgeois morality. Proletarian women, he wrote, were chaste, and sexual relations among workers were more natural than among the bourgeoisie, whose women dressed in crudely alluring ways, and whose men did not respect the honor of working-class women. A year later, he judged that the bourgeois tradition of keeping bride and groom apart before the wedding night was emotionally damaging. In 1905, he argued that the old maid of the middle class and the working girl of the streets were two sides of the same coin, both showing the effects on single women of the morality of bourgeois society: one was forced into prudishness and the other into immorality in order to make a living. So long as prostitution existed, Michels said, "our much praised civilization is nothing but a pretty facade behind which are concealed filth and crime."[48]

In 1909, Michels softened his position on respectability and his attacks on bourgeois society and prostitution, according to Mitzman, who summarized:

Analyzing sexual behavior in Italian cities, he found it difficult in many cases to say who is a prostitute and who is not. There was, apparently, a whole stratum of single girls who would take both sewing work and men in the same room for pay. The ground, of course, for accepting this kind of supplementary income was the low wage for sewing piecework. How, then, were these girls to be economically classed: as dressmakers or prostitutes? And how were they to be morally judged? Clearly, no unambiguous solution was possible. Michels held the same relaxed view of young married middle-class women, who, bored with a purposeless existence, might frequent dance halls and flirt with young men while their husbands were at work.[49]

Michels's book *Sexual Ethics: A Study of Borderland Questions* incorporates the essays just mentioned (with the exception of the 1903 piece).[50] The status of this book is illustrative of the central problem from which I began this study—the hitherto neglected impact of feminist movements on classical sociological theory. The book itself is difficult to find, and there is scant mention of it in the secondary literature. Although Arthur Mitzman refers to articles on sexual morality published by Michels in *Mutterschutz* (*Prenatal Care*) and elsewhere, as well as to his *Problems of Social Philosophy* (1914), he dismisses other articles written from 1902 to 1904 as "a large number of short, generally unimportant pieces [that] appeared in the journals of the movement for women's rights: *Dokumente der Frauen, Die Frau*, and *Neues Frauenleben*."[51] Juan Linz lists a book by Michels entitled *Die Grenzen der Geschlechtsmoral: Prolegomena, Gedanken, und Untersuchungen*, published in 1911 (the same year that *Political Parties* appeared); however, he does not mention the translation into English of Michels's writings on the feminist questions of his time. In 1915, the Walter Scott Publishing Company of London and Charles Scribner's Sons of New York published *Sexual Ethics* as part of a series edited by Havelock Ellis. In this edition, the author stated that although prior to the nineteenth century sexual questions were broached in the field of letters in England as much as in other countries, "during the nineteenth century . . . England became fiercely hostile to all literary study or discussion of questions of sex" (*SE*, v). He noted that at the time he was writing the situation had changed, and England had moved to the front ranks of sexual reform and research (*SE*, v–vi); he hoped, therefore, for a hospitable reception to his work.

Michels observed that the national and economic conflicts in modern Europe were vast in scale and revealed sharply sensed injustices, and also that "sex antagonisms have become and are continually becoming more acute" (*SE*, 196). His explanation for this shift of consciousness was similar to the explanations of Tocqueville and Durkheim (*SE*, 196–219). He presented an argument, consistent with his theoretical position, about the seriousness of women's rights:

Considering in especial the movement for the emancipation
of women, we find that the sense of oppression is now very
strongly felt by certain women who constitute a proportion
of their sex quantitatively small. . . . The woman's question,
when we consider its historical foundation, the diversity of its
social, intellectual, and economic aspects, and the intensity of
feeling that animates the movement, must be recognized as
no fairy tale to occupy the energies of a few unbalanced women,
but a most serious problem, whose relation demands the coor-
dinated efforts of the best of both sexes. (*SE*, 198–99)

Michels's discussions of sexuality, sexual morality, and the relations of the sexes had as its stimulus "the new sexual ethic" advocated by feminists (*SE*, 90). He divided his work into four parts
of several chapters each: (1) General Borderland Problems of the
Erotic Life; (2) Borderland Problems of Extra-Conjugal Erotic Life;
(3) Conjugal Borderland Problems; and (4) Borderland Problems of
the Conjugal Sexual Life. He pointed out that criticisms of "duplex
sexual morality" either demanded equality of rights to sexual liberty for women or demanded chastity prior to marriage for men.
The most advanced feminists in England, France, and Germany,
influenced by doctrines of freedom to develop one's individuality, supported the former (*SE*, 143), whereas the Italians in the
early twentieth century tended to support the latter (*SE*, 283–88).
Michels supported premarital chastity for men as an ideal, but he
doubted that very many would practice it, given the sexual psychology of men and the traditions that supported male polygamy
(*SE*, 137–38, and see *SE*, 144–45). "What a man loves is not a
woman, but women, that is to say, the female of his species" (*SE*,
28). Michels was virtually alone in the sociological tradition in seeking to illuminate the "love struggle" between men and women by
reference to the "erotic coquetry" in the sexual behavior of "lower
animals." As he understood it, "The use of physical force to overcome the object of erotic desire, the forcible attainment of sexual
possession of the female, is one of the normal biological elements of
the erotic function as such, as may be seen daily in animal life" (*SE*,
121–23). Under extreme sexual stimulation, Michels believed, the
sexual nature of men reveals its animality (*SE*, 129–30). Despite his
stand for equality of men and women in sexual matters, a recurrent
theme in *Sexual Ethics* is that men are sexually more aggressive

than women, at least in part due to social structures and cultural traditions.

Michels described the dimensions of power and conflict in the relations of the sexes.

> The psychology of the male is of such a character that the average man does not merely feel that the prostitute, willing or unwilling, should be at every man's disposal; further than this, he thinks that the girl who has once fallen becomes thereby all men's legitimate prey—that she has in the future no moral right to refuse herself to any man who desires her. (SE, 164)

He pointed out that in male-dominated morality the honor of a "violated" woman could be saved only if the man who has "deprived her of virginity" marries her (SE, 165–66). Categorizations of women were rigidly ensconced in law, which recognized only two kinds of women: "regulated prostitutes and respectable women" (SE, 91). The domination of women through a double standard is revealed, Michels wrote, in that "a woman's first act of sexual love, which may also be the last, decides her whole fate" (SE, 167).

Michels described and judged the conflict and power relations evident in marriage. Particularly damning are his words on the violation of married women by their husbands. As he put it, the "original vice of the institution" of marriage is that "the wife is legally and morally bound to lend herself willingly to the sexual desires of her husband." He agreed with the critics of marriage who asserted "that this institution to-day is not infrequently nothing more than the cloak for acts of rape sanctified and authorized by the law" (SE, 38). Thus marriage, according to Michels, reproduced in a worse form than prostitution the vulnerability of women (SE, 38–39).

His discussion of sex-role inequality and its manifestations in human unhappiness is reminiscent of the writings of J. S. Mill:

> It is the widening of the chasm between the intellectual and cultural life of husband and wife which undermines the ideal foundation of marriage. Marriage and love are shattered like a fragile glass vessel when the man continues to experience spiritual growth, whilst the woman is confined within four walls and her interests are limited to the crying of her children, the cares of domestic economy, and the gossip of her neighbors; and no less so when she devotes herself to frivolous

amusement, and meets the aspirations and ideals of her husband with indifference or with open contempt.

He added that men caught up in business concerns were often incapable of appreciating new intellectual interests of their wives (*SE*, 174). In the last chapter of *Sexual Ethics*, on married life, he noted the resistance of husbands to the intellectual cultivation of their wives, especially if the wife had more ability than the husband in the same field, if she differed from him on politics, or if her public pursuits resulted in his having an increased share of domestic duties. He concluded, "Thus masculine egoism imposes limits in many cases to the possibility of women's intellectual development" (*SE*, 268). A wife who is also a mother faces conflicting demands, which vary in intensity, from three sources—her husband, her children, and herself. Beyond the first two "at the same time she will have to give due weight to the often conflicting claims of her own personal development" (*SE*, 282). Michels agreed with Clara Zetkin's advocacy of a "juster apportionment of rights and duties [in domestic chores, including the upbringing of children] which would make that life a better one for both parties" (*SE*, 281). A more egalitarian division of labor, Michels argued, would not only overcome "the comparatively trifling value" placed on housework, but it also would provide the husband "an enlargement of and diversification of his mental horizon" (*SE*, 280, 279). His general stance at the time he wrote was that "the violated [raped] woman is in some way an accessory," because of her poor education and her cowardice in the face of victimization. Against the "fatalistic habit of mind" of such women in married life, Michels said he would choose a modern, independent, "free woman" (*SE*, 131–32).

Michels advocated family planning (but opposed abortion) in the interests of marital and family happiness and economic well-being, especially for the poor. He pointed out that the life of a woman who had a very large number of children was "reduced to a purely animal function" (*SE*, 237). Reductions of the birth rate, he observed, were associated with economic advance and, in turn, with the victory of reason over irrational passion. Finally, he maintained, sexual love exists for its own sake, not solely for reproduction (*SE*, 232–64).

Michels argued that feminists "must not cease to protest against all those external forms of public life which imply a depreciation of woman, or a lower estimation of woman than man" (*SE*, 206). He noted the sexism of speech conventions, particularly the cultural indifference to a man's marital status as compared to the customary requirement of defining a woman's marital status in forms of address. He found speech forms in Russia, the United States, Italy, and Spain more respectful to women's individuality than those in Germany. He summed up, "In this respect, Germany (including German Austria), despite the existence of a vigorous feminist movement, lags greatly behind the rest of the civilised world" (*SE*, 211).

The theoretical and methodological framework that Michels employed when he wrote *Sexual Ethics* is a nice combination of class analysis and attention to cultural variation. He mentioned variations in shame and sexual morality of proletarian and upper-class women (*SE*, 54–57). Women workers, he asserted, are degraded twice—as women and as workers (*SE*, 115). He also saw class variations in the relations of the sexes: proletarian men needed wives to meet sexual and domestic needs for which they could not pay; in contrast, the men of the possessing classes who could afford to pay housekeepers and prostitutes avoided marriage and the consequent loss of freedom. The result, according to Michels, was that the phenomenon of the old maid was to be found almost exclusively in the various strata of the bourgeoisie, whereas it was rare to find proletarian women over thirty who were prostitutes. As mentioned earlier, his thesis was that the working-class prostitute was the old maid of the proletariat. Michels, unlike Pareto (who later became one of his intellectual mentors), argued in a straightforward fashion that these facts were of "purely economic causation" (*SE*, 103). "The enormous majority of women who become prostitutes do so to escape from the joyless life of the working woman" (*SE*, 108) and "as a direct consequence of economic pressures" (*SE*, 111). He stated the connection between class and personal degradation:

> It is a fact of observation that where women's wages rise, prostitution diminishes to a proportionate degree; and conversely, with a fall in women's wages, not merely does there ensue an increase in the number of prostitutes, but, further, as a necessary result of increasing competition, the market price of the prostitute's services fall. (*SE*, 111–12)

His remedy for prostitution was forthright and consistent with his analysis: "The St. George that will slay the dragon of prostitution, as we know the monster of to-day, must be the complete economic and cultural equality of all members of the community without distinction of sex" (*SE*, 119).

Michels's analysis of prostitution and the relations of the sexes in general reveals his sensitivity to the factors of ethnicity and cultural differences—what he termed comparative sexual psychology. His cosmospolitanism attuned him to English prudery, French coquetry and desire for diversity in love, Italian openness in private talk about erotic matters, and the passivity of German women (*SE*, 224–31). He observed that these cultural differences were evident in the varieties of styles of and attitudes toward prostitution. In Italy, England, and Germany (with differences between the mercenary style in the North and the more personal relationship with the client in the South), the prostitute was viewed as a debased creature, an instrument of male pleasure. The prostitutes of the Latin Quarter in Paris were, by contrast, more highly esteemed, according to Michels, and retained a measure of human dignity and independence.[52] These he attributed to the tradition of economic independence of French tradeswomen, a tradition weakened by the economic transformation and general decadence during Louis Bonaparte's reign (*SE*, 63–69). By comparison, Michels accounted for the backwardness of German sexual morality and conceptions of women by the political and social persistence of the power of agrarian feudalism in the midst of developing industrial capitalism (*SE*, 202–6). His analysis of prostitution is distinctive among the theorists in observing the racist and ethnic dimensions of prostitution (see *SE*, 115–17): "Sometimes the nationalists hold that prostitution must be reserved exclusively for women belonging or thought to belong to inferior races, on the ground that prostitution is an unsuitable occupation for the dominant race" (*SE*, 118).

In evaluating *Sexual Ethics*, I must agree with Linz that Michels wrote on topics (sexuality and sexual relationships—in terms of male domination) that were not taken up to the same extent by many contemporary sociologists. He wrote about commercialization of sex in pornography, suggesting that the solution to the problem of obscene literature would not be won by prosecutions but by openness and "a *sincerification* of human sexual relationships" (*SE*, 5, and 1–14). He discussed the issue of sexual education, arguing that since sexuality is part of the natural order of life, instruction should not artificially reinforce sex-role distinctions (*SE*, 15–25, especially 21–22; see also *SE*, 176). Further, Michels poignantly depicted the effects of conventional patterns and beliefs on men and women. He recog-

nized the difficulty for women of the abrupt transition from virginity to married sexual life and early motherhood (*SE*, 177–86).
He clearly pointed out the contradictions of the male fantasy of the
"'pure' woman," who, having had sexual intercourse, is by definition no longer a "pure" woman, and then the man she has made
love with "cannot forgive her for having consented to his wishes"
(*SE*, 214–15). Although Michels's writings might seem to tell us
nothing new, it must be remembered that he was writing some sev-
enty years ago.

Mitzman is on target in his observation that Michels's writings
on the "woman question" prefigure a shift in his political commitment—his disillusionment with German socialism of the type exemplified by the Social Democratic Party and his correlative adoption of an ethical idealism associated with Italian culture (see *SE*,
283–88). Throughout *Sexual Ethics*, he used examples from Italian
and French culture to criticize German society. In 1913, Michels,
like Simmel in 1910, subjected coquetry to a strictly sociological
analysis, noting that it was not primarily sexual but stemmed from
the wish to be favorably noticed. The asexual motives for coquetry
included the love of beautiful clothes and the desire of frigid women
to control men, he wrote. He thought that coquetry functioned socially and pyschologically to render harmless the expression outside
of marriage of sexual drives that monogamy could not suppress
(*SE*, 224–26). As Mitzman has noted, "Characteristic for the evolution of Michels's values is the shifting of responsibility for coquetry
between the first article [1903] and the last [1913], from 'bourgeois
society,' which was an object of attack, to 'monogamous society,' at
most an object of investigation."[53] I hasten to add that this change
in Michels's politics does not vitiate his work from a non-Marxist
feminist standpoint. The shift in his thought is typical of that of virtually the whole of the non-Marxist tradition of classical sociological
theory. Bourgeois social theory embodied and contributed to a decline of faith in the ideas and ideals of the Enlightenment, critical
reason, and any hope for the future of humankind.[54] Positivist or-
ganicism, historicist relativism, or Giambattista Vico's cyclical view
of history as *corsi* and *ricorsi* replaced the belief in progress and
equality.[55] In fact, as Hughes has noted, "Michels adapted himself
quite easily to the Fascist regime, and his later writings contain references to Mussolini's rule that are unmistakably respectful in tone."[56]
Drawing on Weber's pessimistic analysis of bureaucracy, Michels saw
in Mussolini the charismatic leader who would smash the stultifica-

tion of culture and politics brought about by the bureaucratization of social life.[57]

The struggles for and against the emancipation and equality of women were part of the larger historical struggles for socialism and against war and reaction in the twentieth century. In *Les systemes socialistes*, Pareto observed, "It may well prove that in certain countries the Nationalists, the Imperialists, and the Agrarians will be the only parties capable of resisting Socialism, and *vice versa*" (*MS* 3:1145n. 1702). Socialism and the women's movement had both gained ground in the second half of the nineteenth century. Pareto noted that "towards the beginning of the twentieth century came a counter-offensive by the religions differing from Socialism." While sentiments favoring socialism and liberalism weakened in this period, "nationalism underwent a remarkable revival, Catholicism prospered once more, the various metaphysical systems emerged from their eclipse, and even magic and astrology again made room for themselves" (*MS* 3:1145–46). The counterrevolution that began in panic and in earnest in the aftermath of the Paris Commune and later against feminism continued in its struggle against the authentic forces of feminist and socialist revolution.

Pareto anticipated in more than one way the temporary success of the counterrevolution, in particular Fascism in Italy. Mussolini considered Pareto one of his masters. And it was Mussolini who admonished, "Do not let us wander off into discussions as to whether women are inferior to men; let us agree they are different."[58] He believed, as Maria Castellani put it, that women "differ profoundly from men." The Fascists were "laying down a division of duties between the two sexes," women's role being that of the "lubricating oil" of the complicated machinery of modern society. Castellani asserted that in the countries leading the fight against Bolshevism, "women have always been among the first supporters of Fascism."[59] Pareto's work then may offer warnings about the forces raising their ugly heads, hopefully without success, against the human rights of American women.

6

The United States

Contrasting Versions of the Sociological

Tradition on Sex Roles

The absence of a tradition of socialist feminism as it occurred in
Germany or in France is a striking feature of the history of feminism in the United States. A middle-class democracy from its inception, the United States has no history of feudalism and as a result did not experience the same struggle of classes and the clash of
ideologies witnessed in continental Europe in the revolutionary
transition from aristocracy to democracy.[1] Instead, feminism in the
United States, like feminism in England, was more influenced by
the ideas of the Enlightenment and the eighteenth-century age of
democratic revolution, with its themes of rational inquiry and education, liberation from traditional superstitions and tyrannical political authorities, and the strong belief that the rights to equality
and liberty are an inalienable part of the natural order.[2] Slavery and
racism also are pivotal in American history, as Tocqueville astutely
pointed out almost a century and a half ago, expressing his fear of
a revolution by freed blacks denied the exercise of their full civil

rights.[3] From within the movement to abolish slavery, many feminists emerged.[4] Both the lack of a strong tradition of socialism or social democracy as in France or Germany and the crucial issue of racism have shaped and limited the working-class and feminist movements in the United States and the development of American social theory as well.[5]

"The rhetoric of the American Revolution," Nancy Cott has written, "glorified women's role . . . by connecting it with the success of the national experiment."[6] A classic document of early American feminism is the famous letter from Abigail Adams to her husband, John, in which she wrote that "all men would be tyrants if they could," and warned, half-jokingly, that "if perticular care and attention is not paid to the Laidies we are determined to foment a Rebelion, and will not hold ourselves bound by any Laws in which we have no voice, or Representation."[7] However, her voice was unheeded. The Declaration of Independence did not represent slaves or women; in reality, the drafters of the Declaration and of the Constitution meant that only some men—white men of property—were created equal.

In the late eighteenth century, as Cott has stated, "There was extraordinary turbulence in sexual patterns and definitions." The changes were contained and channeled by the idea that women were passionless; Cott suggests that this view "was tied to the rise of evangelical religion between the 1790s and the 1830s."[8] But it was also true that within movements for reform associated with religious revivalism, especially from the 1820s on, the "woman question" became an explosive issue in North American society. The Second Great Awakening, under the leadership of Charles Grandison Finney in New York State, "legitimized the involvement of middle-class women in volunteer reform work in an era when paid employment was frowned upon for them."[9] Alice S. Rossi has observed the "overlap and continuity in the sequence of reform movements that emerged between the 1820s and the 1850s: from evangelical revivals to moral reform, abolition, temperance, and woman's rights." Further, she notes:

> There was nevertheless a distinct contrast between the cause of women and all the other movements. Benevolent reform, applied to people "out there." . . . But when middle-class women demanded changes in the law to give them control over their own persons, their property or their children, or to

receive more and better education, or to participate in government through the franchise, the demands were not only
closer to home—they were *in* the home.[10] (Rossi's emphasis)

To get a sense of the prejudices facing those who advocated
women's rights, there is no better place to look than at the powerful
and exquisite correspondence between Angelina Grimké and her
fiancé, Theodore Weld, who was a convert to Finney's new humanist gospel, an abolitionist, and an advocate of women's rights.
Grimké wrote to Weld (March 1838) that she thought their marriage "was to be my dismission from *public* service" in the antislavery cause. Weld replied, "You are the FIRST woman everywhere
known to be on this ground to whom in the Providence of God the
practical test of married life will be applied (if we are spared)."
With honesty, Weld added, "Married life will be the touchstone to
test me and to show how I reduce to practice what I have long and
perhaps pertinaciously contended for in *theory.*" That they understood each other is evident in Grimké's reply: "Yes, thou art trying a
dangerous experiment, one which I do believe *no other man* would
try because I tho't *no other* understands my principles or myself"
(Grimké's and Weld's emphases).[11]

In the abolitionist movement itself, women encountered resistance to women's rights. The "woman issue" produced divisions
among abolitionists in 1837–38. The Grimké sisters, members of a
prominent southern family, took a lead in the antislavery movement and, in what we could call feminist terms, appealed to women
to join the crusade. Angelina Grimké argued that female slaves "are
our sisters; and to us as women, they have a right to look for sympathy with their sorrows and effort and prayer for their rescue."[12] For
raising the "woman question," the sisters were rebuffed by antislavery clergymen and chastised by officers of the New England abolition society for forgetting "the great and dreadful wrongs of the
slave in a selfish crusade against some paltry grievance . . . some
trifling oppression, political or social, of their own."[13] This argument against women's claims to equal rights has been used, most
often by men, in nearly every historical context I have considered
here.[14] It was just this kind of anti–women's rights stance that led to
the Declaration of Sentiments, which, like Abigail Adams's arguments, paralleled the Declaration of Independence. Alice Rossi
summarizes:

The first woman's-rights meeting in American history took place in a Methodist church in Seneca Falls, New York, on July 19 and 20, 1848. The women responsible for calling this historic meeting had met for a social occasion only six days earlier, in Waterloo, a few miles from Seneca Falls. There, in the home of Jane Hunt, they prepared their now famous Declaration of Sentiments and eleven resolutions covering their aims for presentation at the meeting. The ninth was the demand, revolutionary for its time: "Resolved, That it is the duty of the women of this country to secure to themselves the sacred right to the elective franchise." The most controversial of the eleven resolutions in 1848, suffrage for women, was destined to become a central rallying point as the woman's-rights movement developed over the ensuing decades.[15]

However, many of the one hundred women and men who signed the declaration later removed their names when "the storm of ridicule began to break" in the press.[16]

The revolutionary events of 1848 in Europe also had their effect on American feminists. Sheila Rowbotham has written of Margaret Fuller (1810–50), "the transcendentalist feminist and republican": "Both in her life and writing, [she shows] the manner in which radical ideas were being communicated, not only across national boundaries but across boundaries of colour, class and sex." Fuller traced the beginnings of the idea of women's emancipation to the French Revolution, asserting, "As men become aware that few men have had a fair chance, they are inclined to say that no women have had a fair chance." She urged psychological independence of women from men and saw the need for political mobilization of women to achieve their freedom. Being one's own person, not defining oneself by a relationship with a man, developed into "a crucial theme of feminism," according to Rowbotham. Fuller went to France in 1847 where she met George Sand and "was swept away with enthusiasm for the revolution of 1848, and took an active part in the movement for Italian liberation." Fuller wrote *Woman in the Nineteenth Century* (1845), which Rowbotham has termed "a remarkably perceptive account of the psychological and cultural effects of women's oppression." She knew them well: "Margaret Fuller understood and expressed the tragic exhaustion of the French feminist socialists, who pitted themselves not only against the dominant economic and political values of early capitalism, but also against inhuman sexual relations. Like them she was battered and bruised terribly for her insolence."[17]

However, the central public struggle of women in the United States in the post–Civil War period until 1920 was the struggle for suffrage. According to Rowbotham's synthesis:

> In America . . . the feminist movement came out of the anti-slavery campaign and two tendencies emerged. One group restricted its demand to the vote and were willing to settle for a compromise on total suffrage. But another group based in New York, with Susan B. Anthony and Elizabeth Cady Stanton, not only refused to compromise over the franchise but connected emancipation with change in marriage, clothing, morals and the organization of labour. They produced a short-lived journal called *The Revolution* in 1868. . . . The main wing of American feminism was far more cautious and far more conservative. Its advocates were at once ignorant and contemptuous of organized labour, though later, in the 1890s, a social feminism, connected with the settlements, developed. This was concerned rather to improve the working conditions of girls and women in factories and sweat shops rather than the problem of connecting the liberation of women with the idea of revolution.[18]

Elizabeth Cady Stanton poignantly formulated the problems of being at once a feminist and a married woman with children, unsupported in her activism by the men in her life. Recounting a confrontation with her father over her public activity in support of women's rights, Stanton wrote to Susan B. Anthony: "I never felt more keenly the degradation of my sex. To think that all in me of which my father would have felt a proper pride had I been a man is deeply mortifying to him because I am a woman. That thought has stung me to a fierce decision—to speak as soon as I can do myself credit." She went on to add that her husband, Henry, as well as her friends, opposed "all that is dearest to my heart. They are not willing that I should write even on the woman question. But I will both write and speak." On the suppression of women's anger, she wrote: "I think if women would indulge more freely in vituperation, they would enjoy ten times the health they do. It seems to me they are suffering from repression." And on the topic of childbirth and the male-dominated medical profession: "Dear me, how much cruel bondage of mind and suffering of body poor woman will escape when she takes the liberty of being her own physician of both body and soul!"[19]

Susan Anthony's ability to articulate the consequences of sexism was evident in what she said at a state convention of schoolteachers in 1853—after winning the right to speak:

> It seems to me, gentlemen, that none of you quite compre-
> hend the cause of the disrespect of which you complain. Do
> you not see that so long as society says a woman is incompe-
> tent to be a lawyer, minister or doctor, but has ample ability to
> be a teacher, that every man of you who chooses this profes-
> sion tacitly acknowledges that he has no more brains than a
> woman? And this, too, is the reason that teaching is a less lu-
> crative profession, as here men must compete with the cheap
> labor of woman. Would you exalt your profession, exalt those
> who labor with you. Would you make it more lucrative, in-
> crease the salaries of the women engaged in the noble work of
> educating our future Presidents, Senators, and Congressmen.[20]

Nevertheless, Stanton's and Anthony's increasingly radical feminism remained within the framework of middle-class liberalism. Row-botham has noted that "Emma Goldman showed how the Stanton-Anthony tendency within feminism remained deliberately blinkered about labour movement struggles, even to the point of supporting strike-breaking by women. This earned them the antagonism not only of male but female workers."[21]

The position of women was weaker in the early nineteenth century than it had been in colonial America. When production came to be located away from the household, "women were effectively cut off from participation in the significant work of their society. A woman's labor at home was less valued, and her husband was apt to invest large amounts of time and energy in economic efforts away from the household. As a result, the grounds for a woman's sense of self-worth narrowed during the decades when men's expanded." By the period of Jacksonian democracy, there had emerged the ideo-logical correlate of these changes in the economic foundation of society: the cult of "True Womanhood."[22] Robin Miller Jacoby has observed that economic development was cast in the language of repressed sexuality: thrift was abstinence; an expenditure was an ejaculation. For men economic activity was a measure of virility; for women domesticity was associated with piety, purity, and submissiveness.[23] As Carl N. Degler, a student of the role of women in American history, has argued:

> If the frontier experience helped to create a vague feminist bias that accorded women more privileges than in settled Europe, the really potent force had little to do with the frontier or the newness of the country. It was the industrial revolution that provided the impetus to women's aspirations for equality of opportunity; it was the industrial revolution that carried through the first stage in the changing position of women— the removal of legal and customary barriers to women's full participation in the activities of the world.[24]

The development of industrial capitalism in the United States altered the locus and character of feminist protest. Alice Rossi has noted "a marked change in political ideas, intellectual tone and personal style" in the American feminism emerging in the latter part of the nineteenth century:

> The woman's movement represented by Susan B. Anthony and Elizabeth Stanton drew deeply on its roots in small-town America and reacted far more strongly to what had been lost as the United States embarked on its romance with industrialization than to what the future might hold or to the price attached to industrialism for the millions of women less fortunate than themselves. Though they wrote and spoke as if they were equally concerned with women at all levels of society, the nineteenth-century woman's-rights spokeswomen rarely knew or deeply cared for the lot of women outside their own social class. . . . When the chips were down during the last stage of the suffrage movement, they did not draw back from the anti-immigrant ethos then abroad in the country but bent it to their own political ends, arguing that the best women of the country—middle-class, educated, moral, Protestant—would, if given the vote, help counteract the political power of the growing numbers of new citizens among the immigrants.[25]

Degler has observed yet another effect of industrial capitalism on the conditions of the struggle for women's rights: "As workers outside the home, women buried the Victorian stereotype of the lady under a mountain of reality."[26] The changing focus of American feminism to urban, secular, industrial, and class concerns was evident in the activity of women in working-class, socialist, and trade-union movements.[27] Perhaps the most striking example was feminist and anarchist Emma Goldman, "often described as the finest woman speaker in America," as Martin Green has noted.[28] Born in Lithuania in 1869, she left Russia and arrived in New York in 1889 and was deported to the Soviet Union during the "red scare" following World War I. "Red Emma" became a symbol of anarchism, feared because of its "propaganda of the deed," which included alleged assassinations and bombings. Goldman had attended Freud's lectures in Vienna in 1895. She read Ibsen and Nietzsche and was heavily influenced by Walt Whitman as well as by Peter Kropotkin and Edward Carpenter. She combined in her life personal and political revolution. She was critical of feminists who did not understand the struggles of the working class and also of feminists who thought emancipation was a matter only of removing "external tyrannies." The "internal tyrants" of conventional morality and centuries of slavery and submission had to be overcome, she wrote. She believed that the liberated woman must manifest herself as "a personality, and not as a sex commodity," but that she also must not accept personal relationships with men who were interested in her only as a political or intellectual person.[29]

Other feminists on the left were Mary Harris Jones (Mother Jones) and Elizabeth Gurley Flynn, the "Rebel Girl," who organized with the Industrial Workers of the World and later joined the American Communist Party. Flynn was involved in the efforts by women to combat the prejudices of men during the Lawrence, Massachusetts, textile strike that the IWW led in 1912.[30] Louise Bryant, another outstanding woman, reported on the Bolshevik Revolution in her book *Mirror from Moscow* and interviewed Angelica Balbanov, the Italian feminist and socialist.[31] Bryant traveled to Moscow with John Reed, who described the Russian Revolution in *Ten Days that Shook the World.*

Intellectually, the change in the orientation of feminism can be measured by the work of Charlotte Perkins Gilman, particularly in her book *Women and Economics* (1898), and Florence Kelley, a socialist, who first translated into English Engels's *The Condition of the Working Class in England.* As a young girl, Kelley, whose father was a congressman from Philadelphia, was shocked by the treatment of child laborers in the Pennsylvania glass factories and steel mills. She later became chief inspector of factories for the State of Illinois and worked tirelessly for reform to improve the lives of women and children. Gilman's book—which drew on the nineteenth-century theory of social progress, particularly the work of American sociologist Lester Ward—made her "the leading intellectual in the women's movement in the United States during the first two decades of the twentieth century." Not an activist in reform movements, but a lecturer and publicist, Gilman, who did not characterize herself as a feminist, preferred to be called a sociologist.[32]

Rosalyn Baxandall, Linda Gordon, and Susan Reverby, historians of women of the working class, have noted that the period from the 1880s to the First World War "was richer in radical and reform movements than any in U.S. history," and many of the women who were becoming wage workers in increasing numbers were coming from a heritage of European radicalism.[33] Meredith Tax has agreed: "Socialist housewives, settlement workers, and the left wing of the feminist movement were the main allies in the period."[34] Baxandall, Gordon, and Reverby found that some educated women, "radicalized by their contact with working-class women, . . . joined union organizations [such as the Women's Trade Union League set up in 1903] and the Socialist Party." The Socialist Party "brought together radical intellectuals, big-city immigrant workers, western miners, migrant workers, and many other socialists."[35] Historian Mari Jo Buhle has pointed out that the Socialist Party was the only party at the time that allowed women to participate. The history of the Socialist Party manifested conflicts between feminists, socialists, and socialist feminists similar to those in Germany's Social Democratic Party: socialist feminists were suspicious of middle-class suffragists; the actual behavior of male socialists toward women comrades often belied the party ideal of equality; there were debates about the treatment of women and over autonomous organizations for women; and eventually there was a male backlash. Nevertheless, at its national convention in 1908 in Chicago, when women confronted the party, men gave in and agreed to the formation of a National Women's Committee headed by May Wood Simons; the committee was constitutionally incorporated into the party in 1910 with the blessing of Eugene V. Debs. Women's role in the party began to increase, and at its peak in the 1910–13 period, women's membership reached approximately 15 percent.[36]

From about 1913 on, feminism lost momentum in the party. In

that year the Socialist Party stopped publishing *Progressive Women.* Margaret Sanger, among other radical women, turned to Bill Haywood's IWW for a hospitable climate for her feminist and anarchistic ideas.[37] Sanger is most famous for her advocacy of family planning and birth control so that women might "free themselves from biological slavery." In 1915 and again in 1920, she traveled to London where she confronted the century-long debate between Malthusians and anti-Malthusian socialists about the part played by population growth in the misery of the working class.[38] Although feminism seemed to lose its momentum, "on the eve of World War I a powerful working-class movement and an overlapping socialist movement made radical changes seem likely in the United States."[39] Still, it is difficult to avoid the interpretation that not only the reaction to the Bolshevik Revolution but also the diffuseness of class consciousness among the working class and the absence of radical theory in the United States contributed to the more fundamental weaknesses of socialism, socialist feminism, and the movement of working-class women.[40]

It must be emphasized that middle-class women were the ones who benefited from the industrialization of household chores—such as the commercial processing of food—in the post–Civil War period. As Degler puts it, "These middle-class women became the bone and sinew of the feminist movement, which was almost entirely an urban affair. They joined the women's clubs, organized the temperance crusades and marched in the suffrage parades. With an increasing amount of time available to them in the city, and imbued with the historic American value of work, they sought to do good."[41] Jane Addams's well-known social work, similar to efforts by middle-class women in Europe, was part of this movement. Frances Willard's work with the Women's Christian Temperance Union is another example.[42] In addition, during the period from about 1890 to 1920, the so-called Progressive movement flourished and influenced feminists. As historian Thomas K. Frazier has observed:

The Progressives provided influential support for the women's suffrage movement, which had made little headway since the first women's rights convention in 1848. Ironically, by the time the feminists won the vote with the Nineteenth Amendment of 1920, the women's movement had split into so many factions that the new vote had little effect on existing social, economic, or political policy. Rather, most of the feminists came from the

white middle class and voted in the interest of that group, reflecting the bias of the Progressives in general.[43]

The First World War was the crucial event of the period politically and culturally. To paraphrase F. Scott Fitzgerald in *The Great
Gatsby*, what had been the warm center of the world, America, became the ragged edge of the universe. The war had contradictory
effects on the feminist movement. It broke through some customary and legal barriers to women's employment and provided ideological sustenance for feminist arguments to extend the vote to women;
achievement of suffrage in the United States, as in Germany and
Britain, followed the war. However, the cutting edge of feminism,
as well as that of socialist and working-class movements, was dulled
by this achievement, and by national chauvinism, institutional
change, centralization of power, and repression. The "anticipated
new and broad advances for their sex," in Degler's phrase, did not
materialize for women either economically or politically. After the
Nineteenth Amendment was adopted (the struggle for which had
gone on for nearly three quarters of a century), the organized
women's movement was distilled down to Alice Paul's National
Women's Party, whose main goal was passage of the Equal Rights
Amendment, still unachieved more than half a century later. American women did not use their vote ideologically; instead they "voted
not as women but as individuals," Degler has noted. His thesis is
that the arguments for suffrage came as close as one can get in America "to being a full-blown ideology of feminism," a threatening prospect that accounted for the intensity of the opposition to suffrage.[44]
Winning the right of suffrage in 1920 marked the end of the first
period in the struggle for women's rights in America and the beginning of the second, characterized by Degler as "the participation of
married women in the work force." He observed, "The twenties
witnessed the emergence of the white-collar class, and women were
a large part of it." With the increase in the size and complexity of
firms beyond production and distribution, "new opportunities for
women opened up in business offices." For example, "the telephone
operator, the typist, the clerical worker and the stenographer now
took places beside the seamstress, the cotton mill operator and the
teacher."[45] The entry of women into white-collar occupations was,
as we shall see, perceptively depicted by C. Wright Mills.
With changes in the status of women in the work force came

changes in clothing styles, family relations, education, and sexual
mores. The requirements of work led to alterations in women's dress
and appearance, away from corsets and toward physical freedom.
Women for the first time smoked and drank in public, even during
Prohibition. A popular interest in sexuality, coincident with the
public's discovery of Freud, emerged during the twenties. In educated circles there was talk of a new conception of marriage in
which husband and wife were partners and companions. The clash
between new and traditional notions of marriage was reflected in
the sharp increase in the rate of divorce, up 50 percent from what it
had been just a decade earlier. Two-thirds of the divorces in the
twenties were initiated by women. Degler has concluded that "the
revolution in morals of the 1920's is more accurately a revolution in
the position of women." He summarizes:

> By the close of the twenties the ordinary woman in America
> was closer to a man in the social behavior expected of her, in
> the economic opportunities open to her and in the intellectual
> freedom enjoyed by her than at any time in history. To be sure
> there still was a double standard, but now its existence was
> neither taken for granted nor confidently asserted by men.[46]

At the end of the decade (1929) Sophie Tucker was singing "Aren't
Women Wonderful." Nevertheless, the gains women achieved in the
1920s were depoliticized. During this period what Rowbotham has
termed "the manufacture of beauty" emerged, led by the glamor
industry and a mass culture (especially in films) that marketed a
new image of femininity. The 1920s were not without antifeminist
currents, social amnesia among young emancipated women, and ad-
verse reactions to the gains made by women during the first long
wave of feminism spanning the period from the revolution of the
eighteenth century to the First World War.[47]

In her book *America through Women's Eyes*, historian Mary
Beard has described the political economy of the twenties as follows:

> In the smooth era of "prosperity" for the United States, which
> followed the World War, generally accepted thinking took on
> the nature of the automatic machine. In the Coolidge formula-
> tion of policy, adopted as sound by President Hoover at the

beginning of his administration, lay the pleasing assumption that the economic system would operate flawlessly, shedding its golden blessings in every direction—provided nothing were done by the government to interfere with its divinely appointed mission, save possibly in minor details. . . . The crash of 1929 cast doubts on existing perfection and its intellectual shadow. Then, suddenly, with the force of an earthquake or tidal wave, suspicion of imperfections arose in all quarters and engines of skepticism and criticism were wheeled in position.

Just as women had participated in the social and intellectual changes of the twenties, and, Beard has observed, "Having worked their way into every department of the political and social structure and having a long tradition of feminine criticism as encouragement, women shared in the tempest of discussion which blew at the close of 'the perfect day.'"[48] Women actively shared not only in the travails of the Depression but also in the miseries of the near breakdown of capitalism.

Brief consideration of the condition of women during the Great Depression is in order. Despite the achievement of the vote, women were still affected by numerous discriminatory state laws, such as those requiring their husbands' consent in order to control their own earnings. Three out of ten women workers were employed in personal service and domestic work. At the end of the thirties, fewer than a million out of ten million women workers were members of trade unions. What increase did occur was largely due to the rise of the Congress of Industrial Organizations, organized and led by the left wing of the American working-class movement. As Robert Shaffer has pointed out:

During the early New Deal, the National Recovery Administration codified lower wages for women than for men doing the same work, and some union contracts did the same thing later in the decade. Furthermore, because so many women worked only part-time or in domestic service, proportionally more women than men workers were excluded from New Deal reforms. Married women in the work force faced attack from many quarters, including the Democratic Party, and many, especially teachers and government employees, were fired simply because they were women and married. Despite minimum-wage and other protective legislation in several states which helped some women workers, one historian has concluded that "persistent economic deprivation remained the most striking characteristic of women workers" during this decade.[49]

One of the programmatic conflicts among different types of radical feminism during the 1930s was the one between the supporters of the Equal Rights Amendment (the National Women's Party) and its opponents (the League of Women Voters and the National Women's Trade Union). The American Communist Party offered, as an alternative to the ERA, a Women's Charter that included proposals for full civil and political equality for women, equal pay for equal work, and "protective legislation," such as maternity insurance and a maximum number of working hours.[50] Summing up the position of women in the thirties, Shaffer has written:

> Only about one-fifth of women worked outside the home at any one time during the 1930s. Those who worked in the home were much more subject to the marketplace than their mothers had been; the earlier generation had produced many articles for consumption right in the home. In addition, housework became more isolated in this period. The sexual liberalization of the 1920s, which many had hoped would equalize relations between men and women, led to a commercialization of sex in advertising and other media. Despite some improvement in the availability of birth control, most women still had no real control over their reproductive lives, and public facilities for the care of small children remained almost nonexistent. Overall, in the decade of the 1930s there was relatively little questioning in the society at large of the traditional roles of women and men.[51]

The model of achievements for women in public life was limited to Eleanor Roosevelt.[52] The Great Depression, the rise of fascism, and the beginning of the Second World War caused public concern and energy to shift away from the equality of women.

The condition of some women during the 1920s, 1930s, World War II, and immediately following the war was addressed by Talcott Parsons and C. Wright Mills in their work on sex roles. Juliet Mitchell's description of the period in England can also serve to describe conditions in the United States: "In the period 1940–45 the family as we present it in our dominant ideologies virtually ceased to exist. In wartime the industrial employment of women was once more predominant and fathers were absent."[53] The corresponding cultural image in the United States was Rosie the Riveter. The war brought with it a temporary improvement in attitudes toward women's contributions to the economy and public life.

The cold war[54] and the structural and cultural trends in American society in the postwar period altered again the position of women, reversing wartime advances and all progressive movements in general. As Marxist sociologist Marlene Dixon has put it, "With the end of the war the average age at marriage declined, the average size of families went up, and the suburban migration began in earnest. The political conservatism of the '50s was echoed in a social conservatism which stressed a Victorian ideal of the woman's life: a full womb and selfless devotion to husband and children." In the period immediately following the war, as men returned from military service to reclaim their jobs, "Women were forced back to the kitchen and nursery with a vengeance."[55] Rossi has asserted that postwar (i.e., cold war) social science contributed to legitimizing the unequal status of American women. She argued, "Feminism has been undermined by the conservatism of psychology and sociology in the postwar period. Sociologists studying the family have borrowed heavily from selective findings in social anthropology and from psychoanalytic theory and have pronounced sex to be a universally necessary basis for role differentiation in the family." She concluded:

> The consequences of this acceptance of psychoanalytic ideas and conservatism in the social sciences have been twofold: first, the social sciences in the United States have contributed very little since the 1930's to any lively intellectual dialogue on sex equality as a goal or the ways of implementing that goal. Second, they have provided a quasi-scientific underpinning to educators, marriage counselors, mass media and advertising researchers, who together have partly created, and cer-

tainly reinforced, the withdrawal of millions of young American women from the mainstream of thought and work in our society.[56]

It was the postwar condition of women that Betty Friedan addressed in *The Feminine Mystique,* which marked the rebirth of the feminist movement, in the same way that Rachel Carson's *Silent Spring* launched the environmental movement; Ralph Nader's *Unsafe at Any Price,* the consumer-protection movement; Herbert Marcuse's *One-Dimensional Man,* the New Left and student movement; and C. Wright Mills's *The Power Elite* and *The Sociological Imagination,* a generation of radical sociologists. Nevertheless, despite this postwar regression, the development of American capitalism during the short-lived period of what Henry Luce had hoped would be "The American Century" involved historic changes in women's employment. A major example was that there were more married women than unmarried women in the work force. Degler, writing in 1964, summarized as follows:

> In 1960 the Census reported that almost 32 per cent of all married women were employed outside the home and that they comprised 54 per cent of all working women. No industrial country of Europe, with the exception of the Soviet Union, counted such a high proportion. Today, married women are the great source of new labor in the American economy. Between 1949 and 1959, for example, over four million married women entered the labor force, some 60 per cent of *all* additions, male and female.

He observed that it was Charlotte Perkins Gilman who "recognized that the logic of feminism led unavoidably to the working mother as the typical woman." Gilman believed strongly that women as individuals should not have to choose between work and marriage any more than men have to choose between them. "To make that possible, though," Degler wrote, "would require some way be found to mitigate the double burden which biology and society had combined to place only on women."[57] Despite the fact that the United States is the richest nation on earth, it has yet to find a solution to this problem. What the system offers instead is the feminization of poverty.

Having completed this historical sketch, we are in a position to see how the work of two theorists, Parsons and Mills, stands up to the realities of women's lives in the first half of the twentieth century in the United States.

The U.S. Theorists
Talcott Parsons
Functions of Sex Roles

Talcott Parsons (1902–79) was "the heir of the great European lineage" of bourgeois classical sociology, as Marxist theorist Perry Anderson has put it.[58] Of contemporary professional sociologists, Parsons was certainly one of the most well known, both inside and outside the discipline, and one of the most controversial. During most of his career, his conception of social systems emphasized function and order, naturally focusing on education, socialization, and the family,[59] and consequently on sex roles. Later in his career, the emphasis shifted to development and evolution. I will consider just two of Parsons's numerous writings, one empirical and one theoretical, to illustrate his views about sex roles for women.[60]

In "Age and Sex in the Social Structure of the United States," an article published in 1942, Parsons provided a partial description of sexism in the middle and upper-middle classes.[61] He observed that children of both sexes in the United States were "treated alike"—up to a certain age.

What is perhaps the most important sex discrimination is more than anything else a reflection of the differentiation of adult sex roles. It seems to be a definite fact that girls are more apt to be relatively docile, to conform in general according to adult expectations, to be "good," whereas boys are more apt to be recalcitrant to discipline and defiant of adult authority and expectations. There is really no feminine equivalent of the expression "bad boy." It may be suggested that this is at least partially explained by the fact that it is possible *from an early age* to initiate girls directly into many important aspects of the adult feminine role. Their mothers are continually about the house. . . . It is also possible for the daughter to participate actively and usefully in many of these [household] activities. Especially in the *urban* middle classes, however, the father does not work in the home and his son is not able to observe his work or to participate in it from an early age. ("AS," 605; emphasis added)

Parsons emphasized that "the equality of privileges and responsibilities" of men and women "is seriously modified by the asymmetrical relation of the sexes to the occupational structure" ("AS," 605). Contradicting known facts about differential socialization patterns and expectations in the educational system, he wrote, "It is only in post-graduate professional education, with its direct connection with future occupational careers, that sex discrimination becomes conspicuous" ("AS," 606). He observed that for both males and females the transition to adulthood involved a sharp break with the glamorous aspects of youth culture.

> The symmetry in this respect must, however, not be exaggerated. It is of fundamental significance to the sex role structure of the adult age levels that the *normal* man has a "job" which is fundamental to his social status in general. . . . his occupational status is the primary source of the income and class status of his wife and children. ("AS," 608; emphasis added)

The situation of the adult feminine role was "radically different," he commented. Most upper-middle-class wives did not work, and if they did, the status of their jobs was not competitive with the status of their husbands' jobs. The majority of career women were unmarried, and in the small numbers of cases in which career women were married, "the result is a profound alteration in family structure" ("AS," 609). However, Parsons did not discuss the details of this alteration. He did compare the status of women in rural and urban societies and found that the primary status for urban adult women was that of housewife, a role that produced a great deal of tension:

> From one point of view the emergence of occupational status into this primary position can be regarded as the principal source of strain in the sex role structure of our society since it deprives the wife of her role as a partner in a common enterprise. ("AS," 609)

Women who managed households were stuck with what Parsons thought "may be considered a kind of 'pseudo'-occupation," even though recent calculations have suggested that if housewives were paid at going rates for tasks performed and hours worked, they would make $35,000 per year.

Parsons listed three ways for housewives to escape from the tension produced by the demands made on them. They could dissociate their essential personalities from their drudgery; they could employ domestic servants (if they could afford it); or they could use advertised products to perfect the art of housework. These alternatives were not very successful solutions, and Parsons concluded that "strict adherence to this [domestic] pattern has become progressively less common and has a strong tendency to a residual status." A woman could, of course, also get out of the domestic pattern by taking up what Parsons considered the "masculine pattern" of career, "in direct competition with men of her own class." He added:

> It is, however, notable that in spite of the very great progress of the emancipation of women from the traditional domestic pattern, only a very small fraction have gone very far in this direction. It is also clear that its generalization would only be possible with [he repeats for the second time in two pages] profound alterations in the structure of the family." ("AS," 610)

Once again, Parsons provided no historically grounded discussion of the emancipation of women he referred to, no discussion of why change had gone no further, nor what the implications for the family would be if such change became widespread.

Parsons outlined two alternatives to domesticity, short of pursuit of a career. One was the "infiltration into the respectable sphere of elements of what may be called again the glamor pattern, with the emphasis on a specifically feminine form of attractiveness which on occasion involves directly sexual patterns of appeal"—patterns borrowed from "social types previously beyond the pale of respectable society"—i.e., women of dubious morals ("AS," 610). Parsons noted perceptively the ambiguity of the glamor pattern:

> "Emancipation" in this connection means primarily emancipation from traditional and conventional restrictions on the free expression of sexual attraction and impulses, but in a direction which tends to segregate the element of sexual interest and

attraction from the total personality and in so doing tends to emphasize the segregation of sex roles. ("AS," 611)

(One might also argue that "emancipation" in this sense is more complicated, invading the personality and thereby warping the self.) In addition, he noted, the glamor pattern was also subject to moral censure in the community.

Second, "a woman who takes obligations to social welfare particularly seriously will find opportunities in various forms of activity which traditionally tie up with women's relation to children, to sickness and so on," he wrote. This alternative was part of the pattern of a wife's being a "good companion" to her husband, the ideal during the twenties and thirties. Distinguishing it from the domestic and glamor patterns, Parsons wrote that it involved "far less stress on the exploitation of sex role as such and more on that which is essentially common to both sexes." Such a "peculiar role," in Parsons's phrasing, became most conspicuous after children had grown up, when the husband was most fully involved in his career. However, even this pattern was not without its strains. Parsons thought that a woman's "fundamental status" was determined by marriage, and that within the framework of marriage, her role involved simply "living up to expectations and finding satisfying interests and activities." Strain was introduced because "in a society where such strong emphasis is placed upon individual achievement it is not surprising that there should be a certain romantic nostalgia for the time when the fundamental choices were still open." The problems of women were intensified by the presence of alternative adult feminine roles, and once the possibility of careers had been eliminated, Parsons believed, there "tends to be a rather unstable oscillation" between domesticity, glamor, and companionship. Cultural values emphasized the domestic pattern, and individual choice emphasized alternatives to domesticity. Since the good-companion pattern was not institutionalized, Parsons asserted, "It is quite clear that in the adult feminine role there is quite sufficient strain and insecurity so that wide-spread manifestations are to be expected in the form of neurotic behavior" ("AS," 611–13).[62] His partially accurate assessment of sex-role structure in American society concluded that the differentiation of sex roles made it difficult for married men and women to share common interests and marriages on the "level of human companionship."[63]

In *Family, Socialization and Interaction Process* (1955), Parsons
set forth a more theoretical treatment of sex roles.[64] He opened his
discussion of "The American Family" by denying the thesis, popular at the time, of the "general disorganization" of the family. His
argument was based on statistics for divorces, marriages, birth
rates, and private residential construction trends (*FSIP*, 3–8). He
summarized:

> We think the trend of the evidence points to the beginning of
> the relative stabilization of a *new* type of family structure, in a
> new relation to a general social structure, one in which the
> family is more specialized than before, but not in any general
> sense less important, because the society is dependent *more*
> exclusively on it for the performance of *certain* of its vital
> functions. (*FSIP*, 9–10; Parsons's emphases)

Parsons put this transformation in the context of structural differentiation in the larger society, specifically separating out the occupational from other aspects of society, especially from the kinship
system. Employing his instrumental-expressive distinction, Parsons
argued that "it is fundamentally by virtue of the importance of his
occupational role *as a component of his familial role* that in our
society we can unequivocally designate the husband-father as the
'instrumental leader' of the family as a system" (*FSIP*, 13; Parsons's
emphasis). Put plainly, the man was the boss because he had a job.

Although the number of women participating in the labor force
was increasing, Parsons maintained that "there can be no question
of symmetry between the sexes in this respect [equality of the sexes
in relation to the occupational structure], and, we argue, there is
no serious tendency in this direction" (*FSIP*, 13–14). He gave several reasons. First, many working women were not married or, if
married, had no children. Second, jobs available to women did not
seriously compete for status and income with men's jobs. Further,
he noted that the top levels of typically feminine occupations—
"teacher, social worker, nurse, private secretary"—had a strong
"expressive" component and were often "'supportive' to masculine
roles"; he saw them as analogues to the wife-mother role. Women
were infrequently employed in "top executive" or "impersonal"
technical positions, he noted. He said that "the role of 'housewife'
is still the overwhelmingly predominant one for the married woman
with small children." Finally, "It seems quite safe in general to say

that the adult feminine role has not ceased to be anchored primarily in the internal affairs of the family." Parsons thought that if there came a time when "the average married woman had some kind of a job," role reversals would occur "or their qualitative differentiation in these respects [would be] completely erased" (*FSIP*, 13–15 and n. 13)

The qualitative differentiation of sex roles, according to Parsons, was a consequence of the principal functions of the nuclear family. The family had lost economic production and political power functions: in a highly differentiated society, the family functioned not "directly on behalf of society, but on behalf of personality." In his unwittingly telling words, families "are 'factories' which produce human personalities" (*FSIP*, 16).

> We therefore suggest that the basic and irreducible functions of the family are two: first, the primary socialization of children so that they can truly become members of the society into which they have been born; second, the stabilization of the adult personalities of the population of the society. (*FSIP*, 16–17)

Parsons connected socialization of children and stabilization of adult personality with threads of psychoanalytic theory: socialization had to begin in a small group, that is, the nuclear family; and adult, or genital, sexuality that was productive of marital solidarity was considered the ritual reenactment of pre-oedipal child-mother love, but on a more differentiated level (*FSIP*, 17–22).

The importance of the family for society was precisely the reason, according to Parsons, that "there is a *social* as distinguished from purely reproductive, differentiation of sex roles" (*FSIP*, 22; Parsons's emphasis). From a functionalist perspective, he wrote:

> We will argue that the differentiation of sex role in the family is, in its sociological character and significance, primarily an example of a basic qualitative mode of differentiation which tends to appear in *all* systems of social interaction regardless of their composition. In particular this type of differentiation, that on "instrumental-expressive" lines, is conspicuous in small [task-oriented] groups of about the same membership-size as the nuclear family. (*FSIP*, 22–23; Parsons's emphasis; see also chap. 5)

Parsons queried "why the man takes the more instrumental role, the woman the more expressive, and why in detailed ways these roles take particular forms." The general answer he accepted was the obvious: women bear and nurture infants, and men, being "exempted" from these tasks, therefore specialize in a more instrumental direction. Although roles in the American family ("as we know it") exhibited varied forms, Parsons argued that they were "far from employing an erasure of the differentiation of sex roles" (*FSIP*, 23). Quite the contrary, he believed that they reinforced and clarified sex-role differentiation:

> In the first place, the articulation between the family and occupational system in our society focuses the instrumental responsibility for a family very sharply on its one adult male member, and prevents its diffusion through the ramifications of an extended kinship system. Secondly, the isolation of the nuclear family in a complementary way focuses the responsibility of the mother role more sharply on one adult woman, to a relatively high degree cutting her off from the help of adult sisters and other kinswomen; furthermore, the fact of the absence of the husband-father from the home premises so much of the time means that she has to take the primary responsibility for the children. (*FSIP*, 23)

Given the privatization of child rearing and the increased importance of marriage for the nuclear family and its adult personalities, "the *complementarity* of roles within it tends to be accentuated," Parsons asserted. He inferred "that the increased emphasis . . . on overt, specifically feminine attractiveness, with strong erotic overtones, is related to this situation within the family." Parsons believed that another indication of these trends was "the 'professionalization' of the mother role," that is, "the attempt to rationalize" child rearing on the basis of "scientific" authority. He thought that these changes had been accompanied by strains on families and personalities, as evidenced by "high rates of divorce" and so-called mental-health consciousness ("the immense vogue of psychiatry, of clinical psychology"), most of which was focused on the family (*FSIP*, 24–25; Parsons's emphasis).

In his analysis of sex-role differentiation, Parsons did not differ in principle one whit from the positions found in Durkheim's *The Division of Labor* (but not *Suicide*) or from Herbert Spencer's evolutionary functionalism in *The Study of Sociology* and *The Princi-ples of Sociology.* His brand of functionalism with its instrumental-expressive distinction entailed the conclusion that the inequality of men and women was a biologically based systemic necessity.[65] Par-sons did not let facts get in his way. His work, therefore, can best be taken as a historical document on sex inequality in the period in which he wrote and the reflection of that inequality in the theoreti-cal consciousness of a male sociologist.[66]

C. Wright Mills
Sociological Imagination

If Parsons provided the conservative interpretation of the classical sociological tradition, C. Wright Mills (1916–62) represented its critical, left-wing aspect. In his classic *The Sociological Imagination* Mills castigated "abstracted empiricism" (for example, the work of Paul F. Lazarsfeld) and even more harshly "grand theory" (that is, the work of Parsons). Mills's assessment of Parsons's *The Social Sys-tem* was that "it is only about 50 per cent verbiage, 40 per cent is well-known textbook sociology . . . the remaining 10 per cent is of possible—although rather vague—ideological use."[67] Mills's con-ception of the classic sociological enterprise emphasized its focus on the intersections of biography and history, and of character and so-cial structure—a commitment to seeing private troubles as linked with public issues; in short, he believed that the proper use of the sociological imagination included an endeavor to make a contribu-tion to the role of reason in human affairs. Such an approach ob-viously has relevance to the position of women, individually and collectively. Mills clearly stated his concept of sociology in the ar-ticle "IBM Plus Reality Plus Humanism = Sociology," which antici-pated *The Sociological Imagination:*

> Whatever else sociology may be, it is a result of consistently asking: (1) What is the meaning of this—whatever we are ex-amining—for our society as a whole, and what is this social world like? (2) What is the meaning of this for the types of men *and women* that prevail in this society? And (3) how does this fit into the historical trend of our times, and in what direction does this main drift seem to be carrying us? No matter how small-scale what he is examining, the sociologist must ask

such questions about it, or he has abdicated the classic socio-logical endeavor.[68] (emphasis added)

In "The Salesgirls," a section in his classic *White Collar*, first pub-lished in 1951, Mills contrasted the situation of saleswomen in small towns with that of saleswomen in large department stores in metro-politan areas.[69] In small cities, he wrote, where there was "a person-ally known market," salespersons expressed an ideology of providing a worthwhile service, and they obtained the added benefit of "learn-ing human nature at a gossip center"; they enjoyed dealing with the public (*WC*, 173, 172). In the big-city department store, the sales-woman's attempt to identify with and thus borrow prestige from her customers backfired, Mills wrote, resulting in feelings of "powerless depression" and expressions of hostility toward customers. As Mills formulated it, "Caught at the point of intersection between big store and urban mass, the salesgirl is typically engrossed in seeing the customer as her psychological enemy, rather than the store as her economic enemy" (*WC*, 174).

Mills, following the work of James B. Gale, then described "a range of sales personalities" that could be observed in big-city de-partment stores: "*The Wolf* prowls and pounces upon potential cus-tomers"; the related "*Elbower*" "is bent upon monopolizing all the customers"; the "*Charmer*" "focuses the customer less upon her stock of goods than upon herself. She attracts the customer with modulated voice, artful attire, and stance"; the "*Ingénue Salesgirl*" is [young], "homesick," "self-effacing," overwhelmed by the size of the store and job responsibilities and attaches herself for support to experienced co-workers; the "*Collegiate*" type is a part-time em-ployee from a local college, "a more self-confident version of the ingénue"; the "*Drifter*" is more concerned with interacting with her colleagues than doing her job; the "*Social Pretender*," who has invented a well-bred family background, is of course only selling to get the experience as a planned step in a high-level career; and, finally, the "*Old-Timer*" is one of two subtypes—"a disgruntled rebel" or "a completely accommodated saleswoman"—"who make up the backbone of the salesforce." The rebel old-timer, he wrote, zeroes in on the store: "she is against its policies, other personnel, and often turns her sarcasm and rancor upon the customer." The "accommodated old-timer" is complacent about her position and considers the store to be a good place to work and her employers to have been good to her (*WC*, 174–78).

Mills's portraits of recognizable types of women workers are thought-provoking. The power of his analysis is to be found in his attention to the psychodynamics of white-collar work in a society that has become "the great salesroom" (see *WC*, 161–66, 178–81). Mills pointed out that with the economic shift to servicing and selling, "personal or even intimate traits of the employee are drawn into the sphere of exchange and become of commercial relevance, become commodities in the labor market" (*WC*, 182). In demanding "loyalty," the firm expected the salesperson to be "friendly, helpful, tactful and courteous at all times," but as Mills observed many saleswomen realize that "'sincerity' is detrimental to one's job until the rules of salesmanship and business become a 'genuine' aspect of oneself. Tact is a series of little lies about one's feelings, until one is emptied of such feelings" (*WC*, 183). The personality acceptable to the firm, Mills explained, was determined by "the formulas of 'personnel experts'" and enforced by the floorwalkers who checked on the saleswomen. Like the industrial worker, "In the normal course of her work, because her personality becomes the instrument of an alien purpose, the salesgirl becomes self-alienated." The personality market, like any market, is subject to the laws of supply and demand, Mills wrote: when jobs are scarce and there is a buyer's market, the salesperson must be polite, and the reverse is also true. Thus one's very self is shaped by the swings of the capitalist marketplace (*WC*, 183–84).

One of the themes of *White Collar* is what Mills, following Weber's generalization of Marx's analysis of the factory system, referred to as "the industrial revolution" come to the office (*WC*, 190–98). Between the small, dusty offices of old, where the secretary was close to the boss and possessed a range of skills, and "the new factory-like lay-out" was an "intermediate type," Mills wrote. Drawing heavily upon early twentieth-century American literature ("Ten years on either side of the First World War—that was the time of the greatest literary interest in the white-collar girl"), Mills observed that from the latter kind of office "common stereotypes of the office world and its inhabitants, particularly the white-collar girl, are drawn. Probably the major image is that the office is full of women. Of course, American women work elsewhere; they have had two generations of experience in factories and in service industries" (*WC*, 199–200). But by contrast to the experience of the "white-collar girl," women wage-workers were most conspicuous only during periods of war.

From this literature Mills concluded that "the office is a production plant for old maids, a modern nunnery. The contrast is
between the business college and the glamorous stage, or the profitable, early, lovely marriage" (WC, 201). He continued with the
natural history of the career of the white-collar woman by observing
that "in American folklore, the white-collar girl is usually born of
small-town lower middle-class parents." Upon graduation from
high school, she left for the glamor, lights, and romance of the big
city, the independence that a job for a big firm would presumably
give. But she was usually disappointed; Mills poignantly described
her experience:

> The white-collar girl in the big city often looks back on her
> high-school period in the small town as the dress rehearsal for
> something that never came off. The personal clique of the high
> school is not replaced by the impersonal unity of the office;
> the adolescent status equality is not replaced by the hierarchy
> of the city; the close-up thrill of the high school date is not
> replaced by the vicarious distances of the darkened movie; the
> high-school camaraderie of anticipations is not fulfilled by the
> realization of life-fate in the white collar world. (WC, 202)

Mills outlined the life of the white-collar worker from her first,
low-paying job in the city, to friendship with another young woman
from her small town, to fending off the sexual advances of salesmen
and coming to "believe that all men are after only one thing," to
a failed love affair, after which she settled down in her job (WC,
202–3). "Now she is the mature woman," Mills wrote, "efficient in
her job, suppressing her love for the married boss, to whom she
makes herself indispensable, doing the housework of his business.
This relieves the impersonal business atmosphere and the tension
between superior and employee, but it is also complicated by the
fact that she may feel threatened by the eroticism of younger
women." Mills concluded, "Career has been substituted for marriage; the conflict of the white-collar girl is resolved; she has climbed
the stairway; she is in the nunnery" (WC, 203–4). For any person
who has lived in a small town close to a major metropolis, there is a
familiar ring to Mills's sensitive discussion of the occupational world
of white-collar women. Furthermore, his work was on target in
terms of historical trends: the mechanization and industrialization of

the office, with their particular effects on white-collar women—whose work was "becoming more and more the job of a factory-like operative"—have continued and intensified.[70]

In "Plain Talk on Fancy Sex" (1952),[71] Mills observed the emergence in the postwar period of a new type of prostitute, "the expense-account girl," alongside the two traditional types, the "old-line" prostitute (the hooker of the streets and cheap hotels) and the "upper-class" prostitute (the kept woman, or mistress, of the rich). He suggested that "this newer girl system involves elegant women with light morals and respectable businessmen with heavy expense accounts." Such "part-time" prostitutes succumbed, he said, because they hoped to gain a career in the glamor industries—TV, fashion, films, and so on—while having a "gilded good time" in the process ("PTFS," 324–25). Mills placed the phenomenon of expense-account prostitution in the context of historical trends of social and cultural structure; expense-account sex, he wrote, did not rest on the passions and weaknesses of individual persons of either or both sexes.

> To understand how radically public idols of womanhood have changed, one need only compare the innocent Sweetheart of America, Mary Pickford of 1920, with that newest idol of hip-swinging, breast-dangling eroticism, Marilyn Monroe of 1952. ("PTFS," 325–26)

Through advertising, entertainment, and the national media, such women "set the models of appearance and conduct which are imitated all down the national hierarchy of glamor"—including "the good housewife in the Chicago suburb as well as the salesgirl in the Decatur five-and-ten."

> All this public eroticism which floods the mass media in America is at once a reflection and contributing cause of drastic changes in private morality: there is no doubt but that the value of chastity in the unmarried female has declined, and that the respectability of the experienced woman has gone up. ("PTFS," 326)

Sexual involvement had become common in American firms. It was not just a question of private morality. As Mills bluntly stated,

"Vice, first of all, is one of the service trades that make up the night life of business" ("PTFS," 326–32). Anticipating contemporary feminist concerns, he noted:

> Inside the firm it is likely to be petty, mean, and directly exploitive. There is the boss who uses a girl employee on a threat—direct or indirect—of losing her job, or not getting a pay increase, or not getting a promotion. That sort of thing— which is more likely in smaller than in larger businesses—is directly related to the employment market: when jobs are hard to come by and harder to hold, when wages and salaries are low, then bosses, office managers, foremen, and junior executives have the best chance to demand erotical services along with typing and dressmaking and other skills. ("PTFS," 327)

He continued, "Between firms, girls are used as pawns of the great American game of salesmanship." The potential customer was provided with erotic services to speed the order along, with the funds coming from the expense account ("PTFS," 327).

So the answer to the question "Why do girls go wrong?" was clearly not one of private morality only but also of male domination in American society: "The expense-account girl wants a glamorous career, *and since men largely control the success or failure of such careers*, she wants to be seen by men who hold such positions, or who she thinks hold such positions" ("PTFS," 327; emphasis added; see also 328). With the devaluation of premarital chastity (as exemplified by the public and private lives of those at the pinnacle of the star system), Mills observed, the expense-account girl felt no disgrace. Her fancy hopes for success, the opportunity provided by salesmanship and plutocratic demand, and the means supplied by the expense account resulted in the "crime" of sex at a price ("PTFS," 329).

Mills presented a more theoretical approach to sex roles in "Women: The Darling Little Slaves" (1953),[72] his previously unpublished review of Simone de Beauvoir's *The Second Sex*. The central question to which Beauvoir addressed her book was "How can a human being in women's situation attain fulfillment?" Mills was skeptical of Beauvoir's "faith in social evolution" toward complete social and economic equality and with it the metamorphosis of the inner human being. He criticized Beauvoir's neglect of the "man question":

Under present conditions, many women *are* quite dreadful creatures. So are many men. Many women do not attain the dignity of the independent human being. Neither do many men. But it is about women, and the conditions that make them dreadful, that Simone de Beauvoir cries out. I agree with both her cry and with its humanistic basis. But I cannot help but feel that she often confuses the conditions of women with the generic human condition. ("WDLS," 343; Mills's emphasis)

In the remainder of his review, Mills developed his arguments on sex roles:

In writing about the second sex she really ought to have thought more systematically about the first sex and about human beings in general. For she tends to impute to all men what is in fact true of only very few of them: a transcendent flight, a life of accomplishment. It is true that she at time[s] recognizes that this is not so, but she does not take it into systematic account as she compares "the" situation of men and "the" situation of women. She complains that women are not free "to shape the concept of femininity." But then neither are men free to shape the concept of masculinity. Both concepts are stereotypes and both limit the human being. ("WDLS," 343–44)

In response to Beauvoir's assertion of the universality of women's subordination to men, Mills argued that the "American suburban queens," whose husbands earned between $10,000 and $50,000 a year, clung to their "dependency" because to give it up would be to lose their many privileges. Having children was not enough to redeem them from being anything more than parasites, he claimed, adding that of course it was not their "fault" that they could not make anything of their economic "freedom" ("WDLS," 344). On the war between the sexes, he stated:

Although she does comment on it, I do not think she takes into sufficiently systematic account the intricacy, and the various outcomes, of the power struggle between many men and women. She knows that woman, who in our epoch is losing her femininity, often wishes to retain its privileges while man

wants her to retain its limitations, and they are victims of each
other and of the stalemate between them. But she does not
stress enough the real power that many women have and use:
if man is transcendent and authoritarian, woman is often ma-
nipulative: the form of power for the immanent. If men command, women seduce. Resentment often causes a frigidity,
real or feigned, which is often used as a feminine tool of
power. ("WDLS," 344)

Mills moved next to a more theoretical and methodological critique of Beauvoir's approach to "the second sex." If, as Beauvoir
claimed, "one is not born a woman, but rather becomes one," then,
Mills reasoned, the woman she becomes depends quite largely
on her experienced situation. "Woman stands in these pages all
too often as one generalized type, and the condition that makes
her this type is presumed to be more or less universal in the
West" ("WDLS," 344). Beauvoir provided no adequate set of clas-
sifications of women according to their specific conditions, Mills
thought, which resulted, he felt, in "exasperating" vagueness. For
example, Beauvoir's argument that feminine homosexuality was "an
attitude chosen in a certain situation" did not answer the question
"exactly what situations are most conducive to this choice on the
part of exactly which types of women?" The essence of the matter,
as Mills saw it, was that "after one has eliminated the explanations
of woman according to biological and psychological fate—and this
Mlle. de Beauvoir does well—one must *specify* the necessary and
sufficient social causes which produce the various *types* of women
available to our observation in different societies" ("WDLS," 345).
Commenting on Beauvoir's solution to the "woman question" Mills
wrote:

Mlle. de Beauvoir's solution to the man-woman problem, put
in its briefest form, is the elimination of woman as we know
her—with which one might agree but to which one must add:
and the elimination of man as we know him. There would
then be male and female and each would be equally free to
become an independent human being. No one can know what
new types of human beings would be developed in this historically unique situation, but perhaps in sharing Mlle de
Beauvoir's passion for liberty we would all gladly forego femininity and masculinity to achieve it; and perhaps the best

types would follow Coleridge's adage and become androgynous characters in an androgynous world. ("WDLS," 345–46)

Although Mills disputed the claim that *The Second Sex* was a
classic, he believed that

all this is the more unfortunate because the book is nevertheless indispensable reading for any woman who wishes to become more alert to her own possibilities, and for any man who
wishes to understand what these possibilities might be. She
has written one of those books that remind us how little we
really *think* about our personal lives and problems, and
she invites us and helps us to do so. ("WDLS," 346; Mills's
emphasis)

Comparing Parsons and Mills from historical and feminist stand-
points, it is clear that Mills's work is richer in theoretical possibilities. Both Parsons and Mills drew upon the classical tradition of
sociology and both employed a temporal perspective, Parsons in a
developmental sense (citing differentiation as the major process)
and Mills in a comparative and historically specific sense. It is difficult to refrain from a time-worn criticism of Parsons from a radical
perspective. However, it is almost equally difficult to comprehend
how he could have asserted—in light of historical facts—that there
were no tendencies toward alterations in family structure or in the
social position of women. The key difference between Mills and
Parsons lies in Parsons's positivist-functionalist acceptance of the
sex-role structure and his blindness to centrality of power within it
and Mills's conflict theory and critical, humanistic stance toward it.
I might add that neither Mills nor Parsons has anything to say about
the experience of minority women in the history of the United
States. Mills reminded us not to give up the sociological imagination. But since his time, we have learned that it may be best to shift
emphasis: maybe we really think too much about our personal lives
to the exclusion of personal reflection on public issues. Industrialization and the emergence of corporate capitalism around the
turn of the century involved employment of women in factories and
the appearance of the white-collar woman worker as a social type.
The post–World War II period saw the increasing employment of
married women, with all that this entailed for power and conflict
relations in the family and the stability of marriage. In my judgment

Parsons missed the boat because of his ideological perspective, because of his focus on upper-middle-class women, and because he was a prisoner of his own theoretical perspective. Whatever the basis for the widespread similarities across time and space in sex roles, there is no historical evidence for a single, unilinear pattern of increasing sex-role differentiation. All of the historical cases I have surveyed display, on the contrary, variations over time in the position of women and the relations of the sexes.

7

Conclusion

Now that I have presented the perspectives on women observed in the works of the classical sociological theorists, I will evaluate their answers to the "woman question." I will appraise their treatment of women in society in terms of feminist concerns; second, I will consider two powerful bodies of theory—Marxist and Freudian—and the ways they have been used by feminists to explain the oppression of women. Finally, I will argue that the best approach to a sociological science of women and men is through cross-cultural studies, especially the comparison of histories.

As is evident in the preceding chapters, the separation between sociology and ideology, between fact and value, is in reality not so sharp as the positivist reconstruction of science would have it. Therefore, the question cannot be avoided: From a feminist perspective, how good are the classical theorists? One assessment, given by some feminist critics of the social sciences, is that these theorists, founding fathers of their discipline, were prisoners of the conventional thinking of their times, including the dominant cultural assumptions rooted in male-biased views of the world. However, there are complex and contradictory variations in the writings about women by different classical theorists. Those writings that employed a conflict perspective and displayed a historical sense fare better from a feminist viewpoint than the functionalist theories, which are limited by their lack of historical and class perspectives.

Historians of feminism have revealed that the human and social issues surrounding feminism today were not raised for the first time in the United States in the twentieth century—let alone in the 1960s. Alice S. Rossi has argued that contemporary feminists are closer in perspective to Harriet Taylor Mill and John Stuart Mill than to the suffragists of the early twentieth century.[1] Some contemporary feminists are closer in their aims and outlook to the utopian socialist feminists of the 1820s through the 1840s in England and France. My study has demonstrated that the question of the position of women in society is more important in classical sociological theory than one would gather from a reading of most of the existing literature on the classical theorists. In addition, nineteenth- and early twentieth-century feminist movements had more of an impact on theory than may have been supposed.

Further, it is at least arguable that not only can we learn about the history of the conditions of women from the writings of the classical sociologists but that several of them made contributions that even feminists might find insightful. Why these facets of the history of theory have not been recognized and discussed in one place is itself a problem for the sociology of knowledge. As Marx said, "To understand a limited historical epoch, we must step beyond its limits, and compare it with other historical epochs. To judge governments and their acts, we must measure them by their own times and the conscience of their contemporaries."[2] The same can be said of the writings about women by the classical sociological theorists. Before setting down criteria by which to evaluate their contributions, I will review several contemporary feminist critiques of the social sciences.

The upshot of radical feminist critiques is that sociology has operated within masculine categories of understanding uncritically adopted from the social world—often excluding from its purview the social experience of women, at best seeing women through a distorted, culturally implanted lens. In "Rethinking Sociology Through a Feminist Perspective," Sarah Matthews reviews feminist criticism of social science, especially sociology, according to substance and method: she examines phenomena considered worthy of study—the content, subfields, and direction of the discipline; preferred methods of collecting and analyzing data; and the theoretical structure—the concepts that guide the methodology of the discipline, its assumptions and perspectives about sex roles.[3] With the exception of sociology of the family and newer work on occupations, most fields in the social sciences have not included women until recently. For example, work in the obfuscatingly named area of social stratification has focused on the political power, class, status, ethnicity, and social mobility of males. Quantitative methods generating "hard" data are preferred over the "soft" methods of participant observation and use of historical and literary documents. Hard data are judged to be more scientific but in effect hide masculine interests. As a consequence of the selection of the fields and the preferred methods, differences in socialization of boys and girls are overlooked; and the processes by which the oppression of women originates and is maintained as part of the social structure are denied by functionalist explanations of the family and sex roles. Feminist critics, in Jessie Bernard's words, "pointed out that it is one thing to analyze the way social structures operate—including the way they allocate functions—but quite another to accept the sexual allocations of functions in any given system as intrinsic to social systems."[4] What is required are analyses of the ways in which the maleness of the central concepts of the social sciences colors the vision of those who deploy them.

The ways in which the very conceptual core of one area of social inquiry, political theory, is affected by the neglect of women's roles can be seen in *Women in Western Political Thought,* Susan Moller Okin's lucid analysis of the place of women in the works of four major political theorists: Plato, Aristotle, Mill, and Rousseau. Okin poses the question whether women can be included on equal terms with men in these political theories without rendering the theories inconsistent. She finds that only in Plato's *Republic* were some women (those of the guardian class) treated on the same terms as men. By contrast, as she points out, Aristotle maintained in his *Politics* that all slaves, artisans, and women exist for the purpose of performing their respective functions so that a small number of free males can participate fully in the politics of the city-state. If he had recognized equality for women, his parallel argument about slaves would have been threatened. She concludes, "Aristotle's identification of the hierarchical status quo with the natural, the necessary, and the good, cannot withstand the emancipation of women into political life." The kind of conceptual analysis Okin has contributed to the field of political science has not been made, to my knowl-

edge, for the field of sociology.[5] Many existing suggestions for a sociology that includes women seem to me more empirical than conceptual. These new observations, however, may help form the basis
for rebuilding sociology's theoretical structures.

Georg Simmel said, "Women possess a world of their own which
is not comparable with the world of men.[6] Reflecting the contributions of women's scholarship to sociology, Jessie Bernard's *The Female World* (1981) is grounded in the proposition that most persons
live in separate worlds, one male and the other female. Bernard argues that sociology is concerned only with the male world and that
all it knows of the female world is how it impinges on the male
world. By conceptualizing and describing the autonomous female
world from a woman's perspective, she hoped to right the intellectual balance in the field, breaking through limitations and broaden-
ing the horizons of sociology, which, as it stands, is "a [male] science of male society." Yet it seems to me that describing the female
world—in reality the variety of women's worlds—is only the first
step in constructing a theory of society that includes women. The
relationships of women to men and to the social structure need
to be delineated as well. The problem is a problem of knowledge.
Bernard puts it succinctly: "Not only do men and women view a
common world from different perspectives, they view different
worlds as well." This situation, in her words, "demands that we
[sociologists] include the world women inhabit."[7]

But how are we to know that world? The question can be usefully discussed in terms of competing claims to special validity of
insider and outsider doctrines as alternative routes to knowledge
about social groups (especially oppressed social groups such as
blacks and women). The "extreme Outsider" position is that "one
must *not* be Caesar in order to understand him"; the "extreme Insider" position is that "one *must* be Caesar in order to understand
him." Following Simmel, Weber took the middle position that "one
need not be Caesar in order to understand Caesar."[8] In this study,
the question is whether one must be a woman in order to understand the female world. The more general question is whether social science itself is inherently masculine to its very core.[9] Simmel,
virtually alone among the theorists studied here, pointed out that
cultural categories, even of logic, that appear to represent the objective order of the world are actually male creations. Without pre-
suming to settle these issues in a general way, I believe there are
males who by virtue of their experience and consciousness are ca-

pable of insight into the female world. Nevertheless, propositions about the female world and its relation to the male world stand or fall by meeting established impersonal canons of the context of justification—logic and evidence—regardless of their origin or context of discovery, although the latter may have bearing upon the epistemological status of the former. One does not have to hold steadfastly to a positivistic conception of method to note that the failure to hold on to this distinction is the central weakness of all interpretative and subjective sociologies as claims to knowledge, in contrast to their heuristic value as sources of testable insights. Finally, only a sociology that is truly a science of society, one that includes the experience of women and men, can settle the recent debate about the importance of sex/gender for explaining human conduct, as opposed to more commonly used structural features of society.[10]

A set of questions needs to be asked of any body of writing on society—feminist or not—about its treatment of women.[11] How do women fit into its conception of social structure above and beyond the obvious (sex roles)? Is the treatment sensitive to the place and activity of women in its conception of social organization, in particular in the relationship of women to dominant institutions other than the family? Does it attend to variations in the interplay of social class, race, and ethnicity as well as sex in accounting for socially structured inequalities—in particular, the fact that not all women in society share in identical conditions? Is the treatment sensitive to historical variations in the position of women in society and the relations of the sexes? Or, from a different angle, does the treatment of women in a particular body of writing itself pose these questions: Under what social structures are women more or less oppressed? What are the historical circumstances most conducive to the freedom of women? Only with such general questions in mind can examination of the experience of women and the differences and similarities in the lives of men and women become part of a body of knowledge that advances our understanding and welfare.

In the following section, the classical theorists will be evaluated on how well they illuminated women's world(s)—the term I prefer in order to take into account class and ethnic diversity—and their relationships to men's world(s) and the social structure that includes what men's and women's worlds have in common. I will review the degree to which each theorist's observations about women were distorted by cultural prejudices or broke from those prejudices; whether or

not and in what way the work included women; whether it contributed to an understanding of either the sources of oppression or the
processes by which the oppression of women is maintained or interrupted and challenged; how the work treated the dimensions of the
conflict between men and women. In sum, how, if in any way, the
theorist's work furthered our knowledge in these areas.

Evaluation

In England, the issues raised by women's movements for equality
from the eighteenth century onward were the questions of possible
mental differences between the sexes, specifically the "nature" of
women; legal equality in marriage and the polity, especially suffrage; the public and private consequences of the charitable activities of women, especially religious activities; and women's access to
the professions, especially in the arts and sciences. John Stuart
Mill, in *The Subjection of Women*, pointedly described the reaction
in nineteenth-century social theory to the Enlightenment's attempt
to remake society on the basis of Reason:

> For the apotheosis of Reason we have substituted that of In-
> stinct; and we call everything instinct which we find in our-
> selves and for which we cannot trace any rational foundation.
> This idolatry, infinitely more degrading than the other, and
> the most pernicious of the false worships of the present day, of
> all of which it is now the main support, will probably hold its
> ground until it gives way before a sound psychology, laying
> bare the real root of much that is bowed down to as the inten-
> tion of Nature and the ordinance of God.[12]

Mill subjected to relentless and rigorous logical-empirical analysis
popular and contemporary scientific conceptions about the nature
of women. Taking a position truly outstanding for his time and ours,
he argued that "woman's nature" could only be what would be left
after excluding all the artificial characteristics that are products of
existing social-cultural arrangements of the sexes. Thus, Mill did
not set out to describe the world of women; rather, he concentrated
on refuting male cultural prejudices about the nature of women. In
his writings about women, he exposed some of the nastiness of the
war between the sexes. He understood that the happy bourgeois
family was a fiction. In reality, the family was a school for authori-

tarian moral sentiments and alienation between men and women. He recognized the human unhappiness and wasted potential that resulted from patriarchal dominance in private life and the denial of public careers to women.

A major weakness of Mill's position was his ideological acceptance of the private bourgeois family (albeit with a reformed, companionate marriage) within the context of the class structure of market capitalism; in effect, he would open the public sphere only to women of independent means—those of his own class.[13] Another flaw in his analysis was his belief that the equality of women would be achieved exclusively through law. Mill advocated legal changes that have since come into being: for example, women have the right to control their own incomes and property and, in divorce cases, have rights regarding their children; but in themselves legal changes have not eliminated the subjection of women.

Herbert Spencer spoke to the same issues that Mill addressed, also in response to the women's movement for equality. In his earliest work, in consistent utilitarian-democratic fashion, he favored the rights of women and children. He maintained that the mental differences between men and women were merely "trifling"; he questioned whether a specifically women's sphere existed; and he challenged the notions of propriety that excluded women from public life. But later, in *The Study of Sociology* and *The Principles of Sociology*, Spencer completely changed his mind about women's rights, on the basis of some of the same anthropological and historical evidence he had used before and a "scientific" comparative psychology of the sexes. Caught up in the vortex of the developmental, evolutionary sociobiological thinking that was sweeping England, Spencer defined "woman's sphere" as childbearing and child rearing; he decided that these functions, along with their psychophysiological correlates, made women unfit for public life. Biological differences between men and women served as the basis for Spencer's theory of inequality between men and women and justified the maintenance of second-class status for women. Cultural prejudices about women are embedded in his allegedly scientific work.

Spencer offered little understanding of women's worlds except to record the oppression of women and the not-so-hidden warfare between the sexes and to note their shaping influences on the behavior of women; but he did provide interesting anthropological data on the relations of the sexes, some of which contradict his overall sexist position. What is of value in Spencer's analysis of the conflictful relations of men and women is vitiated theoretically by his functionalism and politically by his liberalism. Not sharing the streak of romantic antimodernism of continental sociologists, Spencer idealized domestic relations in peaceful, modern industrial societies, despite evidence of the disorganization of the traditional family. The nuclear family with connubial happiness at its center was, he believed, the natural adaptive outcome of the processes of social evolution. Only when the highest stage was reached would the activity of women in public life be without pernicious results, he claimed. But then, with the withering away of coercive government, political roles for women might no longer be a matter of public concern. In a formal sense, Spencer and Friedrich Engels were not far apart in their ideal pictures of future private relations of the sexes; the difference, of course, was that for Engels equality and natural love could become a reality only in a socialist future. Probably due to Victorian morality, both Mill and Spencer avoided consideration of sexuality, a topic central to the writings of continental sociological theorists.

French feminism has been intimately connected with France's revolutionary history—a history to which French sociology is a response. Alexis de Tocqueville, who did not sympathize with feminist women, characterized proposals for the full equality of women as "the most disorderly fancy" of his time. Nevertheless, despite his taking for granted the traditional roles of women, Tocqueville's aristocratic sensibility accounts for some interesting observations about the world of women. Especially sensitive were his discussions of contrasting patterns of interaction in families, the decline of forms and property considerations, the relationships of the sexes in general and in marriage, and the ways in which conditions of inequality and equality shaped sexuality and sexual relationships in aristocratic and democratic societies. He was also clearly aware of the variations in relationships produced by economic and cultural differences, noting, for example, that commerce (from which women were excluded), not love, preoccupied men in Protestant, trading nations. It may have been that his observation of the worlds of American women and American men's attitudes toward women sensitized him to the contempt underlying the pedestal on which European women of the middle and upper classes were placed. He noted the looking-glass-self effect on women because of men's treatment of them. On psychological and ideological levels, Tocqueville opposed equality for women in public life because he feared that femininity and the charms of private life would be diminished. For all its limitations, Tocqueville's work has heuristic value in its examination of the tendencies of societies professing legal equality; as he observed, the deprivations felt by those granted *formal* legal rights of citizenship but denied *real* civil rights are a persistent source of movements for equality.[14] Equally powerful is Tocqueville's depiction of the transformation of moral authority and social identities and the resultant interpersonal conflict in periods of revolutionary change.

Auguste Comte displayed the obverse of Spencer's male chauvinism. In Comte's work a distorted, medieval romantic conception of women's worlds is found: he promoted a cult of woman that would restore love to a world rent by conflict and characterized (to use a phrase of Tocqueville's) by an absenteeism of the heart. Comte's proposals for a positive polity based on sociological law contained refutations of communist programs for the reform or abolition of marriage. Women, Comte claimed, like "ordinary people," were too practical and feeling to be persuaded by radicals. He feared that competition between men and women for jobs would destroy the affection the sexes have for one another. Like Spencer at a later date, Comte believed that radical and feminist movements were merely phenomena of transition periods. Order would be restored, he believed, when women and workers, persuaded by sociological science, renounced attempts to gain political authority and accepted their "proper places." The domestic sphere, he believed, was the place nature had made for women. From Comte's exegesis on "the nature of women" we learn more about his fantasies, fears, and wishes than we do about women's worlds. Comte did not reflect upon the worlds of women nor the restrictive and coercive processes by which their social position was maintained.

In his early work, *The Division of Labor in Society*, Emile Durkheim continued the French functionalist conception of sex roles, ignoring the coercive and conflictful features of conjugal solidarity. He noted that to grant women equality would undermine the family and the traditional allocation of functions in society at large. Whatever one may think of the ways in which Durkheim conducted his personal life, his sociological work was clearly affected by the "woman question," especially the debate over divorce law.[15] In particular, the statistics on the differential suicide rates of men and women consequent upon divorce, revealing the costs of marriage for women in contrast to the benefits for men, forced him to face the antagonism between the sexes in contemporary families. He saw no solution, because he was unable to fully accept his emerging recognition that inequality was the source of this war. Durkheim's major purpose was to establish sociology as an autonomous science by providing strictly social explanations of human social behavior— rather than psychological and biological explanations. The undermining of his purpose by sexist stereotypes is evidenced by the fact that he resorted to biological notions about female sexuality to account for the different rates of suicide of men and women.

Although French sociological theorists did not write full or accurate descriptions of women's worlds, they understood that altering the structure of the family and the relations of the sexes would have profound effects on the traditional structure of the social order and its moral underpinnings. French theory exemplified a response Margaret Fuller pointed to that emerged from the debates about women. In Sheila Rowbotham's summary, "As women pressed their claims their opponents changed their tack. Instead of declaring them outright inferiors they granted them affairs relating to the heart. Women were allowed to occupy themselves with all matters that did not concern direct power."[16] As Philip Rieff has pointed out, in French and British cultures, women were viewed as conservators of high ethical standards and traditional culture; in contrast, in German and Russian cultures, women were viewed as antiintellectual and of a lower moral and cultural caliber than men.[17]

In their examinations of the relationships of the sexes and women's worlds, the German sociological theorists manifested a stronger sense of comparative and historical variation and deeper social psychological insight than the English or the French theorists. The German theorists also placed more emphasis on sexuality and prostitution. Max Weber offered clear distinctions among several modes of relationship between women's worlds and men's worlds. The cleavage in his own life between these worlds appeared in his early work as an omission of sociological consideration of the "woman question" (facts) combined with advocacy of liberal reform of patriarchy (values). To educated women he granted a place in the world among male professors. It appears that it was only after his intimate intercourse with the female world and his contact with culturally radical, erotic, and feminist movements that Weber's sociological interests came to include women, or more precisely, the relationships of the masculine and feminine worlds, the sociology of the family, and the place of eroticism and women in major world religions. Unfortunately, he did not include stratification according to sex in his discussion of class, status, and party. Weber's task would have been to explore the differences made by sex for inequalities of class, status, and power (and vice versa for inequalities of sex) in a variety of concrete historical circumstances.

Weber's final historical-comparative discussion of the "woman question" was a critique of the feminist socialism of Engels and August Bebel. Against the theory of matriarchy Weber argued that the apparent rule of women was associated with the institution of the men's house, from which women were excluded. Arguing against the assertion that prostitution is the underside of monogamy, Weber pointed to the phenomenon of temple prostitution. In his final lectures in *General Economic History,* Weber once again kept evaluations separate from facts. In his later work a sociological appreciation of the place of women in society emerged but not a description of the worlds of women, which, in my judgment, he had the resources to write. What is valuable in Weber's work is his use of the comparative method combined with a sensitivity to historical variations in social organization. Working from this approach and his general concern with power and authority, Weber stated the rudiments of a theory of male domination centering on variations in control over economic resources, the implements of warfare, magical and religious practices, the reckoning of descent, and the means of sexual expression. However, he started too late in his life to complete such a theory.

In spite of his occasional disappointing lapses into a Germanic conception that women have a less individuated, darker, more elemental and mysteriously primitive nature than men, Georg Simmel provided more insight into the worlds of women than any of the other classical theorists considered here. For nearly three decades (from 1890 to the year of his death in 1918), peaking at the height of the erotic movement, his work displayed continuous interest in women and the relations of the sexes. The brilliant crescendo of all of Simmel's writings on the position and condition of women was his analysis of the impact of male-dominated culture on the identity and self-respect of women—what might be termed the patriarchal trap in which women were placed. Simmel sensitively depicted the contradictions of the position of women: the separateness of woman's world from man's world, and the fact that women, because their world was dominated by the men's, lived lives full of the experience of otherness. He captured beautifully what he termed the "typical tragedy of femininity," namely that women were not allowed to live up to the standards of male-dominated culture, which at the same time denied them any independent sense of their own value as persons. Given this structure, a woman never could have a sense of herself as an individual human being with personality; she always would be conscious, especially in the presence of men, that she was a woman, not only different from but also unequal to men. Simmel explained that some women applied harsh sanctions to other women who broke with custom because custom represented solidarity and had the function of protecting women from the constant threat of social and sexual exploitation by men. Simmel's work provides us with a model for analysis of the influence of social structure on self, most poignantly on the ways in which individual choice in modern sexual relationships restricts the range of possible mates.

Also powerful is his phenomenology of the interplay of the worlds of men and women as they come together in coquetry, love, and marriage. Once again the interpenetration of opposites was central to his analysis: in modern marriage and love, he wrote, two beings try to overcome, but never can, their radical separateness; and, since they are in love, their very attempt to overcome separateness threatens the autonomy of the intellectual, moral, esthetic, and practical facets of their selves. He did not draw the psychological conclusion that the situation leads to feelings of entrapment and depression. Yet, in a remark that could have applied to Weber's life and work, Simmel observed that the erotic bond can also lead to "the opening-up of those reservoirs of the personality that lie outside the erotic sphere." [18] His work exhibited that rare combination of astute social psychology of sex roles and a sense of historical variations—sociological imagination, if you will. This quality is evident in his discussions of platonic and modern eros, the greater capacity for friendship found in women as they became more individuated in modern times, and the degree of adherence to fashion as a reflection of the oppression or emancipation of women. Simmel stands virtually alone among the classic theorists in going beyond concern with the relationships of women and men to focus not only on the variations of these relationships but also on variations in the relationships between women in different types of societies—tribal, modern, industrial—and the ways in which the emancipation of women created new types of relationships between women.

Finally, Simmel's analysis of prostitution from a Kantian (and Marxian?) standpoint is, in my view, sociologically superior to Weber's "value-free" discussion of prostitution.[19] In Simmel's view, prostitution degraded women by assigning a value in money to "the most private aspects of female persons." Since their business relationships did not engage them as persons, prostitutes often developed more personal, lesbian relationships and/or relationships with pimps, he observed. Underlying most of Simmel's work, as I see it, is the ever present sense of the "typical hostility" between the sexes that stems from male power to use and abuse women. In conclusion, Simmel's analysis of the world of women comes close to qualifying as insider knowledge: his method and style of work seems particularly well suited to the development of a sociology that includes both sexes.

Substantively and theoretically, Ferdinand Tönnies in *Gemeinschaft und Gesellschaft* did little more than translate into a psychological sociology traditional notions of the nature and place of women—their intuitive mode of thought, their specialization in homemaking, their bond with children—all in the context of a benignly conceived patriarchal order. Tönnies' characterization of womanly *Gemeinschaft*, like Comte's, overflows with sentimentality.[20] However, on the positive side of a feminist ledger, Tönnies was keenly aware of the effects of trade, factory employment, and trade unions on the nature, individualization, and position of women, their liberation from the household, and their independence from men. He saw in these changes, combined with the organization of the proletariat, the possibility of a healthy restoration of a cooperative community infused with womanly warmth.

Karl Mannheim's brief analysis of the relations between the sexes manifests the strengths of German and central European sociological theory. In his hands allegedly sex-linked character traits were reinterpreted social-psychologically and placed in the context of social structure, with attention to historical variations in the expression of male sexuality. Mannheim, in his later work, was apprehensive about the release of mass irrationality (such as fascism) consequent upon political disruptions caused by market capitalism and the weakening of the family. In addition to his sociological conception of generations as a tool of historical analysis, Mannheim's formulation of the sociology of knowledge with its emphasis on the ideological and utopian dimensions of social theories is most valuable because it is in the area of the "woman question" that the ideological and the utopian are likely to penetrate social science most deeply and pervasively.

Overall, the centrality of the "woman question" in classical sociology in Germany reflected and expressed aspects of Germany's history: that industrial capitalism began late there, that the German bourgeois revolution was politically incomplete, and that feminism challenged a particularly brutal authoritarian society in a compressed time span. The middle or liberal course on the "woman question" that German intellectuals attempted to steer was a result of the conflicting pressures from the right—traditional and new— and the left—Marxist Social Democratic and radical feminist.

The threat of Marxism also haunted Italian social theory. Vilfredo Pareto's work touched on all the issues concerning the debate about women in the late nineteenth and early twentieth centuries and manifested his traditional belief in the intellectual and cultural inferiority of women and a not-so-hidden notion that woman's proper role was to be a good wife. Misogyny is evident in his statements about women. A persistent motif centered on prostitution and money: women of all classes, he wrote, sold themselves for a few baubles and beads, from which it followed that abolishing capitalism would have no impact on prostitution. Pareto feared the suffragists, and he was hostile to democratic and revolutionary movements, as revealed in his description of the sympathy of some women for revolutionary "criminals." In terms of the criteria I have established to evaluate the theorists, Pareto comes off poorly. The only value of his work is that it is a paradigm of reactionary, antifeminist social theory during periods of decadence. His work may be useful for describing the conditions under which reactionary and antifeminist movements emerge: In periods of change (led, in his terms, by "foxes") when old moral standards and traditional relations of the sexes break down, worry about decadence will become a rallying point for those whose concern is order (the "lions"). At such times cries will be heard to put women back in their place and repress those who spread ideas that threaten "order."

The strength of Robert Michels's *Sexual Ethics* derives from two sources: first, a commitment (marred here and there by the conventional stereotypes of his times) to a sexual morality founded on equal rights for men and women, including women's right to equal sexual pleasure; and second (the result of his early socialist ideas), the adoption of a class analysis of sexual relations. The first provided the standpoint from which he described the ways in which conventional forms of sexual inequality, marriage, and the family frustrate individual happiness and thwart the pursuit of love. The second sensitized him to the ways in which social class interactions conditioned the relationships of men and women outside and inside marriage and the expressions of sexuality within and between classes (e.g., his conception of the working-class prostitute as analogous to the old maid of the bourgeoisie). His exploration of the economic aspect of prostitution has a more solid grounding than Pareto's attempted refutation of economic causes. Also, Michels's cosmopolitanism was a source of sociological strength because through it and his attachment to the Latin countries, especially Italy, he gave proper consideration to cultural variations in sexual relationships.

The writings of Michels's social democratic period idealistically upheld the virtue of working-class women and condemned the hypocrisy of bourgeois men who patronized prostitutes. His analysis of the oligarchical tendencies of democratic movements is useful for understanding feminist movements. Feminist assertions that women would run things differently than men might be tested against Michels's theory. The weakness of the Italian tradition of classical theory, as I have suggested, may be correlated with the relative backwardness of Italian feminism and the traditionalism of much of Italy at the turn of the century. Michels's *Sexual Ethics* documents this backwardness but also reveals that Italians were beginning to discuss the questions feminists had raised in other European countries.

Although liberal and not socialist, feminism in the United States has had a long and militant history influenced by abolitionism and women's equal rights movements in Europe. American sociology, however, has been generally conservative. Herman and Julia Schwendinger have argued that early U.S. sociologists were "sexists to a man."[21] Thorstein Veblen was an exception; an economist of Norwegian extraction, he applied his concepts of conspicuous consumption and conspicuous leisure to the lives of middle- and upperclass women in the late nineteenth-century United States.[22] Among contemporary interpretations of classical sociology, Talcott Parsons's sociological theory of the family did not rise to the historical realities of changes in the family and the position of women in the world of work resulting from industrialization and from women's political struggles. Parsons's conception of sex roles did not differ substantially from Durkheim's in *The Division of Labor,* just as his argument against the breakup of the family bore a striking resemblance to Herbert Spencer's argument in *The Principles of Sociology*. Parsons raised the question of the possibility of fundamental changes in the family resulting from alteration of the traditional pattern of sex roles, only to dismiss it.

Parsons's conclusion was that the existing division of sex roles was biologically based and socially and psychologically necessary and scientifically supported by small-group research, which allegedly demonstrated the requirement for an expressive leader and an instrumental leader in each task-oriented group. His equation was: mother (expressive function) plus father (instrumental function), given the task of socializing children to perform socially required adult sex roles, equals the nuclear family. As Okin has stated, "It is clearly during the oedipal stage that Parsons thinks the clear differentiation of the sex roles of parents is most essential for the child's socialization." Attachment to "social objects"—the first being the mother—is necessary for the child's ego development, Parsons believed, and identification with the same-sexed parent is necessary for the child to internalize the appropriate sex role and the institutionalized values of the social system.[23] I subscribe to Barrington Moore's judgment that Parsons's sociology of the family is yet another example of American sociologists "doing little more than projecting certain middle-class hopes and ideals onto a refractory reality."[24] Theoretically and methodologically, Parsons's approach was flawed by its neglect of the historical and anthropological evidence of variations in kinship structures and child-rearing arrangements—for example, the separation of children from parents in socialist kibbutzim. His work is ideological in its class limitations and in taking for granted the cultural and sexual categories of American society at the time.

C. Wright Mills's writings about women do not suffer from these shortcomings. Mills exhibited a recognition of the changing position of women consequent upon capitalist industrialization, its emerging bureaucratic form of organization, and its market for fashion, glamor, and sex. He wrote about women in the white-collar and pink-collar worlds, wives in suburbia, expense-account sex in the world of business, and transformations of sexual mores and behavior. The strengths of Mills's sociological reflections about women stem in part from his rejection of a functionalist approach and his acceptance of a conflict perspective derived from Weber and Marx. In his proposal for a sociology of women, Mills drew upon the comparative-historical methods of the classical sociological tradition and its central problem of exploring the connections of self and social structure. In this regard, as in others, Mills was ahead of his times.

What general conclusions can be drawn from these assessments of the various theorists of classical sociology? First, in keeping with John Stuart Mill's characterization of the nineteenth-century reaction against the Enlightenment, non-Marxist and anti-Marxist classical sociology involved a critical reevaluation—a watering down, if not an outright rejection—of the Enlightenment's faith that reason and equality are grounded in the natural order and in progress toward a more egalitarian future.[25] However, it might be argued that the more conservative of the classical theorists responded more intensely to the changing position of women in society than either liberal or radical theorists. This apparent paradox may be dissolved when we realize that those classical sociologists who employed a conservative conception of society as their normative theory would thereby be more sensitive to the jolts resulting from involuntary and purposive changes in the traditional patterns of male dominance.[26]

Second, the one perspective that cut across the styles and variations in emphasis of the several cultural traditions in which classical sociological theory took shape, and the one that appeared in all of them, was functionalism. Okin, in *Women in Western Political Thought*, concludes that the philosophical justification for the inequality of women and their restriction from public life was a functionalist view of "woman's nature" and of the patriarchal family as an immutable and necessary institution. On the basis of functionalism, the inequality of women and men was assumed to be inevitable. Said somewhat differently, functionalism took deeply held assumptions about differences in the natures of women and men and turned them into a theory about female and male roles in the maintenance of the social order. The assumptions then were molded into a conception of the family and thereby considered sociological.

Such a functionalist perspective is blatantly evident in Spencer's later work and provides a common thread running through French theory, regardless of individual ideological differences. A break occurred with Durkheim's data-induced realization of the antagonistic interests of the sexes in existing marital arrangements and divorce law, indicated by suicide rates as determined by sex, marital status, and family size. In German theory, with its more conflict-oriented perspective, functionalism, formulated in a more traditionalist psychology of everyday life, is found explicitly only in the work of Tönnies, especially in *Community and Association*—although his ideas of "woman's nature" allowed for some degree of modification in light of capitalist development. Alongside Pareto's sociological exposé of the hypocrisy of democrats on the question of women's suffrage and the utopianism of socialists and sex reformers on the problem of prostitution was his functionalist view of "woman's nature." Parsons's work on sex roles was dictated by his acceptance of the approach of Spencer's late work and Durkheim's early work, with additional support from Freud's work. His position on the "woman question" was therefore derived from the organismic metaphor.

Consequently, it is not quite precise to say that classical theory omitted women. It included women, albeit in a distorted fashion, in its functionalist versions. However, what is valuable in the traditions of classical sociological theory are just those works that break from a functionalist perspective, especially those of Mill,[27] Weber, Simmel, Michels, Mannheim, Durkheim in *Suicide,* and Mills.

Yet another significant and uniform characteristic of virtually all of the classical sociologists' writings is the omission of women of the working class.[28] Most theorists focused on middle- and upper-class women and accepted bourgeois ideals of the family. Exceptions were peripheral. Mill distributed birth-control information to lower-class women, but his writing focused on women of his own class. Comte's appeals to working-class families were sentimental and reactionary. Tönnies and Michels, both of whom were influenced by Marxist ideas or were part of socialist movements, wrote about working-class women. Simmel, who once wrote for the socialist press, wrote a little about the contrasting effects of capitalism on working-class and middle-class women. Mills sensitively portrayed the lives of women, working and nonworking, especially the tragedies in the lives of young, lower-middle-class women trying to get ahead. However, the functionalist tradition represented most recently by Parsons considered the words *normal* and *middle-class* synonymous.

Theoretical Issues

For alternatives to functionalist explanations and justifications of the status of women, I turn now to a brief consideration of the works of Karl Marx, Friedrich Engels, and Sigmund Freud, and some of the feminist interpretations of their work. Marx's work clearly inherited the feminist values of the Enlightenment and revolutionary traditions, especially those developed in Charles Fourier's utopian socialism.[29] Marx's theory as it relates to the "woman question" is different from bourgeois sociological theory in that it does not include a set of assumptions about the "nature" of women nor does it name a "proper," or functional, place in society for women.[30] Indeed, in the Paris Manuscripts of 1844, Marx criticized "crude" communism for its advocacy of a *"community of women"* that opposed the existing form of marriage—"certainly a *form of exclusive private property"*—but maintained the basic condition of women as property.[31]

In their first major collaborative work, *The Holy Family*, Marx and Engels demonstrated their concern for the oppression of women in a sensitive and humanistic social-psychological analysis of a character created by contemporary French novelist Eugène Sue, Fleur de Marie, whose humane and natural attitude toward herself and the world was so transformed by a priest that she became "a *serf of consciousness of sin."* About a central male character of Sue's novel, Rudolph, Marx and Engels commented that in spite of his patronizing concern for women servants, he did not "grasp the general condition of women in modern society as an inhuman one."[32]

Concern with the oppression of women is also evident in *The German Ideology*, considered by many to be the first formulation of historical materialism. The "natural division of labor" in the family was, Marx and Engels believed, the basis of property and inequality. They stated that

the wife and children are the slaves of the husband. This latent slavery in the family, though still very crude, is the first property, but even at this early stage it corresponds perfectly to the definition of modern economists who call it the power of disposing over the labour-power of others.[33]

As a social alternative, Marx asserted in *Capital:*

However terrible and disgusting the dissolution, under the capitalist system, of the old family ties may appear, nevertheless, modern industry, by assigning as it does an important part in the process of production, outside the domestic sphere, to women, to young persons, and to children of both sexes, creates a new economical foundation for a higher form of the family and of the relations between the sexes. Moreover, it is obvious that the fact of the collective working group being composed of individuals of both sexes and all ages must necessarily, under suitable conditions, become a source of humane development.[34]

The analysis of the "woman question" in classical Marxism culminated in Engels's *The Origin of the Family, Private Property, and the State*. This classic analysis of the sources of the inequality of women was based on Marx's notes on Lewis Henry Morgan's *Ancient Society*. Marx stated that "the modern family . . . contains *in miniature* all the contradictions which later extend throughout society and its state." Engels's argument is well known to feminists. Despite the dubious anthropological method and data on which his reconstruction of matriarchy rested, Engels did not rely on the functions of procreation and parenting to account for the origin and perpetuation of women's oppression. He believed that with the emergence of private property, women acquired an exchange value and were captured in war or purchased, became degraded to a condition of servitude in the family, were turned into slaves of men's lust, and became instruments for the production of children. The summary of Engels's position was that the "overthrow of mother-right was the *world historical defeat of the female sex.*"[35] Engels argued:

> The first class opposition that appears in history coincides with the development of the antagonism between man and woman in monogamous marriage, and the first class oppression coincides with that of the female sex by the male.[36]

The marriage contract between equals in bourgeois law really concealed an inequality analogous to that between worker and capitalist in the labor contract, Engels observed. "The modern individual family is founded on the open or concealed domestic slavery of the wife, and modern society is a mass composed of these individual families as its molecules."[37] While Engels did not draw out fully the feminist implications of his statement, he did offer a solution, namely, that the emancipation of women would occur under socialism:

> The position of men will be very much altered. But the position of women, of *all* women, also undergoes significant change. With the transfer of the means of production into common

ownership, the single family ceases to be the economic unit of society. Private housekeeping is transformed into a social industry. The care and education of the children becomes a public affair; society looks after all children alike, whether they are legitimate or not. This removes the anxiety about the "consequences," which today is the most essential social—moral as well as economic—factor that prevents a girl from giving herself completely to the man she loves. Will not that suffice to bring about the gradual growth of unconstrained sexual intercourse and with it a more tolerant public opinion in regard to a maiden's honor and a woman's shame? And, finally, have we not seen that in the modern world monogamy and prostitution are indeed contradictions, but inseparable contradictions, poles of the same state of society? Can prostitution disappear without dragging monogamy with it into the abyss?[38]

Engels's argument was that socialism would create the conditions for real social equality between men and women and relationships not bound by considerations of property, legality, and bourgeois (im)morality but, rather, based on attraction, love, and reciprocity; thus unions without these characteristics would be dissolved, and "the useless mire of a divorce case" would be avoided.[39]

That Engels provided an alternative to bourgeois theorists' accounts of the oppression of women is not sufficient to make it a complete theory of the oppression of women and the relationships of the sexes. Marxism still has the appearance of a theory by, of, and for adult males. If we apply Okin's test of whether a political theory can include women in its categories without inconsiste..cy, we come to two different conclusions about Engels's analysis of the position of women. First, women can be included as equals in his socialist future precisely because it will be a society without social classes. Second, however, because it is primarily a theory of classes, Marxism cannot fully explain in an empirical sense sexism (or racism, for that matter); it was not fashioned to do so. (It is appropriate here to correct a common misconception; Engels did not state that capitalism causes sexism but only that sexism is associated with class societies.)

Against "feminist isolationism," Sheila Rowbotham has pointed out that "in practice, these connections [of sex and class] were grasped by women who by social and political circumstance were involved not simply as women. For a black woman in the Civil War in America, for a Frenchwoman in one of the revolutionary movements, for an English chartist or for an early woman trade unionist to confine their conception of the oppression they resisted simply to their gender was absurd."[40] Nevertheless, as Juliet Mitchell has observed, radical feminism of the 1960s and 1970s emerged as a reaction to the socialist sins of commission and omission against women. The former included the male-chauvinist politics of the Left and the failures of socialist revolutions to combat sexism, and the latter included the absence of an adequate treatment of women in socialist theory. Mitchell argued that a theory of women's oppression requires specific analyses of sexuality, reproduction, and child rearing, as well as production.[41]

Sigmund Freud provided analyses of sexuality, reproduction, and child rearing, but the question is whether he devised a theory of sexism or whether he was a sexist theorist. In *The Dialectic of Sex*, Shulamith Firestone argued that "Freudianism and Feminism are made of the same stuff" and "grew from the same soil." Citing turn-of-the-century literature and early film, she stated, "There was a tremendous ferment of ideas regarding sexuality, marriage and family, and women's role. Freudianism was only one of the cultural product of this ferment. . . . but Freud was merely a diagnostician for what Feminism purports to cure." His was a "misguided feminism," in her designation. Firestone believed that the Oedipus complex must be reinterpreted as the sex-power psychology created by the patriarchal family, which "intensifies the worst effects of the inequalities [of size and strength] inherent in the biological family itself." Accordingly, a theory of what I would term historical sexualism, as comprehensive as Engels's historical materialism, is required. This is where Freud had greater insights than socialist theorists, Firestone argues: "Unlike economic class, sex class sprang directly from a biological reality: men and women were created different, and not equally privileged." The sex-class system is based on reproductive functions; to overthrow that system would require dismantling the family—and thus sexual repression—and applying the technological fix, "the freeing of women from the tyranny of their reproductive biology by every means available and the diffusion of the child bearing and child rearing role to society as a whole, men as well as women." It should be noted that Firestone's explanation of the inequality of women is a biological-functional theory, in that way similar to the functionalism of classical sociological theory.[42]

In her impressive *Psychoanalysis and Feminism*, Juliet Mitchell takes the position that it is irrelevant that Freud held sexist attitudes toward women because, from a scientific viewpoint, he presented us with the elements of a theory of sexism:

> The greater part of the feminist movement has identified Freud as the enemy. . . . Psychoanalysis is seen as a justification for the status-quo, bourgeois and patriarchal, and Freud in his own person exemplifies these qualities. I would agree that popularized Freudianism must answer to this description; but the argument of this book is that a rejection of psychoanalysis and of Freud's work is fatal for feminism. However it may have been used, psychoanalysis is not a recommendation *for* a patriarchal society but an analysis *of* one. If we are interested in understanding and challenging the oppression of women, we cannot afford to neglect it.[43]

Mitchell's argument rests in part on the distinction between the social origin of scientific ideas and the separate, impersonal criteria by which the scientific validity of propositions is established. Some feminist critics of Freud are not persuaded, for they find it difficult to separate so neatly Freud's intentions from his theory. Freud's insistence on the social, psychological, and cultural significance of anatomical differences between the sexes creates the ideological divide between him and most feminists.[44] It is not necessary to recount Freud's well-known remarks on girls and feminine nature but rather to note the larger issue, a problem in epistemology and sociology of knowledge. When statements purporting to be scientific are not warranted, the reason can often be found in the ways in which the social origin and values of the researcher have crept into the results.[45] To borrow a phrase from Kenneth Burke, ways of seeing are at once ways of not seeing.

Nevertheless, despite Freud's disastrously unfortunate remark that biology is destiny, Mitchell maintains that

> [Freud's] theories give us the beginnings of the inferiorized and "alternative" (second sex) psychology of women under patriarchy. Their concern is with how the human animal with a bisexual psychological disposition becomes the sexed social creature—the man or the woman.[46]

In the creation of sexual personalities in early childhood experience in the patriarchal family, the crucial event is the Oedipus complex. As Mitchell has pointed out, Freud rejected a parallel myth for women, the Electra complex, because he "always opposed any idea of symmetry in the 'cultural' making of men and women." She continued:

> At first both sexes want to take the place of both the mother and the father, but as they cannot take *both* places, each has to learn to repress the characteristic of the other sex. . . . *only the boy will one day be allowed to* [take the place of the father]. . . . through the cultural heritage, what the mother desires is the phallus-turned-baby, [and] *both* children desire to be the phallus for the mother. Again, *only the boy can fully recognize himself in his mother's desire.* Thus *both* sexes repudiate the implications of femininity. Femininity is, therefore, in part a repressed condition that can only be secondarily acquired in a distorted form. . . . In the body of the hysteric, male and female, lies the feminine protest against the law of the father. [47]

According to Freud, the oedipal experience for the female is, in Mitchell's words, a "poor, secondary affair." The female child's subjection "to the law of the father entails her becoming the representative of 'nature' and 'sexuality', a chaos of spontaneous, intuitive creativity," she states. In comparison to the "little man," a girl does not develop a strong superego, Mitchell (following Freud) claims, but "can only develop her narcissistic ego-ideal." She concludes that a girl is not "heir to the law of culture. . . . Hers is the sphere of reproduction." In short, "This is the place of all women in patriarchal culture." Mitchell argues that Freud is a cultural, not a biological, theorist and that we live in a "patriarchal culture in which the phallus is valorized and women oppressed." Therefore, "a cultural revolution" against patriarchy is necessary to end the oppression of women. [48]

Freud constructed the most powerful theory of the development of the self; whether that theory—his major contribution—can carry the explanatory weight Mitchell has placed on it is another matter. There is a deeply sexist level in Freud's work that Mitchell does not give its due emphasis. Freud's work can be (re)interpreted as a cultural theory, as many neo-Freudians have done, but the biological component of his thought (for example, the use of the Lamarckian notion of the inheritance of acquired characteristics) and its sexist implications cannot be dismissed. In his theory of the development of female self, anatomy and biology won out. This is one of the grounds of his belief in the universality of his depiction of psychodynamics.

As Nancy Chodorow has pointed out, Freud consciously omitted consideration of female development in his conception of the Oedipus complex. He also measured female sexuality by a male norm and found it deficient. Finally, he rejected feminists' claims to equality as of no scientific relevance. His patriarchal conception of the development of the self, the Oedipus complex, has led psychoanalysis to neglect the active role of mothers in the formation of character, conscience, and neurosis. Clearly, feminists must go beyond what Freud wrote in order to exploit the power of his theory to help explain the oppression of women. His conception of women and his attitudes toward them are similar to many of those found in the works of the classical sociologists. Philosophically, for Freud, women were the locus of irrationality—chaos, sensuality, intuition—in his generally rationalistic outlook.[49] Maintaining a strong and sexist conception of female nature, he thus was theoretically close to classical theory precisely at the point where Marxism departs from it.

In the Marxist tradition, two lines of argument on the "woman question" exist, identified by Lise Vogel as a *family argument* (found in Bebel's *Woman and Socialism* and in Engels's classic), and a *social production argument* (also found in Engels's classic). In Vogel's summary: "The family argument starts from what appears to be empirically obvious: the family, the oppression of women, and divisions of labor and authority according to sex." The social production argument views family relations and the oppression of women as being conditioned by the social organization of production. In this view, the position of women was explained by the fact that maintenance and reproduction of labor power occur at the margins of social production proper, "with specific political, ideological, and psychological effects," the latter two of which have not been sufficiently delineated by Marxists. Vogel reminds us of the obvious: "It is the social production argument that accords most closely with Marx's analysis of the workings of the capitalist mode of production."[50] Wives and mothers contribute, uncompensated, to the production of labor power; their unpaid domestic labor involves the exploitation both of women and of the working class as a whole.

Freud's explanation of the position of women relied exclusively on a family argument (with a biological foundation). For Freud the family is "the germ-cell of civilization." However, his elucidation of psychological mechanisms helps explain how sexism is created and maintained. In Randall Collins's words, "Freud saw, more clearly than anyone else, that conflict underlies the two main dimensions of family life: sexual and power struggles between males and females, and between adults and children. . . . Freud gives us a perspective in which intrapsychic conflict reflects and internalizes social conflict, and social bonds are to be explained by the outcomes of the struggle for emotional gratification. Like Marxian conflict theory, there is the realm of real motives and material conditions [physically based lust and aggression], and a covering ideology or false consciousness that results from domination."[51] Stating the sociological core of Freud's work, Collins points out that it is social conflict and threats from authority that inhibit the striving for sexual pleasure and restrain the use of violence.

However, the central scientific weakness of Freud's theory is its insensitivity to social-cultural variations (demonstrated by Bronislaw Malinowski long ago) in its quest for universals. How, for instance, can it explain historical variations in conceptions of female sexuality, for example, the notion in the 1700s of the "frantic clitoris," or nymphomania (a term first used in 1775), in comparison with the Victorian view that women's sexuality was weaker than men's?[52] I submit that it cannot, unless it takes into account explanatory factors other than its own—that is, variations in social structures as well as familial and psychological variables.

Paradoxically, Marx and Engels's historical sociology of family forms is superior to Freud's. However, from the opposite direction, to strengthen the social production argument, its adherents must specify analytically the common social-psychological processes in the development of the self, how family relations vary with different family structures, and how both of these levels—particularly the ways in which class, gender, and other cultural categories are internalized cognitively and affectively—are causally shaped by the mode of production. Possibly, the more subtle and implicit psychological aspects of Marx's theory of ideology can be formulated to get at the unconscious processes of the internalization of sex roles, the reproduction of sex roles, and the socially constructed reality surrounding them, by which existing social arrangements come to be seen as natural and inevitable.

In general, the question is: Is there any way to integrate the family argument with the social production argument in order to better analyze the subjugation of women? The family argument in isolation runs into its own limits, for *the* family as such does not explain change; the social production argument helps it explain all the influences that shape the development of the self and that determine the relationships of men and women. In addition, social inequality as structured by the interplay of class, race, and sex and as it conditions the relations of the sexes in the organization of families must be studied. It is particular families and types of families in particular historical situations that throw certain (types of) personalities onto the stages of history. The issues cannot be resolved in the abstract; useful concepts must be tested through a comparative-historical sociology of variations in the status of women and the relations of the sexes within the context of society and culture.

Historical Alternatives

The need for a comparison of histories as the method to construct a sociology that is not sex-linked can be illustrated by a brief consideration of two classic assessments of the position of women throughout history written by Mary Beard and Simone de Beauvoir. As Sheila Ryan Johansson has pointed out, in *On Understanding Women* (1931) and *Woman As Force in History* (1946) Beard criticized the conventions of historiography for devaluing the civilizing influences of women in history. But in offering an alternative, "unfortunately, Beard ignored most of the historical evidence relating to the victimization of women." On the other hand, Beauvoir, especially in *The Second Sex*, "is most responsible for reestablishing in recent years the intellectual validity of the 'victim' interpretation," an equally one-sided interpretation, in Johansson's judgment. The problem is that for both Beard and Beauvoir, woman in general, in the abstract, is the unit of analysis in their historical narratives. Quoting Johansson, "Timeless abstractions by their very nature do not have histories, they simply persist without change." It follows that "historians must deal with women, and most important, with well-defined groups of women."[53]

A more fundamental problem is the historical narrative itself as a form of statement for presenting a theory of women. Given the selective nature of narrative, which is related more closely to art than to science, every history of women can be no more than an interpretation; of course, this is not to deny that some interpretations are better than others by virtue of their better correspondence with historical evidence and partially verified theory. Narratives offer interpretations based on one selected case, containing a single series of events. Therefore, a theory of women and men that would more closely approximate a verifiable, scientific explanation must rest on the comparison of histories.[54] With these meta-theoretical and methodological considerations in mind, let us return to the oppression perspective that, until recently, has dominated feminist writing.

Juliet Mitchell has argued that women, "as a sex, despite national, racial or class differences . . . share an overall inferiorization which is total."[55] However, Mitchell's statement misses two essential points, one normative-theoretical, the other empirical. First, a Marxist-feminist perspective must, in Gayle Rubin's words, "maintain a distinction between the human capacity and necessity to create a sexual world [the way a society conceives of and organizes sex and gender, how biological sexual needs get satisfied by cultural activity], and the empirically oppressive ways in which sexual worlds have been organized."[56] Second, since the number of known societies has been estimated to be between 650 and 12,000,[57] ample opportunity exists to examine variations in the oppression of women and historical and structural conditions that interrupt that oppression and favor equality and freedom for women and men.

The issue of the relative and varying subjection of women is, most abstractly expressed, a problem of difference (of culture and social-structural conditions) and a problem of change (historical occasions). There is a long history of debate over the instances of matriarchy, which is most productive when it is not a debate over universal concepts of matriarchy and patriarchy. More limited generalizations about social-structural variations in the conditions of women in tribal societies are useful. With regard to mother rule, Kathleen Gough, a Marxist anthropologist, argues that the physical and cultural anthropological evidence shows that "there is in fact no true 'matriarchal,' as distinct from 'matrilineal,' society in existence or known from literature, and the chances are that there never has been." She adds, "This does not mean that women and men have never had relations that were dignified and creative for both sexes, appropriate to the knowledge, skills, and technology of their times. Nor does it mean that the sexes cannot be equal in the future, or that the sexual division of labor cannot be abolished." Women in matrilineal societies, especially those that are also matrilocal and without states, "tend to have greater independence than in patrilineal societies." But even in these societies, the ultimate authority over the group "is usually a man."[58] There are variations in the status of women in hunting societies; women are more autonomous when they are food providers as well as food preparers, when hunting is not territorially extensive, and when gathering is also important. When men in hunting societies have power over women, it seems to result in part from the exclusive male control over heavy weapons, as well as from the particular sexual division of labor.[59] Women appear to be better off in nonclass societies; without private property, women are not possessed as property.

Feminist theory employs the term *patriarchy* to disentangle the major sources of oppression of women independent of the modes of production and the organization of societies into social classes. There are serious flaws in theories that attempt to depict the essence of patriarchy in "the hierarchical sexual division of labor in the domestic sphere centered on reproduction and housework." As Joan Smith points out in a brilliantly argued critique:

> Thus for each of the theorists I have been discussing (and they represent some of the most serious and interesting of recent feminist scholarship) female subordination cannot be reduced to or explained by the mode of production because it shares common and central features with female subordination as found in a variety of productive systems. Men in all societies have control over the *exchange of women* ([Gayle] Rubin); women do the *mothering* which sets up asymmetrical and exploitive relationships between men and women ([Nancy] Chodorow); no political revolution has yet addressed itself to patriarchal relations, so men dominate women in whatever social formation emerges by continually relegating them to *private spheres* ([Zillah] Eisenstein); and *male control over female labor* can be put to any number of uses in a variety of social contexts ([Heidi] Hartmann). . . . The semblance of universality of male dominance arises from the strategy of divesting its core features of the vast panoply of social arrangements that give it actual, temporal forms. Once these arrangements

are peeled away, the dazzling variety of relationships sub-
sumed under the term "male domination" become examples of
essentially the same thing.[60]

To assign near universality to patriarchy, as the sociobiologists also
do, "renders women's history nonexistent," Smith points out.

> No matter how similar they may look on the surface, the rela-
> tionships between men and women now and six centuries ago
> are not only different, they are antithetical. It was precisely
> the overthrow of family-located obligations and responsibili-
> ties for production and the rise of individualism that were the
> preconditions for the full development of the capitalist wage
> relationship. If we fail to grasp this fact, and instead lump all
> relationships between men and women over the centuries into
> the catch-all category of patriarchy, we ensure that we will to-
> tally misunderstand the most crucial aspect of women's history.

According to Smith, to understand correctly the unpaid labor of
women, as well as other forms of unpaid labor in the modern world,
requires that such labor be placed in the context of a world economy in which capitalist production relations (and their shadows in
noncapitalist economies) are dominant. Capitalist production relations tend to subsume and penetrate all other relations, which
thereby do not exist merely side by side with paid labor outside the
home but are shaped by it.[61]
    Asking questions that can be answered by historical data is, in
the final analysis, the only way ahead for a sociology that includes
both the sexes equally. To pull together more of the strands of the
problems of difference and change, I will add two recent attempts
to conceptualize variations, one in the Weberian tradition and the
other in the Marxian tradition.
    In *Conflict Sociology*, Randall Collins presents an impressively
systematic and theoretically comprehensive attempt to sort out the
variations and variables in systems of sexual stratification. From a
realistic, tough-minded, conflict theory perspective, Collins brings
together considerations of material conditions (such as aggressive
sexuality, size, and strength advantages of men) with economic-
technological levels and control of the means of political domination. To these he adds personal resources, such as attractiveness
(itself making up a system of cultural stratification). He argues that

in several combinations all of these together make for variations in systems of *sexual property*—the form of male dominance—which in turn vary by residence, lineage, and quantity. Each system produces an ideology as a justification and a resource in the bargaining for sexual power.[62]

Collins asserts that "the Victorian Revolution was the first major phase of women's liberation" inasmuch as "women actually acquired at least one source of power they had not had before: the power to withhold their bodies from men as sexual objects." To reinforce this power, women had to combat the double standard (and prostitution) and keep sex within the bounds of marriage, for the marriage bargain "had now become a trade of erotic property for household property." This change, he says, explains the prudery of Victorian morality and the ideology of pure love veiling the increased importance of sex—not property—as the heart of marriage. This channeling of sexuality also explains why Victorian society cried out for a Freud. However, "From another viewpoint . . . the Victorian Revolution was also a dead end. It confined a woman's career to making a good marriage." This was reflected in the nineteenth-century "cult of true womanhood." The twentieth century has witnessed another revolution in the position of women, he observes: coincident with their entry into the world of white-collar work, women became less dependent for their economic security on being members of a family, which membership necessarily confined their sexual activity; as a consequence, marriage became less important. Collins predicted that, except in the eventuality of fascist counterrevolution, "the more the occupational situation shifts toward sexual equality, the more firmly the newer type of marriage market will take hold. The future of the family is more than likely to be on the side of the feminist revolution."[63]

Karen Sacks writes within the Marxian tradition. She believes that to explain variations in the status of women, the relationships of women to one another and to men must be examined, not just the relationships of women to the means of production. She argues that sisterhood and wifehood are "central relations" in the precapitalist world.

Sister is a kind of kinship shorthand term for a woman member of a community of owners of the means of production: an equal, an adult among adults, a decision maker. *Wife* is a shorthand for a woman's relationship to her spouse—she may live with him on her family's productive estate (garden lands or pasture, for example), and he may work for her family—or the reverse—she lives at the estate of her husband's family and works for them. (There are, of course, many more kinds of wifehood.) In the first case wife is generally a relationship of dominance; in the second it is generally one of subordination. In a search for equality, the relationship of sisters—to their brothers and to each other—is the critical one to understand. But the necessary condition for sister relations to exist was a corporation of owners, a social order based on groups of kinspeople who owned the means to their livelihood. Differences in the roles of men and women were compatible with sexual equality.[64]

The rise of private ownership of property and the rise of states in Africa and possibly elsewhere undercut not only the basis of the power of male producers but, in the process, also that of women: "Women were transformed from sisters and wives, to wives (and sometimes daughters), to perennial subordinates. Motherhood, as a social relationship to the means of production, underwent profound changes as a result of changes in women's other relations to the means of production. It went from a relationship of adulthood to one of dependency."[65] Sacks tentatively extends her argument to Europe, where "it appears that the meaning of medieval wife as a productive relationship connoted many of the prerogatives sustained by African sister and, perhaps, by European premedieval sister." This is so because medieval women owned property (their dowries) upon the occasion of marriage. Naturally, the rise of capitalism undercut the proprietorship of the immediate producers, separating the workplace from the household; as a consequence, women lost any control over family estates. Sacks concludes:

In this sense it is possible to see the women's rights movements of the nineteenth century as class-based attempts by women to recreate something of the sisterly prerogatives of preindustrial times by demanding control over such of the new productive means as were associated with their class—to control property and wages and to gain access to the new routes to security that developed in the nineteenth century: education and the licensed professions.[66]

Statements about the past and future of the relations of the sexes, and the prospects for the equality of women and men, must distinguish between several identifiable historical processes: those of persistence of tradition to which the structural variations of tribal societies are relevant; secular trends occurring over longer periods; and those comparatively rapid, fundamental, and discontinuous changes of patterns of social structure, organization, and belief.[67] The effects of capitalism's contradictory laws of motion must be examined also.

The following historical and theoretical propositions have been presented in this book: The development of early capitalism involved excluding women of the bourgeoisie from social production and restricting them to the domestic sphere, injustices that middle-class feminists have fought for the last two centuries. In contrast, the factory system from its inception separated work from the household and employed large numbers of working-class women and children outside the home. Generally speaking, when added to the increasing numbers of women in white-collar occupations in the twentieth century, the development of capitalism has transformed power within the family by virtue of the relative economic independence of women who have their own sources of income from wages or salaries—a secular trend contributing to the rise of feminism and trade-union organization among working women. Punctuating this long-term pattern of secular change have been the recurrent crises of capitalism, those violent reequilibrations of overproduction, in which working men and women are thrown out of work, often women first. Competition for jobs escalated to conflict after wartime, when the larger numbers of women employed during war were driven out of the labor force as a result of demobilization. In such periods, the reassertion of the belief that "woman's place is in the home" has not totally succeeded in eradicating the secular trends toward increasing employment of women outside the home.

Historically, debates over special protective legislation for women workers in England, France, Germany, and the United States have followed the swings in the market demand for female laborers. There has been conflict not only between working-class men and women but between working-class and middle-class women over special protection for women. Robin Miller Jacoby has concluded from an examination of the British and American women's trade-union leagues and suffrage movements that "despite feminist ideology and rhetoric about sisterhood, it was extremely difficult for barriers of class not to come between women."[68] The evidence from France, Germany, and Italy also seems to indicate that sisterhood is not always so powerful.

Referring to the most revolutionary period of the twentieth century—the years after World War I—Sheila Rowbotham writes: "In exceptional periods of class conflict many of the divisions between men and women, work and home, industry and community could be overcome."[69] Such exceptional periods have been occasioned when events have interrupted normal authority relations in the society at large and between men and women—when society's fundamental patterns have been challenged by the appearance of new complexes of action and class relations and, as a result, the dominant intellectual structure no longer informs the consciousness of individuals. Major social revolutions have been both the outcome and the cause of such contradictory historical processes.

Such extraordinary events and processes have provided opportunities for fundamentally altering the relationships of the sexes and the position of women. Friedrich Engels observed one aspect of the process when he stated, "It is a curious fact that with every great revolutionary movement the question of 'free love' comes into the foreground."[70] However, in major nineteenth- and twentieth-century revolutions, important changes in the way men and women relate to each other have not been fully realized. The evidence from the cases covered here indicates that the possibilities for changes in these relations have hinged in part upon alliances of revolutionary men and women. Where such alliances have been broken and revolutionary parties have turned against revolutionary women (or reactionary men and women have suppressed them), feminist hopes and demands have been squashed. Tradition, routinization, institutionalization, and what Otto Kirchheimer once referred to as the "confining conditions" of economic and world-market necessity also prevent revolutionary breakthroughs.

The female world characterized by Jessie Bernard as one of love and duty is itself penetrated by the "cash nexus" formerly restricted to the male world. As Marx and Engels stated in *The Communist Manifesto*, capitalism "has torn away from the family its sentimental veil and has reduced the family relation to a mere money relation." The private, familial, and innermost aspects of life are not exempt from the workings of capitalist production; the production of commodities has come to encompass the commodification of all relationships and aspects of life, including the preparation and consumption of food, the manufacture of beauty, the production of need, and of personal conflicts between wives and husbands and children over money and time. This is what we would expect from a mode of production to which nothing is sacred. On the liberating consequences of capitalism, Mitchell argues that the nuclear form of the family and the socially organized nature of work in a capitalist society make "potentially redundant the laws of patriarchal culture."[71] Technologies in which strength is no longer an occupational prerequisite remove a traditional ground of discrimination against women in employment.

But then there is the matter of the "laws" of class society. It may be, as William Julius Williams has argued in reference to race, that the relative importance of class in comparison to sex and gender is increasing.[72] This process can be seen, for example, in the feminization of poverty and the labor force—most jobs available to women are low-paying clerical, service, and industrial jobs—and in the corporate cooptation of feminism,[73] through which women executives and businesswomen as newly emerging social types legitimate the belief in the increasing equality of opportunity for women. Critical to the emergence of socialist-feminist consciousness is whether the occupations women enter reproduce existing relations of dominance or produce an altered structure of perceptions that collide with them.[74] As Joan Smith has argued, "It is hardly anti-feminist to suggest that a woman in her kitchen, who depends on her husband's wage and thus his goodwill, is in a situation no less determined by the processes that compose the world capitalist system than is an unemployed male Black worker in Detroit, a female Black subsistence farmer in southern Africa, or a white male fully employed computer technician in Menlo Park." She notes that the feminists who hold to patriarchy theory and claim that relations of domination between the sexes are "theoretically immune from capital, although empirically caught up in it" fail to grasp the effects of capitalism on our lives. Her suspicion is that what we "will find when we begin to consider capitalism as the unity of contradictory elements is that unequal and hierarchical gender roles, along with other kinds of system inequalities anchored in nonwaged relations, play a fundamental role in holding those contradictory elements together in a unified system." For feminist theorists to do otherwise, she writes, is to risk "adopting a theoretical framework that is incapable of taking seriously the various non-gender specific forms of oppression."[75] The struggles against exploitation—as well as those against the oppression of women—weaken this contradictory unity and create altered conditions for others in their struggles for equality.

The future of sexual equality will be made—or not made—by women and men under conditions and images handed down from the past and in the unknown circumstances of the future. However, one "certainty" was stated in a letter from Marx to his one-time friend, Dr. Kugelmann (London, 12 December 1868): "Anybody who knows anything of history knows that great social changes are impossible without the feminine ferment. Social progress can be measured exactly by the social position of the fair sex."[76] It can also be said that the "murk of sentimentality" passed down from Victorian ideology, through which sociology has studied and viewed the family, cannot withstand the test of contemporary reality. Collins has observed, "Sociological theory is only starting to become liberated from the self-justifying viewpoints of dominant males and adults."[77] For women and men alike—and for children—this beginning is one of the hopes for a freer and therefore more humane world.

Notes

Chapter 1. Introduction

1. See, for example, Shulamith Firestone, *The Dialectic of Sex: The Case for Feminist Revolution;* Juliet Mitchell, *Woman's Estate* and *Psychoanalysis and Feminism: Freud, Reich, Laing, and Women;* and Nancy Chodorow, *The Reproduction of Mothering: Psychoanalysis and the Sociology of Gender.* For selections of feminist writings, including Marxist and Freudian, see *Feminist Frameworks: Alternative Theoretical Accounts of the Relations between Women and Men,* ed. Alison M. Jaggar and Paula Rothenberg Struhl.
2. Lewis A. Coser pointed out that male scholars neglected Georg Simmel's contributions to the sociology of women until their work was affected by feminism ("Georg Simmel's Neglected Contributions to the Sociology of Women," 870–71). See also Helen MacGill Hughes, ed., *The Status of Women in Sociology, 1968–1972: Report to the American Sociological Association of the Ad Hoc Committee on the Status of Women in the Profession,* and subsequent reports and discussions in *Footnotes,* published monthly by the American Sociological Association.
3. *Signs: A Journal of Women in Culture and Society* probably best exemplifies this large and multidisciplinary universe of feminist discourse. See also *Academe,* Bulletin of the American Association of

University Professors, September–October 1983, which featured essays on "Feminism in the Academy." See also Jessie Bernard, "A Quiet Revolution," foreword to *The Study of Women: Enlarging Perspectives of Social Reality,* ed. Eloise C. Snyder, xiii–xx. Bernard has asserted that feminist scholarship responding to the women's liberation movement has occasioned a paradigm shift in the humanistic disciplines. In the last two decades, there has been intense interest in feminism; what J. A. Banks and Olive Banks wrote in 1963 is no longer true: "Sociologists have, on the whole, been remarkably uninterested in feminism, and it is rare, even in books about social movements generally, to find the subject dealt with in any detail. Yet, changes in the status of women have occurred in all countries where there are sociologists" ("Feminism and Social Change—A Case Study of a Social Movement," 547). For a sophisticated analysis of the place of gender in sociological work by comparison to other social science disciplines, see Judith Stacey and Barrie Thorne, "The Missing Feminist Revolution in Sociology," *Social Problems,* vol. 32, no. 4 (April 1985): 301–16.

4. Gayle Rubin, "The Traffic in Women," 154.
5. Eloise C. Snyder, "The Selective Eye of Sociology," 49.
6. The omission of the classical sociological theorists' treatment of women can be confirmed by a cursory examination of the major histories of classical sociological theory. See the minor exceptions cited throughout the text.
7. For discussions of some of the issues in the preceding paragraphs, see, for example, Jaggar and Struhl, ed., *Feminist Frameworks,* and Lynda M. Glennon, *Women and Dualism: A Sociology of Knowledge Analysis.*
8. Ann D. Gordon, Mari Jo Buhle, and Nancy Schrom Dye, "The Problem of Women's History," 88.
9. Sheila Ryan Johansson, " 'Herstory' As History: A New Field or Another Fad?" 424.
10. Theodore Roszak, "The Hard and the Soft: The Force of Feminism in Modern Times," 87–88.
11. Sheila Rowbotham, *Hidden from History: Rediscovering Women in History from the Seventeenth Century to the Present,* xxxvi.
12. Ibid., 47.
13. "General Introduction" to *Victorian Women: A Documentary Account of Women's Lives in Nineteenth-Century England, France, and the United States,* ed. Erna Olafson Hellerstein, Leslie Parker Hume, and Karen M. Offen, 2.
14. Robert A. Nisbet, *The Sociological Tradition,* 8.
15. Marquis de Condorcet, *An Historical Picture of the Progress of the Human Mind* (1795), in *The Idea of Progress: A Collection of Readings Selected by Frederick J. Teggart,* 351–52.

16. Sheila Rowbotham, *Women, Resistance and Revolution: A History of Women and Revolution in the Modern World*, 58.
17. Hellerstein, Hume, and Offen, eds., *Victorian Women*, 2–3.
18. Ibid., 1, and see 3.
19. Snyder, "The Selective Eye of Sociology," 49.

Chapter 2. England

1. Sheila Rowbotham, *Hidden from History: Rediscovering Women in History from the Seventeenth Century to the Present*, 24, 1–4; see 23–26. See also Sheila Rowbotham, *Women, Resistance and Revolution: A History of Women and Revolution in the Modern World*, chap. 1, especially pp. 31, 35, 23–24. For a detailed treatment of the monographic literature on middle-class women in England and America, see Ruth H. Bloch, "Untangling the Roots of Modern Sex Roles: A Survey of Four Centuries of Change," 237–46. For changes in aristocratic family structure, see Lawrence Stone, *The Crisis of Aristocracy, 1558–1641* (abridged edition, London: Oxford University Press, 1965), chap. XI.
2. Rowbotham, *Hidden from History*, 8–13; Rowbotham, *Women, Resistance and Revolution*, 18–27.
3. Martin Green, *The Von Richthofen Sisters: The Triumphant and the Tragic Modes of Love: Else and Frieda von Richthofen, Otto Gross, Max Weber, and D. H. Lawrence, in the Years 1870–1970*, 150.
4. Rowbotham, *Women, Resistance and Revolution*, 28–35; Rowbotham, *Hidden from History*, 14–16; see also 17–18, for the responses of working-class women to their oppression; and see 6–7. For contemporary feminist analyses of Rousseau, see Susan Moller Okin, *Women in Western Political Thought*, part 3, and Jean Bethke Elshtain, *Public Man, Private Woman: Women in Social and Political Thought*, 148–70. See chap. 3 of this book for a brief discussion of Rousseau.
5. Mary Wollstonecraft, as quoted in Rowbotham, *Hidden from History*, 21; in Rowbotham, *Women, Resistance and Revolution*, 42; and in Rowbotham, *Hidden from History*, 21.
6. William Blake and Percy Bysshe Shelley, as quoted in Rowbotham, *Women, Resistance and Revolution*, 45–46.
7. Rowbotham, *Hidden from History*, 22.
8. Thomas Spence, as quoted in E. P. Thompson, *The Making of the English Working Class*, 163; and see 161–62, 94.
9. Thompson, *Making of the English Working Class*, 414–15.
10. For a concise description of changes in the technology in textiles, see

Neil J. Smelser, "Sociological History: The Industrial Revolution and the British Working-Class Family," 82–85.

11. For the flavor of the revolutionary changes of the period, in addition to sources mentioned in the text, I also rely on Karl Marx's *Capital: A Critique of Political Economy*, vol. 1, *The Process of Capitalist Production*, part 4.

12. Thompson, *Making of the English Working Class*, 9–12.

13. Theresa M. McBride, "The Long Road Home: Women's Work and Industrialization," 282–94, especially 283–84 and 292–93. See also Richard T. Vann, "Toward a New Lifestyle: Women in Preindustrial Capitalism," 192–214; Mary Lynn McDougall, "Working-Class Women during the Industrial Revolution, 1780–1914," 257–78; and Neil J. Smelser's classic *Social Change in the Industrial Revolution*.

14. Rowbotham, *Women, Resistance and Revolution*, 35.

15. Thompson, *Making of the English Working Class*, 248, 250, 234–35, 308–9; and see 198–203.

16. Friedrich Engels, *The Condition of the Working Class in England*, 175.

17. Thompson, *Making of the English Working Class*, 414; and see 327. See also Engels, *Condition of the Working Class in England*, 193–96, 215, 225–26, and 285–87 (for mining).

18. John Wade, as quoted in Thompson, *Making of the English Working Class*, 416; Thompson, quoted from 415, 413, 416.

19. Rowbotham, *Hidden from History*, 32–33.

20. Thompson, *Making of the English Working Class*, 413–14.

21. Rowbotham, *Hidden from History*, 29. For a stronger emphasis on working-class defense of the traditional family, see Smelser, "Sociological History," 76–91.

22. Thompson, *Making of the English Working Class*, 416.

23. Engels, *The Condition of the Working Class in England*, 179.

24. Thompson, *Making of the English Working Class*, 94, 162–63, 179, 414–17, 717–18, 770–71. Rowbotham, *Women, Resistance and Revolution*, 46–47.

25. Rowbotham, *Hidden from History*, 36–38.

26. Ibid., 41–46.

27. William Thompson, as quoted in Rowbotham, *Women, Resistance and Revolution*, 49, and see 47–50; Rowbotham, *Hidden from History*, 40–41, 39.

28. Rowbotham, *Hidden from History*, 46, 43–44; and cf. Rowbotham, *Women, Resistance and Revolution*, 56, 108.

29. Bloch, "Untangling the Roots of Modern Sex Roles," 245–52. Rowbotham, *Hidden from History*, 47.

30. Martha Vicinus, "The Perfect Victorian Lady," introduction to *Suffer and Be Still: Women in the Victorian Age*, ed. Martha Vicinus, ix–x.

31. Rowbotham, *Hidden from History*, 48. The rest of this sketch relies largely on Rowbotham's synthesis.
32. Vicinus, *Suffer and Be Still*, ix.
33. *Saturday Review*, quoted in Rowbotham, *Hidden from History*, 51; and see 49–51.
34. Rowbotham, *Hidden from History*, 48–49, 53–54, 62–63.
35. Martha Vicinus, "New Trends in the Study of Victorian Women," introduction to *A Widening Sphere: Changing Roles of Victorian Women*, ed. Martha Vicinus, x.
36. Josephine Butler, as quoted in Rowbotham, *Hidden from History*, 52; John Elphinstone, as quoted on 53: and see 58, 48–49.
37. Lord Shaftesbury, Henry Broadhurst, and Tom Mann, as quoted in Rowbotham, *Hidden from History*, 56, 61, 64; Rowbotham, quoted from 65; and see chaps. 11, 12, and pp. 70–73, 91; Rowbotham, *Women, Resistance and Revolution*, chap. 4, especially pp. 86–92.
38. Solicitor General, as quoted in Rowbotham, *Hidden from History*, 74; Rowbotham quoted from 75; and see 76.
39. Hannah Mitchell, as quoted in Rowbotham, *Hidden from History*, 81. See Rowbotham, *Hidden from History*, chaps. 15–17; Rowbotham, *Women, Resistance and Revolution*, 130–31; Theodore Roszak, "The Hard and the Soft: The Force of Feminism in Modern Times," 95–98.
40. Perry Anderson, "Components of the National Culture," 219; see also 225, 227. See also Raymond Williams, *Culture and Society, 1780–1950*, part 1.
41. For a brilliant analysis of the formation and transformation of utilitarianism, see Karl Marx and Friedrich Engels, *The German Ideology*, 459–66.
42. Robert A. Nisbet, *The Sociological Tradition*, 17, 14, 12–13, 6–8, 11, 10.
43. Cf. Kenneth E. Bock, *The Acceptance of Histories: Toward a Perspective for Social Science*, 13–16.
44. Okin, *Women in Western Political Thought*, 197. See also Elshtain, *Public Man, Private Woman*, 134–46.
45. Alice S. Rossi, "Sentiment and Intellect: The Story of John Stuart Mill and Harriet Taylor Mill," in *Essays in Sex Equality*, by John Stuart Mill and Harriet Taylor Mill, ed. Alice S. Rossi, 20.
46. Rowbotham, *Women, Resistance and Revolution*, 46.
47. John Stuart Mill, as quoted in Okin, *Women in Western Political Thought*, 219.
48. Mill, as quoted in Okin, *Women in Western Political Thought*, 207; and see 205–8, 330–31 n. 30. Rossi, "Sentiment and Intellect," 19–58.
49. Kate Millett, "The Debate over Women: Ruskin vs. Mill," 121–22.
50. John Stuart Mill, *The Subjection of Women*, in *Essays on Sex Equal-*

ity, by John Stuart Mill and Harriet Taylor Mill, ed. Alice S. Rossi, 139, hereafter cited in the text as *SW.*

51. Millett, "The Debate over Women," 123, 130–39.
52. Rossi, "Sentiment and Intellect," 4–5, 59. See Okin's judgment of Mill at the opening of the discussion.
53. Herman Schwendinger and Julia R. Schwendinger, *The Sociologists of the Chair: A Radical Analysis of the Formative Years of North American Sociology (1883–1922),* 293–95. Cf. Rossi, "Sentiment and Intellect," 59.
54. Okin, *Women in Western Political Thought,* 220.
55. Elshtain, *Public Man, Private Woman,* 136–45.
56. Rossi, "Sentiment and Intellect," 45–46; Millett, "The Debate over Women," 134; Okin, *Women in Western Political Thought,* 204.
57. Elshtain, *Public Man, Private Woman,* 145, 144.
58. Okin, *Women in Western Political Thought,* 228.
59. Ibid.
60. Cf. Millett, "The Debate over Women," 127.
61. Okin, *Women in Western Political Thought,* 226, 334n.86.
62. Rowbotham, *Women, Resistance and Revolution,* 45.
63. Okin, *Women in Western Political Thought,* 205.
64. Rowbotham, *Hidden from History,* 43, 50.
65. Rowbotham, *Women, Resistance and Revolution,* 50.
66. Talcott Parsons credited Herbert Spencer with "three main basic positive theoretical ideas: first, that of society as a self-regulating system; second, that of differentiation of function; and third, that of evolution, all of which remain as important today as they were when he wrote" (Talcott Parsons, introduction to *The Study of Sociology,* by Herbert Spencer, v–vi). For more on Spencer's influence, see Richard Hofstadter, *Social Darwinism in American Thought,* especially chap. 2, and J. D. Y. Peel, *Herbert Spencer: The Evolution of a Sociologist.*
67. Karen Sacks, *Sisters and Wives: The Past and Future of Sexual Equality,* 63; and see 18–20, 22, 32.
68. Herbert Spencer, *Social Statics; or, The Conditions Essential to Human Happiness Specified and the First of Them Developed,* 155, hereafter cited in the text as *SS.*
69. See Schwendinger and Schwendinger, *Sociologists of the Chair,* 296–97.
70. Peel, *Herbert Spencer,* 94. See also Herbert Spencer, *The Principles of Psychology,* 1:581, 583, and 2:603.
71. David Duncan, *The Life and Letters of Herbert Spencer,* 137. Duncan was Spencer's secretary.
72. Spencer, as quoted in Duncan, *Life and Letters of Herbert Spencer,* 138–39.

73. Spencer and Mill, as quoted in Duncan, *Life and Letters of Herbert Spencer*, 139.
74. Vicinus, "New Trends in the Study of Victorian Women," introduction to *A Widening Sphere*, ed. Vicinus, ix.
75. Herbert Spencer, *The Principles of Biology*, 1:594–97, for some interesting passages on the nature of sperm and ova, where the *cultural* relationships of the sexes seem to be applied to *biological* phenomena.
76. Herbert Spencer, *The Study of Sociology*, hereafter cited in the text as *SSoc*.
77. See Sacks, *Sisters and Wives*, 46–50.
78. Herbert Spencer, *The Principles of Sociology*, hereafter cited in the text as *PS*. For my understanding of the underlying set of assumptions governing Spencer's work and the whole tradition of social evolutionary theory, I am indebted to Kenneth E. Bock, my teacher and friend; see his *Acceptance of Histories*.
79. Sacks, *Sisters and Wives*, 24, 32.
80. This puzzle is not addressed by Schwendinger and Schwendinger in their largely ideological analysis, *Sociologists of the Chair*, 310–11.
81. Gordon S. Haight, *George Eliot: A Biography*, 114–19. Duncan, *Life and Letters of Herbert Spencer*, 266–68. Duncan referred to Spencer's "long-formed convictions regarding the intellectual powers of women" and offered the following testimony. In a letter of 10 June 1890 (to Robert Lewins) Spencer praised George Eliot's "high philosophical capacity" combined with extensive knowledge and then went on to say, "I cannot let pass the occasion for remarking that, in her case as in other cases, mental powers so highly developed in women are in some measure abnormal and involve a physiological cost which the feminine organization will not bear with injury more or less profound" (295–96). I am indebted to Mary Jane Elkins, Department of English, Florida International University, Miami, for calling my attention to this material.
82. Duncan, *Life and Letters of Herbert Spencer*, 132–36, 266–68. On Spencer's relationships to his mother and father and aspects of his character, see also pp. 23, 494, and 535.
83. Herbert Spencer, *An Autobiography*, 2:93–94, and 1:361–62, 364.
84. Spencer, as quoted in Duncan, *Life and Letters of Herbert Spencer*, 111–12. Spencer seems to have had a particular disdain for American women. In a letter to T[homas] H[enry] Huxley, 6 February 1888, Spencer gives examples of how improvement generates social protest. One of his examples was "the position of women." He wrote, "While they [women] were slaves and during the long ages when they were ill-treated, not a word was said about their rights; now that they have come to be well treated the screaming sisterhood makes

the world ring with their wrongs, and they scream loudest in America, where women are treated with the greatest regard" (281).

85. Barbara Kanner, "The Women of England in a Century of Social Change, 1815–1914: A Select Bibliography, Part 2," 254.

86. Okin, *Women in Western Political Thought*, 220; Comte, as quoted on 220–21; and Mill discussed, 220–22.

87. Herbert Spencer, "Progress: Its Law and Cause," 436.

88. See Duncan, *Life and Letters of Herbert Spencer*, 64, 101, 140–55.

89. Robert Young, "The Historiographic and Ideological Contexts of the Nineteenth-Century Debate on Man's Place in Nature," 382, 344–438.

90. Lewis A. Coser, *Masters of Sociological Thought: Ideas in Historical and Social Context*, 121–25.

91. Marian Evans (George Eliot), as quoted in Young, "Historiographic and Ideological Contexts," 378, and see 377, 379, 368. Cf. Bock, *Acceptance of Histories*, 5.

92. Stanislav Andreski, introduction to *The Principles of Sociology*, by Herbert Spencer, xvi.

93. See Okin, *Women in Western Political Thought*, 281.

94. Smelser, "Toward a General Theory of Social Change," in his *Essays in Sociological Explanation*, 247–51.

95. Spencer, as quoted in Abram Kardiner and Edward Preble, *They Studied Man*, 39.

Chapter 3. France

1. H. M. Hyndman, as quoted in Sheila Rowbotham, *Hidden from History: Rediscovering Women in History from the Seventeenth Century to the Present*, 95; and see 72.

2. Elaine Marks and Isabelle de Courtivron, eds., *New French Feminisms: An Anthology*, 3–28, especially 10–12.

3. Sheila Rowbotham, *Women, Resistance and Revolution: A History of Women and Revolution in the Modern World*, 28. See also Darline Gay Levy, Harriet Bronson Applewhite, and Mary Durham Johnson, eds., *Women in Revolutionary Paris, 1789–1795*, 6–9. For a discussion of a male advocate of women's rights, see Leon Schwartz, "F. M. Grimm and the Eighteenth-Century Debate on Women."

4. Susan Moller Okin, *Women in Western Political Thought*, 99.

5. Ibid., 100–105.

6. Judith Shklar, as cited in Jean Bethke Elshtain, *Public Man, Private Woman: Women in Social and Political Thought*, 163; and see 148–70, especially 160–63.

7. Rowbotham, *Women, Resistance and Revolution*, 43.

8. Jean Jacques Rousseau, as quoted in Okin, *Women in Western Political Thought*, 103.

9. Rowbotham, *Women, Resistance and Revolution*, 38–39.

10. Claude Adrien Helvétius and Baron d'Holbach, as quoted in Okin, *Women in Western Political Thought*, 103, 103–4.

11. Maurice Bloch and Jean H. Bloch, "Women and the Dialectics of Nature in Eighteenth-Century French Thought," 32–38.

12. Marks and Courtivron, eds., *New French Feminisms*, 15, 3. See also Frank E. Manuel, *The Prophets of Paris*, chap. 2.

13. Petition, as quoted in Levy, Applewhite, and Johnson, eds., *Women in Revolutionary Paris*, 18–21; Levy, Applewhite, and Johnson quoted from 14, 11; and see 9–11, 13–14.

14. Rowbotham, *Women, Resistance and Revolution*, 37.

15. Levy, Applewhite, and Johnson, eds., *Women in Revolutionary Paris*, 16–17, 9–12, 5.

16. Decree, as quoted in Marks and Courtivron, eds., *New French Feminisms*, 16.

17. Levy, Applewhite, and Johnson, eds., *Women in Revolutionary Paris*, 12. For a summary of the documents presented in this work, see Levy, Johnson, and Applewhite, "Women: The Failure of Liberation."

18. J. M. Mogey, "A Century of Declining Paternal Authority," 253. For a more moderate assessment, see Crane Brinton, *The Anatomy of Revolution*, 257–59.

19. Rowbotham, *Women, Resistance and Revolution*, 40.

20. Ibid., 50–51. See also Marks and Courtivron, eds., *New French Feminisms*, 17–18.

21. George Lichtheim, *A Short History of Socialism*, 42–46. For a more detailed consideration, see Manuel, *Prophets of Paris*, chaps. 3, 4.

22. Rowbotham, *Women, Resistance and Revolution*, 52–53; Marks and Courtivron, *New French Feminisms*, 17–18.

23. Rowbotham, *Women, Resistance and Revolution*, 51. For an extended treatment of Fourier, see Manuel, *Prophets of Paris*, chap. 5. See also Marks and Courtivron, eds., *New French Feminisms*, 18.

24. Flora Tristan, as quoted in Marks and Courtivron, eds., *New French Feminisms*, 18. Tristan, as quoted in Rowbotham, *Women, Resistance and Revolution*, 54, 37, 55; Rowbotham quoted from 54. For an extended treatment of Tristan, see S. Joan Moon, "Feminism and Socialism: The Utopian Synthesis of Flora Tristan."

25. Rowbotham, *Women, Resistance and Revolution*, 53–54, 110.

26. Marks and Courtivron, eds., *New French Feminisms*, 19.

27. Henriette D., a working woman, as quoted in Rowbotham, *Women, Resistance and Revolution*, 119; and see 117–24.

28. Rowbotham, *Women, Resistance and Revolution*, 120, 121.

29. The classic treatment of Bonaparte's coup is Karl Marx's brilliant analysis and satire, *The Eighteenth Brumaire of Louis Bonaparte*.

30. Marks and Courtivron, eds., *New French Feminisms*, 19.

31. Edith Thomas, *The Women Incendiaries*, 3–4.
32. Marks and Courtivron, eds., *New French Feminisms*, 19.
33. Proudhon, as quoted in *From Georges Sorel: Essays in Socialism and Philosophy*, ed. John L. Stanley, 19–20.
34. James F. McMillan, *Housewife or Harlot: The Place of Women in French Society, 1870–1940*, 2.
35. Thomas, *Women Incendiaries*, 8; see also 9, 21–23, 28. The following discussion of the 1860s and the early 1870s, including the Commune, relies on Edith Thomas's marvelous and intriguing book, *Women Incendiaries;* quotations are cited, as are sources other than Thomas's book.
36. Ibid., 24–26, 9–14, 13.
37. Maria Deraismes, as quoted in Thomas, *Women Incendiaries*, 27.
38. Jean Daubié, as quoted in Thomas, *Women Incendiaries*, 8; and minister of public education, as quoted on 15. See also 16–20.
39. André Léo, as quoted and discussed in Thomas, *Women Incendiaries*, 28–31; Olympe Audouard, as quoted on 33.
40. Marks and Courtivron, eds., *New French Feminisms*, 20; Thomas, *Women Incendiaries*, 33.
41. Thomas, *Women Incendiaries*, 35–36.
42. Ibid., viii–ix. However, McMillan has written that feminism was a "minority theme in the Commune" (*Housewife or Harlot*, 86).
43. Maxime du Camp and Alexandre Dumas *fils*, as quoted in Thomas, *Women Incendiaries*, ix–x, xi.
44. Benoît Malon and Karl Marx, as quoted in Thomas, *Women Incendiaries*, xi, xii.
45. Thomas, *Women Incendiaries*, chap. 3, pp. 37–51.
46. Ibid., 52–59. See Karl Marx's account in *The Civil War in France*, 46–50.
47. Thomas, *Women Incendiaries*, 68, 60–69.
48. Ibid., 93, 101; and see 88–100, 111.
49. Louise Michel, as quoted in Thomas, *Women Incendiaries*, 107; see 102 for a description of Blanche Lefebvre; and see 99–103.
50. Marx, *Civil War in France*, 65. His prediction is in the last sentence of *The Eighteenth Brumaire of Louis Bonaparte*, 135.
51. Thomas, *Women Incendiaries*, 112–18, 130–32.
52. Léo, as quoted in Thomas, *Women Incendiaries*, 141–42; Thomas quoted from 147; and see 119–30, 133–49, 146–49, 153, and 150–55.
53. Thomas, *Women Incendiaries*, 160; Michel, as quoted on 163; and see 150–62.
54. Captain Jouenne, as quoted in Thomas, *Women Incendiaries*, 178–79. See 165–78 on the issue of the existence of *les pétroleuses*. See also 180–88. Thomas has pointed out that a "large proportion" of women who participated in "the Parisian insurrection of 1871" were "provin-

cials" who had left their villages and moved to Paris. For men "the proportion was less" (155).

55. Michel, as quoted in Thomas, *Women Incendiaries*, 199; and see 189–201.

56. Thomas, *Women Incendiaries*, 204, 222; and see 201–25, 231–41.

57. Verlaine, as quoted in Thomas, *Women Incendiaries*, 229; and see 226–30, 242–44.

58. Marx, *Civil War in France*, 68–69.

59. Ibid., 74–75.

60. Stanley, ed., *From Georges Sorel*, 7.

61. McMillan, *Housewife or Harlot*, 76, 84, 89; and see 2. On some differences between England and France, see Barbara Corrado Pope, "Angels in the Devil's Workshop: Leisured and Charitable Women in Nineteenth-Century England and France."

62. Hubertine Auclert, as quoted in Marks and Courtivron, eds., *New French Feminisms*, 20; and see 21. The material on the French Workers' Party is taken from Werner Thönnessen's *The Emancipation of Women: The Rise and Decline of the Women's Movement in German Social Democracy, 1863–1933*, 35.

63. McMillan, *Housewife or Harlot*, 86–87; see also 95–96. For a sorting out of the several heritages of the French left on the "woman question," see Marilyn J. Boxer, "Socialism Faces Feminism: The Failure of Synthesis in France, 1879–1914," 75–111.

64. Nelly Roussel, as quoted in Marks and Courtivron, eds., *New French Feminisms*, 22; and see 21. Marks and Courtivron's outline of "Histories of France and Feminism in France" is the basis for this brief sketch of post-1871 events.

65. McMillan, *Housewife or Harlot*, 89.

66. Stanley, ed., *From Georges Sorel*, 14.

67. On the conservative sources of French sociology, see Robert A. Nisbet, ed., *Emile Durkheim, with Selected Essays*, 23–28, and Irving M. Zeitlin, *Ideology and the Development of Sociological Theory*, 39–60.

68. Since Le Play's work is empirical rather than theoretical, my discussion of his work is brief. According to Nathan Glazer, Le Play is a central figure in the empirical scientific tradition of sociological research, which, in his view, does not include Marx (see "The Rise of Social Research in Europe"). Glazer pokes fun at Marx's abortive survey of workers. For another discussion of Le Play's work, see Ronald Fletcher, "Fréderic Le Play."

69. See the translation of a brief passage of Le Play's *The European Workers* in *Sociological Research I: A Case Approach*, ed. Matilda White Riley (New York: Harcourt, Brace and World, 1963), 89–90; see also 90–98 and 112–19. See brief selections of Le Play's work in *Victorian*

Women: A Documentary Account of Women's Lives in Nineteenth-Century England, France, and the United States, ed. Erna Olafson Hellerstein, Leslie Parker Hume, and Karen M. Offen, 318–23, 352–55, 480–82.

70. Fletcher, "Fréderic Le Play," 55–56. Mogey's "A Century of Declining Paternal Authority" takes off from Le Play's perspective (250–51).

71. Nisbet, ed., *Emile Durkheim*, 27. That's a nice way to put it. Often, working-class men are more crudely advised to: go to work, stay at home (family), and mind your own business, except for church on Sundays (community); keep your wife in her place, have just enough children (family)—but not too many or you may be out of work and poor (work)—so that the working class is reproduced, i.e., so that there are more than enough workers. Of course, the trinity adds up to capitalism and a few extra workers for a sunny day.

72. Alexis de Tocqueville, *Democracy in America*, 584–89, hereafter cited in the text as *DA*. See also Elshtain, *Public Man, Private Woman*, 129–31.

73. See Robert A. Nisbet, *The Sociological Tradition*, 193–95.

74. This material about Harriet Martineau is taken from a selection in *The Feminist Papers: From Adams to de Beauvoir*, ed. Alice S. Rossi, 125. See also 125–43. John Stuart Mill's analysis is, of course, similar to Martineau's in many respects.

75. Zeitlin, *Ideology and the Development of Sociological Theory*, 75–84, especially 75–79.

76. Auguste Comte, *Cours de philosophie positive, 1830–1842*, in *Auguste Comte and Positivism: The Essential Writings*, ed. Gertrud Lenzer, 267–68.

77. Ibid., 268.

78. The preceding two quotations are from *Cours de philosophie positive* as they appear in *Women, the Family, and Freedom: The Debate in the Documents*, ed. Susan Groag Bell and Karen M. Offen, 1:220, and see 221.

79. *The Letters of Auguste Comte*, 1.

80. Auguste Comte, *System of Positive Polity*, hereafter cited in the text as *SPP*. To spread the gospel of his reactionary project to the masses, Comte developed in 1852 a positivist catechism for women and workers (Manuel, *Prophets of Paris*, 272).

81. Raymond Aron, *Main Currents of Sociological Thought*, 1:111.

82. Lewis A. Coser, *Masters of Sociological Thought: Ideas in Historical and Social Context*, 17–19. See also the quote from Howard Becker and Harry Elmer Barnes: "The woman he chose as his wife was nothing more than a means for the immediate gratification of his crude sexuality," in Ann Oakley, *The Sociology of Housework*, 22. Comte quoted a letter of 11 March 1846 to Clothilde de Vaux, in

which he said, "I was incomplete as a philosopher, until the experience of deep and pure passion had given me fuller insight into the emotional side of human nature" (*SPP*, 175).

83. Manuel, *Prophets of Paris*, chap. 4, for a sympathetic treatment of Comte's life and work.

84. Lewis A. Coser, "Durkheim's Conservatism and Its Implications for His Sociological Theory," 211–32. For a response to the argument that Durkheim's work is conservative, see Melvin Richter, "Durkheim's Politics and Political Theory," in the same volume, 170–210. See also Edward A. Tiryakian, "Emile Durkheim," 187–236, especially 191–93, and Zeitlin, *Ideology and the Development of Sociological Theory*, 250–91, and see vi.

85. A. R. Radcliffe–Brown, "On the Concept of Function in Social Science," 394. He is incorrect in attributing Durkheim's first use of the concept of function to *The Rules of Sociological Method* (1895); Durkheim's first use of the concept of function appeared in 1893 in *The Division of Labor in Society*. Also, Spencer's *A Study of Sociology* (1873) antedates Durkheim's work.

86. Emile Durkheim, *The Division of Labor in Society*, hereafter cited in the text as *DLS*.

87. Emile Durkheim, *Suicide: A Study in Sociology*, hereafter cited in the text as *S*.

88. See Hanan C. Selvin, "Durkheim's *Suicide:* Further Thoughts on a Methodological Classic."

89. This has been done meticulously by Whitney Pope in *Durkheim's Suicide: A Classic Analyzed*.

90. Barclay D. Johnson, "Durkheim on Women," 164n. 1. See also Pope, *Durkheim's* Suicide.

91. Durkheim, *Rules of Sociological Method*, 124.

92. Durkheim did not consider that the relationship may not be completely linear: deprivation below the level of subsistence may produce an increase in suicide.

93. See Johnson, "Durkheim on Women," 167.

94. See Pope, *Durkheim's* Suicide.

95. L. J. Jordanova, "Natural Facts: A Historical Perspective on Science and Sexuality," 64.

96. Richard A. Cloward and Frances Fox Piven, "Hidden Protest: The Channeling of Female Innovation and Resistance," 660.

97. Durkheim, as quoted in Steven Lukes, *Emile Durkheim, His Life and Work: A Historical and Critical Study*, 533; see also 530–34, 18, 186, 188–89, 192, 209, 212, 225. Jessie Bernard has pointed out that "a substantial body of research shores up" Durkheim's conclusion that wives and husbands do not benefit equally from marriage. See her "The Paradox of the Happy Marriage," 86.

Chapter 4. Germany

1. The framework for my interpretation of German history draws upon the Marxist tradition, especially Karl Marx's *Contribution to the Critique of Hegel's "Philosophy of Right"* (1844), Friedrich Engels's *Germany: Revolution and Counter-Revolution*, chaps. 1–3; his *The Peasant War in Germany*; and his *The Housing Question* (1872). See also George Lichtheim, *Marxism: An Historical and Critical Study*. For the neo-Marxist tradition, see Barrington Moore, Jr., *Social Origins of Dictatorship and Democracy: Lord and Peasant in the Making of the Modern World*, chap. 18, "Revolution from Above and Fascism," 433–52. See also Barrington Moore, Jr., *Injustice: The Social Bases of Obedience and Revolt*, chaps. 4–12, on Germany. The opening chapters of Leon Trotsky's *History of the Russian Revolution* are also relevant here.
2. Werner Thönnessen, *The Emancipation of Women: The Rise and Decline of the Women's Movement in German Social Democracy, 1863–1933*, 13. See also Jean H. Quataert, *Reluctant Feminists in German Social Democracy, 1885–1917*, 27–28.
3. Quataert, *Reluctant Feminists*, 28–29.
4. Thönnessen, *Emancipation of Women*, 13–14; Quataert, *Reluctant Feminists*, 28–29.
5. Quataert, *Reluctant Feminists*, 56–57.
6. Thönnessen, *Emancipation of Women*, 20, 15–28. See also Quataert, *Reluctant Feminists*, 154.
7. Thönnessen, *Emancipation of Women*, 28–32.
8. Ibid., 32–36.
9. Quataert, *Reluctant Feminists*, 29–30.
10. Thönnessen, *Emancipation of Women*, 36.
11. August Bebel, as quoted in Sheila Rowbotham, *Women, Resistance and Revolution: A History of Women and Revolution in the Modern World*, 80–84. Adelheid Popp, a trade-union activist in the SPD, was heartened by Bebel's book. She described in her autobiography how she came to understand the "woman question" through her participation in the SPD (discussed in Rowbotham, *Women, Resistance and Revolution*, 80.
12. Thönnessen, *Emancipation of Women*, 37.
13. Ottilie Baader, Luise Zietz, Helene Grünberg, Wilhelmine Kähler, as quoted in Quataert, *Reluctant Feminists*, 59–60, 85, 7.
14. Quataert, *Reluctant Feminists*, 65, 66–67.
15. Thönnessen, *Emancipation of Women*, 44–45.
16. Quataert, *Reluctant Feminists*, 65, 69–71.
17. Thönnessen, *Emancipation of Women*, 39–40.

18. Ibid., 45–47. For a short biography of Ihrer, see Quataert, *Reluctant Feminists*, 57–58, 155.
19. Thönnessen, *Emancipation of Women*, 47–50, 57–59. See also Quataert, *Reluctant Feminists*, 14, 24, 141, 155.
20. Thönnessen, *Emancipation of Women*, 51–56. For biographical material on Hanna, see Quataert, *Reluctant Feminists*, 63–65.
21. Thönnessen, *Emancipation of Women*, 57–58; Quataert, *Reluctant Feminists*, 32–33. The 1912 figure excludes the small number of women in Catholic and other unions.
22. Thönnessen, *Emancipation of Women*, 60–62; Quataert, *Reluctant Feminists*, 77–80, 93–99, especially 96.
23. Thönnessen, *Emancipation of Women*, 64, 60, 65.
24. Edmund Fischer, as quoted in Thönnessen, *Emancipation of Women*, 98.
25. Emma Ihrer and Lily Braun, as quoted in Quataert, *Reluctant Feminists*, 102–4. Zetkin and Braun had been at odds since 1897 over the proper socialist approach to feminist issues. Braun was an upper-class woman and very much an individualist. She had been a part of the bourgeois feminist movement until her conversion to Social Democracy in 1895. Within the SPD, she was an adherent of Bernstein's revisionism and an advocate of class collaboration rather than class struggle, and consequently, Bebel liked Braun and her work. Zetkin believed Braun espoused "vulgar feminist views," which she herself had successfully struggled to overcome before the Gotha Congress in 1896. The difference between Zetkin and Braun was captured by Quataert in two representative quotations. Zetkin said, "I feel first as a comrade"; whereas Braun declared, "When I protest so energetically . . . it is not only as a comrade but as a woman." With the help of Ottilie Baader and Luise Zietz, Zetkin was able to isolate Braun in the party. There were personal antagonisms as well as political differences. It was "Zetkin's 'pride' facing Braun's 'honor,'" as Quataert has termed it. But Zetkin was later to find herself isolated in the party when her leftist views collided with its reformism (Quataert, *Reluctant Feminists*, 109, 130, 109, 107, 107–33).
26. Zietz, as quoted in Quataert, *Reluctant Feminists*, 139; and see 139–60, especially 140–48; Thönnessen, *Emancipation of Women*, 57, 66.
27. Quataert, *Reluctant Feminists*, 146–53; Thönnessen, *Emancipation of Women*, 66–68.
28. Robert Michels, as quoted in Thönnessen, *Emancipation of Women*, 71; and see 69–70. For a biographical sketch of Helene Grünberg, see Quataert, *Reluctant Feminists*, 61–63; and for the SPD's relationship with trade unions, see 161–88.
29. Quataert, *Reluctant Feminists*, 153, 157–58.

30. Rowbotham, *Women, Resistance and Revolution*, 78.
31. Thönnessen, *Emancipation of Women*, 71. Cf. Quataert, *Reluctant Feminists*, 17, 55, 61, 239–40.
32. Quataert, *Reluctant Feminists*, 85; see also 3–4, 229.
33. Richard J. Evans, *The Feminist Movement in Germany, 1894–1933*, 270.
34. Braun, Zetkin, Ihrer, and Grünberg, as quoted in Quataert, *Reluctant Feminists*, 91–92.
35. Auguste Schmidt and Helene Lange, as quoted in Evans, *Feminist Movement in Germany*, 26, 28; and see 24–29.
36. Evans, *Feminist Movement in Germany*, 22; Reichstag deputy Martin Schall, Kaiser Wilhelm II, as quoted on 11, 23; and see ix, 3–4.
37. Evans, *Feminist Movement in Germany*, 30, 8–9, 16–17, 23. Cf. Amy Hackett, "Feminism and Liberalism in Wilhelmine Germany, 1890–1918."
38. Evans, *Feminist Movement in Germany*, 35–37.
39. Evans, *Feminist Movement in Germany*, 41; Minna Cauer, as quoted on 57; Evans quoted from 63; and see 38–63. See also Richard J. Evans, "Prostitution, State, and Society in Imperial Germany."
40. Evans, *Feminist Movement in Germany*, 48–52.
41. Cauer, as quoted in Evans, *Feminist Movement in Germany*, 76; Evans, quoted from 79; and see 71–76.
42. Evans, *Feminist Movement in Germany*, 87, 79–93.
43. Ibid., 92, 99; and see 92–108.
44. Ibid., 115–16.
45. Helene Stöcker, as quoted in Evans, *Feminist Movement in Germany*, 118; and see 116–21. Minna Cauer supported Pappritz's position; Adele Schreiber, who later joined the Social Democrats, supported Stöcker's position. Stöcker eventually backed off from relations with the Berlin liberals.
46. Evans, *Feminist Movement in Germany*, 121, 120–22.
47. Ernst Kromayer and Stöcker, as quoted in Evans, *Feminist Movement in Germany*, 125.
48. Stöcker, as quoted in Evans, *Feminist Movement in Germany*, 132; Marie Stritt, as quoted on 133; and see 130–31.
49. Evans, *Feminist Movement in Germany*, 138–39, 145; and see 133–39.
50. See Friedrich Engels, *The Role of Force in History: A Study of Bismarck's Policy of Blood and Iron*.
51. Martin Green, *The Von Richthofen Sisters: The Triumphant and the Tragic Modes of Love: Else and Frieda von Richthofen, Otto Gross, Max Weber, and D. H. Lawrence in the Years 1870 to 1970*, 8, xi, 3–4.
52. Ibid., 6.
53. Ibid., 6, 9, 17, 66.

54. Ibid., xi, 54, 4, 54, 28, 11; and see 9. On the revolt against positivist materialism, see H. Stuart Hughes, *Consciousness and Society: The Reorientation of European Social Thought, 1890–1930*, 33–66. On the questioning of the classical conception of physics, see Lewis S. Feuer, *Einstein and the Generations of Science* (New York: Basic Books, 1974); on the antipatriarchal and erotic impulses behind Ernst Mach's relativism, see Feuer, 31, 37–41.

55. Green, *Von Richthofen Sisters*, 92, 28, 94; for a discussion of Fanny zu Reventlow and Schwabing, see 88–100, 224.

56. Ludwig Klages, as quoted in Green, *Von Richthofen Sisters*, 77; Green quoted from 73; and see 73–85.

57. Green, *Von Richthofen Sisters*, 35, 38, 46; for a discussion of Otto Gross, see 32–38.

58. Green, *Von Richthofen Sisters*, 46, 99, 47; and see 38–46, 62–72, 90–91.

59. Frieda von Richthofen, as quoted in Green, *Von Richthofen Sisters*, 14; Green quoted from 17; and see 11–17, 20–22, 92–93;

60. D. H. Lawrence, as quoted in Green, *Von Richthofen Sisters*, vii, 84; Frieda von Richthofen, as quoted on 134–35; and see 47–62.

61. Green, *Von Richthofen Sisters*, 16–17, 22–31; see also xi.

62. Ibid., 17, 24, 30; and see 32–33, 90–91.

63. Ibid., 85, 79–80, 92.

64. Sheila Rowbotham, *Hidden from History: Rediscovering Women in History from the Seventeenth Century to the Present*, 106.

65. Green, *Von Richthofen Sisters*, 268–69.

66. Ibid., 167. See also Evans, *Feminist Movement in Germany*, 156.

67. Evans, *Feminist Movement in Germany*, 184; and see 175–83. See also Gloria Steinem, "The Nazi Connection."

68. Green, *Von Richthofen Sisters*, 66–67; and see 161–62.

69. Franz Jung, as quoted in Green, *Von Richthofen Sisters*, 68; Green as quoted on 135; Lawrence, as quoted on 135; see also 67.

70. Evans, *Feminist Movement in Germany*, 207–27.

71. Ibid., 107, 156.

72. Stella Browne, as quoted in Rowbotham, *Hidden from History*, 122, and see 121.

73. Green, *Von Richthofen Sisters*, 164, 220.

74. Ibid., 141, 100.

75. Cf. Evans, *Feminist Movement in Germany*, 229–30, and Barrington Moore, Jr., *Injustice*, chaps. 8, 11.

76. See Robert Michels, *Political Parties: A Sociological Study of the Oligarchical Tendencies of Modern Democracy*, 357–63.

77. Thönnessen, *Emancipation of Women*, 80, 83; Kähler, as quoted on 83; and see 75–85. See also Quataert, *Reluctant Feminists*, 210–19. For detailed consideration of the splits within Social Democracy be-

tween 1905 and 1917 as they were affected by events outside of Germany, especially by the Russian revolutions, see Carl E. Schorske, *German Social Democracy, 1905–1917: The Development of the Great Schism* (Cambridge: Harvard University Press, 1955).

78. Juchacz, as quoted in Thönnessen, *Emancipation of Women*, 86; Thönnessen quoted from 87.

79. Gertrud Hanna, as quoted in Thönnessen, *Emancipation of Women*, 91, 94; and see 93, 89–97. See also Quataert, *Reluctant Feminists*, 219–20.

80. Fischer, as quoted in Thönnessen, *Emancipation of Women*, 98, 105; Zepler, as quoted on 106; Thönnessen quoted from 105; and see 98–106.

81. Thönnessen, *Emancipation of Women*, 108, 107.

82. Quataert, *Reluctant Feminists*, 212–13, 220–26.

83. Anonymous delegate at Görlitz (1921) and Juchacz, as quoted in Thönnessen, *Emancipation of Women*, 109, 111–12; and see 108–16. See also Quataert, *Reluctant Feminists*, 220–27.

84. Juchacz, as quoted in Thönnessen, *Emancipation of Women*, 117; and see 116–17.

85. Thönnessen, *Emancipation of Women*, 118–25.

86. Proceedings of 1924 Berlin SPD party conference, as quoted in Thönnessen, *Emancipation of Women*, 126; proceedings of 1925 Heidelberg meeting, as quoted on 127; resolution of the 1931 Leipzig conference, as quoted on 128; Thönnessen quoted from 128.

87. Proceedings of 1924 Berlin meeting and 1929 Magdeburg Conference, as quoted in Thönnessen, *Emancipation of Women*, 129, 130; Juchacz, as quoted on 130; anonymous woman delegate, as quoted on 131; and see 131–39.

88. Thönnessen, *Emancipation of Women*, 150, 143–50.

89. Zetkin, as quoted in Thönnessen, *Emancipation of Women*, 153, 163; see also 155–56.

90. Renate Bridenthal and Claudia Koonz, "Beyond *Kinder, Küche, Kirche:* Weimar Women in Politics and Work," 303.

91. Evans, *Feminist Movement in Germany*, 235–53. Hackett, "Feminism and Liberalism in Wilhelmine Germany," 135.

92. Peter Gay, as quoted in Green, *Von Richthofen Sisters*, 166. Cf. Arthur Mitzman, *The Iron Cage: An Historical Interpretation of Max Weber*, 10.

93. Green, *Von Richthofen Sisters*, 24. See Arthur Mitzman, *Sociology and Estrangement: Three Sociologists of Imperial Germany*, 32, 283.

94. Rowbotham, *Hidden from History*, 127.

95. Heinrich von Treitschke, as quoted in Evans, *Feminist Movement in Germany*, 17.

96. Friedrich Nietzsche, as quoted in *Masculine/Feminine: Readings in*

Sexual Mythology and the Liberation of Women, ed. Betty Roszak and Theodore Roszak, 5, 3. See also Theodore Roszak, "The Hard and the Soft: The Force of Feminism in Modern Times," 89, for a sample of Weininger's "thought"; and see 4–9, for a selection of Nietzsche's ramblings.

97. Green, *Von Richthofen Sisters,* 168–69, 226–33. Cf. Moore, *Social Origins of Dictatorship and Democracy,* 484–508.

98. Thönnessen, *Emancipation of Women,* 151; see also 10.

99. Adolf Hitler, as quoted in Evans, *Feminist Movement in Germany,* 259. Cf. Steinem, "The Nazi Connection." See also Bridenthal and Koonz, "Beyond *Kinder, Küche, Kirche.*"

100. Cf. Evans, *Feminist Movement in Germany,* 272–75.

101. Hughes, *Consciousness and Society,* 288. On Weber's critique of Marx, see Irving M. Zeitlin, *Ideology and the Development of Sociological Theory,* 111–58.

102. H. H. Gerth and C. Wright Mills, introduction to *From Max Weber: Essays in Sociology,* 26.

103. Julien Freund, *The Sociology of Max Weber,* 183–84.

104. Hughes, *Consciousness and Society,* 288.

105. Green, *Von Richthofen Sisters,* xi.

106. Max Weber, Karl Jaspers, and newspaper report, as quoted in Hughes, *Consciousness and Society,* 290, 334, 326–27.

107. Weber, as quoted in Gerth and Mills, eds., *From Max Weber,* 24.

108. See Gerth and Mills, eds., *From Max Weber,* 29; Green, *Von Richthofen Sisters,* 120. A full-blown analytic interpretation of Weber's life, work, and politics is Mitzman's *The Iron Cage,* upon which Green draws. (See Lewis A. Coser's reservations concerning Mitzman's psychoanalytic interpretation of Weber in his preface to Mitzman's *The Iron Cage.*) I have limited myself to points bearing on Weber's relationships with women. It would be less than intellectually honest, however, not to consider the simpler alternative explanation of hereditary insanity (see Gerth and Mills, eds., *From Max Weber,* 28). His cousin Emmy was committed to an asylum (see n. 118 below). His sister Lily committed suicide when her husband died (Green, *Von Richthofen Sisters,* 124).

109. Guenther Roth, "Weber's Generational Rebellion and Maturation," 7n.1, for biographical literature in English and German on Weber.

110. Green, *Von Richthofen Sisters,* 107, 110, 104, 107; and see 103–14.

111. Gerth and Mills, eds., *From Max Weber,* 29.

112. Green, *Von Richthofen Sisters,* 114.

113. Weber, as quoted in Gerth and Mills, eds., *From Max Weber,* 7.

114. Green, *Von Richthofen Sisters,* 107.

115. Gerth and Mills, eds., *From Max Weber,* 9–10. See also Roth, "Max Weber's Generational Rebellion," 12.

116. Green, *Von Richthofen Sisters*, 117–19, 128. See also Gerth and Mills, eds., *From Max Weber*, 11–14; and Hughes, *Consciousness and Society*, 296.

117. Green, *Von Richthofen Sisters*, 113, 119–20, 118; and see 128. See also Mitzman, *The Iron Cage*, 33, 276; and Hughes, *Consciousness and Society*, 296–97.

118. Gerth and Mills, eds., *From Max Weber*, 29, and see 9–11. See also Green, *Von Richthofen Sisters*, 125–26.

119. Weber, as quoted in Green, *Von Richthofen Sisters*, 118.

120. Weber, as quoted in Gerth and Mills, eds., *From Max Weber*, 12.

121. Green, *Von Richthofen Sisters*, 125, 226, 233, 129–30, 163–64, 170, 172, 214–215, 231–32, 234; and see 366 for a summary statement of the evidence that led Green to believe Else and Max were lovers.

122. Ibid., 114, 116, 228, 126, 159.

123. Marianne Weber, as quoted in Hughes, *Consciousness and Society*, 297.

124. Marianne Weber's life and character are described and her essays quoted and discussed in Green, *Von Richthofen Sisters*, 217–25, 126, 139–40. See also discussion of some passages of Marianne Weber's writings in Roth, "Max Weber's Generational Rebellion," 11–12, 31–32.

125. Mitzman, *The Iron Cage*, 279.

126. Weber, as quoted in Mitzman, *The Iron Cage*, 279.

127. Green, *Von Richthofen Sisters*, 122–23, 127, 217–18, 163, 220, 67. See also Gerth and Mills, eds., *From Max Weber*, 29–30.

128. Gerth and Mills, eds., *From Max Weber*, 28.

129. Weber, as quoted in Green, *Von Richthofen Sisters*, 162n, 163–64; Green quoted from 165–66; see also 161–66.

130. Max Weber, "Politics as a Vocation," 127–28.

131. Cf. Green, *Von Richthofen Sisters*, 121. See also chap. 7 of this book for a discussion of Shulamith's Firestone's treatment of Freud.

132. Max Weber, "Freudianism," in *Weber: Selections in Translation*, ed. W. G. Runciman, trans. E. Matthews, 383–88. See Green, *Von Richthofen Sisters*, 55–58; and Gerth and Mills, *From Max Weber*, 20.

133. Weber in a letter to Edgar Jaffe, as quoted in *Weber*, ed. Runciman, 387.

134. Max Weber, "The Household Community," from *Wirtschaft und Gesellschaft*, in *Theories of Society: Foundations of Modern Sociological Theory*, ed. Talcott Parsons et al., 296–305, hereafter cited in the text as "HC."

135. Max Weber, *The Sociology of Religion*, trans. Ephraim Fischoff from the fourth edition of *Religionssoziologie* from *Wirtschaft und Gesellschaft*, revised by Johannes Winckelmann, hereafter cited in the text as *SR*. See also Mitzman, *The Iron Cage*, 201–8. For useful and com-

prehensive summaries of Weber's *Religionssoziologie*, see Reinhard Bendix, *Max Weber: An Intellectual Portrait*, 83–281.

136. Marianne Weber, as quoted in Green, *Von Richthofen Sisters*, 120.

137. Max Weber, "Religious Rejections of the World and Their Directions," in *From Max Weber*, ed. Gerth and Mills, 323–59, hereafter cited in the text as "RR."

138. Max Weber, *The Protestant Ethic and the Spirit of Capitalism*, 158–59, 62–63. Cf. Hughes, *Consciousness and Society*, 289.

139. Cf. Alvin Gouldner, "Anti-Minotaur: The Myth of a Value-Free Sociology."

140. Max Weber, *General Economic History*, hereafter cited in the text as *GEH*.

141. Gerth and Mills, eds., *From Max Weber*, 46–50, 61–65.

142. Weber, as quoted in Hughes, *Consciousness and Society*, 308; see also 296–314.

143. Reinhard Bendix, "The Age of Ideology: Persistent and Changing," in his *Embattled Reason: Essays in Social Knowledge*, especially 52.

144. Mitzman, *The Iron Cage*, 302, 304. See also Green, *Von Richthofen Sisters*, 41.

145. Ibid., 300.

146. Green, *Von Richthofen Sisters*, 173; see also 142–47, 170–72.

147. See Ann Oakley, *The Sociology of Housework*, 21–22. For a balanced view, see Roth, "Max Weber's Generational Rebellion," 30n.33. For Karl Jaspers's role in the creation of the myth of Max Weber, see Green, *Von Richthofen Sisters*, 172–73, 284–92. For Green's notion of Weber's "patriarchal romanticism," see 126.

148. David Frisby, *Georg Simmel;* Lewis A. Coser, ed., *Georg Simmel;* Donald N. Levine, introduction to *Georg Simmel on Individuality and Social Forms, Selected Writings*. Simmel's work is much more social-psychological and, therefore, more directly concerned with individuality than the work of the other classical theorists.

149. Lewis A. Coser, "Georg Simmel's Neglected Contributions to the Sociology of Women," 869. Simmel's contributions to the sociology of women are neglected in Levine's introduction to *Georg Simmel on Individuality and Social Forms*, which has considerable material relating to women. The magnitude of Simmel's interest in women and their relationships with men is evident in the recently published *Georg Simmel: On Women, Sexuality, and Love*, ed. and trans. Guy Oakes.

150. Lewis A. Coser, *Masters of Sociological Thought: Ideas in Historical and Social Context*, 196. Cf. Green, *Von Richthofen Sisters*, 29–30, 140.

151. Simmel, as quoted in Frisby, *Georg Simmel*, 22; and see Frisby's discussion, 20–44, especially 34–37.

152. Mitzman, *Sociology and Estrangement*, 31–33. Kurt H. Wolff, introduction to *The Sociology of Georg Simmel*, liv, for the articles in *Vorwarts* and *Die Neue Zeit*.

153. Coser, ed., *Georg Simmel*, especially the introduction and parts 1 and 2. Levine, introduction to *Georg Simmel on Individuality and Social Forms*, ix–xii, xliii–lxi.

154. Mitzman, *The Iron Cage*, 4n, 176, 180, 209n, 254n, 263, 266, 271, 275.

155. Oakes, ed., *Georg Simmel*, vii–viii. Frisby, *Georg Simmel*, 27, 39–40. Wolff, ed., *Sociology of Georg Simmel*, liv–lv.

156. Coser, "Simmel's Neglected Contributions." Passages from Simmel's work as quoted in Coser's "Simmel's Neglected Contributions" are hereafter cited in the text as "SNC." Karen Horney recognized the importance of Simmel's writings about women in "The Flight from Womanhood: The Masculinity Complex in Women as Viewed by Men and Women," *International Journal of Psychoanalysis* 7 (1926): 324–29.

157. Kurt H. Wolff, ed. and trans., *The Sociology of Georg Simmel*, 343, hereafter cited in the text as *SGS*.

158. Donald N. Levine, ed., *Georg Simmel on Individuality and Social Forms, Selected Writings*, 91–94, hereafter cited in the text as *SISF*.

159. Evans, "Prostitution, State, and Society in Imperial Germany," 106.

160. This is one thrust of Karl Marx's *Economic and Philosophic Manuscripts of 1844*.

161. Georg Simmel, *Conflict* and *The Web of Group-Affiliations*, trans. Kurt H. Wolff and Reinhard Bendix, 94, hereafter cited in the text and *CW*.

162. Oakes, ed., *Georg Simmel*, 45, 54.

163. Ibid., 25; and see 3–58.

164. Ibid., 44–55.

165. Coser, "Simmel's Neglected Contributions," 870, 874–76. Because of the apparent lack of consistency in the style and character of Simmel's work, it is not easy to discern direction in his analysis of the "woman question": possibly he moved toward more concern with the problem of women and culture as he moved away from left-liberal criticism of society toward a critique of modern culture. For a 1902 essay not discussed in the text in which Simmel offers the radical suggestion of a restructuring of the professions away from their male-dominant orientation, see Priscilla Robertson, *An Experience of Woman: Pattern and Change in Nineteenth-Century Europe, with an Appendix by Steve Hochstadt* (Philadelphia: Temple University Press, 1982), 424–25.

166. Ferdinand Tönnies, *Ferdinand Tönnies on Sociology: Pure, Applied, and Empirical, Selected Writings*, ed. Werner J. Cahnman and Rudolf Heberle, 22, 30, hereafter cited in the text as *OS*.

167. Cahnman and Heberle, introduction to *Ferdinand Tönnies on Sociology*, xvi.

168. Mitzman, *Sociology and Estrangement*, 93–94, 83–84; Mitzman, *The Iron Cage*, 200, for Weber's wavering on the question of the despotic and sexual nature of primitive communities.

169. Cahnman and Heberle, introduction to *Ferdinand Tönnies on Sociology*, xi.

170. Ferdinand Tönnies, *Community and Association*, trans. Charles P. Loomis, 46, hereafter cited in text as *CA*.

171. Statements such as this seem to contradict Tönnies' protestations to von Wiese that his concepts have as their objects ideal types but are not normative (*Ferdinand Tönnies on Sociology*, 9–10). Cahnman and Heberle have accepted this interpretation in the introduction. Tönnies later modified his position. Lynda M. Glennon discusses Tönnies in an appendix on the theoretical background of her use of the instrumental-expressive dichotomy to characterize women's liberation ideologies (*Women and Dualism: A Sociology of Knowledge Analysis*, 213–17). She covers some of the same ground traversed here but from another angle.

172. See Robert A. Nisbet's brief discussion in *The Sociological Tradition*, 76–77.

173. Tönnies' denial of this tone, as well as Cahnman and Heberle's, is simply not persuasive to me. On the one hand, we must distinguish a theorist's personal attitudes from the ideological implications of his/her conceptual apparatus. On the other, Tönnies' background and attachments were rural even if bourgeois (*Ferdinand Tönnies on Sociology*, xiv–xv). For a complete discussion of Tönnies' antimodernism, romanticism, life and work, see Mitzman, *Sociology and Estrangement*, part 2 and pp. 23–25.

174. Coser, *Masters of Sociological Thought*, 441–47, 449–56.

175. Ibid., 441–45, 457–61.

176. Oscar Jaszi, as quoted in Jean Floud, "Karl Mannheim," 206–7.

177. See Zeitlin, *Ideology and the Development of Sociological Theory*, chap. 16, for a summary of Mannheim's work. For a discussion of Mannheim's theory of consciousness, see George Lichtheim, *The Concept of Ideology and Other Essays*, 36–43. See also the brief but excellent discussion in Floud, "Karl Mannheim," 204–13.

178. Karl Mannheim, *Essays on the Sociology of Culture*, ed. Ernest Manheim in cooperation with Paul Kecskemeti, 44–51, hereafter cited in the text as *ESC*.

179. Coser, *Masters of Sociological Thought*, 446.

180. Kurt H. Wolff, ed., *From Karl Mannheim*, 353. See also Coser, *Masters of Sociological Thought*, 447–49, 461–63. For an emphasis on the later works of Mannheim's exile in England, see David Kettler,

Volker Meja, and Nico Stehr, *Karl Mannheim* (New York: Tavistock, 1984).
181. See Mannheim, *Essays on the Sociology of Culture*, chap. 7.
182. Mannheim, *Ideology and Utopia*, 192.
183. On feminist utopias, see "Science Fiction on Women—Science Fiction by Women."
184. Steinem, "The Nazi Connetion."

Chapter 5. Italy

1. John Stuart Mill and Harriet Taylor Mill, *Essays on Sex Equality*, ed. Alice S. Rossi, 209, 139–40.
2. Sheila Ryan Johansson, "'Herstory' as History: A New Field or Another Fad?" 423.
3. To this day Italy has one of the lowest labor-force participation rates for women as well as a low proportion of women in the labor force. See Jean Stockard and Miriam M. Johnson, *Sex Roles: Sex Inequality and Sex Role Development*, 77–78, 89. Recently Italy has had some of the most militant feminists. For recent changes, see James Petras, "Class and Political-Economic Development in the Mediterranean," in *The Sociology of Development in Core and Peripheral Societies*, ed. Michael T. Martin and Terry R. Kandal, a special issue of *California Sociologist: A Journal of Sociology and Social Work*, vol. 8, nos. 1–2 (Winter–Summer 1985): 233–48.
4. Edith Thomas, *The Women Incendiaries*, 96.
5. Tullio Tentori, "Italy," 165, 156, 155, 162, 156–58.
6. Ibid., 160–62, 158.
7. Ibid., 156–57. See also Claire La Vigna, "The Marxist Ambivalence toward Women: Between Socialism and Feminism in the Italian Socialist Party," 179n.62.
8. La Vigna, "The Marxist Ambivalence toward Women," 164–65.
9. Ibid., 164.
10. Tentori, "Italy," 158.
11. La Vigna, "The Marxist Ambivalence toward Women," 166–68.
12. Tentori, "Italy," 158.
13. Carlo Tanzi, as quoted in La Vigna, "The Marxist Ambivalence toward Women," 151; La Vigna quoted from 165; and see 146–81 and 175n.7.
14. Anna Kuliscioff, as quoted in Tentori, "Italy," 159.
15. See Sheila Rowbotham, *Women, Resistance and Revolution: A History of Women and Revolution in the Modern World*, 88, 92.
16. La Vigna, "The Marxist Ambivalence toward Women," 169, 160–61; Tentori, "Italy," 159.
17. Tentori, "Italy," 159.

18. Benedetto Croce, *A History of Italy: 1871–1915*, as quoted in Lewis A. Coser, *Masters of Sociological Thought: Ideas in Historical and Social Context*, 413.

19. Francesco Crispi, as quoted in Coser, *Masters of Sociological Thought*, 416; and see 414–15.

20. Benito Mussolini, as quoted in H. Stuart Hughes, *Consciousness and Society: The Reorientation of European Social Thought, 1890–1930*, 272.

21. See the interesting pamphlet, "Italian Women: Past and Present," by Maria Castellani, a Fascist.

22. Tentori, "Italy," 160.

23. Croce, as quoted in Hughes, *Consciousness and Society*, 249, and see 86; Croce's study of Marx and Marxism was brief; its result for Croce was the heuristic value of Marx's work for historical interpretation (82–89).

24. Hughes, *Consciousness and Society*, 253.

25. T. B. Bottomore, *Elites and Society*, 9. See also Irving M. Zeitlin, *Ideology and the Development of Sociological Theory*, chaps. 12, 13, 14.

26. Coser, *Masters of Sociological Thought*, 407–8; and see 409–10.

27. Ibid., 402–7.

28. Ibid., 417, 402, and see 404–6, 418–22.

29. Vilfredo Pareto, as quoted in Raymond Aron, *Main Currents in Sociological Thought*, 2:215n.12. Mussolini was influenced by the writings of the French theorist of syndicalism, Georges Sorel.

30. See Coser, *Masters of Sociological Thought*, 406; Hughes, *Consciousness and Society*, chap. 7; Aron, *Main Currents in Sociological Thought*, 2: 194–97, 2:215–16n.14; and James H. Meisel, ed., *Pareto and Mosca*, 1–44, especially 14, for the quoted characterizations of Pareto.

31. Werner Stark, "In Search of the True Pareto," 47, 47–49.

32. Pareto, as quoted in Coser, *Masters of Sociological Thought*, 387. My discussion follows Coser's, 388–95.

33. Coser, *Masters of Sociological Thought*, 396, and see 395–400.

34. Ibid., 396. Pareto suggested in 1923 that "France will be able to save herself only if she finds her Mussolini" (quoted in Aron, *Main Currents in Sociological Thought*, 2:215n.14).

35. Pareto, as quoted in Marie Louise Janssen-Jurreit, *Sexism: The Male Monopoly on History and Thought*, 30–31.

36. Vilfredo Pareto, *The Mind and Society*, trans. Andrew Bongiorno and ed. Arthur Livingston, hereafter cited in the text as *MS*.

37. Pareto stated, "There is nothing new under the sun. . . . The religious fanatics of the past and our present-day humanitarians are of the same breed" (*MS* 3:1268n.1819).

38. Pareto cited the poet Carducci's satire of such women, *On the Fadda Case (Poesie)*. It reminds me of the line from a Sylvia Plath poem to the effect that every woman loves a fascist (see "Daddy," in *Ariel* [New York: Harper and Row, n.d.], 49–51).

39. Pareto's attitude toward women in also evident in his scheme for ranking people in elite positions: "To the woman 'in politics' . . . who has managed to infatuate a man of power and play a part in the man's career, we shall give some higher number, such as 8 or 9; to the strumpet who merely satisfies the senses of such a man and exerts no influence on public affairs, we shall give a zero" (*MS* 3:1422).

40. This, despite that in the formerly colonized world (such as Cuba, China, and Southeast Asia) and in the colonized world (including the ghettos of the United States), women are driven by want to prostitution. Relevant here is Karl Marx, *Economic and Philosophic Manuscripts of 1844*, 99–100n.1. Prostitution, Marx maintained, "is only a *specific* expression of the *general* prostitution of the *labourer*" [i.e., selling oneself to stay alive], "*and* since it is a relationship in which not the prostitute alone, but also the one who prostitutes, fall—and the latter's abomination is still greater—the capitalist, etc., also comes under this head."

41. Alvin W. Gouldner, *The Coming Crisis of Western Sociology*, 149–50.

42. Robert Michels, as quoted in Seymour Martin Lipset's introduction to *Political Parties: A Sociological Study of the Oligarchical Tendencies of Modern Democracy*, by Robert Michels, 15, hereafter cited in the text as *PP*.

43. Juan J. Linz, "Michels, Robert," 10:265.

44. Arthur Mitzman, *Sociology and Estrangement: Three Sociologists of Imperial Germany*, 281–82, and 315; see also Linz, "Michels," 10:265, 315.

45. Linz, "Michels," 10:266.

46. Hughes, *Consciousness and Society*, 250–52. See also Coser, *Masters of Sociological Thought*, 420–21.

47. Jean H. Quataert, *Reluctant Feminists in German Social Democracy, 1885–1917*, 63, 75, 117, 128–29, 157.

48. Michels, as quoted and summarized in Mitzman, *Sociology and Estrangement*, 328. Much of this material is drawn from articles later published by Robert Michels in *Sexual Ethics*, which is discussed in the text below; see also n. 50.

49. Mitzman, *Sociology and Estrangement*, 329.

50. Robert Michels, *Sexual Ethics: A Study of Borderland Questions*, hereafter cited in the text as *SE*. I came across this book late in the course of my research. It is not readily available in all libraries; the copy I read was obtained by interlibrary loan from the University of New Mexico.

51. Mitzman, *Sociology and Estrangement*, 286.

52. Ibid., 329.

53. Ibid., 329–30.

54. See Terry R. Kandal, "The Sociology of Knowledge: A Restatement," chap. 7.

55. Lurking behind and linking the antifeminist currents of German, French, and Italian social theory is, in Hughes's characterization, "the almost magical attraction of Georges Sorel." Sorel was one of the few writers Pareto cited favorably; they maintained a long-standing correspondence. Mussolini knew Sorel's work before the war (Hughes, *Consciousness and Society*, 250–52; and for the Sorel-Mussolini connection, see 179–80). For Sorel, progress was an illusion; he sought the violent regeneration of society by the restoration of the ancient heroic virtues of the farmer-warriors of ancient Athens. Such a society was characterized by a strong family with a productive household to which women were restricted and in which men were dominant. Sorel's ideal was unmistakably a man's society (John H. Stanley, ed., *From Georges Sorel: Essays in Socialism and Philosophy*, 24–30, and see 13–24, 30–39).

56. Hughes, *Consciousness and Society*, 272. See Mitzman, *Sociology and Estrangement*, chaps. 26, 27, 227–28, 341–42.

57. See Robert A. Nisbet, *The Sociological Tradition*, 148–50.

58. Mussolini, as quoted approvingly by Castellani in "Italian Women," 8.

59. Castellani, "Italian Women," 8, 36, 33.

Chapter 6. The United States

1. See Alexis de Tocqueville, *Democracy in America*, especially the author's introduction, 9–20. See also Alexis de Tocqueville, *The Old Regime and the French Revolution*. For a work that takes off from Tocqueville's analysis, see Louis Hartz, *The Liberal Tradition in America*.

2. Alice S. Rossi, ed., *The Feminist Papers: From Adams to de Beauvoir*, 3–8, and the rest of part 1.

3. Tocqueville, *Democracy in America*, 639, 316–63.

4. In 1840, for example, Elizabeth Cady Stanton and Lucretia Mott were delegates to an antislavery conference in London—at which women were not permitted to participate in the discussion (Sheila Rowbotham, *Hidden from History: Rediscovering Women in History from the Seventeenth Century to the Present*, 241–42).

5. See Herman Schwendinger and Julia R. Schwendinger, *The Sociologists of the Chair: A Radical Analysis of the Formative Years of North American Sociology (1883–1922)*.

6. Nancy F. Cott, "Passionlessness: An Interpretation of Victorian Sexual Ideology, 1790–1850," 230.

7. Abigail Adams, as quoted in Rossi, ed., *Feminist Papers*, 10–11; and see 11, 13–15 for John Adams's letters stating the views to which his spouse was reacting.

8. Cott, "Passionlessness," 228, 221.

9. Rossi, ed., *Feminist Papers*, 256–57; see also 253.

10. Ibid., 273.

11. Correspondence of Angelina Grimké and Theodore Weld, as quoted in Rossi, ed., *Feminist Papers*, 290, 292; see also 282.

12. Angelina Grimké, as quoted in Rossi, ed., *Feminist Papers*, 286. See also Grimké's "Appeal to the Christian Women of the South," in Rossi, ed., *Feminist Papers*, 296–304.

13. Whittier, as quoted in Rossi, ed., *Feminist Papers*, 287. See also 288, 305–22, for selections from Sarah Grimké's *Letters on the Equality of Sexes* and *The Condition of Women*.

14. Sheila Rowbotham, *Women, Resistance and Revolution: A History of Women and Revolution in the Modern World*, 108.

15. Rossi, ed., *Feminist Papers*, 241.

16. Rossi, ed., *Feminist papers*, 421. See 413–21 for the Declaration of Sentiments and a report on the convention from *History of Woman Suffrage*, 2 vols., ed. Elizabeth C. Stanton, Susan B. Anthony, and Matilda J. Gage (Rochester: Charles Mann, 1881–82).

17. Margaret Fuller, as quoted in Rowbotham, *Women, Resistance and Revolution*, 57; Rowbotham, as quoted on 57–58. George Sand wrote the following, quoted by Karl Marx: "Battle or death; bloody struggle or extinction. It is thus that the question is irresistibly put."

18. Rowbotham, *Women, Resistance and Revolution*, 79.

19. Elizabeth Cady Stanton, as quoted in Rossi, ed., *Feminist Papers*, 386, 381. The consequences for women of a male-dominated medical profession is a recurrent topic in feminist historiography. See, for example, Robin Miller Jacoby, "Science and Sex Roles in the Victorian Era."

20. Susan B. Anthony, as quoted in Rossi, ed., *Feminist Papers*, 391.

21. Rowbotham, *Women, Resistance and Revolution*, 109.

22. Rossi, ed., *Feminist Papers*, 251–52.

23. Robin Miller Jacoby, "Science and Sex Roles in the Victorian Era," 64.

24. Carl N. Degler, "Revolution without Ideology: The Changing Place of Women in America," 654. See also his recent full-length study, *At Odds: Women and the Family in America from the Revolution to the Present* (New York: Oxford University Press, 1980).

25. Rossi, ed., *Feminist Papers*, 473.

26. Degler, "Revolution without Ideology," 656.

27. See Meredith Tax, *The Rising of Women: Feminist Solidarity and Class Conflict, 1880–1917*, part 1.

28. Martin Green, *The Von Richthofen Sisters: The Triumphant and the*

Tragic Modes of Love: Else and Frieda von Richthofen, Otto Gross, Max Weber, and D. H. Lawrence, in the Years 1870–1970, 268; see also 265–67.

29. Emma Goldman, as quoted and discussed in Rowbotham, *Women, Resistance and Revolution,* 96–97. For a sample of Goldman's writings, see Emma Goldman, *The Traffic in Women, and Other Essays on Feminism,* with a biography by Alix Kates Shulman (New York: Times Change Press, 1970).

30. Rowbotham, *Women, Resistance and Revolution,* 110–11.

31. Ibid., 92, 137, 143.

32. Charlotte Gilman, as quoted in Rossi, ed., *Feminist Papers,* 568; see discussion of Florence Kelley, 474–75; and discussion of Gilman, 566–72.

33. Rosalynn Baxandall, Linda Gordon, and Susan Reverby, eds., *America's Working Women,* 129–31.

34. Tax, *Rising of Women,* 20.

35. Baxandall, Gordon, and Reverby, eds., *America's Working Women,* 130–31.

36. Mari Jo Buhle, "Women and the Socialist Party, 1901–1914," 65–81.

37. Buhle, "Women and the Socialist Party," 82–86.

38. Rowbotham, *Hidden from History,* 149–51.

39. Baxandall, Gordon, and Reverby, eds., *America's Working Women,* 130.

40. Robin Miller Jacoby, "Feminism and Class Consciousness in the British and American Women's Trade Union Leagues, 1890–1925," 137–60, especially 150–55.

41. Degler, "Revolution without Ideology," 655.

42. See Rossi, *Feminist Papers,* 473–77; and see the section on Jane Addams in part 3, 599–612.

43. Introduction to *The Underside of American History,* vol. 2, *Since 1865,* ed. Thomas R. Frazier, 5. For a masterly analysis of the major historiography about the Progressives, see Frederick R. Lynch, "Social Theory and the Progressive Era."

44. Degler, "Revolution without Ideology," 660, 664; and see 663, 665.

45. Ibid., 665, 657, 656.

46. Ibid., 656–59.

47. Rowbotham, *Hidden from History,* 125, 123–26. See also Stuart Ewen, *Captains of Consciousness: Advertising and the Social Roots of the Consumer Culture.*

48. Mary Beard, ed., *America through Women's Eyes,* 479.

49. Robert Shaffer, "Women and the Communist Party, USA, 1930–1940," 76–77.

50. Ibid., 77–78.

51. Ibid., 77.

52. Cf. ibid., 103–4.

53. Juliet Mitchell, *Psychoanalysis and Feminism: Freud, Reich, Laing, and Women*, 410–11.

54. Winston Churchill gave the cold war its name in his famous "Iron Curtain" speech at commencement exercise in Fulton, Missouri, 5 March 1946. He spoke at the invitation of Harry S. Truman.

55. Marlene Dixon, "Why Women's Liberation," 320.

56. Alice S. Rossi, "Equality between the Sexes: An Immodest Proposal," 611, 613.

57. Degler, "Revolution without Ideology," 665, 668.

58. Perry Anderson, "Components of the National Culture," 219.

59. The classic critique along these lines is Ralf Dahrendorf's "Out of Utopia: Toward a Reorientation of Sociological Analysis."

60. See also Susan Moller Okin's discussion of these two works in *Women in Western Political Thought*.

61. Talcott Parsons, "Age and Sex in the Social Structure of the United States," hereafter cited in the text as "AS."

62. For what happens to women when they manifest such behavior, see Phyllis Chesler, *Women and Madness* (Garden City, N.Y.: Doubleday and Co., 1972).

63. Parsons included as evidence an observation on segregation of the sexes at faculty parties ("AS," 614n. 6).

64. Talcott Parsons and Robert F. Bales in collaboration with James Olds, Morris Zelditch, Jr., and Philip E. Slater, *Family, Socialization, and Interaction Process*, hereafter cited in the text as *FSIP*.

65. For a critique, see Susan Moller Okin, *Women in Western Political Thought*, 241–46. For the evidence on universality of sex-role differentiation, see the chapter by Zelditch in *Family, Socialization, and Interaction Process*, by Parsons et al.

66. Compare the work of women sociologists for the same period; see, for example, Mirra Komarovsky, "Cultural Contradictions and Sex Roles," and Helen Mayer Hacker, "Women as a Minority Group."

67. C. Wright Mills, *The Sociological Imagination*, 49n. 19.

68. C. Wright Mills, "IBM Plus Reality Plus Humanism = Sociology," 572.

69. C. Wright Mills, *White Collar: The American Middle Classes*, hereafter cited in the text as *WC*.

70. See Harry Braverman, *Labor and Monopoly Capital: The Degradation of Work in the Twentieth Century*, chaps. 15 and 16, on clerical workers, service occupations, and the retail trade. See also recent issues of *Dollars and Sense*.

71. C. Wright Mills, "Plain Talk on Fancy Sex," hereafter cited in the text as "PTFS." This article originally appeared in *New York Journal*,

American-International News Service Syndicate (31 August 1952) with the subtitle "A Peek at Public Morality."
72. C. Wright Mills, "Women: The Darling Little Slaves," hereafter cited in the text as "WDLS."

Chapter 7. Conclusion

1. Alice S. Rossi, introduction to *Essays on Sex Equality,* by John Stuart Mill and Harriet Taylor Mill, 62, and see 50, 52–53.
2. Karl Marx, *The Secret Diplomatic History of the Eighteenth Century,* and *The Story of the Life of Lord Palmerston,* 85.
3. Sarah H. Matthews, "Rethinking Sociology through a Feminist Perspective," 29–30; for "Comments" and her "Rejoinder," pp. 35–39, see Naomi Weisstein's often-reprinted "'Kinder, Küche, Kirche' as Scientific Law: Psychology Constructs the Female," 205–20. See also Marcia Westkott, "Feminist Criticisms of the Social Sciences," and relevant papers in *The Study of Women: Enlarging Perspectives of Social Reality,* ed. Eloise C. Snyder.
4. Jessie Bernard, "My Four Revolutions: An Autobiographical History of the ASA," 778–79.
5. Susan Moller Okin, *Women in Western Political Thought,* 277, 274–89. A notable exception that came to my attention after I completed this work is the sketch by Judith Stacey and Barrie Thorne, "The Missing Feminist Revolution in Sociology," *Social Problems,* vol. 32, no. 4 (April 1985): 301–16.
6. Georg Simmel, as quoted in one of four epigraphs to *The Female World,* by Jessie Bernard.
7. Bernard, "My Four Revolutions," 781, 782, and see 783–89. See also Jessie Bernard, "The Paradox of the Happy Marriage," 85–98. Bernard, *Female World,* 3–15.
8. The formulations are taken from Robert Merton's lucid and literate essay, "Insiders and Outsiders: A Chapter in the Sociology of Knowledge," 31 and passim.
9. Cf. Bernard, "My Four Revolutions," 781. She answers in the negative, but that depends upon men *and* some women sociologists having their consciousness raised through a feminist conversion (787–88).
10. Matthews, "Rethinking Sociology," "Comments" and "Rejoinder," 29–39. I am aware of the interpretive rejoinder: that the canon of the logic of justification itself involves issues of interpretation on several levels.
11. For proposals for a cross-disciplinary feminist sociology, see Mar-

cia Texler Segal and Catherine White Berheide, "Toward a Women's Perspective in Sociology: Directions and Prospects," 69–82.

12. John Stuart Mill and Harriet Taylor Mill, *Essays on Sex Equality*, ed. Alice S. Rossi, 128.

13. See Okin, *Women in Western Political Thought*, 279–80.

14. Bernard, *Female World*, 80, 87, 94–95, 163, 291. Bernard's assertion (343) that Tocqueville's central argument of the historical process of democratization does not apply to the female world is, in my judgment, mistaken. See the conclusion to the discussion of Tocqueville's work in chap. 3 of this book.

15. Ann Oakley, *The Sociology of Housework*, 23.

16. Sheila Rowbotham, *Women, Resistance and Revolution: A History of Women and Revolution in the Modern World*, 56.

17. Philip Rieff, *Freud: The Mind of the Moralist*, 201.

18. *The Sociology of Georg Simmel*, ed. and trans. Kurt H. Wolff, 325.

19. For the classic critique of Weber's position, see Alvin W. Gouldner, "Anti-Minotaur: The Myth of a Value-Free Sociology."

20. See Bernard, *Female World*, 28.

21. Herman Schwendinger and Julia R. Schwendinger, *The Sociologists of the Chair: A Radical Analysis of the Formative Years of North American Sociology (1883–1922)*, 287–334. Julia R. Schwendinger and Herman Schwendinger, "Sociology's Founding Fathers: Sexists to a Man."

22. See the selection of Thorstein Veblen's *The Theory of the Leisure Class*, in *Feminism: The Essential Historical Writings*, ed. Miriam Schneir, 212–27.

23. Okin, *Women in Western Political Thought*, 245, 244–46.

24. Barrington Moore, Jr., "Thoughts on the Future of the Family," 456, and see 467n.2.

25. See Terry R. Kandal, "The Sociology of Knowledge: A Restatement," chap. 7.

26. See Robert A. Nisbet, *The Sociological Tradition*.

27. The Schwendingers criticized Mill for his acceptance of the notion of the complementarity of sex roles even in his ideal of marriage (*Sociologists of the Chair*, 295). However, compared with the distortions in Spencer's and Comte's work, this is a minor flaw in Mill's otherwise admirable analysis of prejudices about women.

28. See Lillian Breslow Rubin, *Worlds of Pain: Life in the Working-Class Family*.

29. See, for example, Karl Marx and Friedrich Engels's praise for Fourier's analysis of marriage and the subjection of women (*The Holy Family; or, Critique of Critical Critique*, 259). See also Karl Marx, *Economic and Philosophic Manuscripts*, 100–101.

30. On Marxism, see Robert Heilbroner, *Marxism: For and Against*.

31. Marx, *Economic and Philosophic Manuscripts*, 99.
32. Marx and Engels, *The Holy Family*, 225–33, 258. See also their defense of Flora Tristan against the criticisms of the Young Hegelians, 29–30, 249.
33. Karl Marx and Friedrich Engels, *The German Ideology*, parts 1, 3, pp. 21–22.
34. Karl Marx, *Capital: A Critique of Political Economy*, 1:536.
35. Friedrich Engels, *The Origin of the Family, Private Property, and the State: In the Light of the Researches of Lewis H. Morgan*, 51, 50, 46–61. In his notebooks drafted in 1857 and 1858—that is, before he read Morgan—in preparation for his work on capital, Marx designated the earliest forms of society "patriarchal" (see Karl Marx, *Grundrisse: Foundations of the Critique of Political Economy* [Translated with a foreword by Martin Nicolaus. New York: Vintage Books, 1973], 146, 157–59).
36. Engels, *Origin of the Family*, 58.
37. Ibid., 65.
38. Ibid., 67.
39. Ibid., 73.
40. Rowbotham, *Women, Resistance and Revolution*, 108, 109. See also Robin Miller Jacoby, "Feminism and Class Consciousness in the British and American Women's Trade Union Leagues, 1820–1925," 137–60.
41. Juliet Mitchell, *Woman's Estate*, 84–96, 99–122; and see 166–72.
42. Shulamith Firestone, *The Dialectic of Sex: The Case for Feminist Revolution*, 44, 43, 47, 8, 206.
43. Juliet Mitchell, *Psychoanalysis and Feminism: Freud, Reich, Laing, and Women*, xiii.
44. See, for example, Barbara Hill Rigney, *Madness and Sexual Politics in the Feminist Novel: Studies in Bronte, Woolf, Lessing, and Atwood*, 6.
45. C. Wright Mills, "Methodological Consequences of the Sociology of Knowledge," 466–67.
46. Mitchell, *Psychoanalysis and Feminism*, 402.
47. Ibid., 404, and see 111–12.
48. Ibid., 405, 361, 406, 409–16. For a formulation based on Mitchell, see Jon Snodgrass, "Patriarchy and Phantasy: A Conception of Psychoanalytic Sociology." See also Alice Miller, *Prisoners of Childhood*.
49. Nancy Chodorow, *The Reproduction of Mothering: Psychoanalysis and the Sociology of Gender*, especially 141–43. On Freud's belief that women are less civilized than men, see Rieff, *Freud*, 199–204, and Sigmund Freud, *Civilization and Its Discontents*, 50–51. Pointing out that when Freud came to study female sexuality later in his career he began to notice the complexities of the development of male and fe-

male selves, especially cross-gender identifications, Lichterman criticizes Chodorow for her uncritical acceptance of Parsons's use of Freud in his theory of socialization. See Paul Lichterman, "Chodorow's Psychoanalytic Sociology: A Project Half-Completed," in Terry R. Kandal, ed., *Theoretical Perspectives from the Edges of Sociology*, a special issue of *California Sociologist: A Journal of Sociology and Social Work*, vol. 9, no. 1 (Winter 1986). It is interesting that whereas Mitchell emphasized the simplicity of female psychological development by contrast to that of males, Chodrow stresses the simplicity of male development.

50. Lise Vogel, "Questions on the Woman Question."

51. Randall Collins, *Conflict Sociology: Toward an Explanatory Science*, 227.

52. See Rowbotham, *Women, Resistance and Revolution*, especially 30, and Robin Miller Jacoby, "Science and Sex Roles in the Victorian Era," 65.

53. Sheila Ryan Johansson, "'Herstory' as History: A New Field or Another Fad?" 401–3.

54. Frederick J. Teggart, *Theory and Processes of History*.

55. Mitchell, *Woman's Estate*, 67.

56. Gayle Rubin, "The Traffic in Women," 156.

57. Margaret T. Hodgen, *Anthropology, History, and Cultural Change*, 34–35.

58. Kathleen Gough, "The Origin of the Family," 54.

59. Ibid., 69–71. See also chap. 4 of this book for Weber's discussion from *General Economic History* of the control of implements and weapons as a source of sexual domination.

60. Joan Smith, "Feminist Analysis of Gender: A Critique," 97–98. For selections of socialist-feminist writings, see Alison M. Jaggar and Paula Rothenberg Struhl, eds., *Feminist Frameworks: Alternative Theoretical Accounts of the Relations between Women and Men*.

61. Smith, "Feminist Analysis of Gender," 99, and see 100–106.

62. Collins, *Conflict Sociology*, 228–59, and see 181–84.

63. Randall Collins, *Sociological Insight: An Introduction to Non-Obvious Sociology*, 147, 146, 147, 148, 153–54.

64. Karen Sacks, *Sisters and Wives: The Past and Future of Sexual Equality*, 6–7.

65. Ibid., 7.

66. Ibid., 245–46, 250. For the impact of North American expansion on Native American women, see Alan M. Klein, "The Political Economy of Gender."

67. For materials on experimentation after the Bolshevik Revolution, see Wilhelm Reich, *The Sexual Revolution*, trans. Therese Pol.

68. Jacoby, "Feminism and Class Consciousness," 154, 150, 154–55, 150.

69. Sheila Rowbotham, *Hidden from History: Rediscovering Women and History from the Seventeenth Century to the Present*, 133. See also Rowbotham, *Women, Resistance and Revolution*, chaps. 6–8; Collins, *Conflict Sociology*, 249.

70. Engels, as quoted in Rowbotham, *Women, Resistance and Revolution*, 59.

71. Mitchell, *Psychoanalysis and Feminism*, 412, and see 413.

72. William Julius Wilson, *The Declining Significance of Race*,

73. See Harry Braverman, *Labor and Monopoly Capital: The Degradation of Work in the Twentieth Century*. See also the growing number of magazines on women in executive positions in corporations.

74. See Jean H. Quataert, *Reluctant Feminists in German Social Democracy, 1885–1917*, 32–41.

75. Smith, "Feminist Analysis of Gender," 105–6.

76. Karl Marx, *Letters to Dr. Kugelmann*, 83.

77. Collins, *Conflict Sociology*, 225.

Bibliography

Anderson, Perry, "Components of the National Culture." In *Student Power: Problems, Diagnosis, Action*, edited by Alexander Cockburn and Robin Blackburn, 214–84. Baltimore: Penguin, 1969.

Andreski, Stanislav. Introduction to *The Principles of Sociology*, by Herbert Spencer. Hamden, Conn.: Archon Books, 1969.

Aron, Raymond. *Main Currents in Sociological Thought*. 2 vols. Translated by Richard Howard and Helen Weaver. Garden City, N.Y.: Doubleday and Co., Anchor Books, 1968.

Banks, J. A., and Olive Banks. "Feminism and Social Change—A Case Study of a Social Movement." In *Explorations in Social Change*, edited by George K. Zollschan and Walter Hirsch, 547–69. Boston: Houghton Mifflin, 1964.

Baxandall, Rosalyn, Linda Gordon, and Susan Reverby, eds. *America's Working Women*. New York: Greenwood Press, 1976.

Beard, Mary R. *Woman as Force in History: A Study in Traditions and Realities*. New York: Collier Books, 1946.

————, ed. *America through Women's Eyes*. New York: Greenwood Press, 1976.

Bell, Susan Groag, and Karen M. Offen, eds. *Women, the Family, and Freedom: The Debate in the Documents*. Vol. 1, *1750–1880*. Stanford: Stanford University Press, 1983.

317

Bendix, Reinhard. *Embattled Reason: Essays on Social Knowledge*. New York: Oxford University Press, 1970.

————. *Max Weber: An Intellectual Portrait*. Garden City, N.Y.: Doubleday and Co., Anchor Books, 1962.

Bendix, Reinhard, and Guenther Roth. *Scholarship and Partisanship: Essays on Max Weber*. Berkeley and Los Angeles: University of California Press, 1971.

Bernard, Jessie. *The Female World*. New York: Free Press, 1981.

————. "A Quiet Revolution." Foreword to *The Study of Women: Enlarging Perspectives of Social Reality*, edited by Eloise C. Snyder, xiii–xx. New York: Harper and Row, 1979.

————. "My Four Revolutions: An Autobiographical History of the ASA." *American Journal of Sociology* 78, no. 4 (January 1973): 773–91.

————. "The Paradox of the Happy Marriage." In *Woman in Sexist Society: Studies in Power and Powerlessness*, edited by Vivian Gornick and Barbara K. Moran, 85–98. New York: Basic Books, 1971.

Bloch, Maurice, and Jean H. Bloch. "Women and the Dialectics of Nature in Eighteenth-Century French Thought." In *Nature, Culture and Gender*, edited by Carol P. MacCormack and Marilyn Strathern, 25–41. London: Cambridge University Press, 1980.

Bloch, Ruth H. "Untangling the Roots of Modern Sex Roles: A Survey of Four Centuries of Change." *Signs: A Journal of Women in Culture and Society* 4, no. 2 (Winter 1978): 237–52.

Bock, Kenneth E. *The Acceptance of Histories: Toward a Perspective for Social Science*. University of California Publications in Sociology and Social Institutions, no. 1, 3:1–132. Berkeley and Los Angeles: University of California Press, 1956.

Bottomore, T. B. *Elites and Society*. New York: Basic Books, 1964.

Boxer, Marilyn J. "Socialism Faces Feminism: The Failure of Synthesis in France, 1879–1914." In *Socialist Women: European Socialist Feminism in the Nineteenth and Early Twentieth Centuries*, edited by Marilyn J. Boxer and Jean H. Quataert, 75–111. New York: Elsevier North-Holland, 1978.

Boxer, Marilyn J., and Jean H. Quataert, eds. *Socialist Women: European Socialist Feminism in the Nineteenth and Early Twentieth Centuries*. New York: Elsevier North-Holland, 1978.

Braverman, Harry. *Labor and Monopoly Capital: The Degradation of Work in the Twentieth Century*. New York: Monthly Review Press, 1974.

Bridenthal, Renate, and Claudia Koonz. "Beyond *Kinder, Küche, Kirche*: Weimar Women in Politics and Work." In *Liberating Women's History: Theoretical and Critical Essays*, edited by Berenice A. Carroll, 301–29. Urbana: University of Illinois Press, 1976.

————, eds. *Becoming Visible: Women in European History.* Boston: Houghton Mifflin, 1977.

Brinton, Crane. *The Anatomy of Revolution.* 1938. Rev. ed., 1952. New York: Vintage Books, 1956.

Buford, Rhea, ed. *The Future of the Sociological Classics.* London: George Allen & Unwin, 1981.

Buhle, Mari Jo. "Women and the Socialist Party, 1901–1914." In *From Feminism to Liberation,* collected by Edith Hoshino Altbach, 65–86. Cambridge, Mass.: Schenkman Publishing Co., 1971.

Carroll, Berenice A., ed. *Liberating Women's History: Theoretical and Critical Essays.* Urbana: University of Illinois Press, 1976.

Castellani, Maria. *Italian Women Past and Present.* Noviissima Roma, 1939.

Chodorow, Nancy. "Family Structure and Feminine Personality." In *Woman, Culture, and Society,* edited by Michelle Zimbalist Rosaldo and Louise Lamphere, 43–66. Stanford: Stanford University Press, 1974.

————. *The Reproduction of Mothering: Psychoanalysis and the Sociology of Gender.* Berkeley and Los Angeles: University of California Press, 1978.

Cloward, Richard A., and Frances Fox Piven. "Hidden Protest: The Channeling of Female Innovation and Resistance." *Signs: A Journal of Women in Culture and Society* 4 (Summer 1974): 651–69.

Collins, Randall. *Conflict Sociology: Toward an Explanatory Science.* With a contribution by Joan Annett. New York: Academic Press, 1975.

————. *Sociological Insight: An Introduction to Non-Obvious Sociology.* New York: Oxford University Press, 1982.

Comte, Auguste. *Cours de philosophie positive, 1830–1842.* In *Auguste Comte and Positivism: The Essential Writings,* edited by Gertrud Lenzer. New York: Harper and Row, 1975.

————. *Passages from the Letters of Auguste Comte.* Selected and translated by John K. Ingram. London: Adam and Charles Black, 1901.

————. *System of Positive Polity.* 1851. Vol. 1. Translated by John Henry Bridges. New York: Burt Franklin, n.d.

Condorcet, Marie-Jean-Antoine-Nicholas de Caritat, Marquis de. "An Historical Picture of the Progress of the Human Mind." 1795. In *The Idea of Progress: A Collection of Readings, Selected by Frederick J. Teggart,* rev. ed., with an introduction by George H. Hildebrand, 321–58. Berkeley and Los Angeles: University of California Press, 1949.

Coser, Lewis A. "Durkheim's Conservatism and Its Implications for His Sociological Theory." In *Emile Durkheim et al., Essays on Sociology and Philosophy,* edited by Kurt H. Wolff. New York: Harper and Row, 1964.

————. "Georg Simmel's Neglected Contributions to the Sociology of Women." *Signs: A Journal of Women in Culture and Society* 2, no. 4 (Summer 1977): 869–76.

————. *Masters of Sociological Thought: Ideas in Historical and Social Context.* 2d ed. New York: Harcourt Brace Jovanovich, 1977.

Cott, Nancy F. "Passionlessness: An Interpretation of Victorian Sexual Ideology, 1790–1850." *Signs: A Journal of Women in Culture and Society* 4, no. 2 (Winter 1978): 219–36.

Dahrendorf, Ralf. "Out of Utopia: Toward a Reorientation of Sociological Analysis." *American Journal of Sociology* 64 (September 1958): 115–27.

Degler, Carl N. "Revolution without Ideology: The Changing Place of Women in America." In *The Woman in America,* edited by Stephen R. Graubard. *Daedalus* 93, no. 2 (Spring 1964): 653–70.

Dixon, Marlene. "Why Women's Liberation." In *The Underside of American History: Other Readings,* vol. 2, *Since 1865,* edited by Thomas R. Frazier. New York: Harcourt Brace Jovanovich, 1971.

Duncan, David. *The Life and Letters of Herbert Spencer.* London: Methuen and Co., 1908.

Durkheim, Émile. *The Division of Labor in Society.* 1893. Translated by George Simpson. New York: Free Press, 1964.

————. *The Rules of Sociological Method.* 1895. Translated by Sarah A. Solovay and John H. Mueller from the eighth edition. Edited by George E. Catlin. New York: Free Press, 1964.

————. *Suicide: A Study in Sociology.* 1897. Translated by John A. Spaulding and George Simpson. Glencoe, Ill.: Free Press, 1951.

Elkins, Charles L. "The Social Order and the Equal Rights Amendment." In *Impact ERA: Limitations and Possibilities,* by the California Commission on the Status of Women, 216–33. Milbrae, Calif.: Les Femmes Publishing, 1976.

Elshtain, Jean Bethke. *Public Man, Private Woman: Women in Social and Political Thought.* Princeton: Princeton University Press, 1981.

Engels, Friedrich. *The Condition of the Working Class in England.* In *On Britain,* by Karl Marx and Friedrich Engels, 1–338. 2d ed. Moscow: Foreign Languages Publishing House, 1962.

————. *The Housing Question.* 1872. 2d ed. Edited by C. P. Dutt. New York: International Publishers, n.d.

————. *The Origin of the Family, Private Property, and the State: In the Light of the Researches of Lewis H. Morgan.* 1884. New York: International Publishers, 1963.

———— *The Peasant War in Germany,* 1850, and *Germany: Revolution and Counter-Revolution,* 1851–52. Edited by Leonard Krieger. Chicago: University of Chicago Press, 1967.

————. *The Role of Force in History: A Study of Bismarck's Policy of Blood and Iron*. Translated by Jack Cohen. Edited by Ernst Wangermann. New York: International Publishers, 1968.

Evans, Richard J. *The Feminist Movement in Germany, 1894–1933*. Sage Studies in 20th Century History, vol. 6. Beverly Hills, Calif.: Sage Publications, 1976.

————. "Prostitution, State, and Society in Imperial Germany." *Past and Present: A Journal*, no. 70 (February 1976): 106–29.

Ewen, Stuart. *Captains of Consciousness: Advertising and the Social Roots of Consumer Culture*. New York: McGraw-Hill, 1976.

Firestone, Shulamith. *The Dialectic of Sex: The Case for Feminist Revolution*. 1970. Rev. ed. New York: Bantam Books, 1971.

Fletcher, Ronald. "Fréderic Le Play." In *The Founding Fathers of Social Science*, edited by Timothy Raison, 51–58. Baltimore: Penguin, 1969.

Floud, Jean. "Karl Mannheim." In *The Founding Fathers of Social Science*, edited by Timothy Raison, 204–13. Baltimore: Penguin Books, 1969.

Frazier, Thomas R., ed. *The Underside of American History*. Vol. 2, *Since 1865*. New York: Harcourt Brace Jovanovich, 1971.

Freud, Sigmund. *Civilization and Its Discontents*. 1930. Translated and edited by James Strachey. New York: W. W. Norton, 1962.

————. *Sexuality and the Psychology of Love*. Edited by Philip Rieff. New York: Collier Books, 1963.

Freund, Julien. *The Sociology of Max Weber*. Translated by Mary Ilford. New York: Vintage Books, 1968.

Frisby, David. *Georg Simmel*. Key Sociologists Series, edited by Peter Hamilton. Chichester, Sussex, England: Ellis Horwood. New York: Tavistock Publications, 1984.

Glazer, Nathan. "The Rise of Social Research in Europe." In *The Human Meaning of the Social Sciences*, edited by Daniel Lerner, 43–72. Cleveland: World Publishing Co., Meridian Books, 1959.

Glennon, Lynda M. *Women and Dualism: A Sociology of Knowledge Analysis*. New York: Longman, 1979.

Goldthorpe, John H. "Vilfredo Pareto." In *The Founding Fathers of Social Science*, edited by Timothy Raison, 110–18. Baltimore: Penguin Books, 1969.

Gordon, Ann D., Mari Jo Buhle, and Nancy Schrom Dye. "The Problem of Women's History." In *Liberating Women's History: Theoretical and Critical Essays*, edited by Berenice A. Carroll, 75–92. Urbana: University of Illinois Press, 1976.

Gough, Kathleen. "The Origin of the Family." In *Toward an Anthropology of Women*, edited by Rayna R. Reiter, 51–76. New York: Monthly Review Press, 1975.

Gouldner, Alvin W. "Anti-Minotaur: The Myth of a Value-Free Sociology."
    In *Sociology on Trial*, edited by Maurice Stein and Arthur Vidich,
    35–52. Englewood Cliffs, N.J.: Prentice-Hall, 1963.
————. *The Coming Crisis of Western Sociology*. New York: Avon Books,
    1971.
Green, Martin. *The Von Richthofen Sisters: The Triumphant and the
    Tragic Modes of Love: Else and Frieda von Richthofen, Otto Gross,
    Max Weber, and D. H. Lawrence, in the Years 1870–1970*. New
    York: Basic Books, 1974.
Hacker, Helen Mayer. "Women as a Minority Group." *Social Forces* 30
    (October 1951): 60–69.
Hackett, Amy. "Feminism and Liberalism in Wilhelmine Germany, 1890–
    1918." In *Liberating Women's History: Theoretical and Critical Es-
    says*, edited by Berenice A. Carroll, 127–36. Urbana: University of
    Illinois Press, 1976.
Haight, Gordon S. *George Eliot: A Biography*. London: Oxford University
    Press, 1976.
Hartz, Louis. *The Liberal Tradition in America: An Interpretation of
    American Political Thought since the Revolution*. New York: Har-
    court, Brace, 1955.
Heilbroner, Robert. *Marxism: For and Against*. New York: Norton, 1980.
Hellerstein, Erna Olafson, Leslie Parker Hume, and Karen M. Offen, eds.
    *Victorian Women: A Documentary Account of Women's Lives in
    Nineteenth-Century England, France, and the United States*. Stan-
    ford: Stanford University Press, 1981.
Hochschild, Arlie. "Emotional Labor in the Friendly Skies." In *Psychol-
    ogy Today* (June 1982): 13–15.
————. "Is the Left Sick of Feminism?" Review of *Public Man, Private
    Woman*, by Jean Bethke Elshtain, and *The Family in Political
    Thought*, by Jean Bethke Elshtain. *American Educator* (Profes-
    sional Journal of the American Federation of Teachers) 7, no. 2
    (Summer 1983): 56–58.
Hodgen, Margaret T. *Anthropology, History, and Cultural Change*. Tuc-
    son: University of Arizona Press, 1974.
Hofstadter, Richard. *Social Darwinism in American Thought*. 1944. Rev.
    ed. Boston: Beacon Press, 1955.
Hughes, H. Stuart. *Consciousness and Society: The Reorientation of
    European Social Thought, 1890–1930*. 1958. New York: Vintage
    Books, 1961.
Hughes, Helen MacGill, ed. *The Status of Women in Sociology, 1968–
    1972: Report to the American Sociological Association of the Com-
    mittee on the Status of Women*. Elise Boulding, chairperson. Wash-
    ington, D.C.: The American Sociological Association, 1973.
Jacoby, Robin Miller. "Feminism and Class Consciousness in the British

and American Women's Trade Union Leagues, 1890–1925." In *Liberating Women's History: Theoretical and Critical Essays*, edited by Berenice A. Carroll, 137–60. Urbana: University of Illinois Press, 1976.

———. "Science and Sex Roles in the Victorian Era." In *Biology as a Social Weapon*, edited by the Ann Arbor Science for the People Editorial Collective, 58–68. Minneapolis: Burgess Publishing Co., 1977.

Jaggar, Alison M., and Paula Rothenberg Struhl, eds. *Feminist Frameworks: Alternative Theoretical Accounts of the Relations between Women and Men*. New York: McGraw-Hill, 1978.

Janssen-Jurreit, Marie Louise. *Sexism: The Male Monopoly on History and Thought*. Translated by Verne Moberg. New York: Farrar, Straus and Giroux, 1982.

Johansson, Sheila Ryan. "'Herstory' as History: A New Field or Another Fad?" In *Liberating Women's History: Theoretical and Critical Essays*, edited by Berenice A. Carroll, 400–430. Urbana: University of Illinois Press, 1976.

Johnson, Barclay D. "Durkheim on Women." In *Woman in a Man-Made World: A Socioeconomic Handbook*, edited by Nona Glazer-Malbin and Helen Youngelson Waehrer, 164–67. New York: Rand-McNally & Co., 1972.

Jordanova, L. J. "Natural Facts: A Historical Perspective on Science and Sexuality." In *Nature, Culture and Gender*, edited by Carol P. MacCormack and Marilyn Strathern, 42–69. London: Cambridge University Press, 1980.

Kandal, Terry R. "The Sociology of Knowledge: A Restatement." Ph.D. diss., University of California, Berkeley, 1974.

Kanner, Barbara. "The Women of England in a Century of Social Change, 1815–1914: A Select Bibliography, Part 2." In *A Widening Sphere: Changing Roles of Victorian Women*, edited by Martha Vicinus, 199–318. Bloomington: Indiana University Press, 1977.

Kardiner, Abram, and Edward Preble. *They Studied Man*. New York: Mentor Books, 1963.

Klein, Alan M. "The Political Economy of Gender." In *The Hidden Half: Studies of Plains Indian Women*, edited by Patricia Albers. Washington, D.C.: University Press of America, 1983.

Komarovsky, Mirra. "Cultural Contradictions and Sex Roles." *American Journal of Sociology* (November 1946): 184–89.

La Vigna, Claire. "The Marxist Ambivalence toward Women: Between Socialism and Feminism in the Italian Socialist Party." In *Socialist Women: European Socialist Feminism in the Nineteenth and Early Twentieth Centuries*, edited by Marilyn J. Boxer and Jean H. Quataert, 146–81. New York: Elsevier North-Holland, 1978.

Lenzer, Gertrude, ed. *Auguste Comte and Positivism: The Essential Writings*. New York: Harper Torchbooks, 1975.

Levy, Darline Gay; Harriet Bronson Applewhite; and Mary Durham Johnson, eds. *Women in Revolutionary Paris, 1789–1795*. Selected documents, translated with notes and commentary. Urbana: University of Illinois Press, 1979.

Levy, Darline Gay; Mary Durham Johnson; and Harriet Branson Applewhite. "Women: The Failure of Liberation." In *The French Revolution: Conflicting Interpretations*, edited by Frank A. Kafker and James M. Laux, 261–66. 2d ed. New York: Random House, 1976.

Lichtheim, George. *The Concept of Ideology and Other Essays*. New York: Vintage Books, 1967.

————. *Marxism: An Historical and Critical Study*. 2d ed. New York: Frederick A. Praeger, 1965.

————. *A Short History of Socialism*. New York: Praeger Publishers, 1970.

Linz, Juan J. "Michels, Robert." In *International Encyclopedia of the Social Sciences*, edited by David L. Sills, 10: 265–72. New York: Macmillan Co. and the Free Press, 1968.

Lukes, Steven. *Emile Durkheim, His Life and Work: A Historical and Critical Study*. New York: Harper and Row, 1972.

Lynch, Frederick R. "Social Theory and the Progressive Era." *Theory and Society* 4 (1977): 159–210.

McBride, Theresa M. "The Long Road Home: Women's Work and Industrialization." In *Becoming Visible: Women in European History*, edited by Renate Bridenthal and Claudia Koonz, 282–94. Boston: Houghton Mifflin, 1977.

McDougall, Mary Lynn. "Working-Class Women during the Industrial Revolution, 1780–1914." In *Becoming Visible: Women in European History*, edited by Renate Bridenthal and Claudia Koonz, 257–78. Boston: Houghton Mifflin, 1977.

McMillan, James F. *Housewife or Harlot: The Place of Women in French Society, 1870–1940*. New York: St. Martin's Press, 1981.

Mannheim, Karl. *Essays on the Sociology of Culture*. Edited by Ernest Manheim, in cooperation with Paul Kecskemeti. London: Routledge and Kegan Paul, 1956.

————. *From Karl Mannheim*. Edited by Kurt H. Wolff. New York: Oxford University Press, 1978.

————. *Ideology and Utopia: An Introduction to the Sociology of Knowledge*. 1929. Translated by Louis Wirth and Edward Shils. New York: Harcourt, Brace and World, 1936.

Manuel, Frank E. *The Prophets of Paris*. Cambridge: Harvard University Press, 1962.

Marks, Elaine, and Isabelle de Courtivron, eds. *New French Feminisms: An Anthology*. Amherst: University of Massachusetts Press, 1980.

Marx, Eleanor, and Edward Aveling. "The Woman Question." *Green Mountain Quarterly*, no. 2 (February 1976): 5–17.

Marx, Karl. *Capital: A Critique of Political Economy*. Vol. 1, *The Process of Capitalist Production*. Edited by Friedrich Engels. Translated by Samuel Moore and Edward Aveling from the third German edition. Revised and amplified by Ernest Untermann according to the fourth German edition. New York: The Modern Library, n.d.

————. *The Civil War in France*. 1871. With an introduction by Friedrich Engels. New York: International Publishers. 1940.

————. *Contribution to the Critique of Hegel's "Philosophy of Right": Introduction*. In *On Religion*, by Karl Marx and Friedrich Engels, second impression, 41–58. Moscow: Foreign Languages Publishing House, 1955.

————. *Economic and Philosophic Manuscripts of 1844*. Translated by Martin Milligan. Second impression. Moscow: Foreign Languages Publishing House, 1961.

————. *The Eighteenth Brumaire of Louis Bonaparte*. Moscow: Foreign Languages Publishing House, n.d.

————. *Letters to Dr. Kugelmann*. Marxist Library: Works of Marxism-Leninism. Vol. 17. New York: International Publishers, 1934.

————. *The Secret Diplomatic History of the Eighteenth Century*, and *The Story of the Life of Lord Palmerston*. Edited by Lester Hutchinson. New York: International Publishers, 1969.

Marx, Karl, and Friedrich Engels. *The German Ideology*. Parts 1 and 3. Edited by R. Pascal. New York: International Publishers, 1947.

————. *The Holy Family; or, Critique of Critical Critique*. Translated by R. Dixon. Moscow: Foreign Languages Publishing House, 1956.

Matthews, Sarah H. "Rethinking Sociology Through a Feminist Perspective." *American Sociologist* 17, no. 1 (February 1982): 29–35.

Meisel, James H., ed. *Pareto and Mosca*. Englewood Cliffs, N.J.: Prentice-Hall, 1965.

Merton, Robert K. "Insiders and Outsiders: A Chapter in the Sociology of Knowledge." In *Varieties of Political Expression in Sociology*, edited by C. Arnold Anderson et al., 9–47. Chicago: University of Chicago Press, 1972.

Michels, Robert. *Political Parties: A Sociological Study of the Oligarchical Tendencies of Modern Democracy*. 1911. Translated by Eden Paul and Cedar Paul. Introduction by Seymour Martin Lipset. New York: Collier Books, 1962.

————. *Sexual Ethics: A Study of Borderland Questions*. 1911. New York: Charles Scribner's Sons, 1915.

Mill, John Stuart. *The Subjection of Women*. 1869. In *Essays on Sex Equality*, by John Stuart Mill and Harriet Taylor Mill, edited by Alice S. Rossi. Chicago: University of Chicago Press, 1970.

Miller, Alice. *Prisoners of Childhood*. Translated by Ruth Ward. New York: Basic Books, 1981.

Millett, Kate. "The Debate over Women: Ruskin vs. Mill." In *Suffer and Be Still: Women in the Victorian Age*, edited by Martha Vicinus, 121–39. Bloomington: Indiana University Press, 1972.

Mills, C. Wright. "IBM Plus Reality Plus Humanism = Sociology." In *Power, Politics and People: The Collected Essays of C. Wright Mills*, edited by Irving Louis Horowitz, 568–76. New York: Ballantine Books, 1963.

———. "Methodological Consequences of the Sociology of Knowledge." In *Power, Politics and People: The Collected Essays of C. Wright Mills*, edited by Irving Louis Horowitz, 453–68. New York: Ballantine Books, 1963.

———. "Plain Talk on Fancy Sex." 1952. In *Power, Politics and People: The Collected Essays of C. Wright Mills*, edited by Irving Louis Horowitz, 324–29. New York: Ballantine Books, 1963.

———. *The Sociological Imagination*. New York: Oxford University Press, 1959.

———. *White Collar: The American Middle Classes*. New York: Oxford University Press, 1956.

———. "Women: The Darling Little Slaves." 1953. In *Power, Politics and People: The Collected Essays of C. Wright Mills*, edited by Irving Louis Horowitz, 339–48. New York: Ballantine Books, 1963.

Mitchell, Juliet. *Psychoanalysis and Feminism: Freud, Reich, Laing, and Women*. New York: Vintage Books, 1974.

———. *Woman's Estate*. New York: Vintage Books, 1973.

Mitzman, Arthur. *The Iron Cage: An Historical Interpretation of Max Weber*. New York: Grosset & Dunlap, 1969.

———. *Sociology and Estrangement: Three Sociologists of Imperial Germany*. New York: Alfred A. Knopf, 1977.

Mogey, J. M. "A Century of Declining Paternal Authority." In *The Family and Change*, edited by John N. Edwards, 250–60. New York: Alfred A. Knopf, 1969.

Moon, S. Joan. "Feminism and Socialism: The Utopian Synthesis of Flora Tristan." In *Socialist Women: European Socialist Feminism in the Nineteenth and Early Twentieth Centuries*, edited by Marilyn J. Boxer and Jean H. Quataert, 19–50. New York: Elsevier North-Holland, 1978.

Moore, Barrington, Jr. *Injustice: The Social Basis of Obedience and Revolt*. White Plains, N.Y.: M. E. Sharpe, 1978.

———. *Social Origins of Dictatorship and Democracy: Lord and Peasant in the Making of the Modern World*. Boston: Beacon Press, 1966.

———. "Thoughts on the Future of the Family." In *The Family and*

Change, edited by John N. Edwards, 455–67. New York: Alfred A. Knopf, 1969.

Nisbet, Robert A. *The Sociological Tradition*. New York: Basic Books, 1966.

———, ed. *Emile Durkheim, with Selected Essays*. Englewood Cliffs, N.J.: Prentice-Hall, 1965.

Oakley, Ann. *The Sociology of Housework*. New York: Pantheon Books, 1974.

Okin, Susan Moller. *Women in Western Political Thought*. Princeton: Princeton University Press, 1979.

O'Neill, William L. "Feminism as a Radical Ideology." In *The Underside of American History: Other Readings*, vol. 2, *Since 1865*, edited by Thomas R. Frazier, 128–48. New York: Harcourt Brace Jovanovich, 1971.

Pareto, Vilfredo. *The Mind and Society [Trattato di sociologia generale]*. 4 vols. 1916. Edited by Arthur Livingston. Translated by Andrew Bongiorno and Arthur Livingston, with the advice and active cooperation of James Harvey Rogers. New York: Harcourt, Brace and Co., 1935.

Parsons, Talcott. "Age and Sex in the Social Structure of the United Morris Zelditch, Jr., and Philip E. Slater. *Family, Socialization, and Interaction Process*. Glencoe, Ill.: Free Press, 1955.

Peel, J. D. Y. *Herbert Spencer: The Evolution of a Sociologist*. London: Heinemann, 1971.

Pope, Barbara Corrado. "Angels in the Devil's Workshop: Leisured and Charitable Women in Nineteenth-Century England and France." In *Becoming Visible: Women in European History*, edited by Renate Bridenthal and Claudia Koonz, 298–323. Boston: Houghton Mifflin, 1977.

Pope, Whitney. *Durkheim's Suicide: A Classic Analyzed*. Chicago: University of Chicago Press, 1976.

Quataert, Jean H. *Reluctant Feminists in German Social Democracy, 1885–1917*. Princeton: Princeton University Press, 1979.

Radcliffe-Brown, A. R. "On the Concept of Function in Social Science." *American Anthropologist* 37 (July–September 1935): 394–402.

Raison, Timothy, ed. *The Founding Fathers of Social Science*. Baltimore: Penguin Books, 1969.

Reich, Wilhelm. *The Sexual Revolution: Toward a Self-Regulating Character Structure*. Translated by Therese Pol. New York: Farrar Straus and Giroux, 1974.

Richter, Melvin. "Durkheim's Politics and Political Theory." In *Emile Durkheim et al., Essays on Sociology and Philosophy*, edited by Kurt H. Wolff, 170–210. New York: Harper and Row, 1964.

Rieff, Philip. *Freud: The Mind of the Moralist*. Garden City, N.Y.: Doubleday and Co., Anchor Books, 1961.

Rigney, Barbara Hill. *Madness and Sexual Politics in the Feminist Novel: Studies in Bronte, Woolf, Lessing, and Atwood.* Madison: University of Wisconsin Press, 1978.

Rosaldo, Michelle Zimbalist. "Woman, Culture, and Society: A Theoretical Overview." In *Woman, Culture, and Society,* edited by Michelle Zimbalist Rosaldo and Louise Lamphere, 17–42. Stanford University Press, 1974.

Rossi, Alice S. "Equality between the Sexes: An Immodest Proposal." In *The Woman in America,* edited by Stephen R. Graubard. *Daedalus* 93, no. 2 (Summer 1964): 607–52.

———. "Sentiment and Intellect: The Story of John Stuart Mill and Harriet Taylor Mill." In *Essays on Sex Equality,* by John Stuart Mill and Harriet Taylor Mill, edited by Alice S. Rossi. Chicago: University of Chicago Press, 1970.

———. "Sex Equality: The Beginnings of Ideology." *The Humanist* (September/October 1969): 3–6.

———, ed. *Essays on Sex Equality,* by John Stuart Mill and Harriet Taylor Mill. Chicago: University of Chicago Press, 1970.

———, ed. *The Feminist Papers: From Adams to de Beauvoir.* New York: Columbia University Press, 1973.

Roszak, Betty, and Theodore Roszak, eds. *Masculine/Feminine: Readings in Sexual Mythology and the Liberation of Women.* New York: Harper and Row, 1969.

Roszak, Theodore. "The Hard and the Soft: The Force of Feminism in Modern Times." In *Masculine/Feminine: Readings in Sexual Mythology and the Liberation of Women,* edited by Betty Roszak and Theodore Roszak, 87–104. New York: Harper and Row, 1969.

Roth, Guenther. "Weber's Generational Rebellion and Maturation." In *Scholarship and Partisanship: Essays on Max Weber,* edited by Reinhard Bendix and Guenther Roth, 6–33. Berkeley and Los Angeles: University of California Press, 1971.

Rowbotham, Sheila. *Hidden from History: Rediscovering Women in History from the Seventeenth Century to the Present.* New York: Vintage Books, 1976.

———. *Women, Resistance and Revolution: A History of Women and Revolution in the Modern World.* New York: Vintage Books, 1974.

Rubin, Gayle. "The Traffic in Women." In *Feminist Frameworks: Alternative Theoretical Accounts of the Relations between Women and Men,* edited by Alison M. Jaggar and Paula Rothenberg Struhl, 154–67. New York: McGraw-Hill, 1978.

Rubin, Lillian Breslow. *Worlds of Pain: Life in the Working-Class Family.* New York: Basic Books, 1976.

Sacks, Karen. *Sisters and Wives: The Past and Future of Sexual Equality.*

Contributions in Women's Studies, no. 10. Westport, Conn.: Greenwood Press, 1979.

Schneir, Miriam, ed. *Feminism: The Essential Historical Writings*. New York: Random House, 1972.

Schwartz, Leon. "F. M. Grimm and the Eighteenth-Century Debate on Women." *The French Review* 58, no. 2 (December 1984): 236–43.

Schwendinger, Herman, and Julia R. Schwendinger. *The Sociologists of the Chair: A Radical Analysis of the Formative Years of North American Sociology (1883–1922)*. New York: Basic Books, 1974.

Schwendinger, Julia R., and Herman Schwendinger. "Sociology's Founding Fathers: Sexists to a Man." *Journal of Marriage and the Family* 33, no. 4 (November 1971): 783–99.

"Science Fiction on Women—Science Fiction by Women." In *Science-Fiction Studies*, vol. 7, part 1, no. 20 (March 1980): 1–72.

Segal, Marcia Texler, and Catherine White Berheide. "Toward a Women's Perspective in Sociology: Directions and Prospects." In *Theoretical Perspectives in Sociology*, edited by Scott G. McNall. New York: St. Martin's Press, 1979.

Selvin, Hanan C. "Durkheim's *Suicide:* Further Thoughts on a Methodological Classic." In *Emile Durkheim, with Selected Essays*, edited by Robert A. Nisbet, 113–36. Englewood Cliffs, N.J.: Prentice-Hall, 1965.

Shaffer, Robert. "Women and the Communist Party, USA, 1930–1940." *Socialist Review* number 45, vol. 9, no. 3 (May–June 1979): 73–118.

Simmel, Georg. *Conflict and the Web of Group Affiliations*. 1908. Translated by Kurt H. Wolff and Reinhard Bendix. New York: Free Press, 1964.

———. *Georg Simmel*. Edited by Lewis A. Coser, Englewood Cliffs, N.J.: Prentice-Hall, 1965.

———. *Georg Simmel on Individuality and Social Forms, Selected Writings*. Edited by Donald N. Levine. Chicago: University of Chicago Press, 1971.

———. *Georg Simmel: On Women, Sexuality, and Love*. Edited by Guy Oakes. New Haven: Yale University Press, 1984.

———. *The Sociology of Georg Simmel*. Edited and translated by Kurt H. Wolff. New York: Free Press, 1950.

Smelser, Neil J. *Social Change in the Industrial Revolution*. London: Routledge and Kegan Paul, 1959.

———. "Sociological History: The Industrial Revolution and the British Working-Class Family." In *Essays in Sociological Explanation*, by Neil J. Smelser. Englewood Cliffs, N.J.: Prentice-Hall, 1968.

Smith, Joan. "Feminist Analysis of Gender: A Critique." In *Woman's Nature: Rationalizations of Inequality*, edited by Marian Lowe and Ruth Hubbard, 89–110. New York: Pergamon Press, 1983.

Snodgrass, Jon. "Patriarchy and Phantasy: A Conception of Psychoanalytic
     Sociology." *American Journal of Psychoanalysis* 43, no. 3 (Fall
     1983): 261–75.
Snyder, Eloise C. "The Selective Eye of Sociology." In *The Study of Women:
     Enlarging Perspectives of Social Reality,* edited by Eloise C. Snyder,
     39–78. New York: Harper and Row, 1979.
Snyder, Eloise C., ed. *The Study of Women: Enlarging Perspectives of So-
     cial Reality.* New York: Harper and Row, 1979.
Spencer, Herbert. *An Autobiography.* 1904. Vols. 1 and 2. Reprint. Osna-
     brück: Otto Zeller, 1966.
———. *The Principles of Biology.* 1874. Vol. 1. Reprint of 1898 edition.
     Osnabück: Otto Zeller, 1966.
———. *The Principles of Psychology.* 1899. Vols. 1 and 2. Reprint. Osna-
     brück: Otto Zeller, 1966.
———. *The Principles of Sociology.* 1876. Vol. 1. New York: D. Appleton
     and Company, 1899.
———. "Progress: Its Law and Cause." 1857. From *Essays, Scientific, Po-
     litical, and Speculative.* 1891. In *The Idea of Progress: A Collection
     of Readings, Selected by Frederick J. Teggart,* rev. ed., with an in-
     troduction by George H. Hildebrand, 435–47. Berkeley and Los
     Angeles: University of California Press, 1949.
———. *Social Statics; or, The Conditions Essential to Human Happi-
     ness Specified and the First of Them Developed.* 1851. New York:
     Augustus M. Kelley Publishers, 1969.
———. *The Study of Sociology.* 1873. With an introduction by Talcott Par-
     sons. Ann Arbor: University of Michigan Press, 1961.
Stanley, John L., ed. *From Georges Sorel: Essays in Socialism and Philoso-
     phy.* Translated by John Stanley and Charlotte Stanley. New York:
     Oxford University Press, 1976.
Stark, Werner. "In Search of the True Pareto." In *Pareto and Mosca,* ed-
     ited by James H. Meisel, 45–55. Englewood Cliffs, N.J.: Prentice-
     Hall, 1965.
Steinem, Gloria. "The Nazi Connection." *MS,* October–November 1980.
Stockard, Jean, and Miriam M. Johnson. *Sex Roles: Sex Inequality and Sex
     Role Development.* Englewood Cliffs, N.J.: Prentice-Hall, 1980.
Tax, Meredith. *The Rising of Women: Feminist Solidarity and Class Con-
     flict, 1880–1917.* New York: Monthly Review Press, 1980.
Teggart, Frederick J. *The Idea of Progress: A Collection of Readings Se-
     lected by Frederick J. Teggart.* Revised edition, with an introduc-
     tion by George H. Hildebrand. Berkeley and Los Angeles: Univer-
     sity of California Press, 1949.
———. *Theory and Processes of History.* 2d ed. Preface by Kenneth Bock.
     Berkeley and Los Angeles: University of California Press, 1977.
Tentori, Tullio. "Italy." Translated by Larissa Bonfante Warren. In *Women*

in the Modern World, edited by Raphael Patai, 153–75. New York: Free Press, 1967.

Thomas, Edith. *The Women Incendiaries*. Translated by James Atkinson and Starr Atkinson. New York: George Braziller, 1966.

Thompson, E. P. *The Making of the English Working Class*. London: Victor Gollancz, Ltd., 1963.

Thönnessen, Werner. *The Emancipation of Women: The Rise and Decline of the Women's Movement in German Social Democracy, 1863–1933*. Translated by Joris de Bres. London: Pluto Press, 1983.

Tiryakian, Edward A. "Emile Durkheim." In *A History of Sociological Analysis*, edited by Tom Bottomore and Robert Nisbet, 187–236. New York: Basic Books, 1978.

Tocqueville, Alexis de. *Democracy in America*. 2 vols. 1835, 1840. Translated by George Lawrence. Edited by J. P. Mayer and Max Lerner. New York: Harper and Row, 1966.

———. *The Old Regime and the French Revolution*. Translated by Stuart Gilbert. Garden City, N.Y.: Doubleday and Co., Anchor Books, 1955.

Tönnies, Ferdinand. *Community and Association [Gemeinschaft und Gesellschaft]*. 1887. Translated by Charles P. Loomis. London: Routledge and Kegan Paul, 1955.

———. *Ferdinand Tönnies on Sociology: Pure, Applied and Empirical, Selected Writings*. Edited by Werner J. Cahnman and Rudolf Heberle. Chicago: University of Chicago Press, 1971.

Vann, Richard T. "Toward a New Lifestyle: Women in Preindustrial Capitalism." In *Becoming Visible: Women in European History*, edited by Renate Bridenthal and Claudia Koonz. Boston: Houghton Mifflin, 1977.

Veblen, Thorstein. "The Theory of the Leisure Class." In *Feminism: The Essential Historical Writings*, edited by Miriam Schneir. New York: Random House, 1972.

Vicinus, Martha, ed. *Suffer and Be Still: Women in the Victorian Age*. Bloomington: Indiana University Press, 1972.

———, ed. *A Widening Sphere: Changing Roles of Victorian Women*. Bloomington: Indiana University Press, 1977.

Vogel, Lise. "Questions on the Woman Question." *Monthly Review* 31 (June 1979): 35–59.

Weber, Max. *From Max Weber: Essays in Sociology*. Edited and translated by H. H. Gerth and C. Wright Mills. New York: Oxford University Press, 1958.

———. *General Economic History*. 1924. Translated by Frank H. Knight. Glencoe, Ill.: Free Press, 1950.

———. "The Household Community." 1922. Translated by Ferdinand Kolegar from *Wirtschaft und Gesellschaft*. In *Theories of Society:*

Foundations of Modern Sociological Theory, edited by Talcott Parsons, Edward Shils, Kaspar D. Naegele, and Jesse R. Pitts. New York: Free Press, 1964.

————. *Max Weber: Selections in Translation*. Edited by W. G. Runciman. Translated by E. Matthews. Cambridge: Cambridge University Press, 1978.

————. "Politics as a Vocation." 1919. In *From Max Weber: Essays in Sociology*, edited and translated by H. H. Gerth and C. Wright Mills. New York: Oxford University Press, 1958.

————. *The Protestant Ethic and the Spirit of Capitalism*. 1904–5. Translated by Talcott Parsons. With a foreword by R. H. Tawney. New York: Charles Scribner's Sons, 1958.

————. "Religious Rejections of the World and Their Directions." 1915. In *From Max Weber: Essays in Sociology*, edited and translated by H. H. Gerth and C. Wright Mills. New York: Oxford University Press, 1958.

————. *The Sociology of Religion*. 1922. Translated by Ephraim Fischoff. Boston: Beacon Press, 1963.

Weisstein, Naomi. "'Kinder, Küche, Kirche' as Scientific Law: Psychology Constructs the Female. In *Sisterhood Is Powerful: An Anthology of Writings from the Women's Liberation Movement*, edited by Robin Morgan. New York: Vintage Books, 1970.

Westkott, Marcia. "Feminist Criticism of the Social Sciences." *Harvard Educational Review* 49, no. 4 (November 1979): 422–30.

Williams, Raymond. *Culture and Society, 1780–1950*. New York: Harper and Row, 1966.

Wilson, William Julius. *The Declining Significance of Race*. Chicago: University of Chicago Press, 1978.

Young, Robert. "The Historiographic and Ideological Contexts of the Nineteenth-Century Debate on Man's Place in Nature." In *Changing Perspectives in the History of Science: Essays in Honor of Joseph Needham*, edited by Mikulas Teich and Robert Young, 344–438. Boston: D. Reidel Publishing Co., 1973.

Zeitlin, Irving M. *Ideology and the Development of Sociological Theory*. 2d ed. Englewood Cliffs, N.J.: Prentice-Hall, 1981.

Index

Adams, Abigail, 213, 214
Adams, John, 213
Addams, Jane, 221
Anderson, Perry, 228
Andreas-Salomé, Lou, 115, 157, 178
Anthony, Susan B., 216–17, 218
Antifeminism, 116, 121, 170–71, 198, 214,
    258; in Germany, 92, 97, 98, 115,
    116–17, 126, 185; in Italy, 195–201, 211;
    proletarian, 90, 99, 120
Aristotle, 72, 247
Aron, Raymond, 77
Auclert, Hubertine, 65, 66
Audouard, Olympe, 58
Augspurg, Anita, 102, 103, 104, 106, 116

Baader, Ottilie, 93, 95, 96, 98, 118
Bachofen, J. J., 110, 112, 133, 178
Bakunin, Mikhail, 62, 91, 190
Balabanov, Angelica, 190, 219
Baum, Marie, 114
Bäumer, Gertrud, 114, 116, 125
Baumgarten family, 131
Baxandall, Rosalyn, 220
Beard, Mary, 223–24, 271
Beauvoir, Simone de, 29, 240–42, 271

Bebel, August, 91, 92–93, 98, 124, 125,
    147, 190, 255, 269
Bentham, Jeremy, 23, 47
Bernard, Jessie, 247, 248, 278
Bernstein, Eduard, 96
Besant, Annie, 21
Bieber-Böhm, Hanna, 102
Birth control, 16–17, 21, 23, 96, 105, 117,
    210, 221, 225, 262
Bismarck, Otto von, 92, 94, 100, 108–9,
    116; opposition to, 111, 112, 113, 115,
    131, 132, 157; and patriarchy, 110,
    128–29, 134, 135
Blake, William, 12
Blanqui, Auguste, 58, 61, 62
Blatchford, Robert, 20
Bloch, Jean H., 51
Bloch, Maurice, 51
Bonaparte, Louis-Napoléon (Emperor
    Napoléon III), 56, 57, 108, 209
Borgius, Walter, 106
Bradlaugh, Charles, 21
Braun, Heinrich, 96, 106
Braun, Lily, 96, 97, 99, 106, 124
Bré, Ruth, 105–6
Brinton, Crane, 201

Brion, Hélène, 66
Broadhurst, Henry, 20
Brochon, Victorine, 57
Browne, Stella, 117
Bryant, Louise, 219
Buhle, Mari Jo, 220
Butler, Josephine, 19, 102

Cabet, Étienne, 56
Capitalism, industrial, 5, 7, 10, 13, 32, 67,
    89, 101, 173, 186; and family, 97, 180–
    82, 257, 277, 278–79; and feminism, 8,
    218, 224, 227, 243, 258; and oppression
    of women, 58, 93, 216; vs. socialism,
    94, 122–23, 177; and status of women,
    31, 126, 139, 181–82, 200, 260, 274,
    276–77, 279
Carlile, Richard, 16–17
Carlyle, Jane, 24
Carlyle, Thomas, 30
Carpenter, Edward, 20, 219
Castellani, Maria, 211
Cauer, Minna, 102, 103, 106
Chodorow, Nancy, 269, 273
Christianity, 66, 77, 83, 105, 136, 140,
    141, 142, 154, 190, 197
Civil Code (Germany), 102, 103
Civil Code of 1804 (France), 53, 187
Collins, Randall, 270, 274, 275, 280
Combination Law (Germany), 91, 94,
    95–96, 97
Communism, 77, 90, 112, 114, 219, 263
The Communist Manifesto (Marx and En-
    gels), 278
Comte, Auguste, 3, 6, 7, 32, 46, 47, 51,
    74–79, 80; Cours de philosophie posi-
    tive, 74, 78; evaluation of, 253, 262;
    and Pareto, 193, 194; and Tönnies, 177,
    178, 257
Condorcet, Marquis de, 5–6, 51–52
Coser, Lewis A., 78, 156–60, 176–77,
    184, 193, 194, 196
Cosmic Circle (Germany), 110–11, 115
Cott, Nancy, 213
Crispi, Francesco, 191
Croce, Benedetto, 189, 191, 192, 194
Cunow, Heinrich, 147

Darwin, Charles, 46, 47, 48
Daubié, Julie, 57–58
David, Eduard, 106
Debs, Eugene V., 220
Degler, Carl N., 218–19, 221, 222, 223,
    227
Demar, Claire, 54
Democracy, 68–74, 115, 117, 127, 192,

212, 217; and feminism, 125, 198; in
    Greece, 142, 148
Deraismes, Maria, 57, 58, 65
Deroin, Jeanne, 56, 62
Diderot, Denis, 51
Dilthey, Wilhelm, 105, 128
Divorce, 84, 85, 200, 223, 251, 253, 265;
    in England, 17, 19, 43; in France, 7, 51,
    53, 54, 58, 66, 77, 88; in United States,
    234
Dixon, Marlene, 226
Dmitrieff, Elizabeth, 60, 63
Domination, male, 158–59, 186, 240,
    256, 257, 261, 273–74; theories of, 2,
    138–39, 185, 255, 280. See also Family,
    patriarchal; Patriarchy
du Camp, Maxime, 59
Dumas, Alexandre, fils, 59
Dunker, Käthe, 118
Durand, Marguerite, 66
Durkheim, Emile, 7, 48, 50, 64–65, 66,
    67, 79–88, 140, 204; The Division of
    Labor in Society, 79–81, 88, 234,
    253–54, 259; The Elementary Forms of
    Religious Life, 139; evaluation of,
    253–54, 261, 262; Suicide, 79, 81–88,
    168, 176, 234, 254, 261, 262

Education, 41, 50–51, 56, 61, 76, 178,
    187, 228, 229; debates over, in France,
    50, 52, 57–58, 61; equal, 5–6, 7, 24,
    25, 166; exclusion of women from, 10,
    12, 44, 100; feminine, 26, 117; in Ger-
    many, 124, 133, 158
Eisner, Kurt, 135
Elshtain, Jean Bethke, 30, 50
Ender, Emma, 125
Enfantin, Barthélemy Prosper, 17, 54
Engels, Friedrich, 29, 49, 90, 116, 159,
    190, 252, 255, 265, 278; The Condition
    of the Working Class in England, 219;
    on family, 16, 151–52, 153, 198; feminist
    interpretations of, 262–65, 270; The
    Origin of the Family, Private Property,
    and the State, 93, 264–65, 269; and
    theory of mother-right, 133, 147
England, 6, 7, 10–48, 204, 222, 250; the-
    orists in, 22–48, 254
Enlightenment, 4, 49–54, 127, 143, 196,
    261; and feminism, 5, 12, 49–53, 67,
    212, 263; reaction against, 74, 183, 210,
    250, 261
Equality, 7, 8, 11, 18, 27–28, 33, 43–45,
    72–73, 141; and family, 68, 77, 86, 253;
    legal, 124, 250; in marriage, 162, 275;
    and natural order, 5, 212; and sex dif-

ferences, 70–71, 75, 77, 86, 88, 152, 198, 209, 269, 276, 280
Equal pay, 9, 90, 91, 94, 95, 225
Equal Rights Amendment, 222, 225
Erotic movement (Germany), 89, 108–18, 126, 134, 135, 136, 142, 158, 167, 174, 176, 255
Esquiros, Adèle, 58
Evans, Marian (George Eliot), 45, 47
Evans, Richard J., 100, 101, 102, 104, 106, 107, 167
Excoffon, Béatrix, 60, 63

Family, 2–3, 5, 10, 261, 269, 271, 280; abolition of, 20, 54; authoritarian German, 109; effects of democracy on, 68–72; extended, 130, 153–54; and factory system, 10, 15, 20, 97; and feminism, 67, 275; and French Revolution, 53; and morality, 67, 76; nuclear, 3, 17, 41, 137, 185, 233–34, 252, 260, 279; origins of, 39–40; propaganda for, 117; and public life, 92, 99; as social unit, 3, 8, 13, 67, 74, 184, 189, 226, 228, 265; vs. state, 40–41; and suicide rates, 83; in tribal life, 171–72; and women's rights, 19, 130, 155, 253; and work, 3, 13, 16, 223, 227
Family, patriarchal, 3, 11, 15, 47, 67, 71, 81, 130, 163; criticism of, 74, 86, 105, 266, 268; universality of, 3, 198, 261. See also Domination, male; Patriarchy
Fascism, 124, 125, 185, 191, 194, 210, 211, 225, 257, 275
Femininity, 3, 91, 99, 223, 241–42, 252–53, 256, 268
Feminism: and capitalism, 8, 66, 74, 182, 218, 222, 224, 227, 243, 246, 258; and classical sociological theory, 1–9, 204, 246; and conservatism, 226–27; and Freudianism, 266; and labor movement, 217, 219; and liberal social theory, 7, 10–22, 89, 90, 99–107, 114, 174, 185, 211, 217, 258; and Marxism, 269, 272; middle-class, 96, 100–107, 116, 126, 173, 174, 217, 218, 221, 222, 277; and radicalism, 65, 124, 217, 219, 221, 225, 258; and revolution, 49–67, 278; scholarship of, 1–2, 3, 246, 272, 273; socialist, 7, 58, 65, 89, 90–99, 118–26, 185, 190, 211, 212, 215, 220–21. See also Antifeminism; Socialism: and feminism; individual countries
Finney, Charles Grandison, 213, 214
Firestone, Shulamith, 266
Fischer, Edmund, 97, 120

Flynn, Elizabeth Gurley, 219
Fonseca, Eleonora de, 187
Fonseca, Fornarina de, 61, 187
Fourier, Charles, 16, 17, 54–55, 263
Fox, William J., 12, 23
France, 5–6, 7, 24, 49–88, 212, 213, 215; theorists in, 67–88, 254, 261; tradition of sociology in, 67, 252, 254. See also French Revolution
Franco-Prussian War, 59–60, 64, 116
Frazier, Thomas K., 221–22
French Revolution, 187; and feminism, 4, 5, 6, 12, 16, 52, 54, 215, 252; women in, 52–53, 59
Freud, Sigmund, 3, 8, 106, 268–69, 270, 275; feminist interpretations of, 1, 2, 245, 262, 266, 267, 268, 270; influence of, 111–12, 135–36, 139, 141, 176, 185, 200, 219, 223
Freund, Julien, 127
Friedan, Betty, 227
Frisby, David, 157
Fuller, Margaret, 215, 254

Gay, Désirée, 56
George, Stefan, 111, 114, 158
German Communist Party, 123
The German Ideology (Marx and Engels), 200, 263
Germany, 6, 7, 89–185, 208, 258; anti-Semitism in, 111, 115, 125; erotic movement in, 108–18; Heidelberg as anti-Bismarck center, 114–15, 117; liberal feminism in, 99–107, 162; New Morality in, 106–7, 116; revolutions in, 89, 119, 258; socialist feminism in, 90–99, 185, 212, 213; theorists of, 126–85, 197, 254, 257, 261–62; women's associations in, 90, 100, 102, 103, 104, 107, 116, 125
Gerth, H. H., 127, 131, 154
Gilman, Charlotte Perkins, 29, 219, 220, 227
Godwin, William, 12
Goethe, 145, 164
Goldman, Emma, 217, 219
Gordon, Linda, 220
Gouges, Olympe de, 53
Gough, Kathleen, 272–73
Green, Martin, 108, 109, 111, 113, 116, 132, 219; on Heidelberg, 114–15, 117; on Weber family, 128–29, 132–37, 156
Grévy, Jules, 65
Grimké, Angelina, 214
Gross, Frieda Schloffer, 112, 116, 134
Gross, Hanns, 111, 116

Gross, Otto, 111–12, 113, 114, 142, 155,
    156; arrest of, 116; on Bismarck, 134;
    death of, 117; and Freud, 135–36; and
    Platonism, 164; *The Secondary Func-
    tion of the Brain*, 111
Grünberg, Helene, 93, 98, 100, 120

Hanna, Gertrud, 95, 98, 119, 120
Hays, Mary, 12
Helvétius, Claude Adrien
Henderson, L. J., 201
d'Héricourt, Jenny, 57
Heuss, Theodor, 115
Heuss-Knapp, Elly, 115, 157
Heymann, Lida Gustava, 102, 103, 104,
    106, 116
Hindenberg, Paul von, 125
Hitler, Adolph, 126, 135
d'Holbach, Baron, 51
The Holy Family (Marx and Engels), 263
Homans, George, 201
Homosexuality, 20, 111, 112
Honigsheim, Paul, 157
Hughes, H. Stuart, 126–27, 132, 192, 210
Hugo, Victor, 63, 64
Hyndman, H. M., 49

Ibsen, Henrik, 99, 110, 219
Ihrer, Emma, 94, 95, 97, 98, 100
Industrial Revolution, 4, 5, 10, 13–16, 20,
    42–43, 218, 237. *See also* Capitalism,
    industrial
Italian Socialist Party, 190, 202
Italy, 6, 7, 8, 24, 185, 186–211; theorists
    in, 192–211, 258–59. *See also* Fascism

Jaclard, Anna, 60–61, 63
Jacoby, Robin Miller, 217–18, 277
Jaffe, Edgar, 114, 117, 132, 136, 163
Jaffe, Elsa. *See* Richtofen, Elsa von
Jaspers, Gertrud, 114
Jaspers, Karl, 127
Jaszi, Oscar, 183
Johansson, Sheila Ryan, 4, 186, 271
Jones, Mary Harris (Mother Jones), 219
Juchacz, Marie, 93, 118, 119, 121, 123
Jung, Carl G., 116
Jung, Franz, 116

Kähler, Wilhelmine, 93, 119
Kant, Immanuel, 96, 136, 159, 167, 257
Kantorowicz, Gertrude, 158
Kautsky, Karl, 94, 96, 98
Kelley, Florence, 219–20
Klages, Ludwig, 110–11, 115
Knowlton, Charles, 2

Kromayer, Ernst, 106
Kropotkin, Peter, 112, 219
Kuliscioff, Anna, 190

Labriola, Antonio, 194
Lacombe, Claire, 53
Lafargue, Paul, 66
Lamarck, Jean-Baptiste, 40, 269
Lamber, Juliette, 57
La Mettrie, Julien, 51
Lange, Helene, 100, 103, 114, 116
Lassalle, Ferdinand, 90, 91
La Vigna, Claire, 188, 189, 190
Lawrence, D. H., 111, 113–14, 116, 156,
    167
Lebensphilosophie movement, 110, 126
Lefebvre, Blanche, 61
Legislation, 19, 124, 153; and control of
    property, 11, 19, 66, 174, 224; and
    equality, 52, 95, 124, 251; and mar-
    riage, 60, 107, 206, 253; protective, 9,
    20, 94, 95, 190, 277. *See also* Divorce
Lemel, Nathalie, 57, 61, 63
Lemonnier, Élisa, 57
Lenin, V. I., 99, 115, 134
Léo, André, 58, 59, 62, 63
Léon, Pauline, 53
Leo XIII, Pope, 190
Le Play, Frédéric, 67
Liebknecht, Karl, 118
Liebknecht, Wilhelm, 91
Lindner, Gisela, 202
Linz, Juan, 202, 204, 209
Lombroso, Cesare, 189
Louvet, Victorine, 62
Lukács, Georg, 9, 115, 118, 183
Luther, Martin, 140, 145
Luxemburg, Rosa, 93, 96, 98, 118

Machiavelli, 186, 192, 193, 194, 195
McMillan, James F., 65, 66, 67
Malon, Benoît, 59
Malthus, 17, 21, 46, 96, 221
Mannheim, Karl, 7, 126, 182–85, 257,
    262
Marcuse, Herbert, 112, 227
Marriage, 7, 39, 51, 83–88, 160, 205–7,
    253; attacks on, 54; Christian, 17, 140,
    144; companionate, 183, 184, 251; and
    equality, 30, 33, 86–87, 223; and femi-
    nism, 49, 57, 58, 214; Greek, 161, 183;
    group, 152; in history of family, 80, 137,
    154, 180, 275; and love, 70, 106, 161–
    63, 183, 259; and new morality, 175,
    223; and property, 19, 69, 154, 263,
    275; Roman, 154; and subordination of

women, 69, 74–75, 183; and suicide
rates, 83–84, 87, 88, 253–54; and
women's suffrage, 19; and work, 13,
223, 227, 229, 243; and working class,
57, 208. *See also* Family, patriarchal;
Legislation: and marriage; Monogamy;
Patriarchy
Martineau, Harriet, 24, 47, 73
Marx, Karl, 1, 2, 57, 60, 66, 90, 118, 159,
170; *Capital*, 263; *The Civil War in
France*, 59, 64; criticisms of, 96, 146,
154; *The Eighteenth Brumaire of Louis
Bonaparte*, 61, 171; on family, 263–64;
on feminism and social change, 280;
feminist interpretations of, 262–64,
270; on history, 13, 246; on humor, 156;
influence of, 177, 190, 260; on love,
164; Michels and, 202, 210; Pareto and,
194, 201; Paris manuscripts of 1844,
167, 263; and patriarchy, 182; and
reformism, 202; and women workers,
91, 93
Marxism: in England, 21, 29; and feminism, 245, 257, 258, 261, 262, 265,
269, 270, 274; in France, 66; in Germany, 7, 98, 119, 125, 126, 257; in Italy,
8; in United States, 226, 228
Massin, Caroline, 78
Matthews, Sarah, 246
Matriarchy, 110–11, 133, 146–47, 151, 154,
163, 264, 272
Mazzini, Guiseppe, 88, 193
Mead, Margaret, 184
Mehring, Franz, 118
Meisel-Hess, Grete, 115
Michel, Louise, 57, 58, 61, 62, 63, 64
Michels, Robert, 98, 125, 192–211; on
bourgeois society, 203–4; on coquetry,
210; evaluation of, 258–59, 262; on
family planning, 207; on feminism, 202,
207; on male psychology, 205, 206, 210;
on Marxism, 202; and Mussolini,
210–11; on oligarchy, 118, 201–2; *Political Parties*, 97, 201, 202–3, 204; on
pornography, 209; *Problems of Social
Philosophy*, 204; on prostitution, 203,
206, 259; on sex role inequality, 206–7;
Sexual Ethics, 8, 204–10, 258, 259
Mill, James, 17
Mill, John Stuart, 7, 11, 12, 16, 17–18,
22–32, 33, 247; and birth control, 23,
262; and contemporary feminists, 246;
death of, 21; on education of women,
26–27, 31, 186; evaluations of, 29–32,
250–51, 261, 262; and family, 27, 29,
30–31, 42, 250–51; and marriage, 28,

30; on nature of women, 25–26, 31; on
patriarchy, 24, 251; on sex roles, 24–
25, 29; and Spencer, 34, 46; *The Subjection of Women*, 19, 22–32, 34, 35,
189, 250; utilitarianism of, 23, 28, 33;
and women's suffrage, 31–32, 34
Mills, C. Wright, 8, 127, 131, 154, 235–
44; compared with Parsons, 243, 260;
evaluation of, 260–61, 262; "IBM Plus
Reality Plus Humanism = Sociology,"
235; "Plain Talk on Fancy Sex," 239;
The Power Elite, 227; on sex roles, 226,
241; *The Sociological Imagination*, 227,
235; *White Collar*, 222, 236–37, 260;
"Women: The Darling Little Slaves,"
240–43
Minck, Paule, 58, 63
Mitchell, Hannah, 21
Mitchell, Juliet, 226, 266, 267, 268, 272,
279
Mitzman, Arthur, 133, 136, 155, 158, 178,
203, 204, 210
Mommsen, Theodor, 128
Monogamy, 10, 11, 40–43, 97, 112, 140,
154, 210, 265. *See also* Marriage
Montesquieu, 50, 67
Moore, Barrington, Jr., 260
Morality, sexual, 69, 200–201, 204, 205,
209, 258; and class, 20, 208; double
standard in, 17, 23, 71, 102, 104, 161,
169, 206, 223, 275; freedom in, 54,
104–5
Morgan, Lewis Henry, 146, 178, 264
Mosca, Gaetano, 127, 202
Mozzoni, Anna Maria, 189
Müller, Moritz, 90
Mussolini, 125, 191, 194, 210, 211
Mutterschütz League, 105, 107

Napoléon, 53–54, 125, 129, 186
Napoleonic Code. *See* Civil Code of 1804
National Council of Italian Women, 189,
190, 191
Naumann, Friedrich, 106, 115
Nazism, 115, 124, 125, 126, 184, 185
Niboyet, Eugénie, 56
Nietzsche, Friedrich, 105, 112, 219

Oakes, Guy, 175, 176
Okin, Susan Moller, 22, 30, 50, 247, 260,
261, 265
Otto-Peters, Luise, 90
Owen, Robert, 16, 17

Pankhurst, Emmeline, 19, 20, 21
Pankhurst, Sylvia, 21, 49

Pareto, Vilfredo, 7, 8, 127, 186, 193–201, 202, 211; on circulation of elites, 195–96, 202; critique of democracy, 127, 192, 198; evaluation of, 258, 262; on feminism, 196–97, 198–99; and Machiavelli, 192–93, 194, 195; *Manual of Political Economy*, 193, 196; misogyny of, 195, 196–97, 201, 258; and Mussolini, 191, 211; on patriarchy, 197–98; on prostitution, 199–200, 208–9, 262; *Les systemes socialistes*, 193, 211; *Treatise on General Sociology*, 194, 195, 197, 201; on women's suffrage, 198

Paris Commune (1871), 7, 59, 60–65, 187, 211

Parsons, Talcott, 8, 81, 201, 228–35, 243; "Age and Sex in the Social Structure of the United States," 228; evaluation of, 259–60, 262; *Family, Socialization and Interaction Process*, 232; on family, 41, 232–34, 259–60; on sex roles, 226, 228–35, 243, 244, 259–60, 262; *The Social System*, 235

Paterson, Emma, 20

Patriarchy, 18, 19, 24, 50, 53, 148–49, 151, 153, 257; and democracy, 68, 71; and feminism, 126, 133, 182, 267, 268; feminist theorists of, 2, 176, 272, 273, 274, 279; in Germany, 7, 108, 132, 135, 185; and household community, 139, 179–80; and Industrial Revolution, 5, 15, 20, 67; and men, 132, 159; and political despotism, 42; and prostitution, 105; resistance to, 11, 20, 109–11, 114, 115, 116, 134, 136, 148; and suicide, 83; and World War I, 116. *See also* Family, patriarchal

Paul, Alice, 222

Pissarjevsky, Lydia, 66

Place, Francis, 16

Plato, 247

Poirier, Sophie, 60–61, 63

Population and Birth Control (Eden and Cedar Paul), 117

Potter, Beatrice, 19

Property, 18, 20–21, 57, 147, 151–52; control of, 11, 19, 153, 154, 160, 224, 251; and marriage, 69, 154, 263, 275; women as, 39, 151, 263, 264, 273

Prostitution, 8, 9, 15, 17, 148, 175, 183–84, 206; campaign for abolition of, 102–3, 104, 105; condemnation of, 147–48; and cultural differences, 209, 259; expense-account, 239, 260; and French feminism, 53, 57, 61, 65; and male sexuality, 86; in Middle Ages, 140, 147; and middle-class women, 19, 102, 199, 258; and militarism, 101; and monogamy, 147, 255, 265; in nineteenth century, 167, 275; and racism, 209; state control of, 103; and working-class women, 57, 203, 208

Proudhon, Pierre-Joseph, 56–57, 91, 97, 182

Puritanism, 11, 69, 129, 134, 139, 141, 144, 145–46, 148

Quataert, Jean, 93, 99, 203

Reed, John, 219

Reich, Wilhelm, 112

Reventlow, Fanny zu, 110, 111, 114, 117

Reverby, Susan, 220

Revolutions of 1848, 56, 59, 62, 89, 90, 100, 101, 108, 215

Reynaud, Colette, 66

Richer, Léon, 65

Richtofen, Else von, 111, 112–13, 114, 115, 117, 132, 133, 134–35, 136, 137, 156, 163

Richtofen, Frieda von, 111, 113–14, 117, 156

Rieff, Philip, 254

Rilke, Rainer Maria, 115

Rimbaud, Arthur, 63

Roland, Pauline, 56, 61

Roosevelt, Eleanor, 225

Rossi, Alice S., 23, 29, 213–14, 215, 218, 226, 246

Roszak, Theodore, 4

Rousseau, Jean-Jacques, 11, 12, 50, 247

Rowbotham, Sheila, 11, 18, 31, 49–50, 52, 56; on feminism in America, 216, 217, 223; on feminism and capitalism, 4, 10, 13, 15; on feminism and revolution, 6, 12, 20–21, 278; on Margaret Fuller, 215, 254

Rubin, Gayle, 2, 272, 273

Ruskin, John, 18, 27

Sacks, Karen, 32, 43, 275–76

Sade, Marquis de, 53

Saint-Simon, Henri de, 16, 17, 31–32, 54, 177, 193

Sand, George, 54, 57, 215

Sanger, Margaret, 117, 221

Schloffer, Frieda. *See* Gross, Frieda Schloffer

Schmidt, Auguste, 100

Schreiber, Adele, 106

Schuler, Alfred, 111, 115

Sexism, 94, 121–23, 168, 201, 217, 228; Freud on, 267, 270; in language, 152,

208; and Marxism, 265, 266; and suicide, 82–84, 85, 88
Sex roles, 6, 10, 37–38, 70, 211, 226; and division of labor, 79–81, 149–50, 159; and education, 209; and functionalism, 261–62; and household authority, 138; internalization of, 270–71; and love, 167, 206–7; and marriage, 206–7; and socialism, 92, 97, 98, 99, 120; and sociology, 247, 253, 256; and suicide, 84–88; and women's freedom, 12, 24–25, 29, 159, 182
Sexuality, 8, 155, 223, 252, 254, 259, 275; and ethics, 136, 205; female, 105, 168, 267, 270; male, 7, 104, 184, 257, 269, 274; and religion, 127, 139–42, 201
Shaffer, Robert, 224, 225
Shaftesbury, Lord, 20
Shelley, Percy Bysshe, 12
Simmel, Georg, 7, 125, 126, 131, 156–77, 183; "Adventurer," 166; Conflict and the Web of Group Affiliations, 170–74; "The Conflict of Modern Culture," 174–75; on coquetry, 164–66, 210, 256; on custom, 170–71, 256; "Eros, Platonic and Modern," 163; evaluation of, 255–57, 262; "Fashion," 165–66, 256; on individuality, 163–64, 166, 169–70, 256; on love and marriage, 160–64, 175, 256; on male domination, 158–59, 255–56; on modern culture, 158, 174; The Philosophy of Money, 167–70; on prostitution, 167–70, 175, 257; on sexism, 158, 168–69; view of women, 159–60, 164, 165–66, 175–76, 179, 248, 255–56
Simmel, Gertrud, 114, 157, 158
Simons, May Wood, 220
Smith, Joan, 273, 279
Snyder, Eloise C., 2, 6
Social Democratic Party (Germany), 91, 115–16, 118, 135, 202–3, 210, 258; membership of, 119, 121, 123; party conferences of, 120, 122, 123; party newspapers, 91, 95, 96, 122; and war, 118; women's movement in, 93, 96–99, 122, 220; and women's suffrage, 95, 119, 121; and women workers, 94, 118, 122, 124
Socialism, 18, 20, 115, 117, 192, 202, 210; vs. capitalism, 108, 177; and feminism, 21–22, 49, 58, 66, 88, 90–99, 118–26, 185, 211, 213, 220–21, 264; and Marxism, 98, 99, 202; and World War I, 21–22, 99, 118, 203, 219, 221
Solomon, Alice, 114

Sombart, Werner, 106
Sorel, Georges, 202
Spence, Thomas, 12
Spencer, Herbert, 11, 16, 19, 32–48, 79, 152, 177, 193; change of views of, 7, 34–35, 39, 45, 46, 48, 251, 253, 261, 262; death of, 21; evaluation of, 251–52, 261; on family, 3, 20, 47, 48, 80; on future status of women, 43–44; and J. S. Mill, 29, 34, 46; on nature of women, 35–39, 44; The Principles of Biology, 34–35; The Principles of Psychology, 33–34; The Principles of Sociology, 39, 40, 41–43, 235, 251, 260; Social Statics, 32–33, 34, 35, 45, 46; and Social Darwinism, 32, 38, 39, 47; The Study of Sociology, 35, 44, 235, 251; and women's suffrage, 34, 37
Staël, Mme. de, 53–54, 125
Stanton, Elizabeth Cady, 216, 218
Steinem, Gloria, 185
Stirner, Max, 112
Stöcker, Helene, 105, 106, 107
Storm, Theodor, 178
Stritt, Marie, 102, 103, 107
Sue, Eugène, 263

Taylor, Harriet, 23, 34, 246
Tentori, Tullio, 187, 189
Thiers, Louis-Adolphe, 60, 64
Thomas, Edith, 57, 58–59, 60, 62, 63, 187
Thompson, E. P., 13, 14, 15
Thompson, William, 17, 18
Thönnessen, Werner, 90, 91, 92, 95, 96, 119, 120, 123, 124
Tinayre, Marguerite (pseud., Jules Paty), 57
Tocqueville, Alexis de, 7, 68–74, 80, 172, 181, 204, 212; evaluation of, 252–53
Tönnies, Ferdinand, 126, 132, 158, 177–82; Community and Association, 177, 178–82, 262; evaluation of, 257, 262; on nature of women, 7, 179, 257, 262
Trade unions, 14–15, 20, 56, 90, 95, 96, 99, 119, 124, 219, 224, 257, 277, 278
Treitschke, Heinrich von, 125, 128, 131
Tristan, Flora, 55

United States, 6, 8, 68–74, 82, 185, 212–44; depression in, 224, 225; first woman's rights meeting in, 215, 221; 1920s in, 223–24, 225; Progressive movement in, 221–22; public eroticism in, 239–40; reform movements in, 213, 221; theorists of, 228–44, 259. See also Democracy; Tocqueville, Alexis de

Valette, Aline, 66
de Vaux, Clothilde, 78, 79
Veblen, Thorstein, 259
Verlaine, Paul, 63
Vicinus, Martha, 18, 19
Vico, Giambattista, 210
Vogel, Lise, 269
Voilquin, Susanne, 54, 56

Ward, Lester, 220
Weber, Alfred, 109, 114, 126, 131–32, 183
Weber, Helene, 129, 142
Weber, Lily, 131
Weber, Marianne Schnitger, 114, 117, 125,
    128, 130, 132–33, 135, 147
Weber, Max, 7, 103, 106, 108, 111,
    126–56, 185, 197, 202, 274; attitude to
    Bismarck, 109, 110, 134, 135; on bu-
    reaucracy, 210; death of, 117, 135;
    Economy and Society, 137, 139; on
    eroticism, 142–44, 155, 254; evaluation
    of, 254–55, 256, 257, 262; family back-
    ground of, 45, 115, 127–30; General
    Economic History, 146–54, 255;
    Heidelberg circle of, 113, 114, 117, 157;
    on household community, 138–39,
    146–47, 152–53; Jugendbriefe, 128;
    and Mannheim, 183; and marriage, 145,
    148, 152, 163, 254; and Marx, 127, 237,
    260; and matriarchy, 145–47, 148, 151,
    255; opposition to irrationalism, 115;
    and patriarchy, 109, 132, 133, 134, 136,
    148–49, 150, 151, 152, 153, 254, 255;
    "Politics as a Vocation," 135; on prosti-
    tution, 147–48, 257; The Protestant
    Ethic and the Spirit of Capitalism, 145;
    "Religious Rejections of the World and
    Their Directions," 142; "Science as a
    Vocation," 185; on sex roles and divi-
    sion of labor, 149–50; on sexuality and
    religion, 127, 139–46; and Simmel, 158,
    248; The Sociology of Religion, 139–42,
    254–55; and Tönnies, 178
Weber, Max, Sr., 128–30
Weekley, Ernest, 113
Weekley, Frieda. See Richtofen, Frieda
    von
Weimar Republic, 89, 117, 118–26
Weininger, Otto, 125
Weise, Leopold von, 158
Weld, Theodore, 214
Wheeler, Anna, 18
Wilhelm II, Kaiser, 101
Willard, Frances, 221
Wolfskehl, Karl, 111

Wollstonecraft, Mary, 11–12, 16, 26, 31,
    50, 58, 169
Women: access of, to professions, 7, 8–9,
    10, 11, 24, 77, 250; American vs. Euro-
    pean, 71–72; and chastity, 187, 203,
    239, 240; and competition for jobs,
    119–20, 121–22, 253, 277; and custom,
    170–71, 256; and democracy, 125; dur-
    ing depression, 224, 225; economic in-
    dependence of, 14, 119, 122, 181–82,
    275, 277; and fascism, 211; in Franco-
    Prussian War, 59–60; in French Revo-
    lution, 52; frontier, 218; history of,
    4–9, 271–72, 274; hysteria in, 58, 112,
    268; and love, 160–64, 167; and male
    culture, 158, 159, 176–77, 216–17,
    255–56; minority, 243; and moth-
    erhood, 97, 100, 105, 120, 207, 210,
    234, 251, 276; and pacificism, 125, 141,
    176; as persons, 100, 182, 256; and phi-
    lanthropy, 19, 29, 188, 231, 250; and
    poverty, 227, 279; and power, 33,
    36–37, 38, 242, 275; and property, 39,
    151, 263, 273; relationships between,
    256, 275; and religion, 108, 139; sexual
    drive in, 97; sexual liberation of, 20,
    53, 97, 134, 148, 205; and slavery, 17,
    20, 24, 40, 73, 212–13, 247, 263; and
    socialism, 125, 176, 190; and suicide,
    81–88; and war, 45, 48, 89, 116, 135,
    211; white-collar, 236–39, 243, 260,
    275, 277; and work, 4–5, 11, 13–16, 94,
    95, 96, 97, 100, 119, 122–23, 145–46,
    222, 224–25, 227, 236–37, 274, 275.
    See also Education; Family; Marriage
Women, nature of, 2, 7, 8, 11, 261, 262;
    debates in France on, 49–50, 58, 75,
    76, 80, 83; Freud on, 267; Hitler on,
    126; Mill on, 25–26, 250; Simmel on,
    159–60, 167, 168, 176, 177; Spencer on,
    34–38
Women, working-class, 16, 20, 55, 88, 95,
    262; and Industrial Revolution, 42–43,
    89–90, 173, 277; and middle-class, 19,
    114, 203, 259; and prostitution, 57, 208;
    and revolution, 61, 62, 216; and so-
    cialism, 91, 99, 119, 122; in United
    States, 74, 219, 220, 221
Women's Liberation Movement, 72–73,
    107
Women's rights, 7, 11, 32–33, 39, 117,
    204, 276; and "birth-strike," 96; and
    evolutionary biology, 47–48; and Ger-
    man militarism, 101; and German so-
    cialism, 120–21, 176; and Industrial

Revolution, 13, 174; in Italy, 186–88, 190, 192, 201; and liberal parties, 104, 175–76; and Marxism, 154; in revolutionary France, 62; and sexual liberation, 19; in United States, 213–44. *See also* Women; *individual countries*
Women's suffrage, 7, 8, 21, 116, 246, 278; in England, 19, 20, 24, 31, 32, 250; in France, 56, 65; in Germany, 91, 94, 95, 98, 99, 102, 103, 104, 116, 117; in Italy, 190–91, 258, 262; opposition to, 19, 34, 37, 65, 198, 215, 222; and socialists, 21, 58, 121, 125; in United States, 215, 216, 220, 221, 222

Zepler, Wally, 119, 120
Zetkin, Clara Eissner, 93, 94, 95, 96, 97, 98, 100, 118–19, 124, 190, 207
Zietz, Luise, 90, 93, 97, 98, 118